Orientalism and Empire

DATE DUE

Brodart Co.   Cat. # 55 137 001   Printed in USA

Orientalism and Empire

*North Caucasus Mountain Peoples
and the Georgian Frontier,
1845–1917*

AUSTIN JERSILD

McGill-Queen's University Press
Montreal & Kingston · London · Ithaca

© McGill-Queen's University Press 2002
ISBN 0-7735-2328-6 (cloth)
ISBN 0-7735-2329-4 (paper)

Legal deposit second quarter 2002
Bibliothèque nationale du Québec

Printed in Canada on acid-free paper that is 100%
ancient forest free (100% post-consumer recycled),
processed chlorine free, and printed with vegetable-
based, low VOC inks.

Publication of this book has been made possible by a
grant from Old Dominion University.

McGill-Queen's University Press acknowledges the
financial support of the Government of Canada
through the Book Publishing Industry Development
Program (BPIDP) for its publishing activities. It also
acknowledges the support of the Canada Council
for the Arts for its publishing program.

**National Library of Canada Cataloguing
in Publication Data**

Jersild, Austin
Orientalism and empire: North Caucasus mountain
peoples and the Georgian frontier, 1845-1917
Includes bibliographical references and index.
ISBN 0-7735-2329-4 (bound)
ISBN 0-7735-2329-4 (pbk)
1. Caucasus, Northern (Russia) – History.
2. Caucasus, Northern (Russia) – Ethnic
relations.   3. Caucasus, Northern (Russia) –
History – Religious aspects.   4. Mountain people –
Russia – Caucasus, Northern – History.   I. Title.
DK509.J47 2002   947.5'2   C2001-902856-3

This book was typeset by Dynagram Inc.
in 10/12 Palatino.

For Annika and Kirsten

Contents

Preface

Russia's relationship to the North Caucasus has again turned violent, as it has so many times in the past, and a collection of ideas and images in the Russian press about mountain banditry, crime, and savagery has again emerged to explain and facilitate the war. Federation troops can do no wrong against the "terrorists" of Groznyi, who, "[e]ven though [they] by day seem like peaceful inhabitants, at night are merciless fighters."[1] The Russian checkpoint at Asinovsk in Chechnia, reports a Georgian journalist, greets travellers with an enormous sign in big red letters: "We will cure you of the disease of terrorism!"[2] "In Russia we will always be outsiders," complains Chechen Islam Saidaev, " 'low' [*chernye*] people of the second sort."[3] Even the new president of the Russian Federation, Vladimir Putin, has emerged in part because of his belligerent response to the North Caucasus crisis.[4] An official from the Russian Federal Frontier Service sounds like a general in the nineteenth-century Caucasus Army when he explains, "We must not leave places to which previous generations have made way with sweat and blood."[5] As this study will show, contemporary publicists and politicians draw on a long history of imperial discourse about Islam, savagery, and the mountain peoples of the North Caucasus.

To study the formation of the empire on its southern frontier in the nineteenth century, I have utilized a variety of materials in both the Russian and the Georgian languages from libraries and archives in St Petersburg, Moscow, and Tbilisi. In the text and notes I transliterate Russian according to the standard system employed by the Library of

Congress, and Georgian according to the simplified, rather than "scientific," system. Georgian does not have capital letters, but generally in the text I follow English convention and render Georgian names and places with the first letter capitalized. The endnote references to Georgian materials, however, do not include capital letters. The endnotes are also abbreviated, but readers can refer to the bibliography for full citations. The city of Tbilisi (Tiflis in Russian) is generally referred to by its Georgian name, except in those cases where the name is used in an imperial designation, such as "Tiflis Theatre" or "Tiflis province." Dates for events before 31 January 1918 generally correspond to the Julian calendar in use in imperial Russia, rather than the Gregorian calendar of the West. For the rendering of ethnonyms from the region in English, I follow the usage adopted by Ronald Wixman in *Language Aspects of Ethnic Patterns and Processes in the North Caucasus* (Chicago: University of Chicago Press, 1980).

For the support of five different research trips over a period of nine years, I am grateful to the Education Abroad Program of the University of California, the Department of History at the University of California, Davis, and the American Councils on International Education. Eric Johnson and the Tbilisi office of the American Councils on International Education supported and facilitated my study of the Georgian language and my work in Georgian archives and libraries in both 1999 and 2000. I am especially grateful to my language teachers, Ramaz Kurdadze, Tamuna Koshoridze, and Tamara Chakhtauri, for their excellent instruction in Georgian, and also to Rezo Khutsishvili and his dedicated staff at the Georgian National Historical Archive in Tbilisi, Larisa Isinovna Tsvizhba of the State Military Archive in Moscow, Serafima Varekhova of the Russian State Historical Archive in St Petersburg, Neli Melkadze of the Tbilisi Public Library, and Aleko, Maia, and Nutsa Khutishvili of Tbilisi. In the United States several stimulating and productive summers were made possible by the Kennan Institute of the Woodrow Wilson Center in 1997 and the Hoover Institute of Stanford University in 1995. The Social Science Research Council (New York) supported my dissertation work for an entire year in 1992–93. The Office of Research and Graduate Studies and the College of Arts and Letters at Old Dominion University generously supported the project in its later stages.

For critical responses to portions of my work, as well as for their organizational initiative, my thanks go to Tom Barrett, James Brooks, Michael David-Fox, Wayne Dowler, David Hoffman, Harsha Ram, Ron Suny, Yuri Slezkine, Ted Weeks, and Dov Yaroshevskii. Marc Raeff, Anthony Rhinelander, Richard Wortman, and my anonymous readers at McGill-Queen's University Press read the entire manuscript at different points along the way, and I am grateful to all of them for their efforts to focus my interests and for their suggestions for improvement to the manuscript. Margaret Levey, Philip Cercone, Joan McGilvray, and the staff at McGill-Queen's offered much-appreciated support and guidance through the process of publication. I was especially fortunate to benefit from the careful and intelligent editorial work of Elizabeth Hulse. Don Emminger of Academic Technology Services at Old Dominion University prepared the maps. Various regional and national conferences of the American Association for the Advancement of Slavic Studies, the Midwest Russian History Workshop, the Maryland Workshop, the Berkeley Center for Post-Soviet Studies, and the Post-Colonial Studies Group and the Faculty Research Seminar at Old Dominion University offered productive forums and camaraderie over the past several years. Robert Crummey and Reginald Zelnik read the work as a dissertation at UC Davis. My dissertation adviser, Daniel Brower, shared his knowledge of Russia and other topics as well as his general enthusiasm for scholarship, travel, and family, and I am lucky to count coffee drinking with Professor Brower among my other fond memories of Davis, California.

Scholarly work is the product of many happy moments of learning and exploration, bringing to my mind the presence over the years of my parents, Paul and Marilyn Jersild, my daughters, Annika and Kirsten, and especially my wife, Heather.

Portions of chapters 6 and 3 have been previously published as "Who Was Shamil? Russian Colonial Rule and Sufi Islam in the North Caucasus, 1859–1917," in *Central Asian Survey* 14, no. 2 (1995): 205–23, and "Faith, Custom, and Ritual in the Borderlands: Orthodoxy, Islam, and the 'Small Peoples' of the Middle Volga and the North Caucasus," in the *Russian Review* 59, no. 4 (October 2000): 512–29, and I am grateful to the editors for allowing me to reproduce the material here.

Church in Imeretia; from *Kavkazskii Kalendar' na 1853 god* (Tiflis, 1852)

Restoration Society church in Svanetia; from Platonov, *Obzor deiatel'nosti*

Khevsur armed for battle, artist S. Zhivotovskii; from Kaspari, *Pokorennyi Kavkaz*

Mountain Georgian family; photograph in possession of author

Georgians; from Kaspari, *Pokorennyi Kavkaz*

Khertvisi, 2nd century BC; postcard in possession of author

Mountain Georgians; photograph in possession of author

"The Caucasus: A Mountaineer," artist Selivanov; from Kaspari, *Pokorennyi Kavkaz*

Adygei; from Kaspari, *Pokorennyi Kavkaz*

Lezgin; from Kaspari, *Pokorennyi Kavkaz*

Monument to Bariatinskii, Gunib; from Kaspari, *Pokorennyi Kavkaz*

Mountain road in Dagestan, artist S. Zhivotovskii; from Kaspari, *Pokorennyi Kavkaz*

Ossetians and Tushin, artist N. Ol'shanskii; from Kaspari, *Pokorennyi Kavkaz*

Svan woman weaving, artist N. Ol'shanskii; from Kaspari, *Pokorennyi Kavkaz*

Meeting of General Kliuke von Kliugenau with Shamil, artist G.G. Gagarin; from Kaspari, *Pokorennyi Kavkaz*

Capture of Shamil, 25 August 1859, artist F. Rubeau; from Kaspari, *Pokorennyi Kavkaz*

Murder of Prince Tsitsianov in Baku, artist M. Andreev; from Kaspari, *Pokorennyi Kavkaz*

Presentation of the captured Shamil to Bariatinskii; from Zisserman, *Fel'dmarshal Kniaz'*

Grand Prince Mikhail Nikolaevich; from Kaspari,
Pokorennyi Kavkaz

Adol′f Petrovich Berzhe; from Bakradze, *Arkheoloqicheskoe puteshestuie*

Restoration Society church in Ajaria; from Platonov, *Obzor deiatel'nosti*

Restoration Society school in Svanetia; from Platonov, *Obzor deiatel'nosti*

Palace of the Caucasus viceroy; Tbilisi; from Kaspari, *Pokorennyi Kavkaz*

Russian officer in the Caucasus; photograph in possession of author

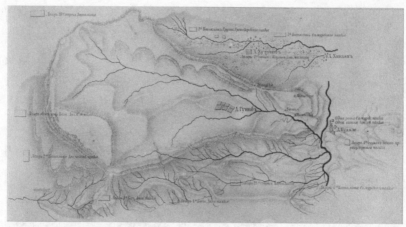

Gunib; from RGIA

Monument to Vorontsov, Tbilisi; photograph in possession of author

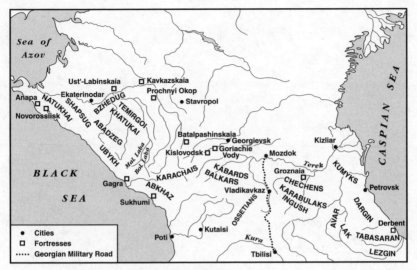

The Caucasus in the early nineteenth century

The contemporary Caucasus

Orientalism and Empire

1 The Discourse of Empire

> Our activities in the Caucasus are reminiscent of the many
> tragedies of the early conquest of America by the Spaniards; but
> without any heroic victories or military successes such as those
> of Pizarro or Cortés. God forbid that the conquest of the
> Caucasus might leave a similar bloody legacy to Russian history,
> such as that left by these conquerors to the history of Spain.
>
> Nikolai N. Raevskii to Minister of War
> A.I. Chernyshev, 1841[1]

INTRODUCTION TO THE NORTH CAUCASUS

In 1872 O. Iosseliani, a Georgian missionary and educator in the employ of the Society for the Restoration of Orthodoxy in the Caucasus, attended the funeral of a wealthy prince in the Okum region of Abkhazia. Accompanied by a local imperial official, he witnessed elaborate rituals of mourning and despair. The privileged Abkhaz women separated from the men and collectively beat their heads and cried. They bowed to the ground for ten minutes at a time before the family and relatives of the deceased. The men processed by the body and placed their hands on the forehead of the body and cried, "A-a! a-a! a-a!" The body was draped in a white cloth and brought to the courtyard, where the commoners were given their opportunity to wail, tear at their hair, and put their hands to their foreheads. They chanted their various cries of sympathy to the family of the deceased, who responded in kind.

The intriguing aspect of this story of a funeral is the fact that Iosseliani felt compelled to recount his afternoon in such detail to officials and missionary colleagues in the imperial bureaucracy. "On my trip I witnessed an extremely interesting scene," he explained, "not because the event was particularly remarkable but because it was simply novel."[2] To convey his experience he adopted an ethnographic mode of representation, communicating his distance from virtually unknown peoples on a remote colonial frontier: "The official and I remained in the courtyard and viewed this spectacle."[3] Iosseliani successfully transformed his experience and the event into a story, comprehensible to officials in Tbilisi. "And so concluded the funeral scene which I saw two weeks ago."[4] A Georgian viewing the "novelty" of an Abkhaz funeral, an event in geographic and cultural terms on the imperial frontier as well as the Georgian frontier, found a ready audience for his story among both Russians and non-Russians in the Caucasus.

The transformation of the conquest of the North Caucasus into a story is the subject of this book. Iosseliani filed his teacher's report only a decade or so after the conclusion of the long and brutal Caucasus War. Members of educated society (*obshchestvo* in Russian, *sazogadoeba* in Georgian) on the frontier felt the need to render historically "savage" mountaineers, with their *kinzhali* (daggers), blood feuds, radical Sufi brotherhoods, and episodes of bride-kidnapping, as new subjects of the empire. Even North Caucasus mountaineers, famously exotic and the subject of literary Orientalism from Pushkin to Tolstoy, might find their place and function within an imperial narrative, a story about the purpose and meaning of both the region and the Russian Empire.[5] Multi-ethnic borderland communities from the frontier made important contributions to the growing consciousness of Russia as an empire that emerged and developed from the 1840s on.

The diversity of the North Caucasus contributed to the imperial dilemma of imagining the region anew. The mountain range itself helped to advance this diversity, extending roughly 720 kilometres across the region from the Black Sea to the Caspian. Beyond the range lay the Transcaucasus (South Caucasus) and the Armenians, Georgians, and Azerbaijanis.[6] The Russians actually conquered these more distant lands first, while the vast mountain range shielded its inhabitants from Russian rule. Linguistically the range appears to be the site of the original Babel: one branch of the Ibero-Caucasus languages includes the Adygei-Abkhaz and the Kabards, who live to the northwest; another is the Dagestan-Veinakh branch of the northeast Caucasus, which includes the Chechens, Ingush, and Karabulaks, and the Avar, Dargin, Lak, Lezgin, and Tabasaran (the primary languages of Dagestan); the region is also host to the Turkic branch of the Altaic family, which includes the Karachais, Balkars, Kumyks, and Nogais; and as well, it contains the Iranian branch of the Indo-European language family, which includes the Ossetians, Kurds, and Tats ("mountain Jews").[7] And mountain tribes themselves were further divided. The internationally famous "Cherkes" (Circassians), or the Adygei tribes of the northwest Caucasus, were composed of thirteen primary groups: the Zhaneev, Shefak, Natukhai, Shapsug, Abadzeg, Bzhedug, Temirgoi, Khatukai, Egerukai, Adamiev,

Mamkheg, Makhosh, and Beslenei.[8] In sum, the region presented to
the Russians a series of "barely comprehensible incongruities and
contradictions" in every imaginable way, as G.V. Sollogub wrote.[9]

ORIENTALISM

The dilemmas posed for the makers of empire by the remarkable geographic, ethnic, and religious diversity of the North Caucasus and the
long opposition of the mountaineers to Russian rule make the region
an excellent borderland setting for the study of the formation of the
empire. Just as the North Caucasus complicates the work of the
makers of the federation today, so the region posed special challenges
to Russians intent upon imagining a workable empire in the nineteenth century. Difference and opposition stimulated the imperial
imagination and provoked a plethora of plans, projects, and visions
concerning the future of the empire. This study explores this conceptualization of empire by considering the work and ideas of Russian
and non-Russian administrators and state-builders, colonial officials,
travellers, literary figures and thinkers, and ethnographers and geographers as they administered and thought about the North Caucasus
from the 1840s to 1917. Imperial visions of the region and its mountain inhabitants were a response to the tragic and extended war, and
they serve as examples of the search for imperial cohesion, integration, and identity during and after the Great Reforms. Multi-ethnic
educated society visualized empire in order to justify the conquest
and offer some greater purpose or civilizing mission in the wake of
the military expansion.

Edward Said's imaginative application of diverse currents within
French post-structuralist thought to colonial history has inspired numerous rereadings of the history of Europe's textual reproduction of
foreign lands and cultures.[10] Colonialism throughout the globe was
often violent and coercive, but it was also importantly a set of discur-
sive practices that represented Europe's effort to confirm in a global
context the truths of the hierarchy of peoples established by the
eighteenth-century Enlightenment. Scholars from a variety of disciplines have explored the manner in which colonial writers were determined to impose or create some form of order and meaning out of
the confusing chaos they perceived in other lands, and thereby affirm
some greater truth about themselves and their historical role in the
world.[11] One scholar has even extended this discussion to Western
Europe's "invention" of Eastern Europe.[12] The exploration of knowledge and rule has included fascinating histories of disciplines such as
geography and anthropology.[13] Numerous scholars have recognized

the significance of exploring a culture at its edges or margins in order to gain insight into its values, preoccupations, and even fears.

The comment of Ann Laura Stoler and Frederick Cooper about the British in India applies to the imperial borderland experience as well: "A large colonial bureaucracy occupied itself, especially from the 1860s, with classifying people and their attributes, with censuses, surveys, and ethnographies, with recording transactions, marking space, establishing routines, and standardizing practices."[14] In this study I adopt from Said his attention to the significance of Europe's interest in the sacred antiquity of the East as a contrast to the degenerate present. If the Orient was a problem in the present, as the North Caucasus certainly was to an expanding Russia in the nineteenth century, then it "needed first to be known, then invaded and possessed, then re-created by scholars, soldiers, and judges who disinterred forgotten languages, histories, races, and cultures in order to posit them – beyond the modern Oriental's ken – as the true classical Orient that could be used to judge and rule the modern Orient."[15] The colonizing power justifies its presence through its supposed role as the restorer of a pristine and Romanticized past. British scholars and officials took their purpose to be the recovery of India's "magnificent" past, long since mired in the familiar process of Eastern stagnation and deterioration.[16] France's "Kabyle myth," or the French colonial notion of a Latin Africa of indigenous Berbers free from the influence of the conquering Arabs and their faith, offers the closest comparative example from this history of European mythmaking.[17]

RUSSIA AS EMPIRE

The conceptual debt of imperial empire-builders to worlds of Western colonialism such as that of Algérie française will be clear from the discussions that follow on Shamil, Islam, customary law, ethnicity, and other topics. Russia's general recognition of the diversity and especially the "Oriental" character of its borderland regions in the nineteenth century introduced new concerns and a new imperial purpose, especially in the wake of Russia's own eighteenth-century clarification of its "Western" location on the modern map of the globe.[18] On the other hand, the Russian context of empire was, of course, quite different from that of the Western powers. Historians in particular point out that Said's very preoccupation with a series of epistemological dilemmas is a method by definition likely to obscure the particular historical context of each colonial relationship.[19] Russia did not possess distant "colonies" but contiguous borderlands, and its enduring *ancien régime* social order and its "emperor of all the

Russian (*rossiiskoe*) lands" pose a series of contrasts to the European experience. For good reason, scholars of the history of Russia as an empire have explored the impact of geographic "core areas" in struggle for control of "frontier zones," the importance of social structure and its impact upon the process of the incorporation of a multi-ethnic service elite, and the role of crucial borderland administrators such as Mikhail S. Vorontsov in Odessa and Tbilisi.[20] Along with nineteenth-century scholars of the "Eastern question" such as Sergei Zhigarev, these scholars possess a keen sense of the way in which affairs on the steppe frequently blurred the boundaries between foreign and domestic policy.[21] Soviet scholarship was somewhat different, with otherwise competent scholars continuing the nineteenth-century tradition of writing about the "Caucasus War" (*Kavkazskaia voina*) but stifled by an institutional setting that demanded attention to a series of narrow socio-economic questions regarding its history.[22]

The traditional story of tsarist military conquest and colonial expansion, presented in positive terms by nineteenth-century Russian historians but then as one of conquest and rapacity by scholars as diverse as John Baddeley in 1908, Soviet historians, and Moshe Gammer more recently, does not do justice to the complexity of inter-ethnic relations and the shared nature of many of the ideas and assumptions of colonial discourse.[23] This book addresses numerous instances of Russian and non-Russian cooperation in the construction and making of empire in the Russian Caucasus. Georgian educated society was a world of discussion and debate similar in important respects to Russian worlds of educated society throughout the Caucasus, which themselves were always multi-ethnic (*rossiiskii* rather than *russkii*). Like Russians in St Petersburg from the 1830s on, Georgians were proud of their emerging press and vibrant community of numerous "educated readers," who were increasingly interested in Georgian plays, Georgian books, and Georgian history.[24] And again as in the capital cities of Russia, Georgian intellectuals in a time of new ideas about civic participation and the nation worried about their distance and estrangement from the lower orders and the people of the countryside. In the wake of the ten-year anniversary of the Georgian newspaper *Droeba* in 1876, the editors chose to bring attention to the continuing problem of the distance of Georgian educated society from the people, a problem of "ignorance" that was also a "weakness" which inhibited the process of national development.[25] Some Georgians blamed the imperial system itself, which offered a little too much comfort to the Georgian upper classes.[26] Traditional Russian social dilemmas were evident throughout the lands of the empire, as were cultural terms of debate, themselves appropriated by

Russians from the German Romantics. Ilia Chavchavadze frequently reviewed new trends in literature and the arts that qualified as something which served the "motherland, the people and the [father]land" (*samshoblo, khalkhi da mamuli*).[27] He drew on his educational experiences in Russia and his exposure to its own efforts to clarify the nature of their unique and "original" (*samobytnyi*) contribution to humanity. The depiction of the "genuinely national" and uniquely "Georgian" for Chavchavadze in fact constituted a contribution, to continue with these allusions to the Romantic tradition in Germany and Russia, to humankind in general. Authentic and indigenous poetry, he argued, was the opposite of that which was "imitative" (*mibadzva*).[28] Georgians viewed Russia as their bridge to Europe, and themselves as the chief representative of the "West" on the "Eastern" frontier of the Caucasus.

The shared cultural concerns among Russians and Georgians were especially obvious when the topic at hand was the North Caucasus, Islam, and the mountaineers. Georgians contributed to imperial debates about the virtues of the cultivation of custom and native language, the effectiveness of customary law, the remarkable story of Shamil, the threat of Islam in the North Caucasus, the significance of archaeological exploration, and other topics discussed in this study. Eastern Orthodoxy obviously created some natural affinities between Russia and Georgia, but the cooperation extended beyond matters of faith and the church. From the work of Andreas Kappeler and others we know about the multi-ethnic character of privilege and bureaucratic service in the Russian Empire, and Georgians too, of course, were influenced by the primary avenues of social mobility and privilege. The rhetoric of empire, however, was also a product of shared cultural experience, and the Georgian experience and contribution were crucial to the viability of a discourse that made colonial expansion and control possible. And Georgians are not the only non-Russian characters pertinent to the discussion that follows. Numerous nationalities such as Ossetians, Abkhaz, Dagestanis, and others worked as teachers, missionaries, and officials, and contributed to the formation of empire on the southern frontier.

While Georgians shared many ideas and assumptions with Russians, they also, along with other non-Russian educated communities of the imperial era, stretched and defined for their own purposes the parameters of debate.[29] If mountain peoples were often the savage "other" of the presumably civilized and Europeanized imperial imagination, mountain Georgians for Georgian educated society offered a glimpse into the past of a historically hardy and enduring Georgian identity. Aleksandre Qazbegi, who along with Vazha-Pshavela and others transformed folk tales and ethnographic reports into literature, explained to a reviewer in the 1880s: "I saw that the highland [*mtiuli*] region of Georgia was barely considered to be Georgian, and I tried to make these people known to Georgians, to acquaint the public with their innermost feelings, which they have since ancient times devoted to the common cause."[30] Giorgi Tsereteli and numerous others depicted "frontier" inhabitants such as the Khevsur as "well-off and distinguished tillers of the soil, brave and freedom-loving" peasants who stood their ground in the face of Georgia's many historic enemies.[31] Georgian nativists claimed to see Georgians everywhere on the edges of Georgia, in need of cultural, religious, and linguistic direction and support.[32] They appealed for attention to the matter from the new scholarly societies and from Georgian educated society generally, and lobbied the imperial state to school their frontier peoples in the Georgian language and culture. While the Russian journey to the imperial frontier, as was common to Europeans in the colonial context, was not just a movement through space but also backward in time, the Georgian exploration of this frontier was a journey to a specifically Georgian past. Georgia's historic dilemmas on the frontier of Islam provided a local colouring and urgency to Russia's visions of empire in the Caucasus. The nativism that emerged as a product of the encounter with Islam was a version of the empire that foreshadowed the Soviet ethno-territorial state of the twentieth century.

Russia's growing consciousness of its exotic borderlands and peoples, evident in the Caucasus especially from the 1840s and 1850s, meant a rethinking of the historic practices and mentality of what Geoffrey Hosking has called the "Asiatic imperial style."[33] Traditionally, diverse "men of power" offered loyalty to the throne in exchange for local wealth and privilege.[34] The introductory discussion of the history of the conquest addresses historic traditions of allegiance and "subjecthood" (*poddanstvo*) on the frontier. Loyalty to the "nation" was irrelevant in a world of big states, small peoples, and local elites accustomed to careful alliances with the surrounding empires. The emergence of new and more modern ideas about civic participation and the social order inspired genuine efforts to think through the nature of the multi-ethnic community and the role of Russia and its empire in its eastern borderlands.

Several issues form the background to this rethinking of empire. Educated society and officialdom reacted negatively to the long and destructive history of military conquest and exile in the North Caucasus, hardly a sign of "enlightened" imperial policy, and they were frustrated by the failures of imperial integration. The next chapter describes this history, the background to the efforts to reimagine the imperial community. A more distant but also important source of inspiration for the rethinking of empire was the general Great Reform effort to reconceive the character of the social order in Russia. The encounter with the Caucasus and Central Asia happened to coincide with this crucial period of social and cultural exploration in Russia. But the most important notion, distant in location yet somehow ever-present in the minds of both Russians and non-Russians, was that of "Europe" itself as an idea. Notions of enlightenment, progress, and Russia's relationship to Europe were especially important among multi-ethnic educated society on the frontier. Perhaps this is not surprising, given that "educated society" was by definition a community marked by literacy and varying degrees of education.

The preoccupation on the frontier with Europe's notion of progress reminds us of two different issues related to the work of Said and the interdisciplinary scholarship increasingly known as "post-colonial" studies of the history of colonialism. In the Russian context it is clear that the corpus of ideas, attitudes, and policies identified by Said as "Orientalist" were indeed significant and especially crucial to understanding the incorporation of eastern borderland regions such as the North Caucasus, the Volga-Urals, and Turkestan. The problem of Russia's torturous relationship to the West was especially complex and also especially promising on the frontier, as Mark Bassin has recently emphasized. The East, in his rendition, was a location where Russians might prove their worth as promoters of Europe's enlightenment and civilization, and where they might even alter the playing field. The "original Russia-Europe juxtaposition – so unfavorable for the former – could be reconsidered and, ultimately, readjusted."[35] "The historical tasks of Russia lie to the East," announced a Batumi newspaper on 1 January 1900, "which itself is eager to meet us."[36] Russia's greatness might be revealed and exhibited in the process of imperial expansion. The "second Renaissance," as Raymond Schwab liked to refer to Europe's discovery of the East, offered Germans the opportunity to "recapture the first Renaissance from the Latins by undisputedly possessing oneself of the Orient."[37] Russia too was offered a unique field upon which to develop its emerging nationalist consciousness, a matter closely tied to the process of imperial expansion.[38]

On the other hand, the Russian imperial experience also illustrates, in a way similar to the conclusion of numerous scholars studying the Western empires, that Said's "Manichean opposition between East and West" inadequately captures the experience of "cultural hybridity that necessarily informs both colonizing and colonized cultures."[39] Shared experiences and ideas made the level of "entanglement" so significant as to often obscure ethnic differences among the peoples of the region, reminding us that the empire was indeed "rossiiskii" rather than "russkii."[40] Russians and non-Russians together served the tsar, fought wars, conducted archaeological expeditions, propagated the Christian faith, transcribed alphabets, founded schools and worked as teachers, read about Shamil and mountain crime, and did numerous other things. Like Russians in the Far East, in the depiction of Bassin, Georgians too were particularly sensitive about their relationship to the idea of "Europe." As long as Russia was perceived, and as long as Russians perceived themselves, as the bringer of European civilization and progress to backward peoples beyond the reach of civilization and society itself, the colonial impulse familiar to the West remained strong and persuasive. But that same impulse continued to be uniquely a product of the "Russian" empire, shaped by its multi-ethnicity, contiguous expansion, imperial competition, historically charged and ambiguous relationship to European civilization, and encounter between Christianity and Islam.

2 Conquest and Exile

In this year of 1864 a deed has been accomplished almost without precedent in history: not one of the mountaineer inhabitants remains on their former places of residence, and measures are being taken to cleanse the region in order to prepare it for the new Russian population.

Main Staff of Caucasus Army, 1864[1]

Gunib is high, Allah is higher still, and you remain below.

Shamil to Bariatinskii, from Gunib, August 1859[2]

ARMY, TERRITORY, CHURCH

In 1828 the Russian playwright Aleksandr Griboedov presented a plan to I.F. Paskevich-Erivanskii, the high commander of the Caucasus, for the creation of a Russian Transcaucasus Trading Company. The plan, composed in Tbilisi with the help of a colleague in the imperial bureaucracy, envisioned a human economy as productive and rich as the famously abundant natural resources of the region. Such growth and activity would bring honour to Russia, the authors emphasized, and were the logical next stage of development in the wake of the recent military victories. Griboedov criticized officials who thought only about military victories and the "raising of rank."[3]

The authors of the plan were roughly twenty-five years ahead of their time, and the trading company was never established. The Caucasus was still principally a theatre of imperial competition and conquest for the Russian military. Russia's subjugation of its southern frontier was somewhat similar to its historic incorporation of other frontier regions such as Siberia. The conquest of Siberia was accomplished through the construction of forts and stockades (*ostrog*) manned by Cossacks, who fought hostile tribes, and more organized rivals such as Khan Kuchum. Forts gradually became administrative centres and towns, whose chief purpose was the exaction of fur tribute (*iasak*).[4] Minus the iasak, the military conquest of the southern borderlands was somewhat similar to that of Siberia.

On this frontier also, Cossacks fought the elements, constructed and manned fortresses, and defended themselves from hostile Crimean Tatars, Kalmyks, and mountaineers. In the North Caucasus the military gradually expanded the series of fortress-building begun in the early eighteenth century. In the northeast Peter the Great actually had captured Derbent (Dagestan) in 1722, and the following year the Persian shah ceded control of a strip of land along the Caspian, from Dagestan to Baku, to the Russians. In contrast to the earlier conquest of Siberia, Russians faced powerful rivals in the Persian and Ottoman empires, and they were also far more conscious of the prestige and power associated with big states. After Peter's success, his senators "toasted joyfully the health of Peter the Great, who had entered upon the path of Alexander the Great."[5] The Persians regained control of this area after Peter's death, but the general Russian advance continued. The Russians constructed fortresses at Kizliar in 1735 and Mozdok in 1765, and they took Azov and Taganrog in 1769. Catherine the Great and Potemkin referred to this string of fortresses as the "Caucasus Line," a moving frontier of Cossacks in defence of Russian gains.[6]

This edge of the empire was a site of imperial rivalry and war. The Russian defeat of the Ottoman Turks in the war of 1768–74 left Catherine as sovereign of new southern borderlands, and she directly annexed Crimea in 1783. In that same year the monarch of Kartli-Kakheti (Georgia), Irakli II, requested Russian protection in the face of pressure from Turkey, Persia, and the surrounding mountain population. The Russians built the fortress of Vladikavkaz, meaning "ruler of the Caucasus," in 1784 on the Terek River as a gateway to the Caucasus range and a path to Georgia. P.S. Potemkin declared the existence of the provinces of the Caucasus and Astrakhan in 1785 and made provisions for the organization of Cossack settlements along the Kuban River.[7] The question of security along the border and relations with Turkey and Persia dominated the correspondence of important St Petersburg officials with their frontier military governors, as B.V. Vinogradov reports.[8]

In 1801 Georgia was directly incorporated into the Russian Empire by Alexander I. It served as the Russian base for a further series of wars, against Persia (1804–13) and Turkey (1806–12), and for the gradual pacification of the Muslim regions of the Transcaucasus (Azerbaijan).[9] In the northeast Caucasus, Governor A.P. Ermolov, appointed in 1816, continued the construction of Russian fortresses, with names intended to express the power of the Russian military: Groznaia ("menacing" or "terrifying") on the Sunja in 1818, Vnezapnaia ("sudden") in 1819, and Burnaia ("stormy") in 1821.[10] The

Russian Empire's southern borders were clarified by 1828 after a further series of wars. The Russians again defeated the Turks in the war of 1826–28, and they took Erevan in 1827 and declared themselves the rulers of the southern steppe in the Treaty of Turkmenchai, which concluded the Russo-Persian War of 1826–28.[11] Paskevich was honoured with the name "Paskevich-Erivanskii" as a result of these military victories. The southern frontier remained principally a theatre of conquest and military conflict. Tsar Nicholas I expressed his "sincere gratitude" to Paskevich in a letter of 20 August 1828, for illustrating the strength of "Russian guns in Asia."[12] The incorporation of Georgia offered the empire a useful ally against the mountain peoples and a military and administrative foothold on the southern frontier.[13]

This pattern of imperial war and competition continued throughout the nineteenth century. France and Britain joined Turkey in the defeat of Russia in the Crimean War, and Turkish vessels and troops again appeared in the North Caucasus during the war of 1877–78. From the eighteenth century to the Cold War the Caucasus remained subject to the claims and pretensions of rival empires. From as far away as England, Lord Palmerston said in 1837, "No one values the important significance of the Cherkes for the maintenance of political equilibrium in Europe as much as I do."[14] Palmerston also feared Russia's conquest of the Caucasus as a potential challenge to Britain's control of India.[15] The British did not recognize Russian control of the Black Sea and sent armed schooners under the cover of trading flags, such as the one carrying James Bell, which was intercepted by the Russians in 1836.[16] Bell fled the Russians, spent three years among the mountaineers, and returned to write about it for his English-speaking audience.[17]

Russian military officials in the Caucasus were deeply disturbed by any such activity throughout the nineteenth century. They participated in a minor episode in the "Great Game" of imperial contest and intrigue that covered India, Central Asia, and other regions of the colonized world. Military officials of the Black Sea-Shore Line, such as General Nikolai N. Raevskii and Admiral Serebriakov, spent a great deal of their time pursuing Bell and others associated with what they understood as contraband trade with Turkey. Battling mountaineers in the summer of 1839 along the left bank of the Shakhe River, for example, Raevskii confirmed his suspicions: "From the fortress was visible a person with a European hat, moving from one gun to another and distributing ammunition. This was Bell."[18] Russian cruisers of the Black Sea Shore Line pursued an assortment of Englishmen and Turks who transported cannons and other weapons from Constantinople to the Caucasus coastline.[19] Raevskii felt that he was fighting a losing battle against Turkish contraband ships, as one successful run could make up for the cost of nine other ships captured by the Russians.[20]

Officials who conducted imperial wars on the frontier understood the value of the control of land and the expansion of the state to be self-evident, and aside from their interest in influential tribal leaders, many of them gave little thought to the inhabitants of the region. During the Russo-Turkish War of 1826–28, General Emmanuel issued a "proclamation" to the Adygei to inform them of the circumstances of Russia's war with Ottoman Turkey. The Ottoman government was guilty of breaking its agreement with the Russians, he explained, and the resulting imperial conflict was likely to be resolved on Adygei soil. "However, this war does not concern you," he assured the Adygei, "and the Russian government will not confuse you with the Turks."[21] Russian arms were to be directed only against the Turks and the "rebels" of the region. For Emmanuel, this was an imperial conflict that did not concern the local inhabitants of the region beyond the Kuban. The Adygei were to remain "completely quiet in their homes and calmly occupy themselves with their domestic matters." The Turks were the enemies of the Adygei, he emphasized in his proclamation, and if victorious, would deprive them of their property, privileges, and "your very life itself!"[22] Much to the chagrin of Russian officials, in 1843 the Adygei united to send a delegation to the Turkish sultan with a request for aid in the fight against the Russians. Some Russian officials optimistically expected the Porte to reject their plea, as, according to the Adrianople Treaty of 1829, the Ottoman government had "conceded" control of the Black Sea coast to Russia. "The articles of the Adrianople Treaty have never been announced to the Adygei," noted one military official, "but then how could this be done anyway?" They knew neither authority nor responsibility, he claimed, and answered to no one.[23] The land belonged to Russia, and it mattered little to Russian officials if the Adygei were unable to comprehend or accept this fact.

Russia's expansion south also brought the regime into conflict with Islamic peoples. Muslims were not new to the Russian Empire, of course, as the conquest of the khanates of Kazan and Astrakhan dated from the time of Ivan the Terrible in the sixteenth century. Russians had been in continuous contact with Muslims in one form or another since Prince Vladimir encountered the Bulgars of the Volga in the tenth century.[24] Russia's expansion in the eighteenth and nineteenth centuries in the southern and eastern borderlands was part of the general global process in which newly powerful Christian colonial states confronted the frontiers of the Islamic world. Russian policy was not eternally hostile, but vacillated from what Andreas Kappeler calls "pragmatic flexibility" in the sixteenth and seventeenth centuries to the extreme intolerance of the early eighteenth century, prompted by the desire of Peter the Great and his successors to make uniform the administrative regulations of the empire.[25] During Catherine's reign the government formed a series of ecclesiastical administrations that regulated the activities and property of Muslim religious leaders and institutions in a way similar to the policy of Muslim empires such as Ottoman Turkey and Persia. Conversion of Muslims was also a relatively low priority for the Russian state, and by comparison to the British or other colonial powers, Russian expansion in the borderlands was not characterized by a vigorous Bible distribution program or missionary fervour. In the Caucasus the Society for the Restoration of Orthodoxy in the Caucasus was not founded until 1860, and before then the regime sponsored only the modest Ossetian Spiritual Commission, which was created in 1746.

However, the encounter between faiths and religious traditions was frequently understood by Russians in the Caucasus as a matter of military conflict and imperial competition. Many Russians conceived of expansion as part of the historic campaign to push back the frontiers of Muslim "savagery" from the lands of Christendom. Orthodox churches accompanied the conquest, and they functioned not as centres of missionary conversion but as symbols of the historic identity of the Russian Empire. The fortress established by Peter outside of Derbent in 1722 was called "Fortress of the Holy Cross."[26] Mozdok had an Orthodox church from 1763, a church was constructed a year after the building of the fortress at Vladikavkaz, and a monastery was established at the Kizliar fortress in 1788.[27] Some Russian military commanders, such as General Nesselrode, hoped to appeal to fellow Christians such as the Armenians for support in Russia's effort to push the frontier farther south.[28]

Newspaper accounts of the history of Russian expansion emphasized the religious theme far more dramatically than the military reports of the Caucasus Army. The history of the Muslim presence in the Caucasus, whether in the form of local khans, mountaineers and Sufi Islam, or the Persian or Ottoman empires, was understood by the expanding Russian reading public of Tbilisi and the Caucasus to represent a threat to the religious integrity of Georgia, a neighbouring Orthodox land that apparently shared with Russia a common Byzantine heritage. For Russians, an event that best exemplified this relationship was the expansion north and plundering of Tbilisi in 1795 by Iranian shah Aga Mohammad while Empress Catherine the Great directed her attention toward events in the Balkans (the second

Russo-Turkish War) and France (the revolution of 1789).[29] The savagery of this event would frequently be remembered and alluded to by Russians throughout the nineteenth century as an example of what the Caucasus could expect, were it not for their presence. Cruelty and plunder, many Russians assumed, were typical facets of life under an "Oriental" and Muslim despot. General Tsitsianov's murder was another incident of considerable pedagogic significance for Russians. Pavel D. Tsitsianov (Paata Tsitsishvili), a Russian-educated Georgian who was remembered during Vorontsov's time for his fair treatment of the Georgian nobility, was murdered by the Baku khan, Hussein Kuli, in Baku in 1806.[30] In the retelling of this story, Georgia again appeared as Russia's ally against the Muslims. Tsitsianov, the Russian press emphasized, had arrived in Baku in anticipation of negotiation and had previously written to Hussein Kuli as "brother to brother," hoping that they would "eternally remain friends."[31] Yet the incorrigible khan took advantage of the truce to murder the well-intentioned Tsitsianov, or so the story went. The fortieth anniversary of his death was commemorated by the newspaper *Kavkaz* in 1846.[32]

PODDANSTVO

The inhabitants of the frontier found themselves caught between rival empires. For the mountaineers, sometimes there were money and contacts to be made as a result of the conflict. Tsebel'din (Adygei) prince Skhotsa Temurkva, in return for a significant financial reward from Baron Rozen, helped Russian forces along the Black Sea coast in their attack on the Abkhaz in 1837.[33] Bell supposedly offered the Ubykhs 1 million rubles for the head of Raevskii.[34] Early Russian interest in the mountaineers was thus motivated by such concerns. Local rulers, such as Prince Mikhail Shervashidze of Abkhazia, were often useful to the Russians because they informed them of the activities of British ships along the Abkhaz shore.[35] As Russian military officials encountered the different tribes of the North Caucasus, they attempted to secure affirmations of "loyalty" from their tribal leaders. From the Russian point of view, these often consisted simply of a commitment not to engage in "predatory" raids upon Cossack regiments or tribes whose previous pledge of loyalty to Russia made them "subjects" (*poddannyi*) of the Russian tsar.[36]

The interest of the regime in securing the loyalty of prominent mountain leaders was prompted by Russia's difficulties in prosecuting what rapidly developed into a protracted guerilla war in the North Caucasus. The practice was also a logical extension of traditional imperial ideology, where the state sanctioned the privileges of the noble estate in exchange for its loyalty. Especially since Catherine the Great, the state had attempted to strengthen the corporate identity of the nobility, hoping to increase its role in the fostering of social creativity and productivity.[37] In the borderlands, as Kappeler in particular has shown, the expanding old-regime state continued this practice and accepted non-Russian elites "as partners."[38] The state historically invited the nobility of non-Russian lands into the Russian service, including Muslim Tatars from Kazan, Astrakhan, Siberia, Crimea, and the Nogai Hordes, Kabard princes in the sixteenth century, and the Ukrainian nobility in the eighteenth century. After defeating Cossack hosts from the frontier, the imperial state in time created a privileged nobility from among Cossack elders, such as those of the Don. The seventeenth-century Muscovite regime even permitted Tatar nobility in the former khanate of Kazan to hold Russian peasants as serfs.[39] The Georgievsk Treaty of 1783 granted the Georgian nobility prerogatives similar to those of the Russian nobility.[40] Early officials such as Tsitsianov and Ermolov granted a broad autonomy to Georgian nobles and Muslim (Azerbaijani) khans, and provided positions in the Russian imperial service to Georgian nobles and places in the military for their sons.[41] From the early nineteenth century the sons of the most powerful families in the Caucasus were sometimes educated in St Petersburg.[42]

Old-regime custom aside, securing the loyalty of the powerful made for common sense on the part of regime policy. Local rulers who submitted to the Russians presumably brought their "families and subjects" with them, as the government of Paul I assumed at the end of the eighteenth century.[43] Grigorii Shvarts understood the task bestowed upon him by Viceroy Vorontsov to be "to attempt to win over to our side" those mountaineers with "influence upon the unsubjugated mountaineers."[44] Much of the correspondence between Generals Ol'shevskii and Raevskii on the Black Sea coast chronicled their efforts to determine the reliability and authority of the various Adygei and Abkhaz princes with whom they initiated negotiations.[45] After Daniel-Bek, the Elisuiskii sultan, fell out with Shamil in 1845, Russian officals such as General Gurko moved quickly to guarantee his personal safety and well-being in return for his loyalty and service.[46]

Native elites had their reasons to be attracted to imperial service. Money, payments in silver, the confirmation of landholdings, and service careers offered "respectable" natives a variety of motives. These were logical and realistic choices for small peoples between empires, in a world where everyone was presumably subject to some big state. Georgia's nobility had long enjoyed the privileges of service careers, and important families such as the Orbeliani, Chavchavadze, and

Eristavi were accustomed to using their positions to procure educational and career advantages for family members.[47] Combining traditions of loyal service, an excellent "higher military education," and a "familiarity with the Caucasus," as officials recommended a young man from the Baratashvili family, Georgians were particularly useful to the administration of empire in the region.[48]

The Georgian example offered an important model of incorporation to apply to the North Caucasus, even if among the Chechens, as an official from Shatov fortress reasoned in 1861, "there is no higher estate [soslovie] by birth, but [nonetheless] there are people who by virtue of their position should naturally exercise the rights of this estate."[49] Service records surviving in archives illustrate the imperial cohesion created by the religious divide, the long war against the mountaineers, and the experience of service. The better mid-level service careers among Georgians, Armenians, Ossetians, and many others included military decorations in the Crimean War, the Caucasus War, and the war of 1877–78 against the Turks.[50] Mountaineers won awards for their work as teacher inspectors in Dagestan and translators in Abkhazia.[51] Certain Adygei from Kuban oblast were generously rewarded in the midst of the massive exile of their people between 1861 and 1864.[52] The question of "poddanstvo" (subject-hood) for frontier elites was a fluid and ambiguous one of loyalty, faith, intrigue, realism, ambition, and fear.

MUSLIM RESISTANCE

The conquest of the Caucasus continued in the tradition of the expansion of the Russian state into the southern borderlands. The Russian military countered Western influence, defeated the surrounding empires of Ottoman Turkey and Persia in war, carved out the borders of the empire further to the south, encouraged the spread of Orthodoxy, took little interest in the cultural and religious differences of the new inhabitants of their realm, and worked to court non-Russian elites into the service of the empire. In time, that expansion was threatened more by the development of a Muslim resistance movement in the North Caucasus than by foreign powers such as Ottoman Turkey or Persia.

Sufi orders, which were at the forefront of this resistance movement, inspired North Caucasus Muslims to wage holy war (jihad, or ghazawat, as it was called in the Caucasus and Central Asia) in defence of Muslim lands or for the return to the world of Islam of territory lost to infidel rule. Sufi orders are informally organized mystical collections of brothers devoted to a spiritual director or leader. In the

North Caucasus the Sufi disciple was known as the "murid," and the Russians referred to North Caucasus Sufism as *muridizm*. Through various prayers, spiritual excercises, and disciplinary injunctions, the murid seeks progress along the mystical way or path (*tariqa*) toward God. The imam, or the religious leader recognized as the divinely designated successor to the prophet, is the leader of the Sufi order or brotherhood. Imam Shamil was the greatest of a long line of North Caucasus imams dating from Sheikh Mansur, who appeared in the North Caucasus in 1785 and was captured by the Russians in 1791 and eventually executed, to Gazi Muhammad, who declared holy war against the Russians from Gimri in 1829, and the short-lived tenure of Hamzat Beg.[53] Shamil became imam of the Naqshbandiya Sufi order in 1834.

Founded by Baha' al-Din Naqshband in Bukhara in the fourteenth century and active throughout the Muslim world, the Naqshbandiya order spread into the North Caucasus in the late eighteenth century. Long before the onset of European colonial rule, throughout the Muslim world such versions of mystical Sufism, sometimes called "popular" Islam, were radical in their challenge to the orthodoxy of the urban ulema (Muslim religious leaders). In the early and middle nineteenth century, for example, followers of Muhammad ibn Abd al-Wahhab contested Ottoman rule in central Arabia.[54] European expansion and the prospect of infidel rule presented an even greater threat and intrusion to believers within the Muslim community. The Sufi brotherhoods and other revivalist movements were more likely than the ulema to respond to the Qur'anic duty of either emigrating to Muslim territory or waging holy war.[55] Frequently, regions distant from the great city mosques of Islam were the most likely to possess active and radical Sufi traditions. Amir Abd al-Qadir frustrated French aims in western Algeria in the 1830s and 1840s, as did the Mahdists in Sudan for the British, before the latter reconquered the country in 1898.[56]

Shamil and the Sufi orders of the North Caucasus were thus part of these broader histories of Islamic renewal, and of contact and conflict between new empires and old. Russian officials such as Minister of War Alexander Chernyshev followed events in North Africa with great interest.[57] Like the Russian Caucasus, what was to become French Algeria was a distant frontier of the Ottoman Empire and subject at an early date to pressure from an expanding Christian power. Like Shamil, Abd al-Qadir inspired several Sufi orders by his call to holy war against infidel rule, and he led a protracted guerilla war against the French and the brutal scorched earth tactics of Marshal Bugeaud. In an effort to unite groups of different background as "one armed hand raised against the enemy," proposed Abd al-Qadir to a Turk in 1823, "[l]et us therefore efface all the racial differences among the true Muslims."[58] Shamil's imamate included the many different ethnic groups of the northeast Caucasus, and he tried to bolster his campaign by sending emissaries such as Magomet-Amin and Sel'men Efendi to the Adygei of the northwest Caucasus as well as to Ottoman territories near Erzerum.[59] In their respective colonial metropoles, both Shamil and Abd al-Qadir became the objects of extensive Orientalist curiosity and speculation. After his surrender in 1847, Abd al-Qadir spent several years in French prisons and eventually lived on an annual French pension of 150,000 francs in Damascus. In July 1860 he intervened to help alleviate a conflict between Muslims and Christians in Damascus and was credited with saving the lives of many Syrian Christians. He was the subject of great interest and fanfare during his visit to Paris in 1865.[60]

To the great fascination of readers of the Russian press, Shamil toured the major cities of Russia after his capture in 1859. As revered leaders of Muslim resistance movements, both he and Abd al-Qadir were simultaneously courted and contained by the colonizing powers. Their paths even crossed in the fall of 1865, when Abd al-Qadir, en route to France, presented N.P. Ignat'ev and the Russian embassy in Constantinople with a request that the Russian government allow Shamil to leave Kaluga for a visit to Mecca.[61] He even suggested that Shamil might stop in Damascus on his way home from Mecca. The North African leader was hoping to increase his prestige in the Muslim world by serving as a "protector for his fellow Muslims [*coreligionnaires*]," wrote Ignat'ev.[62] The ambassador used French to describe the religious interests and values held in common by Abd al-Qadir and Shamil. More important, however, was his recognition of the nature of the conflict prompted by Russia's expansion into Muslim lands. Along with other European powers, Russia participated in the history of conflict between Christian and Muslim empires.

The southern borderlands repeatedly frustrated Russian officials. They were defeated in the Crimean War, and the Caucasus War lasted some thirty years longer than most military officials expected. The conclusion of the Crimean War in 1856 allowed the Russian army the opportunity to divert forces from that theatre of conflict to the North Caucasus. Viceroy Aleksandr I. Bariatinskii reorganized the Russian military forces and implemented a more aggressive policy toward the forces of Shamil in Chechnia and Dagestan. The Caucasus Line was divided into two flanks, with the "right wing" in the west Caucasus commanded by General Filipson, and the "left wing" in the east Caucasus by General Evdokimov. General Orbeliani and then General Baron

Wrangel headed the region between these two wings – Stavropol province and the Transcaspian Region – and Baron Vrevskii commanded the Lezgin Cordon Line.[63] Shamil was driven further into retreat.

In the summer of 1859 the march of the left flank of the Caucasus Army drove him to the mountain village of Gunib, an enclave accessible only from one direction. Russian progress was rapid through late June and July, as valleys and villages which had for years been associated with Russian losses and tragedies now announced their submission to Russia. On 13 July in Dargo, where fourteen years earlier Viceroy Vorontsov had almost been killed, Bariatinskii now had breakfast and anticipated future progress.[64] August brought Bariatinskii and the Russian troops through further legendary sites of the Caucasus War: on the 6th to Karata, the place considered by Shamil to be his second capital and where his son and successor Kazi-Magomet lived, and on the 15th to Khunzakh, the capital of Avaria and the site of Hamzat Beg's death and the historic transfer of power to Shamil.[65] The advance of the Russians was initially tempered by an offer of compromise: Shamil would be allowed to travel to Mecca with whomever he pleased and helped to Turkey, or he might settle in another location in Dagestan.[66]

He retreated to Gunib, however, where he was temporarily safe but trapped. Backed by a contingent of some 40,000 men, Bariatinskii sent Colonel Lazarev and Sultan Daniel-Bek to Shamil with an ultimatum: surrender within twenty-four hours or face a full-scale Russian assault. Shamil still boasted in response, "Gunib is high, Allah is higher still, and you remain below."[67] After a series of threats had passed between Shamil and Bariatinskii through their messengers and translators, Shamil unexpectedly appeared on the 24th on horseback, led by two murids and surrounded by forty others around him. In an encounter made famous in illustrated chapbooks and pamphlets, Bariatinskii announced to him: "You did not want to come to me, so alas, I myself came to you. Now there will be no conditions. It is finished: you have been taken in battle, and I am able to grant you only your life, and that of your family; everything else depends upon the sovereign emperor."[68] On 26 August Bariatinskii sent his second telegram of the past four days to the tsar, this time with the momentous news: "Gunib has been taken; Shamil has been captured and will be sent to St Petersburg."[69]

EXILE

But the war was far from over. Perhaps buoyed by the defeat of the famous Shamil, the Russian army set upon the northwest Caucasus with a vengeance. Seventy battalions, a dragoon division, and twenty Cossack regiments were diverted from east to west. The Russians began preparing what officials repeatedly called the "cleansing" of the northwest Caucasus well before 1864. The practices and mentality of earlier regime officials in the southern borderlands again offered an important precedent to military officials of the Caucasus Army. Forced exile and massive population transfer had an extended history in the Russian Empire. Between 1784 and 1790 an estimated 300,000 Crimeans left the peninsula for Turkey out of a total population of 1 million.[70] Catherine the Great and her adviser Potemkin transferred Cossacks and Russian peasants to the southern steppe and the North Caucasus as a means of enhancing the security of the state. In their view, local populations were useful to the extent that they served these larger issues of imperial security.[71]

In the Caucasus Mikhail T. Loris-Melikov was sent to Constantinople to discuss plans for coordinating the emigration as early as 1860, and Bariatinskii had considered exiling some of Shamil's east Caucasus mountaineers to Turkey, before he was deterred by the prospect of attempting to transport them across the region.[72] Important military officials felt that exile was the only resolution to the conflict. General Kartsov, for example, emphasized that mere "pacification" was in this case insufficient. War would quickly be renewed, he complained, "with the first shot on the Black Sea, or even as a result of some senseless letter from the sultan, or the appearance of a self-described pasha."[73] Russia's plan for the "Cherkes," formulated sometime in the fall of 1860, was fairly simple. The mountaineers were to leave and might choose as a residence either Ottoman Turkey or a special region on the left side of the Kuban River.[74] The tsar himself informed an Adygei delegation of these intentions of the military during his visit to the Caucasus in 1861.[75]

Forced exile complemented the Muslim tradition of *hijra* (*makhadzhirstvo*), or voluntary migration in times of trouble. Muslims sometimes left by choice. After the Russian military victories in 1828–29, some 10,000 Abkhaz had left the North Caucasus. This emigration continued in the late 1830s and early 1840s, in particular after the Russian suppression of the rebellion in Guria in 1841 resulted in increased pressure upon Abkhazia as well.[76] The 1850s witnessed further Abkhaz emigration, with the population in decline from 98,000 in 1852 to 89,866 in 1858. After the Crimean War the Turkish government offered Caucasus emigrants freedom from military service and the tax-free use of land for up to six years, or twelve years in Anatolia.[77]

The most tragic phase of the mountaineer exile took place between 1858 and 1864. Over 30,000 Nogais were expelled from 1858 to 1860, and 10,000 Kabards from 1860 to 1861. Adygei exile included 4,300 Abaza families in 1861–63 (from the Kyzylbekov, Tamov, Bagov, Bashilbai, and Shakhgirei tribes), 4,000 Natukhais, 2,000 Temirgoi families, 600 Beslenei families, and 300 Bzhedugs. In the winter of 1864 there was extensive Ubykh and Abadzeg emigration, and by this time the Natukhais and the Shapsugs had virtually disappeared.[78] In 1865 some 5,000 Chechen families from the northeast Caucasus were sent to Turkey. They became subject to conflict between Russian and Turkish officials, who argued about their eventual destination. The Russians wanted them to continue into Anatolia, while the Ottoman officials initially hoped to keep them near the Russian border. Viceroy Grand Duke Mikhail accused the Ottoman officials of being unprepared to supervise the mountaineers after they crossed the border. While mountaineers waited for instructions and settlement preparation from Ottoman officials near the village of Musha, in search of food they began to threaten the local inhabitants. Captain Zelenyi, a Russian official assigned to oversee the process in Turkey, actually intervened to convince Turkish officials not to raise arms against the mountaineers. A similar event led to the death of at least fifteen Karabulaks (Ingush) and several Turks.[79] Russians later in the century often emphasized the difficulties encountered by mountaineers as they attempted to rebuild their communities in the Ottoman Empire. North Caucasus mountaineers eventually settled in Turkey, Syria, Jordan, Libya, and even Egypt.[80]

Military officials were proud of their concern for the mountaineers in the process of exile. The regime formed a special commission to oversee the process, tried to aid the mountaineers in their sale of belongings, and helped the most impoverished mountaineers to pay for the price of the journey.[81] Other witnesses, however, emphasized, a different story. "A striking spectacle greeted our eyes on our route back," wrote N. Drozdov of a village thirty versts from the Black Sea: "the scattered corpses of children, women, and old people, half torn apart by dogs, emigrants emaciated from hunger, barely supported by their weak legs, falling from exhaustion, but still alive and representing booty for the starving dogs."[82] Terrified by the rapid success of General Evdokimov and the Caucasus Army, the majority of the mountaineers gathered in dire conditions at the mouths of the mountain rivers that flowed into the Black Sea, such as the Shakhe, Vardane, and Sochi. Women and children, Drozdov noted, bore a disproportionate share of the toll of hunger, disease, and the effects of the war.[83] The date of 20 February 1864 was set as the deadline for their emigration, and the starving and beleaguered mountaineers were faced with rapidly falling prices as they sold what remained of their possessions and livestock.[84] Cossacks obtained bulls for just 3–5 rubles and cows for 2–3 rubles.[85] Many would soon perish on the shoddy vessels that carried them to Turkey.[86] The Russian regime instructed its consulate in Trapezund to encourage the process of exile by temporarily allowing Turkish contraband ships to cross the Black Sea if their booty included mountaineers from the North Caucasus.[87]

Many regime officials and other Russians in the Caucasus and throughout Russia quite simply believed that the Adygei and the mountaineers in general did not belong in the empire. Generals Kartsov and Evdokimov saw exile as the only resolution to the long Caucasus War, and officials of the Main Staff of the Caucasus Army continued to worry more about new imperial conflicts than about the needs, concerns, or rights of the Adygei.[88] Viceroy Grand Duke Mikhail looked forward to the end of the war as the achievement of the "complete cleansing [ochishchenie] of the Black Sea shoreline and the resettlement of the mountaineers to Turkey," and he told the tsar in a letter of March 1864 that he assumed the majority of the mountaineers would choose Turkey over the Kuban steppe.[89] Kavkaz informed its readers in 1864 that the Ubykhs had announced their submission, but their untrustworthiness required the authorities to continue to "cleanse the country" (ochistit stranu).[90]

The conclusion to the war resembled something like a mismatched hunting expedition in which the heavily armed aggressors pursued their desperate prey. The Main Staff reported in 1863 that the battle was basically won, but many tribes such as the Ubykhs still eluded Russian forces by retreating deep into mountain ravines and gorges. The "final cleansing" of the region was a matter of hunting down the families who held out, some at the very heights of the mountains.[91] Russian losses were few in 1863–64, during these final stages of "cleansing work," in contrast to the battles of 1861–63.[92] Military officials were unabashedly proud of these accomplishments of the Caucasus Army. "In this year of 1864 a deed has been accomplished almost without precedent in history," reported officials of the Main Staff of the Caucasus Army with satisfaction: "not one of the mountaineer inhabitants remains on their former places of residence, and measures are being taken to cleanse the region in order to prepare it for the new Russian population."[93] A military chronicler, K. Geins, emphasized that the total destruction of Adygei villages was required in order to dissuade the exiled from the thought of any eventual return.[94] In April the viceroy personally arrived at the mouth of the Sochi to thank and congratulate the Russian troops for their successful work.[95]

This work amounted to the expulsion of roughly 450,000 west Caucasus mountaineers in the course of just several years. G.A.

Dzidzariia, who has devoted an entire book to the problem of emigration from Abkhazia in the nineteenth century, concludes that 470,703 people left the west Caucasus in 1863–64.[96] N.G. Volkova provides figures of 312,000 west Caucasus mountaineers in 1863–64 and 398,000 from Kuban oblast from 1858 to 1864.[97] Nineteenth-century scholars offer comparable numbers. Adol'f Berzhe, chargé d'affaires of the Caucasus Department of the Imperial Russian Geographic Society and editor of numerous volumes dedicated to the history of the region, estimated the emigration at 493,194 from 1858 to 1864, or one-eleventh of the total Russian and non-Russian population of the Caucasus, and Vs. Miller, an ethnographer of the later nineteenth century, put the figure at 470,453.[98] Early-twentieth-century students offered similar figures.[99] In a Caucasus Department publication of 1866, N.I. Voronov put the number at 318,068 for the winter and spring of 1863–64 and at 400,000 in all.[100]

A detailed file on the emigration left by the Main Staff of the Caucasus Army confirms these figures: 332,000 mountaineers left in the fall of 1863–64 and an additional 86,000 from 1861 to 1863, for a total of 418,000 from 1861 to 1864.[101] Soviet and Turkish scholars tend to insist on much higher figures, and Western scholars often further confuse the matter by adopting one or more of the many available figures.[102] The question of counting is complicated by the fact that not all mountaineers fell under the control of the special commission designated by the regime to oversee the process. Some left on Turkish ships without the knowledge of the Russians, and a significant emigration took place from rivers such as the Tu, Nechepsukho, Dzhub, and Pshad, which empty into the Black Sea.[103] Given the circumstances of the war, as Berzhe implied in his 1882 *Russkaia Starina* article, who was counting anyway?[104] Roughly 90,000 mountaineers, approximately one-sixth of the total mountaineer population, received six desiatins of land per person to resettle in what was to become Kuban oblast.[105] Loyal imperial officials were rewarded with approximately 240,000 desiatins of land in Terek and Kuban oblasts.[106]

Many Russian writers in the nineteenth century were inclined to ignore the role of Sufi Islam in the North Caucasus and to deny that the greater Muslim world indeed possessed a significant influence within Russia's imperial borders. N. Drozdov suggested with condescension that the average mountaineer possessed a "knowledge of geography [that] ended at the borders of the village," making him susceptible to rumours and lies about the benefits of life in Turkey.[107] Adol'f Berzhe also stressed Turkey's deception of the ignorant mountaineers, such as the proclamations about the advantages of life there issued by

Mukhammed Nasaret to the west Caucasus mountaineers in June 1861.[108] Russian views in the nineteenth century coincide with the otherwise different assumptions of scholars writing in the late Soviet period, who explained the emigration with reference to the manipulative role played by "feudal" elites, the role of English and Turkish provocateurs, and the brutal policies of the tsarist government.[109] Yet Sufi Islam and the lands of the sultan remained a central factor in the politics and culture of the region.

In fact, when some mountaineers tried to return from Ottoman Turkey, officials enjoyed exploiting the issue for the purpose of propaganda, but they generally tried to close the border. Ignat'ev from Constantinople, along with other officials, rejected the efforts of 8,500 Adygei to return in 1872.[110] An official in Tbilisi reported in 1876 that roughly eighty parties of Chechens had returned to the Caucasus from approximately 1866 to 1873, or 5,857 people. This development dismayed local officials, who had already disposed of their land for a "different purpose." Officials resolved the matter in 1871 by sending them first to Vladikavkaz, from where some were sent again to Turkey, while the majority were returned to rural communities in Chechnia.[111]

THE UNFINISHED CAUCASUS WAR

The defeat of Shamil and the exile from the northwest Caucasus hardly diminished the presence of Sufi Islam. Russian troops captured Shamil and virtually destroyed the Naqshbandiya Sufi order, but the Qadiriya tariqa quickly filled the vacuum of religious authority. This order dated from the twelfth century and was introduced to the North Caucasus in the 1850s by a Kumyk shepherd named Kunta Haji Kishiev.[112] Sufi-inspired opposition continued to complicate Russian rule in the North Caucasus. There were rebellions in 1860 in Argun and Benoev, in 1861–62 at Tabasavan and Unkrable, in 1864 at Shalin, in 1865 at Kharachoev, and in 1866 in Madzhalise.[113] Kunta Haji returned from Mecca to Chechnia in 1861 and quickly established what a Russian official, A.P. Ippolitov, described as a "special secret administration" that appointed its own village elders beyond the influence of Russian rule.[114] His arrest and deportation in 1864 inspired the gathering of approximately 4,000 murids in Shalin, of whom 200 were killed and 1,000 wounded by Russian gunfire. Central Dagestan witnessed a revolt in 1871 which resulted in the exile of 1,500 people. Eighteen revolts in all took place in Dagestan alone between 1859 and 1877.[115] Kabard witnessed a rebellion in 1867.

Neither was the northwestern Caucasus free from rebellion. There were significant disturbances in Zakatal'skii *okrug* (district) in 1863 and in Abkhazia in July 1866.[116] The commander of Sukhumi *otdel* (section), Colonel Kon'iar, was killed, along with four officers and several Cossacks. The rebels destroyed the customs station in Lykhny and engaged the Russian garrison in Sukhumi.[117] Over 6,000 firearms were confiscated from the Abkhaz in the suppression of their revolt.[118] Faced with such threats, many Russian officials continued to think of the tradition of exile. Viceroy Grand Duke Mikhail noted in 1870 that the vast exile from Abkhazia made government objectives there easier to accomplish, and he advocated the expulsion of the "most troublesome portion of the Chechen population" as a regular means of dealing with the persisting difficulties in Chechnia.[119]

Shamil and his family, now in exile in Kaluga, were not oblivious to events in the North Caucasus. His keepers in Kaluga were dismayed to discover that the father of Zaidat, and Shamil's father-in-law, was in contact from Kars with rebellious Dagestani mountaineers in the early 1860s. Naib Umma-Duev, subsequently active in such activity in Dagestan, managed to visit Shamil in Kaluga.[120] The regime was careful to respect the Muslim sensibilities of Shamil and his family while they were in captivity. Kazi-Magomet was quickly sent back to Dagestan to assure the mountaineers of Shamil's comfortable and respected position in Kaluga.[121] Like the French with Abd al-Qadir, the Russian regime was generous in its subsidy to Shamil and his family. In addition to a 10,000 ruble yearly payment and rent subsidy, funds were routinely allocated to him for home construction, furniture, Kazi-Magomet's various trips, a new bathroom, and the almost yearly lease of a dacha outside Kaluga for the summer.[122] Now minister of war, Dmitrii Miliutin reminded the officials responsible for Shamil that their surveillance was to be "constant, but not inhibiting for him."[123] The terms were strict, but at the same time Miliutin and his ministry emphasized that Russian officials were never to obstruct the fulfillment of Islamic religious rites by Shamil or anyone else in his party, and in general were not to interfere in their domestic arrangements.

Shamil wanted to leave Kaluga, however, and repeatedly wrote to Russian officials of his hope to visit the holy places of Islam before his death.[124] But the relationship of the conquering regime to Sufi Islam remained uneasy. Viceroy Grand Duke Mikhail strongly opposed one such request of Shamil in 1868 because he feared the effect of such an announcement upon the mountaineers of the North Caucasus.[125] With the health of his family in serious decline, Shamil was finally allowed a move south on 28 November 1868.[126] The family went to Kiev, where they lived for a year, and then abroad in 1869, without Kazi-Magomet and his family, on a one-year journey of pilgrimage to

Mecca and Medina. On 4 February 1871 Shamil's life came to an end, appropriately during a second journey to Mecca, when the religious leader died after a fall from the special seating arranged for him between two camels.[127] By then most of his remaining family were with him in the Ottoman Empire. The sultan granted Shamil a home in Constantinople, and Kazi-Magomet was allowed a six-month visit to attend to his father's deteriorating health.[128] There most of the family lived out their lives, including Shamil's Armenian wife, Shuanet, who did not die until 1878, in Constantinople.[129] Zaidat had died in 1871 some months after Shamil, near Mecca.[130]

Kazi-Magomet returned to Russia only to help transport remaining family members to their new home in Turkey.[131] Because of excitement among North Caucasus mountaineers over Kazi-Magomet's presence in the Ottoman Empire, Ignat'ev vowed to maintain a "secret surveillance" over his activities abroad.[132] He felt that Kazi-Magomet would generally remain "loyal to Russia," although he conceded that it was unclear what "influence the trip to Arabia would have on the thought and behaviour of Kazi-Magom[et], or his meeting with his father and his contact with the fanatical Muslim clergy."[133] Throughout the 1870s Kazi-Magomet maintained contacts with mountaineer pilgrims on their way to Mecca and, as some Russian officials reported with dismay, performed various Sufi rituals and encouraged North Caucasus emigration.[134] He would not return to Russia until the war of 1877, when he commanded the Turkish division that laid siege to the Russian fortress at Baiazet and starved the trapped Russian garrison of Captain Shtokvich. Designated by Shamil as his successor, Kazi-Magomet continued in the tradition of Muslim resistance to infidel rule.

The rebellion of 1877 that accompanied the outbreak of another Russo-Turkish War was an additional instance of Sufi opposition to Russian rule. In many respects this was simply a continuation of the Caucasus War. Sheik Haji Mohammed, who led the revolt in Dagestan, was a Naqshbandi, while in Chechnia the Qadiriya order was particularly active.[135] Early reports of disturbances in May 1877 in Dagestan were dismissed by Russians in Tbilisi as rumour and hearsay and as the work of small groups of discontented Ichkerians and Aukhovs (Chechens).[136] Yet in late April all of Ichkeriia was in revolt, which included forty-seven villages and roughly 18,000 people. By June the Russians judged the threat to Georgia to be real. In the beginning of that month a Russian writer in *Kavkaz* confessed that the reasons for the disturbances were "still unknown," while by late June he attributed the matter to "Muslim fanaticism."[137] Colonel Nurid informed the fortress at Groznyi that "there is no doubt that all of

Chechnia is for the mutineers, and only awaits their appearance in order to openly act against us."[138] By August newly pronounced imam
and rebel leader in Dagestan Alibek-Khadzhi Aldanov commanded
an army of 30,000, and by October the Russian population was flee-
ing to safer havens, such as Astrakhan and Temir-Khan-Shura.[139]

The extensive character of the rebellion, covering 504 different locations in Dagestan alone, prompted among Russians a reassessment of
the legacy of Russian rule in the North Caucasus after 1859.[140] "We
are unable to say that the region has been subjugated and that we,
Russians, are the complete masters here. The sad circumstances suggest the exact opposite," an editor in *Kavkaz* noted in the wake of the
rebellion.[141] The readiness on the part of the mountaineers to act in
concert with Turkey raised further questions about the viability of
Russian rule over Muslim regions that bordered Muslim empires. In
the Middle Volga, by contrast, officials only noted the prevalence of
rumours among the Tatars about Russian plans for their religious
conversion.[142] But in Ichkeriia (Chechnia), rebellious mountaineers
gathered immediately after Alexander II's announcement of the beginning of another Russo-Turkish War on 12 April.[143] Fazli-pasha arrived in Sukhumi (Abkhazia) with an explicitly religious appeal to
his Muslim "brothers" to oppose the enemy "Muscovites," who
wished to "wipe Islam from the face of the earth."[144] The Turks maintained control of Sukhumi from May through July of 1877.

The 1877 rebellion was again a revival of the tradition of religious
warfare, the efforts of Soviet scholars to depict the uprising as motivated by grievances of a social and economic nature notwithstand-
ing.[145] Russian administrator N. Semenov recalled in his memoirs of
the event that he and other officials noted an increase in Sufi activities
in Chechnia in early 1877.[146] And the rebellion was neither isolated
nor local. Chechnia and Dagestan were most active in the rebellion,
but it was also felt in Ossetia, Ingushetia, Abkhazia, Svanetia,
Kakhetia, Mingrelia, and the provinces of Baku and Elisavetpol'.
Georgian prince Chavchavadze, the military governor of Dagestan,
later reported that the imperial administration in a district such as
Kazi-Kumukh completely disappeared in the course of the rebellion.
The rebels destroyed the materials and documents of the district commander, who worked out of his home in any event, and easily over-
powered the local police force, a contingent of forty men for the entire
district.[147]

Officials were dismayed that they had to divert forces from the war
with Turkey in order to quell a rebellion in the rear. General Komarov
converged upon southern Dagestan, General Murav'ev upon central
Dagestan, and Colonels Tukhonov and Kvisinsk upon the west. By

September the 26,000 Russian troops mobilized for the occasion regained control of Chechnia, and by October they took Dagestan. Five
thousand mountaineers were exiled, and 370,000 desiatins of land
that belonged to them were expropriated by the state.[148] The roster of
Russia's potential rebels increased as a result of the war, as it acquired
22,330 new versts of land and transformed them into the oblasts of
Kars and Batum.[149] Accustomed to the reality of massive population
movements in this part of the world, Russian and Turkish representatives met in December 1878 to establish a three-year time period for
the expected migration. Those who remained after 8 February 1882
were considered subjects of Russia.[150] Russian policy in Kars oblast
was oriented to the Christian population after its incorporation into
the empire. In 1893 "Turks," "Kurds," "Karapapakhs," and other
Muslims accounted for 56.6 per cent of the population of the oblast,
while Muslim students took up only 3.7 per cent of the space in the
eight educational institutions founded by the government, in contrast
to the larger number of Armenian, Greek, and Russian students.[151]

Many military officials advocated a harsh response to the uprising.
"The Abkhaz people betrayed Russian authority in the recent war,"
reported an official in Tbilisi, "joined the ranks of the Turkish troops,
and took an active part in the military activities."[152] General
Svistunov suggested exile to Russia for untrustworthy mountaineers
and Muslims from all over the Caucasus and particular severity for
Dagestani and Chechen villages. He wished to see the entire villages
of Benoi and Zandak sent to Siberia and recommended that, "if these
scoundrels refuse, freeze them in the winter like beetles and starve
them to death."[153] N. Butkevich, in an unpublished essay, offered the
astonishing proposal of the relocation of as many as 1 million Muslim
and mountaineers from the Caucasus.[154] Forced exile to Ottoman
Turkey was no longer an option, but the Russians identified
5,000 mountaineers whom they declared unfit for continuing residence in the North Caucasus. Approximately 1,000 mountaineer families were quickly sent first to Opochki in Pskov province and
Medved in Novgorod province in October 1877, and another
2,650 mountaineers were moved from the mountains of Dagestan
and Chechnia to the plains, where they awaited Russian exile.[155] Entire families and even villages were sent into exile. This was a necessity, explained Viceroy Grand Duke Mikhail, because rebellion was
woven into the very fabric of mountaineer culture, and a stern example had to be set for the benefit of those mountain villages that remained intact.[156] The unfortunate mountaineers were eventually
transported to Saratov province, where the regime laid plans to orga-
nize and administer them like Russian peasants. Even in Saratov,

however, their faith continued to inspire their opposition to Russian rule and the world constructed for them by the regime. The mountaineers refused to conform to the rhythm and life of settled agriculture in a Russian setting, and they complained that it interfered with their daily prayer schedule.[157] The provincial authorities resorted to the use of Cossack detachments to quell a growing number of demonstrations.[158] In 1883 the remaining Dagestanis won the right to return home.

THE LIMITS OF IMPERIAL INTEGRATION

Given this extended history of war and continuing opposition to Russian rule, it is not surprising to learn that imperial officials were tentative and frustrated in their efforts to impose the administrative norms of the empire upon the North Caucasus. The Petrine model of state-building, the "well-ordered police state" described by Marc Raeff, in its ideal form stressed uniformity. "Russia" itself was not an administrative unit within the empire, and Catherine the Great's 1775 statute on the provinces did not distinguish between the older Russian regions and the new provinces of Arkhangel'sk, Olonets, and Kavkaz (the Caucasus), created in 1784–86.[159] Ukrainians lived in nine different provinces to the west, Lithuanians were in three different western provinces, Chuvash territory was divided among Kazan and Simbirsk provinces, and Georgians, Armenians, and Azerbaijanis resided in *gubernii* such as Tiflis, Kutais, Erevan, Baku, and Elisavetpol'.[160]

Gradually the conquering state worked to abolish the previous forms of rule common to the North Caucasus. In the northeast, Russian officers replaced the local khans and naibs with themselves and the districts (*okrugi*) of Dagestan region (*oblast*). General Wrangel, for example, used the 1858 death of Alagar-Bek, the ruler of Kazi-Kumukh *khanstvo* (khanate), as a pretext to place the administration of the khanstvo in the hands of a Russian officer. General Iusuf-Khan, who had ruled the Kiurin khanstvo since 1842, was replaced in 1862 by a Russian officer, and in 1864 the khanstvo was made an okrug and governed like the rest of Dagestan oblast. Colonel Ibragim-Khan Mekhtulinskii and the Avar khanstvo met a similar fate in 1864, as did the Dagestan regions of Kaitak and Tabasaran. The Russians put their respective khans on government pensions. The Tarkov region became part of Temir-Khan-Shura okrug in 1867, and the Dargin societies, left alone since 1860, became Dargin okrug that year.[161] In Abkhazia the Russians severed their relationship with Prince Mikhail Shervashidze in 1864.[162] A similar process took place in Mingrelia, which continued under the special rule of Prince David Dadiani until

1867, when he was removed and Mingrelia became part of Kutaisi province.[163] After 1859 the Chechens resided in several districts (Chechen, Argun, Nagornyi, and Ichkeriia) of Terek oblast, which were in turn divided into sections (*uchastki*) and administered by a Russian police officer (*pristav*).[164] Kuban oblast covered the northwest Caucasus and the lands of the Adygei tribes. Khanstvos, naibstvos, and other forms of local rule were gradually becoming okrugs within oblasts as the imperial administration extended its practices onto the southern frontier of the Caucasus.

The mix of motives, ambitions, and fears that signified "poddan-stvo" for frontier elites was most evident in this time of transition, a process perhaps similar to the transition from indirect to direct colonial rule of tribal and patrimonial societies described by Michael Doyle in his comparative work on empires.[165] Prince Mikhail Shervashidze and his family, the Abkhaz ruling family, were outraged by the turn of events begun in 1864. "[I]n his words, he had been driven out of Abkhazia like some sort of Ubykh," he told imperial envoy Prince D.I. Sviatopolk-Mirskii.[166] Shervashidze's defence was the customary mix of the desperate plea, the appeal to past loyalty and service, and a few mild threats. "I fulfilled the will of the tsar and passed on the administration of my domains to my successors," he justified himself to Sviatopolk-Mirskii.[167] And in the course of forty years of service, he added on another occasion, he had been "significantly useful to the Russian throne."[168] His children's only defence was an appeal to their status as "the first family in this land."[169]

Sviatopolk-Mirskii, however, was unmoved and felt no need to negotiate. Change was necessary "for the preservation of state interests and general peace" in Abkhazia, he explained.[170] He wrote to Viceroy Grand Duke Mikhail without remorse over the transition, adding that the conquest of the west Caucasus finally made it possible. Imperial officials, however, were themselves products of the "old regime" system, where the state rewarded and sometimes penalized its nobility as it saw fit. Sviatopolk-Mirskii was also a "prince," and he communicated his general respect for noble privilege throughout this exchange through the fall and winter of 1864–65. And as an experienced borderland official, he also recognized the potential treachery of the frontier. He recommended against exile abroad for Shervashidze, which might easily become "harmful for us," and instead placed the ruling family in nearby Imeretia (Georgia).[171]

The desperate appeal of the surviving family members of the Kazi-Kumukh and Kiurin khanstvo in Dagestan was similar to that of the Shervashidze children from Abkhazia. The daughter of the last khan was virtually impoverished by 1883 in Temir-Khan-Shura, from where she appealed for financial support. She told a story of loyalty and service, of historic "poddanstvo" to the Russian throne since 1812, of a grandfather made khan by Ermolov in 1823, and of the imminent and unjust demise of this princely line.[172] The tentative exploration of something closer to a modern form of empire left the offspring of many previously privileged families in new and unfamiliar conditions.

In spite of this emerging transformation, the North Caucasus generally remained different from the interior provinces of the empire and continued to pose special problems for administrators. The region continued to be a distant colony, rather than an integral part of the empire. Until 1917, except for the fortresses that were becoming towns, the region remained in what the Russians called "military-native administration" (voenno-narodnoe upravlenie). Officials felt that this special form of rule was still necessary, even long after the conquest.[173] The system was suggestive of the colonial relationship and was similar to the methods of the French in the Maghrib, who left mountaineer and nomadic regions under military administrations such as the Algerian bureaux arabes or the Moroccan Service des Affaires Indigènes.[174] The imperial norm, applied to the cities, was called "civil rule" (grazhdanskoe upravlenie).

Military-native administration left the North Caucasus in a holding pattern, with the regime tentative and unable to extend its administrative traditions to distant mountain villages. The far more integrated Georgia, by contrast, felt the impact of the Great Reforms, including the abolition of serfdom in Tiflis province in October 1864, Kutaisi province in October 1865, and Mingrelia in 1866.[175] In Ossetian, Kabard, and other regions the regime generally sought stability in the wake of the war by guaranteeing the holdings of "reliable" and privileged families, and providing security to the landless through village and communal institutions.[176] Like French officials in Africa, however, reformers understood the need for compromise.[177] In Dagestan, for example, further from the Georgian frontier, imperial officials were reluctant to undercut the order imposed by local khans and beks.[178] Early-twentieth-century administrators such as A. Nikol'skii were disturbed by the absence of imperial traditions at so late a date and complained about the enduring agricultural dependency in mountain regions as "remnants" of a previous historical epoch and a "complete anachronism."[179] It was not until 1 January 1913 that the regime declared the dependent classes in Dagestan to be free of obligation to their beks.[180] As a result of the war and the collapse of the empire, these continuing discussions of tsarist administrators on land reform became irrelevant.[181]

A variety of issues illustrate the distance of North Caucasus peoples from the imperial system. They did not serve, for example, in the imperial army. Historically, there had been a limited form of mountaineer military service, dating to a special branch of the imperial convoy established by Catherine the Great in 1775. The Imperial Convoy of Caucasus Mountaineers, formed in 1828, featured primarily Kabards, Chechens, Kumyks, and Adygei, all fastidiously dressed in the Romanticized version of mountain military garb.[182] Like the special Bashkir squadron, however, this was a very limited and privileged form of military service.[183] Aware of the sensitive nature of military service for newly conquered mountain peoples, Bariatinskii in 1860 declared that the claims of the Russian military would never be extended to Chechen and Dagestani mountaineers.[184] Instead, North Caucasus mountaineers, according to a 1864 statute, paid a 3-ruble-per-person tax in exchange for their exemption from military service.[185] Reformers within the Ministry of War, who conceived of the imperial army as a potential site of education and exposure to the values of Russia, often initiated discussions about extending military service to the mountaineers. Even at the onset of the First World War, however, the regime remained unable to compel the mountaineers to serve in the army, although there were various voluntary and special divisions that served up to the collapse of the old regime.[186]

Mountaineers were not in imperial schools. Drawing upon the heritage of the eighteenth-century state, where education, claimed Catherine's adviser Betskoi, would create a "new type of people" and provide "for the sovereign, zealous and faithful servants; for the empire, useful citizens," early educational decrees were directed at the nobility in the Caucasus and emphasized the needs of the state.[187] The state granted various "Caucasus stipends" to Georgians in particular throughout the early nineteenth century, "directed toward the creation of a native administrative intelligentsia," as one historian put it.[188] An 1849 statute on education in the Caucasus emphasized that the purpose of schooling was to "prepare the sons of the Caucasus and Transcaucasus privileged estates to occupy different levels, even the highest levels, of state service in the Caucasus and the Transcaucasus."[189]

While the impact of the tsarist educational system was profound in Georgia, it was far less so in the North Caucasus. "All they lack is education," optimistically wrote a student of the North Caucasus in 1847, but its impact remained minimal before 1917.[190] Schooling was the uncoordinated product of a variety of institutions, such as the General Staff of the Caucasus Army, the Ministries of Education and the Interior, the Holy Synod, and the Georgian Synodical Office.[191] During Vorontsov's reign, secondary schools existed in Tbilisi, Kutaisi, Stavropol, and Ekaterinodar, and twenty district institutes functioned in many smaller cities such as Derbent, Erevan, Gori, Mozdok, Kizliar, Elisavetpol', Kuba, and Anapa. By the late 1850s the regime had reached further into the mountain regions to sponsor the educational and living expenses of mountain students, most of them from "respected" families, at institutes in Vladikavkaz, Nal'chik, Temir-Khan-Shura, Ust Lebin, Groznyi, Sukhumi, and other places.[192] Among the 142 students at the Stavropol Gymnasium in 1847, for example, 30 were the children of Russian nobles and officials, 47 were from the families of Cossack officers, and 65 were the sons of mountain princes and other privileged families.[193] Scholars such as Petr K. Uslar hoped to reach beyond this limited audience, and he provided written scripts for mountain languages and compiled primers for reading and elementary education. He also established schools in many mountain regions, and his alphabets and readers were adopted for use in the schools founded by the regime's missionary society.[194] Such efforts resulted in the founding of schools in even more remote mountain regions in Dagestan, Abkhazia, and Kabarda, although they were no match for the thriving Muslim primary and secondary schools, in particular in Dagestan.[195]

The bloody and protracted resistance of numerous North Caucasus mountaineers to Russian rule prompted regime officials to tread cautiously in the region, and the state moved slowly on sensitive matters such as military service and land reform. Military-native administration was left intact because officials feared new outbreaks of rebellion to their rule, and they also were unable to implement the judicial and urban reforms of 1864 and 1870.[196] The Muslim Ecclesiastical Administration that Catherine had established for Muslims in Siberia and Crimea, and that her successors had extended to Azerbaijan, was also not introduced in North Caucasus regions.[197] In terms of military service, the North Caucasus was similar to other borderland regions such as Central Asia, Siberia, Astrakhan gubernii, and the oblasts of Turgaisk and Urals, where inorodtsy ("aliens") remained exempt from the 1874 decree on military service.[198] The North Caucasus posed special problems for imperial state-builders, and it was perhaps most similar to recently conquered and still-rebellious Turkestan. Tatars in the Volga region, Tatars in the Transcaucasus (Azerbaijan), Georgians, and others were far more integrated into the imperial system. The North Caucasus remained relatively untouched by imperial rule before 1917, a sensitive and rebellious frontier region with cultural links to worlds beyond the borders of the Russian Empire.

The tenuous nature of Russian rule in the North Caucasus crossed the divide of revolution, as both the Naqshbandiya and Qadiriya orders continued to grow under Soviet rule. Contemporary researchers estimated that 70–80 per cent of the men over eighteen in Chechnia in 1925 possessed some sort of a connection to a Sufi brotherhood.[199] After the mass deportations of Chechens, Ingush, and others to Central Asia in February 1944, Sufi-led fighting continued in the mountains until 1947. The Soviet regime revived the tradition of the Muslim Ecclesiastical Administration, whose officials carefully appointed the most important figures within the Muslim hierarchy and persecuted what they called "self-proclaimed" religious leaders and "unregistered cult members."[200] As with their colonial predecessors, the language of Soviet officialdom was intended to deny the legitimacy of popular Sufi traditions. The events of the past decade suggest that the long Caucasus War has not yet ended.

The conquest of the Caucasus followed the annexation of Crimea by Catherine in the eighteenth century, in the continuing story of the Russian state's conquest of its steppe frontier. In both Crimea and the Caucasus the Russian military defeated rival empires, clarified borders, and exiled large numbers of the indigenous inhabitants. Military officials and most other Russians felt no need to apologize for the expansion of the state or for the exiles they created. Expansion increased the strength of the state, which in turn glorified the tsar and his nobility. Continuing with their early modern traditions on the steppe, Russian officials sought to identify, accommodate, and reward the interests of non-Russian elites. The general inhabitants of the borderlands were hardly relevant to this equation; they in any case were, in the Russian view, self-evidently better off as subjects of the Orthodox tsar rather than the Muslim sultan. Christian expansion was a victory against Muslim savagery. Like Habsburg domains to the west, Romanov rule was a "patchwork of disparate territories, brought together in largely piecemeal fashion."[201] The incomplete nature of the conquest and the unsatisfactory character of imperial integration provided a particular urgency to the Orientalist project of imagining and visualizing empire.

3 Orthodoxy: The Society for the Restoration of Orthodoxy in the Caucasus

I don't remember the crosses, but I heard that we once professed
some other faith, but as to what it's called I don't know.
                                elderly Chechen to Nikolai Dubrovin, 1871[1]

ORTHODOXY AND ISLAM ON THE FRONTIER

Conservative writers such as the Slavophiles were famously preoccupied with the past, of course, and studied Russian history for unique traditions that, in their view, also heralded a special future. As numerous scholars have shown, thinkers such as Ivan Kireevskii and Alexei Khomiakov explored the special Russian traditions of social harmony, communal peasant institutions, customary law, the Muscovite heritage, and the Orthodox faith, which they felt served as a reservoir of Russia's special "narodnost'"and "originality" (*samobytnost'*).[2] While there is obviously not a direct connection between the classical architects of Slavophile thought such as Kireevskii and Khomiakov and distant colonial communities on the frontier, a series of general conservative notions about tradition, the past, and cultural authenticity predominated among borderland communities and hence shaped the expansion and formation of the empire. "Conservative" thought was especially important on a frontier where officials and members of educated society were intent on conserving Orthodox tradition in the face of a historically expansive Islam.

For Slavophiles, Orthodoxy in particular held the key to Russia's special future. Khomiakov, for example, deplored a Western tradition in his view centred on rationalism, legalism, and the worship of "science" as an end in itself. Orthodox Christians, by contrast, "stand on entirely different soil."[3] Russia's special promise for Slavophile thinkers was a product of its fidelity to genuine Christian tradition.

Christians who fell away from the faith were those who neglected their tradition, which was the unforgivable sin of the western half of the Roman Empire. Latin Christians, wrote Khomiakov, were the "schismatics" whose deviant tenets, practices, and popes were followed by the continuing disintegration fostered by Luther and Calvin at the Reformation, when every individual took it upon himself to define the faith "according to his own taste."[4]

The Slavophiles were profoundly critical of foreign borrowing and "imitation" (*podrazhanie*), which left them in an antagonistic relationship to the Petrine state and its Westernized nobility. Because Peter the Great "destroyed a lot that he shouldn't have touched," as Khomiakov put it, and saddled Russians with a "foreign way of looking at things," in the words of Iurii Samarin, contemporary educated Russians hardly recognized their own indigenous cultural past.[5] The situation was not hopeless, however. The eastern half of the empire outlasted the Latin West, and Russia was its heir. In depicting the collapse of the vast and powerful Roman Empire in the West as a product of spiritual weakness rather than military disintegration in the face of Germanic tribes, Khomiakov must have also had in mind the expansive but secular empire founded by Peter the Great and his successors.[6] The contrasting endurance of Byzantium was not a product of favourable physical geography or commercial networks but was "purely spiritual" and a "fruit of its previous spiritual life."[7] "The East was for centuries rich in intellectual and original [*samobytnoiu*] activity."[8] This contrast was also emphasized strongly in the polemical "Letter to the Serbs, sent from Moscow," signed by Khomiakov along with Mikhail Pogodin, Iurii Samarin, Konstantin and Ivan Aksakov, and others. "The spiritual pride of the Greeks corresponds to the intellectual pride of all the western people," the Russians told the Serbs.[9] "Christianity was transformed into an institute [in the West]," while genuine personal belief endured in the East.[10]

Russia as the heir to Byzantine Christianity also seemed to inherit the historic struggle with Islam. The preservation of the past and the respect for tradition and "originality," mixed with a dose of Greek pride, recounted Khomiakov, allowed the Byzantine Greeks to fortify themselves in the struggle with the "Muslim conquerors."[11] Khomiakov's depiction of the deleterious impact of the Mongol invasions upon Russian historical development was hardly unique, of course, but his continuing hostility to the "remnants of the former Tatar power" had disturbing temporary implications.[12] Ivan the Terrible's taking of Kazan and Astrakhan in 1552 was a moment of "glory" for Russia: "Russia took for itself all of the Volga, seized the Muslim tsardoms, and extended its hand to its fellow Christian believers in

Georgia and on the slopes of the Caucasus."[13] Since that time the "peaceful," "agricultural," and "trading" Slavic tribes had been assaulted by their "militaristic neighbours" and protected only by the Cossacks, whose "single goal was to stand in defence of Christian land against Muslims and Tatars." This encounter was "repeated almost everywhere on the borders [of the empire]."[14] Following a well-beaten path through the Caucasus of the Russian literary imagination, at the age of twenty-four Khomiakov was inspired to experience this encounter personally, and he accompanied the Russian army as far south as Adrianople in 1828.[15] The many Muslims of the empire also posed a threat to Russia's cultivation of its native soil.

Russia's version of Latin Europe's crusading impulse was wrapped up with its memory of Byzantium. While Constantinople after 1453 remained distant from medieval Russia's rulers, by the eighteenth century Russia's expansion south brought its frontiers close to those of early Christianity. Islam, according to this crusading mentality, was historically illegitimate, an intruder into Christian holy lands and regions formerly held by the city of the first Christian emperor, Constantine. Russia's rulers were eager to claim for themselves the role of the protector of Orthodoxy during their many subsequent conflicts with the declining Ottoman Empire.[16] Catherine the Great concluded that Russia had the right and duty to defend the faith "in the places of its upspringing, protected from all oppression and violence."[17] However unlikely was her "Greek project," or the notion of restoring some form of the old Byzantine Empire based in Constantinople (Aleksandr Pypin referred to it as a "grandiose plan," Zhigarev as a "dream"), it included a prominent role for Russia, and the southern expansion initiated during her reign was presented by the regime as part of this project of recovery.[18] The new territories included Kherson (after the Greek Khersones), Odessa (Odysseus), and Taurida province (after Tauris, the Greek name for the Crimean region). The fortress at Kherson proclaimed, as Richard Wortman notes, the "Route to Byzantium," and a medal created in honour of the second grandson of Catherine featured the cathedral of St Sophia from Constantinople.[19] The boy was named Constantine, and the medal presented the St Sophia with Christian crosses rather than Muslim minarets. This imperial impulse endured through the nineteenth century. At the start of the fourth Russo-Turkish War of the century in 1877, Tsar Alexander II proclaimed: "Our faithful and beloved subjects know the lively interest which we have always devoted to the destinies of the oppressed Christian population of Turkey."[20] While officials in the Ministry of Foreign Affairs were skeptical of the viability of Russian control over the straits of Constantinople, the imperial family, Pan-

Slavists, and other conservative Russians belligerently continued to bring attention to this issue throughout the imperial era.[21]

Educated society and officialdom on the frontier made their own contribution to the ideas of intellectuals and empire-builders in St Petersburg and Moscow. Russians and Georgians throughout the nineteenth century depicted Muslim Turks as the source of "oppression and violence," and viewed the Russian conquest of the Caucasus as an opportunity to counter the historic rise of Islam in the Mediterranean and Black Sea regions. "Yes! We live in a wonderful place / Our warlike Kavkaz," sang Iablochkina at the Tiflis Theatre on 21 October 1853, "Protecting Kavkaz is Orthodox Rus'."[22] She used the medieval designation (Rus') to refer to Russia and performed in front of eight dragoon squadrons and numerous officers and other representatives of the Russian military, in honour of yet another war with the Muslim Turks, the Crimean War of 1853–56. The Russian military thus promoted religious conversion, and the assumptions that informed the missionary efforts of the regime reflected an acute awareness of the historic encounter between an expansive Islam and a retreating Christianity. Eventually the mountaineers would learn Russian, emphasized Aleksandr A. Begichev of the Ministry of War in 1846, and "beyond the Kuban unfrightening Cherkes" would stand in prayer before an image of Christ.[23]

The distant and unique setting of this imperial frontier, however, also a borderland region in the global encounter between Christianity and Islam, produced an unusual set of ideas about the North Caucasus and its mountain dwellers. The ideas of missionaries and sympathetic officials were shaped by a powerful set of assumptions about identity, tradition, and Eastern Orthodoxy. Mountaineers, some of whom would contest Russian infidel rule for some thirty years, were apparently not Muslim at all. The colonial context of French officials and scholars in Algeria, who were similarly opposed by hostile Berber mountaineers from rugged mountains in the northeast, Sufi orders, and a powerful emir, offers a helpful comparative example. Proponents of what is since known as the "Kabyle myth" held that this rugged and isolated Berber existence had left the mountaineers free of the influence of Islam brought by the expanding Ottomans.[24] In its most extreme form, French administrators and scholars claimed that the Berbers even had a common past with the French, that of the ancient Roman Empire. French colonial administrators attempted to divorce contemporary Berber identity from the history of Islam. The secret to the colonial future lay in the distant past.

Educated society in the Caucasus also hoped to "restore" the historical faith of the North Caucasus and hence create a more promising future. Russians, Georgians, and many others emphasized the foreign, non-indigenous, and therefore illegitimate character of Islam. The provocative notion of "restoration" was part of the name of the missionary society founded in 1860, Obshchestvo Vostanovleniia Pravoslavnago Khristianstva na Kavkaze. In this context the term had a Slavophile flavour, suggesting that history had not been given its due respect. Authentic tradition had decayed, betrayed by the indigenous peoples, who failed to maintain it, and usurped by foreigners determined to supplant it. Slavophiles such as Khomiakov and Kireevskii attributed a similar problem to Russia itself after Peter the Great, which in their view was even regularly producing "foreigners" in its own midst. Not just Orthodox Christianity but tradition itself was the primary victim of the rise of the Muslim empires. Administrators of both French and Russian colonial regimes held similar notions about the significance of tradition, and about the relationship of their rule to the preservation of this imagined past. Islam, in both cases, was the enemy of cultural authenticity. In the Russian case, however, missionaries looked to remedy the issue through the promotion of quasi-Slavophile notions about genuine faith, correct ritual, and the heritage of custom. Russian missionaries were guided by these ideas in other parts of the empire as well. Among North Caucasus mountaineers, the "weakly Islamacized" peoples such as the Mordvinians, Chuvash, and Cheremis of the Volga basin, the Kazakh nomads of the steppe, and the native Siberians, Russians attempted to counter the comparatively recent gains of Islam by promoting native language literacy and education, understood by officials and missionaries as crucial to the maintenance of indigenous tradition.[25]

THE HISTORY OF THE SOCIETY

In 1743 the Georgian archbishop Ioseb and other prominent Georgian churchmen informed Empress Elizabeth that some 200,000 people called the Ossetians lived not far from Kizliar and "at one time professed the Orthodox faith," evident from their old stone churches containing Christian icons.[26] The efforts of the Ossetian Spiritual Commission, which was founded in 1746, provided a base for the activities of the Society for the Restoration of Orthodoxy as well as a precedent for treating the religious heritage of the Caucasus as problematical. The Ossetian Spiritual Commission was accompanied by a school for Ossetian children, which was set up in Mozdok in 1775 and functioned until the temporary closing of the commission in 1792. Of the eight to forty-five Ossetian children per year who attended the school, fifteen continued their education at the Astrakhan Seminary.[27]

In 1815 the commission began work again, this time with greater resources and as part of the Georgian-Imeretian Synodical Office. Though its primary focus remained the Ossetians, its mission was expanded to the Caucasus mountaineers in general and by the 1830s also included the construction of schools. The Ossetian commission left a legacy upon which the society could build, including the construction of thirty-three churches and fourteen schools, six of which were in Ossetia. One of these was an ecclesiastical institute with six teachers in Vladikavkaz, where students were taught Ossetian grammar and sometimes went on to study at the Tiflis Spiritual Seminary.[28] The commission also issued prayer books, catechisms, and short histories of the church in Ossetian.[29] The Moscow Committee of the Bible Society contributed to this work by translating and printing an edition of the Gospels in Ossetian in 1824.[30] At the conclusion of the war in the east Caucasus, supporters of missionary work judged these efforts insufficient and noted that many of the churches restored by the commission had already fallen into disrepair by mid-century.[31] The missionaries of the commission, reported Evsevi, the (Georgian) archbishop of Kartli, to the Holy Synod, were poorly educated and trained, and understandably reluctant to serve in mountain Ossetia because of the harsh conditions, low pay, and possible danger.[32]

The conclusion of the war allowed the regime to pursue the "moral subjugation of the Caucasus," as an early supporter of missionary work put it.[33] Viceroy Aleksander Bariatinskii stressed that the Russians would now change the tactics of battle, engaging the mountaineers, "not with the sword in one hand and a firearm in the other, but with the weapon of Christianity, with the word of evangelical love and mercy."[34] Charity and humanity, he claimed to Metropolitan Isidor, would replace fanaticism and barbarism on the shores of the Black Sea.[35] Like many officials in the Ministry of War, Bariatinskii stressed the relationship of the spread of Orthodoxy to the security of the Russian state. He explained to the Caucasus Committee in 1857 that the religious beliefs of the Ossetians, Abkhaz, Khevsur, and Svan remained beyond the influence of Russian rule and culture, "as if the Caucasus did not belong to a Christian state." Bariatinskii reminded the committee that Russian inattention to the problem had resulted in the spread of Sufi orders into Ossetia and left the Georgian Military Road as dangerous as the hills of Dagestan.[36]

The tsar, ruler of Orthodox Russia, was particularly supportive of the project of the "restoration" of Orthodoxy to the North Caucasus. Bariatinskii and Alexander II had been friends from youth, and as a young colonel from a prominent aristocratic family, the viceroy had had the honour of presenting to Nicholas I the news of Alexander's marriage to Maria Aleksandrovna.[37] A friend of Bariatinskii in St Petersburg who gained an audience with the imperial couple at Tsarskoe Selo was impressed by their support for missionary work in the Caucasus, in particular the support of the tsar's wife: "she has such warm sympathy for the success of Christianity in the Caucasus!" he reported to Bariatinskii.[38] The tsar and Tsarina Maria hoped that all of Russian society would respond to this challenge to propagate Orthodoxy in the borderlands. The Holy Synod allowed for the formation of special circles (*kruzhki*) in Russian churches far from the Caucasus, which would contribute funds required for the work of the society. It awarded a special cross decorated with the name of St Nino, Georgia's fourth-century evangelist, to supporters of the missionary project. The tsar was initially skeptical of offering the cross in exchange for money, but quickly changed his mind when confronted with the need for resources to fulfill the society's ambitious plans.[39] The cross varied in complexity and grandeur according to the size of the donation, which might range from 20 to 1,000 rubles.[40] The society was made official by a charter of 2 June 1860, with the tsarina serving as its special patron. From the point of view of Metropolitan Filaret and Tsarina Maria, the Russian state as the bearer of Orthodoxy had a special relationship to the former lands of the Eastern Roman Empire. The imperial family and other high church officials continued to imagine missionary work in terms of the grandiose project of imperial restoration suggested by Catherine the Great.

FAITH, THE PAST, AND THE EXAMPLE OF GEORGIA

The impact of these ideas about cultural authenticity and fidelity to the past, Orthodoxy, and the problem posed by Islam significantly shaped the imperial conception of the mountaineers. North Caucasus mountain communities in this rendition were perpetually confused, cut off from their true heritage. Nikolai Raevskii, for example, observed of his adversaries in 1839, "Calling themselves Muslim, the inhabitants of the Black Sea shore are unfamiliar with any kind of faith."[41] The military historian Nikolai Dubrovin lamented of the Ossetians, "All the rules and church regulations are mixed up and confused."[42] Christians held pagan rituals for weddings and funerals, Muslims ate pork and drank wine, and pagans performed many Christian practices. The Svan presented a similar problem for Dubrovin. "One can say that all the Svan are baptized, but this is far from saying that they are all Christians," he wrote.[43]

Idol worship, fortune-telling rituals, and superstitions about faith healing were extremely popular. Their lack of literacy in the past had prevented them from reading the holy books, and in the view of Dubrovin, "they lost the genuine idea of religion."[44] They remained, as Dimitri Bakradze said, an "enigmatic tribe" for whom a history of religion needed to be written.[45] Rapiel Eristavi depicted the Tushin, Pshav, and Khevsur as neither Christian, Muslim, nor pagan. They performed Christian rituals, but also a festival on Saturday as if they were Jewish, and a number of Armenian practices, and like many of their Muslim neighbours, "whom they hate and despise," they refrained from pork, shaved, and practised polygamy.[46] They worshipped a variety of gods, yet they believed in a single God. Orthodox revival had to be quick: "the long neglected spark of Christianity is close to going out, if it is not ignited by the pastors of Christianity. The priest needs a lot of energy and a little courage as well, if he is to lead these mistaken creatures to the path of truth."[47]

Imperial rule, then, was a remedy for religious confusion, and the cure was to be found in the study of the past. "Several centuries ago the majority of the Caucasus mountaineers, today cursed enemies of Christianity, were illuminated by the light of the true faith," proclaimed one of the early founding statements of the society.[48] History was thus so important that it could not be left to historians. Ethnographers explained the present via extended discussion of the ancient past, travellers and archaeologists searched for the physical traces of the Christian heritage, and both the Russian and the Georgian press frequently devoted extended attention to the religious history of the Caucasus. P. Khitsunov's essays in *Kavkaz* in 1846 were a typical Russian contribution. History began in the sixth century BC, when early Greek colonists settled the eastern shore of the Black Sea and allowed for an eventual Christian presence in the region in the form of subsequent Byzantine Greeks and then the Georgians. Russia participated in this tradition: Prince Mstislav Udaloi baptized the sons of an Adygei prince in the late tenth century, an Abkhaz prince accepted Christianity in 1333, numerous Adygei and Kabard tribes sought Russia's protection in the time of Ivan the Terrible, and the Ossetian Spiritual Commission was founded during the reign of Elizabeth in the eighteenth century.[49] This religious history was far from a scholarly matter. V.O. Gurko was leading a Russian military expedition into Chechnia in August 1844 when his regiment came upon an enormous stone cross almost seven feet high on the left bank of the Argun River near the village of Chakhkirin. This counted as an archaeological discovery, a remnant of the past that provided a clue to the true identity of the region in the present, and the military commander slowed his troops to ponder the origins of the cross.[50]

Imperial rule, in this vision, included an almost populist respect for the culture of the common people. Writers portrayed Turkish emissaries, Muslim mullas, and Sufi teachers as illegitimate outsiders who obstructed the expression of the true and indigenous culture of the mountaineers.[51] The Adygei, claimed Dubrovin, maintained "their own religion, consisting of a mixture of paganism, Christianity, and Islam," in contrast to their thoroughly Muslim clergy.[52] Adygei folk songs, he discovered, contained many themes and melodies similar to Georgian church music.[53] While time worked toward the "destruction of the remnants of Christianity," wrote L. Ia. Liul'e of the Adygei lands, he found evidence that this tradition had endured: the ruins of old Christian temples still stood in parts of Adygei, such as along the upper Kuban and along the road to Abkhazia through the main Caucasus range. A Christian temple at Pitsunda had "stood up against the destructive influence of time."[54] Adygei beliefs and rituals, Liul'e emphasized, bore many similarities to the world of early Christianity. Adygei and Georgian words for the cross were almost identical, as they were for the days of the week.[55] For Liul'e, these ethnographic discoveries were evidence of an ancient Orthodox past that was not completely forgotten, that Islam had not entirely destroyed. The Abkhaz offered similar possibilities. Christianity was introduced in the sixth century by the Byzantine emperor Justinian, and Islam was later spread by the Turks. Yet the Turks, claimed Dubrovin, failed to "completely erase Christianity from the memory of the people," and the hope of revival remained. Kartvelians (Georgians) too had "to a great extent preserved their ancient character," he wrote, and Russian rule would allow the region's historic and "genuine" cultures to grow and thrive.[56] The indigenous Christian faith of the *narod* endured through time, in spite of foreign rule and the foreign borrowing characteristic of the elite.

Georgia was the shining light in this historical debate, perpetually true to its Christian heritage and past in the face of a long history of invasion and misfortune frequently brought by Islamic empires. The depiction of Georgia by Georgians as "the nation justifiably called the *avant-garde of Christianity in Asia*," as G.N. Kazbegi put it, was an important source of inspiration for a Russia in the process of imperial expansion into Asian borderlands.[57] Georgian essayists frequently outlined a history of Christianity in the region under threat from the Mongols, Turks, and Persians, culminating in the fortunate circumstances of Russia's annexation and protection of Georgia's historic Christian identity.[58] Church writers predictably emphasized the centrality of the Christian heritage to Georgia's past and present identity, and they chronicled an early history of proselytizing from the time of St Nino in the fourth century that extended to the Georgian frontier and mountain peoples such as the Tushin, Pshav, and Khevsur.[59] The special cross awarded by the Holy Synod to Restoration Society supporters throughout the empire, as previously mentioned, was decorated with the name of St Nino. Even more enthusiastic Georgian commentators claimed that not just Paul but Peter himself had evangelized in the region and communicated the teachings of Jesus to the mountain peoples.[60] And from a place like mountainous Tushetia, emphasized society missionaries, the "mountain Muslim tribes" nearby could be reached next.[61] Important Georgian church officials such as the Georgian exarch, Archbishop Evsevi, also presented familiar arguments about the relationship of education and literacy to the ability to adhere to the doctrines and rituals of the Christian faith.[62] The Christianizing project was closely related to the general civilizing effort to ameliorate and transform the most savage aspects of alpine culture. "In order to accept Christianity, one must be capable of self-control," Evsevi advised.[63] Georgia was at the locus of all these positive elements in the region, and the imperial project of Christian restoration nicely coincided with emerging Georgian concerns about the preservation and cultivation of Georgian identity.

LANGUAGE AND THE "IL'MINSKII METHOD"

Where historic Christianity beyond the Georgian frontier faltered, missionaries suggested that this was because the common people proved unable to master the true essence of Christianity and instead merely practised its ritual form. Slavophiles contrasted the true spirituality of the Russian peasant, or the "deep secret of his soul," as Khomiakov claimed about Hellenistic Easterners, to the "external" character of the faith of the Latin Christian.[64] Latin Christians repeated prayers they did not understand and watched in isolation as their priests conducted ceremonies for themselves. In contrast to the communal experience of Orthodoxy, argued Ivan Aksakov, Latin priests "sometimes even performed liturgy *alone*, by themselves and for themselves, even in a whisper."[65] Instead, missionaries visualized a heartfelt Christianity practised in common by the common people. In the Middle Volga, Nikolai Il'minskii even discouraged missionaries from persecuting various forms of paganism. Il'minskii was the well-known missionary, scholar, and linguist who advocated schooling for baptized non-Russians in the Kazan region in the native languages, transcribed in the Cyrillic alphabet, of the students. Shamanism, he argued, was a form of religious expression character- istic of "young tribes," but nonetheless a genuine example of the "striving toward the divine and the unseen" that, in his view, made up the most important component of human nature.[66] Il'minskii con- cluded that small peoples in the Middle Volga had fallen into "apos- tasy" because of the absence of literacy, written scripts in the local language, and missionary instruction in the native language.

Similarly, in the North Caucasus missionaries and officials agreed that the absence of literacy and written scripts among the mountain peoples in the past had encouraged a formulaic relationship to faith. Mountaineers forgot the essence of the faith because they were un- able to transmit the tradition to subsequent generations. The Ossetians lacked their Cyril and Methodius, proclaimed travel writer Evgenii Markov, and over time had adopted Islamic practices and traditions. No one wrote down their language, he lamented, and they were left "without a single comprehensible prayer, without liturgy, without the gospel."[67] "Unable to distinguish A from B," added Dubrovin, the Chechens "blindly fulfilled religious rites they did not understand, the quickest path to superstition and fanaticism."[68] The Adygei had mastered "only the ritual aspects of Christianity and completely mixed these up with pagan rites," argued V. Novitskii.[69] Christianity via the incomprehensible Byzantine Greek, wrote Dubrovin, had failed to influence the "moral understanding and in- ternal life" of the Adygei.[70]

Again in a way similar to the experience of Il'minskii, the turn to native language instruction as the most effective means of education and the transmission of the Christian message was a product of diffi- cult experiences and frustrations. Educators and missionaries such as Il'minskii had trouble communicating with those they were deter- mined to enlighten. In the North Caucasus, what were Russians with- out a knowledge of the local tongue to do in remote mountain villages? Russian Grigorii Beliaev found himself in such dire straits among the (Ossetian) Digors in 1861 that he could not "even get a piece of bread" and practically starved. The poverty and isolation, he claimed, made it "impossible to be a Russian person." He did not have any materials to aid him in his work, and "Beyond this I didn't know the Digor language, and without a priest or a translator – what could I do?"[71] He was recalled and replaced by an Ossetian speaker. A Russian graduate of the Tiflis Women's Gymnasium, Kinopleva, taught at the Tionetsk Women's School without the ability "to pro- nounce even one word in the Georgian language." She conducted church singing in Old Church Slavonic, which was completely incomprehensible to both the students and their audience.[72] The language barrier was not just a problem for Russians. Georgian teachers in Abkhazia found themselves with a similar dilemma and often requested a transfer from the area.[73]

Numerous missionaries in the mountains thus pushed for native language instruction. A (Svan) Restoration Society missionary to the Svan, for example, complained that church services "were exclusively conducted in Georgian," which made them "understandable" to the Svan but unable to inspire genuine conviction. Instead, "as is done in Ossetian parishes," the services should be conducted in Svan, he argued.[74] Similarly, an Abkhaz missionary reported in 1886: "If church services were conducted in a language comprehensible to the population, then it would not be difficult to maintain among them the rules of our Holy Faith." This missionary was unusually explicit about the implications of the "Il'minskii method" for regional autonomy and more: missionary work, he wrote, might serve as the "chief means of facilitating a comprehension of the national [natsional'nyi] language."[75] This was still an unusual use of this term on the frontier at this time, and his reasoning was of course anathema to a developing Russian conservatism.

Regional autonomy, separatism, and nationalism, however, were far away on the horizon. The missionaries and officials were visualizing and constructing an empire. Nation-building was still unimaginable at this time. Missionaries posed the question of language, not in the spirit of self-determination, but as a means to gain access to the true faith. Like Il'minskii, Restoration Society missionaries drew on the experience of the Apostle Paul, the original Christian evangelist. Paul had offered the message of Jesus to everyone, emphasized society missionaries, but how could they accept what they could not understand? Like the Roman Empire, the Russian Empire contained peoples without access to the message. "The Gospel has never been translated into the mountain languages, and without priests it remains lifeless and stale, especially as a result of the present illiteracy of the mountain tribes."[76] Access to the Gospels in one's native language would allow for a genuine and enduring Christianity, making Russia's imperial subjects on the edges of Islamic culture immune from the possiblity of "apostasy" (ostupnichestvo) or conversion back to Islam among the newly baptized Christians of the Middle Volga.

This term was less frequently used in the North Caucasus than in the Middle Volga, but the issue was similar. Calls to prevent the further Islamization and Tatarization of small Middle Volga peoples and Kazakhs and Bashkirs from the Kazan Tatars were frequent throughout the imperial era. In the Caucasus, Governor-General G.S.

Golitsyn reported to Konstantin Pobedonostsev, ober-procurator of the Holy Synod, in 1901 with alarm about a "massive movement of the Abkhaz to Islam" in Abkhazia, a matter "especially dangerous on a frontier that borders Muslim states."[77] The neighbouring big states of the Ottomans and Persians frightened imperial officials even more than the Kazan Tatars among the "small peoples" of the Middle Volga. Missionaries closer to the village wondered about numerous "Muslim sons of Orthodox parents" in Ossetia or the absence of a Christian burial after the death of a baptized girl because the mother had "returned to Islam."[78] Even conservative state officials were convinced of the efficacy of the Il'minskii method. Il'minskii, of course, had his important patrons, such as Dmitrii Tolstoi and Konstantin Pobedonostsev, and important officials in the Caucasus such as Viceroy I.I. Vorontsov-Dashkov went along as well.[79] Conservative officials in the borderlands, such as Governor-General Golitsyn, managed to reconcile support for school instruction, reading materials, and religious services in Abkhaz with the traditional goals of respect for labour, order, and imperial loyalty, or the effort, as Golitsyn explained to Pobedonostsev, "to fuse [the Abkhaz] with the Russians and make of them loyal and faithful subjects."[80] Officials high and low, for a variety of reasons, concurred about the use of the native language and the transformation of "inorodtsy" and small peoples throughout the empire, and the "method" became standard policy in the education of the "aliens" of the eastern borderlands by the early twentieth century.[81]

Christian services, religious materials, and Christian education in the local language would also remedy the problem of historic mountaineer "indifference" to the true faith. The eclectic mix of religious customs and traditions so troublesome to numerous commentators would be resolved in favour of a firm adherence to true ritual, faith, and tradition. Missionaries in frontier villages echoed the work of scholars in Tbilisi who argued that the religious eclecticism of the mountaineers illustrated their inablity to preserve correct ritual over time. The Svan, for example, claimed a Svan missionary in 1886, mixed numerous "superstitions" and pagan rites into their observances of Lent, Easter, and Christmas. The clergy, he emphasized, must encourage among the Svan a more accurate conception of Christian notions such as the Holy Trinity and encourage them to abstain from burying their deceased infants in the house or mourning so long after the death of a spouse.[82]

Mountaineer religious eclecticism alarmed the missionaries because it suggested an inability to discriminate and distinguish the "correct faith" from the many frontier alternatives. The Lezgin

(Dagestan), pointed out Ossetian missionary Vitalii Dizhaev, are "indifferent" to questions of doctrine and correct belief. "One of the more influential Lezgin honestly told me," he reported, "that in general the Lezgin believe the salvation of the soul can take place through either the Gospels or the Qur'an."[83] But this problem only made missionaries more unsure of their work. If the mountaineers were indeed so eclectic and unconcerned about matters of doctrine, how could missionaries be sure about the true state of the heart in the matter of conversion?

The very practices of conversion on the frontier posed a similar dilemma. Christian conversion in the Middle Volga and Siberia in the early modern period had usually occurred in exchange for clothes, boots, flour, and temporary exemptions from taxation.[84] Eighteenth-century baptisms in Siberia sometimes meant "being herded into rivers at gunpoint."[85] In such circumstances, could missionaries be sure that the newly expressed Christian sentiment was genuine? Many missionaries in the mountains were eager to report an enthusiastic response back to Tbilisi. Georgian missionary Ioseb Vatsadze claimed that the Svan expressed a "genuine desire" for Christian conversion, and he proceeded to baptize the entire village of Tserimi. His preparatory instruction included a brief explanation of the Lord's Prayer and several Christian symbols and ten stories from the Gospel.[86] Abkhaz missionary Geromonakh Gona of the Mazukhsk parish in Pitsunda (Abkhazia) was delighted that entire villages were apparently eager for conversion. They asked him to let them know when he was ready and they would "bring the chicken and the wine" for the ceremony. "We ourselves now see," the villagers explained, "that the Christian faith is better than Islam, and to be a Christian is better than being a Muslim. The Turks have deceived our Abkhazians who emigrated to Turkey, and they suffer there, while we, thanks to our dear tsar and grand prince, live peacefully."[87] Could small peoples caught between powerful empires so easily be believed? Gabriel, the (Georgian) *episkop* of Imeretia, did not think so, especially after a few tense encounters with local elders on his own trip to the area. He concluded that Gona had been "deceived" and was insufficiently "acquainted with the character and customs of the Abkhaz."[88] Sometimes cynical priests contributed to the confusion. Ossetian Vitalii Dizhaev was disturbed by the work of a priest, left unnamed, who advised villagers: "If you don't want to be Christian, then just find some smart lawyer, pay him well, and instruct him to get the authorities to allow you to return to Islam."[89]

Undeterred by conservatives who were alarmed by the implications of sanctioning linguistic diversity in the polyglot empire, or

especially belligerent officials who considered "savage" mountaineers beyond the reach of any civilizing or Christianizing mission, military and church officials in the North Caucasus welcomed the end of
the war as an opportunity to implement their vision. When the council of the Restoration Society met in 1868, it invited Generals
Bartolomei and Starosel'skii to contribute to the formulation of a set
of basic goals in education for the society. Bartolomei and
Starosel'skii were both scholars as well as generals. Bartolomei had
completed his *Abkhaz Reader* in 1865, and Starosel'skii worked in the
Caucasus Mountain Administration. Military officials and missionaries met to coordinate their efforts and clarify their goals, which in education were reading and writing in the local language; reading and
writing in Russian; the mastering of religious history and Orthodox
liturgy (in Russian); and basic arithmetic, also taught in Russian. By
this time the group was already making use of readers and primers in
Svan, Ossetian, Chechen, and Abkhaz, which "facilitated the gradual
weakening in the Caucasus of Arabic and the Qur'an – the sources of
Muslim fanaticism and antagonism to us from among the mountain
population."[90] In 1865 the official printing house of the main administration of the viceroy in Tbilisi had cooperated with the Restoration
Society to issue 2,400 copies of Bartolomei's *Abkhaz Reader*, 1,500 copies of the Bible in Ossetian, and 3,000 copies of a prayer book in
Ossetian, as well as 1,200 copies of the teachings of Episkop Gabriel
in Georgian. The financing of the project was handled by Prince
Orbeliani, a general and imperial official, which meant that Georgian
officials were heavily involved in this imperial project of encouraging
Ossetian and Abkhaz literacy.[91] Georgian priest M. Iluridze, to pro-
vide another example, applauded the increasing use of Ossetian over
Russian in Restoration Society schools in a church journal in 1889.[92]

Native language instruction in Restoration schools put a premium
on the training and development of a cadre of native instructors. The
society was learning from experience as well in this matter. As
Beliaev attested, unable "even to get a piece of bread," the missionary
post demanded a hardy mental and physical constitution. Teachers
and missionaries frequently complained about the absence of support
and funding which made their service almost impossible and prevented them from appearing as an example of "imperial" and civilized culture on the savage frontier. One teacher wondered how he
could serve as role model "of the entire village, and not just of the
school," when inadequate pay and administrative support made it
difficult for the villagers to distinguish the teachers from the surrounding villagers.[93] Teachers struggled with dilapidated classrooms,
insufficient teaching materials, collapsing tables, broken chairs, and

so on.[94] Georgians (perhaps especially) considered mountain out-posts a career demotion. A Georgian teacher complained about his work in the "backwater" of Abkhazia in 1872 with condescension: "Try to imagine what sort of life is here. Where is polite society? Where is the theatre?"[95] And missionaries faced hostility from the lo-cal population, in particular if their work took them closer to the northeast Caucasus and the seat of Shamil's former imamate. Priest Tukuzhev, an Armenian missionary associated with the society, was in the Lezgin village of Toipalo when two Chechens accosted him, ex-claimed, "Again the devil has arrived," and spat in his face.[96] Ossetian Vitalii Dizhaev put the struggle for resources and respect in the terms that counted: "Our forefathers were Christian, and we wish to maintain the faith of our ancestors; but under conditions in which we are not so needy in the religious sense. Now the Muslims laugh at us, because we don't have any priests, we don't have churches, and we don't conduct Christian services on our holidays."[97]

The suspicions of mountain peasant families about schooling, like those of Russian peasants, presented another difficulty for teachers.[98] Parents were suspicious of the intentions of educators, sometimes suggesting that the purpose of schooling for boys was preparation for military service.[99] Rumors persisted among the Ossetians that the girls who attended the Vladikavkaz Girls' School were actually being trained in order to be presented as wives to soldiers and Cossacks.[100] A teacher among the Tushin and Pshav had trouble getting any sup-port from the local imperial official (*pristav*), a Georgian named Zov Tsiskarishvili, for the construction and maintenance of a school. Tsiskarishvili finally explained to the frustrated teacher that Pshav el-ders from the valley had refused to cooperate in procuring materials and providing labour for the construction of the school. "What am I to do! You can see for yourself that orders, threats, and even punish-ments have no impact upon the Pshav elders."[101] The elders frankly told the official and the teacher that they were unwilling to spare the material, time, or labour. And besides, they explained, "There's hardly one man among us that's going to send his son to your school."[102] Schooling conflicted with the rhythm of the agricultural season and the important role played by even young boys in the fam-ily economy. Vakhar Kubalov reported the sudden loss of ten boys to agricultural labour during the harvest of 1871.[103]

The tough conditions made suitable teacher candidates difficult to find. Especially unqualified priests might for that very reason find their way to the frontier. Church officials in Tbilisi discovered that a certain Karzhilov, a priest from Saratov province, had abandoned his wife and children there, wandered through several borderland towns such as Kishinev and Odessa, was briefly incarcerated for an unknown crime, and received administrative exile for a false accusation of murder in 1839. Officials in the Georgian Ekzarkh discovered all this and then wisely rejected his application to serve as a missionary in the mountain regions.[104] The "civilizing" work that put priests in conflict with local customs sometimes even provoked violence, as had been the case for the missionaries of the earlier Ossetian Spiritual Commission.[105] Georgian priest Ioseb Surguladze in the Ossetian village of Chetorsi was murdered in the early 1860s when he refused to sanction the arranged marriage of two children.[106] Or sometimes missionaries suffered from the problems they brought upon themselves. Romantic liasons between teachers and village girls were a frequent source of tension. A Khevsur father killed a priest in the village of Sno in 1853 over such an issue concerning his daughter.[107] A Tushin priest, a former student at the Tiflis Spiritual Seminary, was killed in 1887 by Lezgin in the village of Bash-Suagal after he "abducted a Muslim girl."[108] With embarassment, in 1864 the society was compelled to establish a special fund to support village orphans that were the offspring of village priests.[109]

For all these reasons, but chief among them the language problem, Restoration Society officials looked for native speakers as teachers and missionaries. They were the most likely to be comfortable in the mountains, develop a productive rapport with the local population, and communicate effectively the truths of the Christian message and the virtues of the imperial world of civilization. Society teaching rosters reveal that by 1880 predominantly Georgian teachers (with names such as Natenadze, Geladze, and Khmaladze) worked in "mountain Georgian" areas, Ossetian teachers (Sadzagelov, Sanakoev, Khatagov) staffed the village schools in the countryside surrounding Vladikavkaz, and Abkhaz teachers (Charaia, Eshibaia, Narkebiia) worked in Abkhazia.[110] Teacher seminaries such as the Tiflis Spiritual Seminary and other such institutions in Vladikavkaz and Mozdok concentrated on training native students from the mountains for future work with the Restoration Society. Consequently they adjusted their own curriculum to adopt to the need for mountain language instruction and literacy. Some officials wondered about the possibility of an entirely separate course for the Ossetian students at the ecclesiastical seminaries. Instead, church educators eliminated Greek and Latin study for the Ossetian children, so as to give them more time to master literacy in Ossetian with the Cyrillic characters. They also tried to teach a pure Ossetian, not mixing in words and phrases of the nearby Pshav ("mountain Georgian"). Like officials administering affirmative action programs in the United

States, church educators described their struggles to find and keep viable Ossetian and Svan students, in contrast to the much larger pool of Georgians and Russians.[111] They also worried about Ossetian and Abkhaz students who were reluctant to return to the mountains after their training, instead preferring a career within the multi-ethnic service elite of the empire. Graduates of the Tiflis Teaching Institute supported by the society were obligated to serve at least four years in the North Caucasus in return for their education.[112]

In the classroom the teachers implemented the concerns common to borderland educated society about the correct practice of ritual and the cultivation of a genuine faith that would deter the influence of paganism, Islam, and foreign faiths. A teacher's lesson plan for the primary school children at the Kakhsk school in 1870 included a discussion of the following issues and questions:

- What is a prayer?
- How do we pray? Where does one pray?
- Why it is best to pray in the morning.
- Why are we called Christian and Orthodox?
- What do our names mean?
- Why do we pray in front of icons?

Somewhat more complicated was a discussion of the "essential qualities of God" and more in-depth discussions with the older students on the life of Jesus from the New Testament and on Old Testament stories about Creation, Hebrew law, Abraham, and the Jews in Egypt.[113] These were in addition to their studies in arithmetic and the Russian language. Teachers were particularly proud if they could get the older students to learn enough Old Church Slavonic to sing in church.[114]

Native language instruction on the difficult North Caucasus frontier was contested by Russian conservatives, who viewed the Russian language as a source of cohesion and identity important to the stability of empire, and ironically, by a few non-Russian families themselves. Ossetian teacher Vakhar Kubalov in the Batako-Iurtovsk school shared this exchange with a skeptical father from the village: "'And what are you teaching your students?' an Ossetian father of one of my students asked. 'Everything that is necessary to him in life,' I answered. 'That's good: teach him whatever you want, but my son wants to learn Russian.'"[115] Given that the imperial service elite was multi-ethnic but that the language of administration was Russian, we can assume that many ambitious non-Russian families saw knowledge of Russian as a top priority for their sons. The state's promotion of native language instruction was viewed by some non-Russians themselves as not entirely useful, an odd situation that perhaps parallels the otherwise very different contemporary debate in the American Southwest over Spanish language instruction for Hispanics.

Conservative critics alarmed by the implications of concessions to native language instruction on the frontiers of the empire were increasingly vocal in the later nineteenth century. Proponents of "Russification" looked for imperial administrative conformity and were suspicious of diversity and innovation in method and practice on the frontier. By 1885 the Restoration Society could claim credit for the construction of 52 churches, the restoration of 24, the support of 137 church parishes, the building of 46 primary schools for mountain children, where in some cases enrolment reached 65 students, the founding of the Aleksandrov Men's Teaching Seminary and the Ossetian Vladikavkaz Girls' School, the support of some 70 students in institutions of higher education, support for the writing of mountain languages, and the translation of the Bible and religious literature into mountain languages.[116] In search of administrative uniformity, however, Konstantin Pobedonostsev in that year curtailed the activities of the society and made it subordinate to the Holy Synod by placing it within the Georgian Exarchate. He objected to its continuing autonomy and administrative distance from the concerns and practices of St Petersburg.[117]

The notion of faith and its relationship to the preservation of the past that informed the work of the Restoration Society granted the Russian state and the educated community in the Caucasus an imperial purpose and mission of world-historical significance. Russians found themselves in continuity with the great imperial heritage of Orthodox Christianity, the builders of the "Third Rome" and the successor to Constantinople. As a result of their expansion into the southern borderlands, Russians could congratulate themselves on their new-found ability to counter the historic decline of Christianity in its confrontation with Islam. Pan-Slavists, such as Ivan Aksakov, who drew on the Slavophile tradition posed a similar problem for Russia regarding the Balkans, where small peoples needed the Russian "hand of salvation" against "Muslim barbarism and tyranny" and "Asian hordes" in order to maintain their Orthodoxy and recover a glorious past.[118] In the North Caucasus the "Eastern question," so to speak, could be pursued within the borders of the empire, and the preservation of the past was the chief means of countering the strength of Islam and the Ottomans. Orthodoxy and the recovery of tradition facilitated the conquest and served as the basis for empire, in particular for the imperial family, high officials, and many Russians in the military. Georgia's own struggles to maintain its historic Christian identity in the face of Islamic threats served as an important example and guide in the region. Georgians themselves worked as teachers, missionaries, and officials in the society, and they frequently contributed to the official, newspaper, and scholarly discussions.

Missionaries in the schools founded by the society associated the waning of Christian tradition and the rise of Islam in the region with intellectual stagnation among dormant, backward, and "Eastern" peoples. The absence of written scripts, literacy, and a literate tradition contributed to the making of a culturally stagnant frontier. Mountaineers who could read, they reasoned, had access to the enduring textual truths of the Christian tradition; those who could not were left to suffer the ravages of time and the backwardness of their culture. Knowlege of texts offered continuity with the heritage of Orthodoxy and civilization itself, while oral traditions and illiteracy promised confusion and a belief system that served to deny access to that heritage. The Russian imperial and Orthodox community, in the view of these missionaries, was a literate one, united by common assumptions about the character of civilization and the relationship of Orthodox Russia to its growth and development. "Literacy is the basic foundation of history," wrote Khomiakov; "therefore enlightened peoples who have forgotten their writing were reduced to a forgetfulness on a par with savages."[119] Literacy allowed for access to the message of the Gospels and a genuine and heartfelt Christianity that would make one immune from the temptations of other traditions in the borderlands. The restoration and recovery of the past was crucial to the imperial future, as well as to the maintenance of the true faith and its rituals.

The work of the Restoration Society serves as an illustration of the impact of a series of conservative concerns about the practice and maintenance of the correct faith. This matter was an especially delicate question in borderland regions influenced by Islam and close to Muslim empires. The society's work also serves as an example of a form of empire-building that stressed religious conformity as a kind of imperial identity while sanctioning linguistic diversity. The North Caucasus also reveals that the extent and reach of the "Il'minskii method" and the imperial concern about "apostasy" went beyond the eastern borderlands of the Middle Volga and Central Asia. The method emerged from some of the basic concerns of Russian intellectual history and transcended the famous Il'minskii. The encouragement of native literacy and education also had implications not yet

comprehensible to its religious-minded proponents. Religious thinkers such as Khomiakov or Il'minskii could not yet imagine a world in
which the fruits of literacy might conflict with the values of
Orthodoxy. The cultivation of native soil, however, a prerequisite for
a people's eventual participation in the community of civilization,
need not include the revival of Orthodoxy. The next two chapters ex-
plore the dimensions of secular nationality or ethnicity as part of
what we have identified as the imperial preoccupation with cultural
authenticity and tradition on the frontiers of the empire.

4 Narodnost': Russian Ethnographers and Caucasus Mountaineers

> If a substantial seed of the spiritual life of a people [*narod*] falls on historical soil and receives the opportunity to develop on its own – then the natural poetry of the people will be reborn as art, its folklore – as literature.
>
> V.G. Belinskii, 1842–44[1]

"ORIGINALITY" AND EMPIRE

Russia's enthusiastic appropriation of the German Romantic tradition meant that the empire in principle or at least potentially was home to many peoples. All peoples possess folklore (*slovesnost'*), wrote Vissarion Belinskii, and "[w]hen a people becomes acquainted with the culture of literacy, its literature takes on a new character, depending on the spirit of the people and the stages of its civilization and education."[2] "Westerners" like Belinskii shared with Slavophile thinkers many common concerns and interests, although they tended to cast the question of Orthodoxy to the side. Slavophiles such as Khomiakov and Iurii Samarin foresaw that in the modern era it would be possible to cultivate tradition without faith, and they often reminded readers that the development of Russian narodnost' drew its sustenance from its close connection to Orthodoxy.[3]

As for the question of faith, the exploration of narodnost' on the frontier had implications for regional autonomy and the eventual "national question," but this was not on the agenda in the 1850s and 1860s. Russia itself was not a nation. A literary critic such as Aleksandr Pypin was wishfully recasting Russian cultural history in Western terms when he associated the Russian interest in narodnost' with Europe's reorganization of itself according to the "principle of nationality."[4] Instead, the debates about narodnost' were informed by a nativistic respect for local custom and indigenous culture rather than the new forms of mass culture, parliamentary politics, and civic participation that scholars usually associate with the rise of national-ism in Europe. Ivan Kireevskii was enthusiastic about what he thought of as Pushkin's gradual move toward narodnost', away from "Italian-French" to "Byronic" to "Russian-Pushkinian," and he saw Gogol's work as a "complete turn around in our literature in this re-gard."[5] Like samobytnost' ("originality"), which Belinskii defined in 1834 as "the way of thinking and viewing things, in religion, lan-guage and above all in *customs*," narodnost' was something native and indigenous, "something inexpressible, comprehensible only to the Russian heart," as Kireevskii put it.[6] The question of "identity" as Russians imagined it in the nineteenth century was very different from the developing "principle of nationality" in Europe.

The expansion of the imperial system also meant the expansion of similar concerns, ideas, and attitudes. Educated society (*obshchestvo/sazogadoeba*) was a multi-ethnic educated world shaped and informed by a common imperial discourse. Georgian intellectuals such as Akaki Tsereteli, Sergo Meskhi, Ilia Chavchavadze, and many others absorbed these ideas in St Petersburg itself and returned to Tbilisi to establish new newspapers, discussion groups, and scholarly societ-ies.[7] Fifty-five Georgians studied in St Petersburg alone from 1857 to 1861, points out Oliver Reisner.[8] For Chavchavadze, in a manner fa-miliar to students of Russian intellectual history, the "truly national" was something that reflected the "genuine face of the people."[9] Like Belinskii in search of an emerging Russian literature, he profiled works of writers such as Nikoloz Baratashvili, "our Byron," who in his writing "depicts genuinely Georgian portraits."[10] Russia's Romantic discourse was particularly inspiring to small peoples dis-tant from the world of the eighteenth-century Enlightenment. As in Russia, however, this emerging nativistic movement was compatible with empire. "Nationalism" in an imperial context did not mean a so-cial movement in search of the independent nation-state, but instead a cultural nativism fostered and cultivated, even promoted, under the umbrella of empire.

This relationship between nativism and empire in Georgia was on display on 22 October 1895, when Russians, Georgians, and many others gathered to commemorate the life and work of Rapiel Eristavi. His prose offered a "truly Georgian speech, enriched and made pleas-ant to the ear by the beautiful language of the people."[11] The criterion for excellence in the arts was the ability to depict "everyday peasant life." Telling the story of the nation meant the writing of ethnography, a vision of the peasant "in peasant fields and prairies, plains and mountains, in work and play, in good times and bad, alone and among family and hearth."[12] The celebration commenced at the

St Giorgi Church in Tbilisi and was attended by prominent Russians, Georgians, and Armenians from the ecclesiastical hierarchy, the military, the imperial service, and the worlds of culture, the arts, and journalism. Scholarly societies, literary societies, folk music collectors, and Georgian culture generally flourished throughout the imperial era.[13] The Russian and Georgian relationship to "tradition" shaped imperial discourse about the highlanders of the North Caucasus, and "tradition" in the wake of the Romantic era meant not just the history of Orthodoxy but the history of indigenous custom.

ROMANTICISM AND TRAVEL LITERATURE

Susan Layton has described the misgivings of famous Russian literary figures about the conquest of the Caucasus. While Romantic writers were unable to visualize an alternative to the march of Russian "civilization," they were ambivalent about the demise of mountain (noble) savages and alarmed at the callous destructiveness of Russian military policy. Pushkin and his heirs created a world of frontier escape and "freedom," perhaps as a means of personal rebellion in response to the strictures of the imperial state and the world of officialdom.[14] Leo Tolstoy most notably revived this impulse at the turn of the century with powerful novellas such as *Hadji Murat* and *The Wood Felling*. This fundamental ambivalence about the course of the conquest extended beyond the world of literature to educated society generally. The Decembrist M.O. Orlov, for example, criticized the work of Ermolov in a 1820 letter to Pushkin and suggested that peace would come to the region via not "the bayonet but time and enlightenment."[15]

Russian Romanticism put the mountain peoples on the map of Russian cultural history. The "imaginative geography" of the region remained close at hand as officials conquered and incorporated the North Caucasus.[16] "In general one of my dearest hopes is to take an extended trip to the Caucasus," wrote the brother of the tsar, Grand Duke Konstantin Nikolaevich, to the office of the viceroy in Tbilisi.[17] Aleksandr Bestuzhev-Marlinskii served in the Caucasus from 1829 until his death in a skirmish with mountaineers on the Black Sea coast in 1837. A.S. Griboedov served in Turkey and in the Caucasus under Ermolov; A.I. Polezhaev participated in Vel'iaminov's 1832 expedition into Chechnia; and Aleksandr Odoevskii spent two years in the Nizhegorod dragoon regiment until he died of fever at Pzeuapse on the shore of the Black Sea in 1839.[18] Russians throughout the century needed to see and experience what Pushkin referred to as the "burning border of Asia," a place "fascinating in all respects."[19]

They also drew on the general thirst for colonial travel and exploration beyond the boundaries of "civilization" that informed European colonial expansion. "I was still very young," recalled A.P. Berzhe, "when the desire to travel to the most remote places arose within me."[20] He studied Farsi in Tehran and hoped to serve in the diplomatic corps in places such as Persia, Arabia, Turkey, or Egypt, but instead landed in Tbilisi. The Russian ambassador to Persia, D.I Dolgorukov, was an active member of the Caucasus Department of the Imperial Russian Geographic Society and frequently sent news of European travel expeditions in Iran that he thought would be of interest to department members.[21] Their library included a ready supply of numerous classics of European exploration and adventure, such as *An Account of the Mission to the Court of Persia in 1807* by Harfourd Brydges, Wilhelm Heine's work on Commodore Perry in Japan, Thevenot's *Reisen in Europa, Asien und Africa*, Sir Gore Ouseley's *Epitome of the Ancient History of Persia*, and numerous other works.[22] In 1862 the department library began permanent subscriptions to *Nouvelles annales des voyages* and *Journal asiatique*.[23] Members of this Orientalist and colonial community centred in Tbilisi thought of themselves as participants in a general global process of colonization, and they followed with particular interest the policies and experiences of the French in North Africa.

A Russian readership for the drama of discovery and exploration gathered strength throughout the nineteenth century. Jeffrey Brooks has described the new interest in empire, among other themes, evident in popular literature and chapbooks before the revolution, and Daniel Brower has described the Russian interest in the adventures of Nikolai Przhevalsky in Central Asia, an imperial equivalent, perhaps, of David Livingstone or Richard Burton for European readers.[24] Russians read popular publications such as *Vsemirnyi Puteshestvennik* (Global traveller), where they learned of the journey of the Englishmen Speke and Grant through North and central Africa in search of the source of the Nile, French progress in New Caledonia, General Sherman's attempts to subdue the Native Americans, the growth of San Francisco from its rugged beginnings in the American West, the growth of Australia in spite of its humble origins as a penal colony, or the construction of a railway in Central America.[25] The general structure of these tales – the willing departure from the civilized world, the deprivations of travel, the encounter with the natives, glimpses of exotic women, and hunting in the wild – were familiar to Russians and non-Russians raised on Romantic travel literature. Patagonian nomadic tribes, for example, living solely by robbery seemed to have much in common with "Cherkes" tribes who swept down from the mountainside to terrorize the plain.[26] Russian Romanticism and European travel literature provided a ready formula for the visualization of the mountaineers and the borderlands during the incorporation of the North Caucasus into the empire.

M.S. VORONTSOV, THE STATE, AND ENLIGHTENMENT

Tsar Nicholas 1 was long frustrated with the Caucasus and the interminable war, and he adopted a novel administrative approach by granting extended authority and the special position of viceroy (*namestnik*) to Mikhail S. Vorontsov in 1845.[27] Vorontsov possessed a strong imperial vision concerning the European Enlightenment, the role of Russia, and the integration of the borderlands. He was extremely wealthy, and was experienced in the borderlands as a result of his tenure as governor-general over the province of New Russia in the 1820s and 1830s. His father, Simon, had been Catherine's ambassador to England, and his uncle, Alexander Romanovich Vorontsov, was the primary author of a charter of individual rights, a Russian liberal response to the Declaration of the Rights of Man and the Citizen of the French National Assembly.[28] During these years Tbilisi and its population grew dramatically, and the city emerged as a centre for the prosecution of the war against the mountaineers.[29]

Vorontsov's transformation of Tbilisi was in the tradition of the Petrine state of the eighteenth century. Peter himself had initiated the first issue of the *Vedomosti* on 2 January 1703, and had established a theatre with a director and troupe supported from Danzig.[30] His administration posed new questions about the purpose of expansion with his support for the founding of the Academy of Sciences and his interest in new fields such as geography and cartography, which led to the great expeditions of the eighteenth century. Scholars catalogued the flora and fauna of the distant borderlands, and increasingly took interest in the peoples of the empire as well.[31] The Academy of Sciences was an expression of the enlightened eighteenth-century state, its work shaped by emerging discussions about *obshchestvennost'* and *grazhdanstvennost'*.[32] The enlightened state in Catherine's day intended to take the lead in the production of good citizens, as a school reader illustrates.[33] Educated Russians understood the direction, tutelage, and impact of the state itself in frontier regions as a crucial component of the civilizing process. "Backward" borderland regions in particular offered officials the perfect opportunity to witness progress in their promotion of the "common good."[34] By the early nineteenth century, innovative officials such as Mikhail Speransky and Mikhail Vorontsov were determined to use this emerging scholarship in order to promote the social and cultural transformation of the inhabitants of the realm. Influenced by notions of the role of the enlightened monarchy as a promoter of social change, these officials believed that the task of government was to provide the foundations for the eventual social and political maturing of the population.[35] The scholarly reconfiguration of empire included a strong civilizing mission.

Catherine the Great extended this vision beyond St Petersburg and Moscow with her Fundamental Law on provincial town life, which was intended to develop provincial centres of "government, commerce, and civilized social life."[36] Nineteenth-century Russian scholars such as N. Chechulin and M.I. Demkov emphasized that provincial society had barely existed before Catherine. The cities were tiny and their inhabitants impoverished, the streets were dangerous and filthy, the bridges were dilapitated, administration was non-existent, and drugstores, doctors, and post offices were nowhere to be found.[37] The emergence of provincial town life since the late eighteenth century was thus a source of pride and a mark of progress to Russians in the nineteenth century, who were now, at least in their view, bestowing a similar gift on the borderland regions of the empire.

Vorontsov's attention to the growth of public life in Tbilisi was in the spirit of this Enlightenment project of provincial uplift. His attention to questions of public hygiene and sanitation, for example, put him in correspondence with the St Petersburg Water Filtration Company and its French suppliers. A water filtration system, a certain M. de L'Thomas informed Vorontsov, would "benefit the entire city of Tiflis" and was a "matter of great importance for public well-being" (*de la plus haute importance pour la salubrité publique*).[38] Vorontsov and his administration debated matters of policy with a strong sense of the values of the Enlightenment and its optimistic vision of cultural change for barbarous and frontier lands outside the realm of public life and civilization. An Italian opera yearly performed in Tbilisi from 1851, and in late 1853 the first full-scale ballet was performed on the Tbilisi stage.[39] "How can one not be joyful at such a rising, developing social life in Tiflis, which still carries upon itself the imprint of Asia," the editorial staff of *Kavkaz* exclaimed.[40] Artists, Russians in Georgia reported with enthusiasm, were making the move from Nevskii Prospect in St Petersburg to Erevan Square in Tbilisi.[41] A young Leo Tolstoy was one of the many who applauded the efforts of Tbilisi to imitate St Petersburg.[42] Enlightened high culture was to play an integrative function on the diverse frontier, as the efforts of the Tiflis Theatre to encourage Georgian and Armenian participation and productions suggest.[43] As late as 1893, Giorgi

Tsereteli applauded the work of Viceroy Vorontsov for his establishment of the theatre in Georgia, which served as the "soil" for subsequent Georgian cultural development.[44]

Vorontsov's role was also heralded by the many officials long frustrated with the Caucasus War. One such official was Arnol'd
Zisserman, a young man initially inspired by the prose of Marlinsky
to seek a civil post in the bureaucracy in Tbilisi in 1842.[45] His subsequent service as district commander of the Tushetia-Pshav-Khevsuria
district and then as *pristav* (police officer) in the army in the Lezgin
Line brought him to the attention of Viceroy Vorontsov, who com-
mended him for his commitment to the study of local cultures and
traditions. "I hear, dear Zisserman," Vorontsov greeted him in
Shemakha, "that you have managed in a short time to learn Tatar?
Well, thank you for not spending any time in vain ... Imagine, Boris
Gavrilovich [General Chilaev] ... among the Tushin he learned
Georgian, and here in only several months Tatar – remarkable talent.
If we had more of such young people, our administration would be
much better."[46] Once in Tbilisi, Vorontsov requested of Zisserman an
interview in his travelling outfit. "Well, my dear Zisserman, have a
look at yourself; yes, a perfect Chechen," Vorontsov greeted him.[47]

Zisserman was an example of the kind of local adminstrator judged
by Vorontov and other officials to be crucial to the enlightened
administration of the region. In his memoirs Zisserman expressed
frustration with the general ignorance and disinterest among "the so-
called educated class" about affairs in the southern borderlands. One
such Russian, "like many others, imagined the Caucasus in the form
of one large castle surrounded by Cherkes, whom our soldiers shoot
at day after day."[48] His extensive experience instead led him to con-
ceive of the task of colonization in broader terms, encompassing far
more than military matters and the winning of the Caucasus War. Enlightened administrative, economic, educational, and judicial institutions, staffed by capable administrators with an understanding of the
region and willing to discuss matters "openly" with the local population, were necessary, Zisserman believed, if Russia was to justify its
colonial presence in the Caucasus.[49] Scholarship, Orientalist knowledge, and a recognition of the diversity of the empire were important
aspects of Vorontsov's vision.

A.P. BERZHE, SCHOLARLY SOCIETIES, AND ANTIQUITY

Orientalist scholarship flourished in the remade Tbilisi of Vorontsov.
Most important, the Imperial Russian Geographic Society opened a
Caucasus Department (Kavkazskii otdel) in 1851, which regularly

issued its *Zapiski Kavkazskago Otdela Imperatorskago Geograficheskago Obschestva* (Memorandum of the Caucasus Branch of the Imperial Geographic Society). As several scholars have recently explained, the Geographic Society was at the centre of a series of debates about reform, expansion, and Russian nationalism.[50] "Science" (*nauka*) would be put to the service of the "fatherland," explained Vorontsov at the opening meeting.[51] There were numerous other avenues for research on the North Caucasus as well. The Caucasus Society of Agriculture sponsored exhibits, a museum, and its own publication from 1850, and Vladimir Sollogub, Adol'f Berzhe, G.A. Tokarev, and others provided the initiative for the opening of the Caucasus Museum of Regional Studies in 1856, an outgrowth of the work of the local branch of the Geographic Society.[52] This rapidly became a repository for the efforts of collectors throughout the region, and in 1867 the collection formed the basis for the Caucasus Museum, led by Gustav Radde, a German transplanted to Tbilisi after a childhood in Danzig and participation in a Siberian expedition sponsored by the Geographic Society. Other sponsors of Orientalist research and scholarship included the Caucasus Statistical Committees, founded in the 1860s and issuing the *Sbornik statisticheskikh svedenii o Kavkaze* (Collection of statistical information about the Caucasus), and the Caucasus Mountain Administration, headed by Dmitrii S. Starosel'skii throughout the 1870s and producing the *Sbornik svedenii o Kavkazskikh gortsakh* (Collection of information about the Caucasus mountaineers). Later in the century other state-sponsored institutions contributed to this tradition, such as the Caucasus Education District and its *Sbornik materialov dlia opisaniia mestnostei i plemen Kavkaza* (Collection of materials toward the description of the regions and tribes of the Caucasus), and the Main Staff of the Caucasus Military District, the publisher of *Kavkazskii sbornik* (Caucasus collection).[53]

The question of the purpose of imperial expansion informed the growth of the Geographic Society in the borderlands. Supporters of Vorontsov's initiatives in St Petersburg such as Fedor Petrovich Litke (Ferdinand Lütke) viewed the collection of artifacts and information, "although isolated," as "valuable for that very reason, because after they are gathered into a whole they will serve as important material for a knowledge of Russia."[54] Litke was enthusiastic about the prospect of provincial supporters of the "fatherland's enlightenment" from around the empire who might participate in this communal effort to clarify the imperial purpose.[55] And just as collectors situated in St Petersburg envisioned the borderlands in this way, so scholars gathered in Tbilisi and made similar calls to the smaller cities, forts, and villages of the Caucasus. At present, material in private libraries from around the empire "lies around unused," as an early Geographic Society proclamation emphasized.[56] In time, the society would provide intellectual coherence to the chaos of the frontier.

If the Geographic Society proposed to make sense of the empire's vast expanse, the Archaeological Commission promised to compose order out of the imperial past. This group routinely issued calls to borderland communities to aid in the collection of numerous objects, from ancient church icons to paintings, mosaics, and musical instruments.[57] The commission, emphasized Baron A. Nikolai to the viceroy in 1864, was transforming "a mass of paper" into scientific collections covering statistics, history, geography, politics, law, and "administration in the broad sense of [this] word."[58] Such a project held special significance in the "savage" North Caucasus, where the story of Russian rule would illustrate the continuing development of "civil administration." The Caucasus Archaeological Commission was formed on 11 March 1864. Under the editorial direction of A.P. Berzhe, it diligently but selectively published archival documents in the multi-volume *Akty Kavkazskoiu Arkheograficheskoiu Kommissieiu.*

Adol'f Berzhe's very name and personal experience illustrate the important role played by the peculiar Russian service nobility and its "European" background in the formation of the empire. Berzhe was born in Russia, but of a father from France and a mother from Germany. In his training and practice he thought of himself as part of a general European Orientalist community. Besides his work as chairman of the Caucasus Archeological Commission, his many scholarly posts in the colonial administration included the editorship of *Kavkazskii Kalendar'*, chargé d'affaires of the Caucasus Department of the Geographic Society, and director of the Tiflis Public Library.[59] For his labour he was decorated by the more prominent scholarly and Orientalist societies in Europe, such as the Société orientale de France and the Deutsche Morgenlandische Gesellschaft.[60] He was part of the Caucasus delegation that brought its knowledge, artifacts, and even a few mountaineers, including a Chechen, to the Third International Congress of Orientalists, held in 1876 in St Petersburg.[61] Like the codification of legal documents as an illustration of administrative regularity and the growth (for some) of legality, Berzhe and his commission's production of the massive volumes (*Akty*) served witness to the emergence and development of "civil rule" and society itself in a land historically struggling to join the community of "civilization." Scholars conceived of all of their respective but hardly distinct disciplines in a similar fashion. New statistical work, announced Nikolai I. Voronov, would improve the administration of newly colonized regions and represented a "new epoch of civic life" in the borderlands.[62]

A preoccupation with antiquity informed the interests of scholars in the region. Their obsession with antiquity and the process of collecting and ordering it amounted to a familiar colonial and "Orientalist" vision of a dormant and degraded land long after its fall from grace, although their vision possessed a uniquely Russian and imperial flavour. Scholars in St Petersburg and Tbilisi, for example, were extremely excited about an archaeological find in 1868 near the Cossack settlement of Khada-Finskaia in Kuban oblast. The find included gold and silver buttons, belts, remnants of clothing, jewellery, silver utensils, and dishes. General Bartolomei concluded that the inscriptions were similar to those of fifteenth-century Byzantine churches. Scholars in St Petersburg struggled with Radde of the Caucasus Museum for control of what they referred to as the "so-called 'Classical' materials."[63] One of the stated goals of the Archaeological Commission, formulated in an early 1859 document signed by Count Adlerberg, was the collection and analysis of "folk [narodnyi] [materials], as well as other monuments of antiquity."[64] The deeply disturbing nature of this vision should be readily apparent. The commission collected and displayed "folk" life through archaeological excavation, just a few years after the virtually entire destruction of contemporary "folk" life among the Adygei. Scholarship legitimated the recent colonial conquest by portraying the present as suspect and locating true culture in the past.

A set of assumptions about a glorious past that might be rescued by colonial rule motivated numerous scholarly projects on the region. The work of Berzhe and the study of archaeology by definition suggested that some greater truth lay buried underneath the bothersome accumulation of more historically recent sediment. "Nowhere else, it seems, has there been so strikingly preserved the traces of deep antiquity," claimed the Georgian scholar Dimitri Bakradze.[65] Were the mountains hiding "fragments of a prehistoric European race?" wondered Petr K. Uslar.[66] The region was of great interest to all the principal peoples of the ancient world, emphasized Bakradze, Uslar, and many others. The geographical diversity and the location between Europe and Asia, wrote Bakradze, made the North Caucasus the home of "numerous special peoples [narodnostei], for which it has been called the 'anthill of peoples.' "[67] Uslar argued for a long and indigenous ethnohistory in the region, and he surveyed Greek and Roman myths and travelogues to illustrate the antiquity of peoples.[68] To the minds of Orientalist scholars in particular, the rescue of this antiquity alone justified the Russian colonial project, and the "classical" antiquity they memorialized was that of the Byzantine heritage of the Eastern Roman Empire.

Berzhe's essay on the Chechens, *Chechnia i Chechentsy* (Chechnia and the Chechens), published in Tbilisi in 1859 and recently reissued in Groznyi, set the tone for the general respect for the past over a degraded present in Russian scholarship on the region. Chechens in the ethnography were undoubtedly "savage" in a way familiar to imperial readers: the authority of the father in the family, Berzhe claimed, is all-powerful until the children reach the age when they too can wield a weapon, at which point the relationship between "father and children is shaped by the rights of the stronger"; children also lack respect for their mothers, he wrote, who in turn are reduced to a state of "slavery" in relation to their husbands, and so on.[69] And his points of reference were perpetually imperial, meaningful to members of imperial educated society. To orient the reader to the Valerik River, for eample, he refered to the 1839 victory of General Galafeev there and to the poem written by Lermontov of the same name. In other places the work reads like a manual for Russian military planners.[70]

Primitive peoples, however, in spite of their savagery, might be rescued and set straight by imperial rule and its influence. Islam, Berzhe emphasized, was a recent event, historically alien to Chechnia and brought only by missionary mullas and, even more recently, the murids of Shamil. He depicted Chechen customary law (the *adat*) as a distinctive aspect of Chechen ethnic identity, historically constituted by the Chechens in order to free themselves from the domination of Kabard and Kumyk princes, an indigenous, genuinely Chechen cultural practice, in contrast to the foreign *shari'a* (Muslim law). Muslim traditions threatened the indigenous and genuine customs of the Chechens. Primitive life was thus not entirely negative. Like missionaries and educators such as Nikolai Il'minskii on the eastern frontier, Berzhe thought that primitive expressions of culture and faith were at least indigenous and hence superior to the foreign influence of Islam, and the basis for progress along the path toward civilization. Customary law was for him the first step in the formation of social life, which required a firm and stable state to enforce social norms above the mere individual caprice that ruled in primitive society. The absence of such a state, he maintained, resulted in the widespread and pernicious mountain traditions of the blood feud. What the Chechens needed was guidance and exposure to the "educated peoples," which in time would raise them from their present situation of "half-savagery" to the pursuit of "peaceful civilization [*grazhdanstvennost'*]."[71] Berzhe was even kind in places to Shamil, who was a "genius" for his efforts to mould a people of primitive instincts and mentality, "by nature foreign to order and subservience," into "something similar to a correctly organized state."[72]

The Orientalist preoccupation with antiquity put Georgia in a special relationship to the expanding regime, even a scholarly inspiration for the exploration of the North Caucasus. It was thus again an important model shaping the colonization of the North Caucasus. Its heritage of noble service and incorporation, for example, was fresh in the minds of officials as they sought similar arrangements with leading mountain families. Among the antiquities of Georgia, of course, was the Christian heritage, and scholars such as Bakradze and numerous officials moved naturally from searching for the remnants of Christian churches, structures, and rituals in Georgia to the North Caucasus. Archaeology was a science of empire, and military officials were not just supportive but were actively involved in the process of the archaeological exploration of Georgian antiquity. Berzhe and Radde benefited from the active contributions of military figures to a series of archaeological conferences in Tbilisi, where one of the principal topics was the archaeology of ancient churches in the region.[73] Georgian church officials and commentators declared their appreciation and support of the work of the Imperial Archaeological Commission and its local branch and emphasized the common ground between the two religious and secular institutions.[74] In the Georgian case, the question of Christian antiquity again posed Islam as a problem and impediment to the preservation of the authentic past. With a perpetual refrain, as we discussed in the last chapter, Georgians themselves contributed to this imperial preoccupation: "For thousands of years, with the sword in one hand and the cross in the other, [Christian Georgia] has defended its fatherland and the Orthodox faith from the hands of Muslims," declared the Georgian ekzarkh, I. Aleksei, in 1905.[75]

The imperial preoccupation with history, archaeology, and Christianity in the Georgian context coincided with the efforts of Georgian nativists to recover their own frontier peoples lost to Islam and conquering empires. In an essay presented to the Academy of Sciences in 1873, Dimitri Bakradze was careful to insert a case for the historically Georgian character of numerous peoples in his discussion of these matters.[76] The Udis (near Dagestan), explained Ingalo Janashvili in a similar vein, deserved schooling in Georgian because they "formerly lived in Georgan cities, which were then destroyed in Mongol times." The truths of history and archaeology outweighed the practices of the present: "Their contemporary existence is Tatar, but the Udis were formerly Georgian."[77] The situation to the south of Georgia was similar, emphasized Z. Mtatsmindeli, where Georgians in the regions of Kars and Batumi remained, in his estimation, disturbingly Muslim even after Russia incorporated the area following the defeat of the Ottoman Turks in 1877.[78] Ancient cemeteries among "our ancestors," the Khevsur, to move to Georgia's northern frontier, revealed a Christian presence deep in the mountains, in the "villages of the fatherland," perpetually threatened by the "hostile" and "powerful" Chechens.[79] Georgians provided a local and contemporary colouring to the imperial exploration of antiquity.

ETHNOGRAPHIC REALISM

The glorification of an enduring "folk" identity from antiquity spurred the emergence of ethnography in the borderlands. Ethnographers of Russia itself were engaged in a similar sort of exploration, which Hans Rogger dates to the eighteenth-century interest of Romantic writers in the unique tales, songs, and legends that they believed represented the most faithful expression of the character of the Russian people.[80] Russian educated society was looking to the "lower orders" for revelation, as Belinskii put it, and by the 1850s intellectuals in general, from Alexander Herzen to Fyodor Dostoevsky, shared similar ideas about the importance of the world of the Russian peasant to what it meant to be "Russian."[81] Russian peasants appeared to educated Russians to inhabit a different world, and the questions and concerns brought by Russian ethnographers to the Russian peasantry were not far removed from the methods employed upon the mountaineers.[82] Georgia's encounter with Russia's version of "originality" stimulated a similar preoccupation with the culture of the common people. A "literature of the people," suggested a commentator in *Droeba*, might be identified, "rescued," and transformed from its inevitably rough state into a "poetical work" by members of educated society.[83] As in Russia, the development of a Georgian ethnography emerged from literary writing and newspaper essays inspired by these new ideas about custom, tradition, and the dilemmas of an "educated society" divorced from its primary source of sustenance.

In the more isolated and distant North Caucasus, the principal discovers of tradition were often Russian and Georgian imperial officials. Arnol'd Zisserman, the previously mentioned district supervisor in Tushetia-Pshav-Khevsuria, was initially inspired by Marlinsky. His first essays for *Kavkaz* read like Marlinsky, and they emphasized harrowing rides on horseback, the excitement and danger of combat, and the indecipherable geography of the region.[84] Sometimes Zisserman passed through "half-subjugated" regions, guided by mountaineers and dressed as a Chechen, or he participated in dances and festivals in mountain villages: "I was unable to sleep; I lay in a half-conscious state, my ideas gathering in a chaotic way ... I will never forget that night!"[85] Zisserman recalled a trip on horseback along the Aragva River with a group of Pshav: "A gorgeous ravine: woods and mountains, small villages here and there. A turn to the right, and our road went along the shore; still for 10 versts it was tolerable, but further on – you hold the reins of your horse, close your eyes, and make a prayer ... Ukh! What a deafening roar! The waves crash in ... your head spins ... the waves crash against the shore, the horse exerts all its strength and you make it to dry land ... Such, or almost such, is how we moved on to the Pshav village of Shuapkho."[86] The yearly migration of the Tushin from the Alazan lowlands to the mountains in May and June, Zisserman informed readers of *Kavkaz*, was, "in a word, a remarkably diverse mixture, a picture worthy of the brush of Rembrandt!"[87] The young Zisserman found his audience among the rapidly growing borderland educated community in Tbilisi.

That audience was also interested in a different form of representation, one that more closely served its new sense of imperial purpose. Ethnographers quickly rethought the very Romantic tradition that had initially inspired them.[88] Romantic writers traditionally emphasized human insignificance before the natural beauty and power of the extended Caucasus mountain range. In the first issue of the Caucasus Department *Zapiski*, by contrast, G.V. Sollogub suggested that the deep ravines of those "colossal phenomena" might instead offer insight into the fragmentation of the Adygei tribes.[89] "On the peaks of the Caucasus are hidden the solutions to many important historical questions about the fate of many disappearing peoples," he wrote.[90] The editors of the first issue of *Kavkaz* announced that readers of Russian in the Caucasus needed to be acquainted with the curious lands beyond Tbilisi, "still in a young state and little known."[91] Of particular interest to the literate community in the Caucasus were ethnographic reports or, as the editors of *Kavkaz* wrote a week later, "descriptions of the ways and habits of the Caucasus peoples [*narody*]."[92] By 1851 Zisserman could fulfill this mandate as well, and he described the customs of religion, courtship and marriage, feuding, singing, and socializing that were unique, he emphasized, to the Khevsur.[93] Initially captivated by the elaborate costumes, dances, songs, and cultural practices of the people whose affairs he managed and "about whom in Russia barely anyone has heard," he was compelled to ethnographic study, as he recalled later in his memoirs, in order "to acquaint the reading portion of society with them when the opportunity presented itself."[94] The agenda of the newspaper *Kavkaz* was similar. In 1858 the editors announced the creation of a special "rubric" of the newspaper, to be devoted to the "study of our interesting region." The editors looked for reader response. "[L]et everyone bring their stone to the construction of this building," they suggested, the edifice for a future "museum of the nature, peoples, and history of the Caucasus."[95] Ethnographic description promised to create a form of order out of the chaos of the frontier.

The military in particular was sympathetic. Military officials such as Nikolai Raevskii, Admiral Serebriakov, Lieutenant Stamm, Kashutin, and others criticized the overly aggressive tactics of the Russian army and devised plans for peaceful forms of cooperation with the mountaineers.[96] Raevskii had a long career of service in the borderlands, in his younger years a general in the Black Sea Shore Line and many years later a supporter of Pan-Slavism and General Cherniaev in the Balkans. His experience on the Black Sea Shore Line prompted him to rethink imperial policy and the prosecution of the war. Toward the end of a two-hour battle with about a thousand Adygei along the Shakhe River in 1839, for example, Raevskii was approached with a request from their elders to allow them to bury their dead. He knew the elders by name and understood that to deny such a request would needlessly antagonize the mountaineers, since they had taken various pledges to bury their fallen in battle. "As I did last year, I informed them that I do not profit from the dead and will return them at no cost," Raevskii reported. He ordered his soldiers to offer carts and help as necessary to collect the dead, and generally tried to convince the elders that "poddanstvo" to Russia, or the "favours they could expect, if they would subject themselves to our Sovereign Emperor," was far better than needless military conflict.[97] Raevskii became an active critic of the military and even departed the region because of these concerns. As we have seen, in 1841 he informed the minister of war in St Petersburg, A.I. Chernyshev, "Our activities in the Caucasus are reminiscent of the many tragedies of the early conquest of America by the Spaniards," and he expressed the hope that the experience would not leave a similar "bloody legacy" to Russian history.[98]

The military officials understood increased ethnographic knowledge as the key to an improvement in the prosecution of the war and to the formulation of more appropriate Russian military policy. To them, mountaineers were more than simply the "enemy," as General Emmanuel wrote to General Paskevich in the late 1820s.[99] Such officials imagined an empire populated by a diverse number of peoples. In their view, a culturally, linguistically, and even territorially defined narod, safely situated within an empire and led by the more developed

Russian narod, possessed the necessary attributes to prosper and progress. Early Russian writers of ethnography within the Caucasus Army attempted to convince themselves and their superiors that the identities of the mountaineer narody were fairly clear. Although he was unable to determine the origins of the word "Cherkes" or the history of the various tribes of the northwest Caucasus, Lieutenant Stamm assured the General Staff that the many Adygei tribes in fact constituted a single people.[100] They possessed a single physiognomy and physique, and spoke a similar language.[101] A North Caucasus populated by narody, Stamm believed, was a more comforting prospect than the confusing situation that the region typically presented to the Russians. Russian military commanders, for example, like American officials in relation to Native tribal organizations, were often surprised at an attack from an Adygei tribe just days after the negotiation of a ceasefire, only to discover that the treaty was not honoured by nearby mountaineers who belonged to a different tribe.[102] In an 1843 discussion of muridizm in the northeast Caucasus, a military official named Neverovskii despaired of Russian failures to establish peace in the region and stop the spread of Muslim "fanaticism." He described how Sufi leaders told the populace that Russian cannons and bayonets could not harm the faithful, and that death in battle against infidel rule was for the Muslim a great honour. Neverovskii remained optimistic, however, and foresaw a different kind of secular unity in the future. Religion and the experience of war had merged the diverse tribes of Chechnia and Dagestan into "one people" (narod), he said.[103] Early ethnographers in the military attempted to offer coherent pictures of narody rather than to emphasize tribal distinctiveness.

Missionaries in the Restoration Society shared their interests. Teaching and evangelizing meant participation in imperial educated society, which included the adoption of the traditional modes of writing about the frontier. Ossetian teacher Nikolai Khatagov from the Sadonsk school entitled one of his yearly reports to the Restoration Society in Tbilisi "Travels in the Dargav Valley."[104] Amateur ethnography was the most common format, and teachers routinely included sections in their reports on "local customs."[105] Ossetian Boris Khetaurov called his 1872 report "An Ethnographic Portrayal of the Ossetian People."[106] O. Iosseliani's description of the funeral, recounted in chapter 1, was part of his report for 1872. There was nothing unusual about such a report, except perhaps its quality and liveliness. Some teachers were too impressed with themselves to communicate anything of interest. The Georgian teacher in Abhazia previously noted for his condenscension and snobbery entitled his report for 1872 "Notes of a Young Man."[107]

The teachers were responding to the initiatives of their colleagues in Tbilisi, who specifically requested this sort of material in the reports. The question of the religious beliefs and practices of the mountaineers was only one among many questions or issues. The first issue at hand, according to the guide for the teachers composed by Inspector N. Likhachev, was a "description of the village, locality, or city" and the "history and archaeology of the area." The reports were to resemble the standard ethnographic accounts published by the numerous scholarly societies and to include descriptions of geography, climate, livestock, domestic implements, the "physical and moral characteristics of the inhabitants," their "way of life," and their "hygenic and sanitary conditions."[108] For these missionaries and educators, the question of faith and religious practices would be understood and encouraged through the creation of this sort of composite picture of "custom" or culture.

The evolution of imperial cartography illustrates the interests of these travellers, military officials, and missionaries. Over time, Russian maps of the North Caucasus became populated by peoples and thus served, as J.B. Harley suggests, as "communicators of an imperial message."[109] Eighteenth-century maps showed the provinces of the empire. New Russia, Azov, Taurida, and Astrakhan stretched close to the North Caucasus.[110] A 1744 map of the region lacked any notion of ethnicity whatsoever; Kabard was marked by the princely households (*dvor*) and the forty-eight villages that belonged to them.[111] Early military maps, such as the one composed for General A.P. Ermolov (1816–27), referred to the North Caucasus as the "Land of the Mountain Peoples" and lacked a conception of ethnicity as territorially and culturally distinct.[112] Cartographers marked the rugged territory that served as an obstacle to the Russian army. Fortresses, bridges, and Cossack settlements competed with mountain villages and the different "tribes" known to the cartographers.[113] Military maps of 1806 and 1807 offered a prominent place to the Kabards, Chechens, and Karabulaks, an Ingush tribe subsequently exiled to Ottoman Turkey in 1865.[114] The random character of the early maps reflected the experiences and encounters of Russian military officials. "A village of the Kazelbekovsk people," explained the key to one such map.[115] This "people" was presumably an Abaza tribe called the Kyzylbekovs, who either were killed in the war, left in the emigration, or were, as a contemporary scholar writes, "assimilated" by the Abkhaz.[116]

Later maps offered a more coherent vision of ethnic identity. In an 1842 map, narody such as the Abkhaz, the Dagestanis, or the Cherkes were not represented as a whole, but the table to the left of the map contained an early attempt to list the various "Abkhaz tribes," "Cherkes [Adygei] tribes," "Tatar tribes," and so on.[117] The 1870 map of the Caucasus Military District's Topographic Department represented with a single colour groups such as the Cherkes, Ossetians, Chechens, Dagestani mountaineers, and Abkhaz, and provided a key that listed the many tribal distinctions among these groups.[118] Tribes, Russians believed and hoped, were soon to be peoples. There were deviations from this trend, of course. A 1790 map was strangely modern, almost similar to a Soviet map of the autonomous regions in the 1920s. "Dagestanis" was even used by the makers of this map ("Dagestani mountaineers" was the norm in the nineteenth century), although the "Lezgin" (one of the primary languages of Dagestan) were also identified.[119] Some cartographers had a greater interest in ethnicity than others. The general trend, however, was toward the more prominent and precisely defined presentation of "peoples." This interest in ethnicity was probably unique to the colonizers. After Khalat Efendi killed the murid of Shamil who had robbed his home and injured his wives, a series of events that forced him to flee Chechnia in 1852, he arrived before the Russians with maps of Vedeno and the lands of Shamil's imamate. "Although these drawings are very crude and done without any rules," noted an official in the viceroy's office, Russians will be "curious to see these examples of the geographic conceptions of the mountaineers."[120] Ethnic distinctions were irrelevant to the concerns of the mountaineer cartographers. The makers of the Russian Empire, ironically, were sometimes more interested in the representation of what we have come to call ethnicity than the non-Russian peoples themselves.[121]

In direct response to the rich tradition of literary writing about the region, ethnographers imagined themselves as producers of realistic accounts of mountain culture, which in their view amounted to a clarification of the imperial mission. The concerns of ethnography were matters of great "practical interest" to the administration of the empire, noted Voronov, and the statistical committees reminded their research helpers that only "truthful, actual, and genuine figures have meaning for statistics."[122] The search for "facts" was an effort to clarify the imperial mission. By the later nineteenth century, journals, scholarly societies, and even university departments accompanied and fostered a more precise sense of purpose among ethnographers. The Society for the Amateurs (*Liubiteli*) of Nature at Moscow University became in 1867 the Imperial Society for the Amateurs of Nature, Anthropology, and Ethnography. *Etnograficheskoe Obozrenie* (Ethnographic review) was founded in 1889. The scientific classification of peoples was the primary issue for the contributors to these new journals. "People of science gather and classify [*gruppiruyt*] ethnographic facts according to the central manifestations of a people's world outlook, morals, and way of life [*byt*]," stated the editors of *Etnograficheskoe Obozrenie* in an early issue.[123] "[I needed] to orient myself amidst this mass of tradition," wrote P.S. Nazarov of his work with Bashkir legends and folk tales.[124] The search for folk culture on the frontier resulted in a new conceptualization of the empire.

In the Caucasus, ethnographers were armed with more "scientific" methods, and scholars such as Gustav Radde criticized Zisserman's early essays on the Khevsur, which were far too personal and self-absorbed for his taste. Zisserman wrote too much about himself, complained Radde.[125] Zisserman's experience was central to the telling of the story, such as when he accompanied a group of nomadic Tushin and helped hold off an attack from a band of Dido (Dagestani Avar). "This was a day not to be effaced from my memory," he proudly told his Tbilisi readers.[126] For Zisserman, inspired by the traditions of Russian Romanticism, the strange clothes, turbans, and long stockings of the Khevsur were reminiscent of "the middle ages, and the time of knights, fighting for their faith."[127] His early work might have been intriguing, but for Radde much more was at stake. Scholarly objectivity, he stressed in 1880, was required for a truthful picture of the Khevsur, and ethnographic description had advanced since Zisserman's time. Radde's ethnographic essay was devoted to the "main moments in the lives of the Khevsur: birth, marriage, and death," and also covered religious beliefs and church buildings, customary law, and Khevsur clothes, decorations, and domestic implements and utensils.[128] Late-nineteenth-century ethnographers such as Radde believed that the administration of the multi-ethnic empire demanded a form of ethnographic knowledge that could facilitate progressive cultural change. Ethnographers attempted to understand and thereby transform the practices of the blood feud (*krovomshchenie*), and they frequently compiled and studied examples of crimes committed by mountaineers.[129] Their effort to codify mountaineer customary law (*adat*) was an example of the interest of the regime and educated society in the identity of the mountaineers as "peoples." "Peoples," ethnographers and administrators believed, possessed legal traditions, a history of laws, and a court system. As in Siberia and on the Kazakh steppe, the Russian regime established special courts (*narodnyi gorskie sudy*) that were primarily based on customary law.[130] Russian ethnographers served as the compilers and interpreters of this tradition.

The process of collecting initiated by the Caucasus Department in Tbilisi became the basis for the Caucasus Museum, a site for the display of the many peoples of the Caucasus and the surrounding region. Radde founded the museum in 1867. Before this, the smaller museum of the Caucasus Department had rapidly become a repository for the efforts of collectors throughout the region, who supplied gold and silver coins, belts, necklaces, buckles, a Turkish inkstand, Persian spoons, a Persian breastplate for a horse, hairpins, pendants, rings, and other artifacts.[131] Initially dedicated to natural history, the collection expanded to include historical and ethnographic sections, and by 1855 the Ethnographic Section included 3,300 representative objects of the Caucasus "peoples."[132] The Caucasus Department collected human skulls and thus participated in early physical anthropology, although local workers, who possessed "superstitions and understandings foreign to scientific interests," were often reluctant to help.[133] As a result of a landslide in 1854, I.A. Vrevskii found the skeleton of a Chechen woman which was decorated with gold bracelets and elaborate necklaces, and buried with gold ingots. He sent the skeleton to Tbilisi, where it became part of the department museum's collection.[134] After 1867, Radde's curators identified thirteen suitable categories for collection for the Ethnographic Section, including clothes, kitchen and domestic ware, "instruments of domestic use," musical instruments, furniture, jewellery, agricultural implements, and children's toys.[135]

The representation of empire as a collection of peoples featured the constant collaboration of scholars and institutions in both St Petersburg and Tbilisi. Officials and collectors in St Petersburg relied on local Orientalists and collectors from the frontier. For the Third International Congress of Orientalists in 1876, hosted by the Russians in St Petersburg, Radde, Berzhe, N.I. Voronov, and General Stebnitskii gathered materials from the Caucasus Museum for presentation at the congress.[136] They even sent four "natives" to the imperial capital as representatives of Dagestanis, Kabards, Chechens, and Abkhaz. Interestingly, these individuals were required to be fluent in Russian but dressed in local costume.[137] The Academy of Sciences Museum of Ethnography and Anthropology was a key institution in St Petersburg for the representation of empire. The academy president alerted the high commander in Tbilisi about the camera as a new technology of representation in 1880 and noted that "photographs of *narodnyi* types" accompanied museums and collections throughout Europe. He needed help from Tbilisi to fulfill his goal of representing all the "diverse tribes inhabiting the empire."[138]

Tsar Nicholas II announced in 1909 a new exhibit sponsored by the museum dedicated to a "collection of figures portraying all the peoples [*narodnosti*] of Russia."[139] The visionaries of empire struggled with the realities of modernity, of course, as the debates over the process of collection illustrate. Local officials from around the region informed Tbilisi that locating the "genuine dress of the given nationality [narodnost']" would require significant expenditure and effort, as few people wore or even possessed what the Academy of Sciences identified as authentic and native to the people in question.[140] Addressing this dilemma was one of the purposes of the exhibit – the "preservation for the future of rapidly disappearing ethnographic particularities of the Caucasus peoples."[141] Ethnographers in Russia itself faced similar dilemmas.[142]

The power to name, collect, and represent had its political consequences. Russian representations of the region were backed by the authority of imperial power, and hence proved quite durable. The literate makers of texts shaped subsequent knowledge of borderland peoples and Russian peasants as well. Svan elders were astonished at ethnographer A.I. Stoianov's knowledge of their historic customs: "And the elders in a whisper informed the others that I had a remarkable notebook, in which was described everything about their church."[143] The Chechens did not refer to themselves as Chechens, a word that derived from the name of a village in the foothills on the Argun River, but Nokhchi (singular, Nokhchuo).[144] Nearby communities each used a different designation for the Chechens, complained researchers associated with the Geographic Society. The Kumyk called them Michikiz; most Georgians used Kistebi (which could also refer to the Ingush); the Salatavi of north Dagestan said Nakbak; and the Ossetians referred to the Chechens as Tratsan.[145] Zisserman thus encountered Kistebi (Kist), as he followed the term used by the Tushin, Pshav, and Khevsur with whom he lived. Not just Romantic Georgian writers but the regime itself called the Tushin, Pshav, and Khevsur "mountain Georgians," as the makers of the 1897 census associated language with ethnic identity.[146] In a similar fashion, the census counted the "Lezgin," which was one of the primary languages used by the mountaineers in Dagestan. Imperial representation, of course, did not need to correspond to mountaineer conceptions of identity. Mountaineer ideas and stories were dismissed by the Russians as legend and misleading hearsay, mountaineer maps were different from Russian maps, and mountaineers did not even know their own ethnic names. As Adol'f Berzhe commented in a footnote to one of his works on the region, "All these names, including even the word Lezgin, are unknown to the Dagestani mountaineers."[147] And it was "highly probable," he wrote of the Chechens with prescience, that in time the tribal names would disappear and the Chechens would "hold on to one general name for themselves."[148]

TRANSCRIBING LANGUAGES

Missionaries viewed native languages as the best means for the transmission of the Christian message. For scholars interested in narodnost', the indigenous tongue was also the historically authentic one.
Johann Gottfried Herder's interest in primitive and folk culture and
his insistence on the importance of language as the vehicle for the expression of the character of a people found a ready audience in
Russia. Herder advocated studies in comparative anthropology and
comparative linguistics, and he inspired what would become the rich
tradition of German philology in the nineteenth century.[149] "[Civiliza-
tion] grows best, and I would say only," he wrote to Joseph II in 1793,
"in the peculiarity of the nation, in its inherited and constantly trans-
mitted vernacular. One wins the heart of a people only by using its
language. Is it not inspiring to plant seeds of well-being for the re-
motest future among so many people in their own way of thought, in
the manner which is most peculiar and most cherished by them?"[150]
In the latter eighteenth century, Russian writers were preoccupied
with the development of their own language and emphasized its capacity to measure up to the literary potential of the languages of the
West.[151] Almost a century later, Russian scholars associated with the
Caucasus Department were united in their belief about the importance of the study of mountain languages. While Arabic was the language of the Qur'an and the mulla, most mountaineers were
illiterate, and their languages were yet to be transcribed.

Like Zisserman and in the spirit of Herder, Petr K. Uslar emphasized the significance and value of the study of the many languages
of the North Caucasus. Uslar briefly served in Dagestan in the late
1830s as a young man, and he returned in 1850 with the task of preparing a study of Erevan province. He stayed in the Caucasus for
twenty-five years, committed to his linguistic and ethnographic research. His wife and eldest daughter died of scarlet fever in 1843
while Uslar was working at the General Staff in St Petersburg, and his
younger brother had died many years earlier, at the age of twenty-
two, in a battle with the mountaineers.[152] "The view about the extreme impoverishment of these languages is completely mistaken,"
he argued. "These languages are incredibly rich in their grammatical
forms and allow one the possibility of expressing the most refined
and nuanced ideas."[153] As Herder had suggested a century earlier, all
languages were capable of abstraction and "bear the stamp of reason,
the tool of which it has been formed."[154] Uslar contested the views of
conservatives who were skeptical of the capacity of non-European
languages to express significant concepts and ideas.

Closer to the region than European thinkers such as Herder was again the example and experience of Georgia. Members of the new generation of the 1860s criticized their predecessors for their lack of attention to explicitly Georgian forms of cultural expression in the Georgian tongue, a language, in their view, certainly sufficient to express the nuances of Molière.[155] The Romantic impulse coincided with modern notions of the civil order and of the importance of higher levels of popular literacy and educational attainment, all of which was "useful" (*sasargeblo*) to the tasks of cultural renewal and awakening.[156] Like Russians, Georgians were struggling to extend "literacy to the lower segments of the population," as Georgians pointed out to (Russian) school inspector V.V. Levashev in 1865. "The desire of the natives to know their own language is completely natural and logical" and should be supported by the state, they explained.[157] If Georgian students faced a "Chinese alphabet" in the classroom, complained B. Petriashvili, reading comprehension and educational progress would be severely inhibited.[158] If the native tongue was important for the communication of the Gospel, as we saw in the last chapter, it was also central to the concerns of Georgian educators interested in ethics, "morality," and the "soul" of the student.[159] Contributors to *Droeba* frequently complained about the insufficient number of Georgian instructors in the gymnasiums.[160] The Society for the Spread of Georgian Literacy was founded in 1879, although the Ministry of Education in the Transcaucasus remained reluctant to challenge the supremacy of Russian in its schools before 1914.[161]

In the North Caucasus, Uslar and other linguists hoped to equip each narodnost' with its own written language. Uslar was not the first linguist to attempt this task, but he was the most successful. Earlier scholars such as Andrei Shegren of the Academy of Sciences in St Petersburg had been reluctant to modify the Russian alphabet. Shegren simply rendered in Russian transcription what he understood to be the equivalent sound supplied by his local informants, with occasional directives, such as "pronounce gutturally."[162] Vorontsov hoped to initiate further study, and he requested input from a number of Academy of Sciences scholars. The ethnographic implications of their program of linguistic study were clear from the start, as the project was intended "to explain the dark and confusing ethnographic interrelationships among the Caucasus peoples."[163] Time was of the essence, as languages, like peoples and their cultures, could disappear.[164] Adol'f Berzhe began work on the project in 1856, but he failed to expand significantly on Shegren's method and dropped the matter in 1860.[165] Uslar, by contrast, devised a new "Caucasus alphabet" based on Cyrillic, with several additions to accommodate the guttural mountain sounds.[166] He insisted on the use of Cyrillic for the new alphabet, even while admitting at the 1861 Caucasus Department meeting that Georgian would provide a more suitable alphabet. Uslar started with Abkhaz in 1861, Chechen in 1862 (with the help of two Russian-speaking Chechens who lived in Tbilisi), and Kabard with the help of Kazi Atazhukinym. He eventually worked on Avar, Lak, Dargin, and other northeast Caucasus languages and composed a linguistic map of all the languages of Dagestan oblast.[167]

Uslar had many native helpers in his work. Early pioneers were usually the sons of prominent princes who had been educated in a privileged setting in St Petersburg. Khan-Girei, for example, left his influential Bzhedug (Adygei) family for Tbilisi and then the St Petersburg Cadet Corps. His manuscript, "Zapiski o Cherkesii" (Memorandum on Cherkesia), written at the behest of Russian military planners and read by General A.A. Vel'iaminov and Baron G.V. Rozen, told the story of the "Cherkes" people.[168] Their past was a time of savagery, he argued, an insignificant prelude to the real beginning of Adygei history, which coincided with the arrival of Russian colonial rule. He hoped the Russians would help the Adygei develop a written script for an Adygei alphabet. "The Cherkes do not have books in their own language," he wrote, "and have been deprived of the best means of attaining human reason – writing."[169]

Others from among this growing cohort of educated and bilingual mountaineers helped transcribe North Caucasus languages, served as teachers in Restoration Society schools and small schools founded by Uslar, and even contributed ethnographic essays about their respective peoples for readers of Russian. Aideemir Chirkeev taught Avar children in Khunzakh, and Abdulla Omarov conducted lessons in Lak at Uslar's school in Kumukh. Omarov shared his personal history for readers of *Sbornik Svedenii o Kavkazskikh Gortsakh*. This was a story satisfying to imperial educated society – a personal struggle in search of education and a progressive future, in which he surmounted the obstacles presented by mountaineer backwardness, rule of the khans, and Muslim medresses.[170] His father was even a Sufi adept.[171] Omarov noted that his descriptive material referred to just one tribe (the Lak), but "all the same the Dagestanis are so similar that, based on the life of the Laks, one can arrive at a picture of the Dagestani way of life in general."[172] By the time he moved to the "new world" of Tbilisi in the 1860s, he was part of a growing collection of educated non-Russians who participated in one way or another in Russia's rule of the Caucasus.[173] With the voice of "native" authenticity, they affirmed the importance of Russia's work in the region. Omarov understood his scholarly efforts to be for the benefit of "Dagestan," in contrast to the Sufi leaders, who were motivated by religious fanaticism and hatred. The murids, he wrote, offered little to those moved by "patriotic and national feelings."[174] Imperial rule was to include this form of respect for non-Russian "patriotism," and ethnographic representation was helping to turn Laks and Avars into Dagestanis.

Omarov not only shared his own story but sought out those of other mountaineers. Russian publications are interested in everything "regarding the mountaineers of Dagestan," he wrote to Mirza Suleiman in 1868. Omarov suggested to Suleiman that he share the story of his childhood and early education, his memories of Dagestan before the arrival of the Russians, and his knowledge of mountain customs, administration, and judicial traditions. "They [Russian readers] genuinely do not know anything about our past," Omarov emphasized to Suleiman, and he promised to translate the story from Arabic to Russian and bring it to the attention of the administration.[175] In another translation Omarov offered the work of Muheddin Mahomed-Khanov, a mulla who denounced the teachings of the Sufi orders as false interpretations of the Qur'an.[176] Berzhe introduced with satisfaction the work of Shora Nogmov, an Adygei educator and student of his people's past.[177] "All peoples are preserved in the memory of their historical legends," wrote Nogmov, who thus "greedily listened" to the stories of the elder generation.[178] Like Russians who sought to clarify the relationship of Russian history and culture to the global process of "universal history," Omarov, Khan-Girei, and Nogmov worked to place Dagestan and Adygei on the map of the empire.

Literacy and education were again central to this cultivation of custom and the past. The Society for the Restoration of Orthodoxy adopted Uslar's alphabet for its own efforts to transcribe mountain languages such as Abkhaz and Svan. The *Abkhaz Reader* sponsored by the society, published in 1865 by a trio that included I.A. Bartolomei, the military general previously mentioned, contained a mix of educational and practical admonitions for the "good pupil" with occasional forays into the larger implications of literacy and education.[179] When a learned elder (*starik*) advised his son of the virtues of a serious and studious life, the son retorted that the older generation had done just fine without schooling. The starik replied that members of his generation had never been offered the opportunity of reading or writing in their native language. "We had to refer to someone who knew Georgian or Turkish," he complained.[180] Other short vignettes taught the students about the evils of greed,

the power of God, and the virtues of sitting "quietly during lessons." Literacy and hard work apparently offered the opportunity of
upward mobility, as was evident from the story of the poor peasants
whose progress in their studies eventually enabled them to help
their parents out of poverty.[181] Bartolomei's reader was also intended to acquaint Russians with Abkhaz language and culture, and
it included a collection of Abkhaz proverbs.[182] Bartolomei also
worked on a *Chechen Reader* which was sponsored by the Restoration
Society and contained similar lessons about the importance of native
education and literacy, as a counter to the Arabic of the mullas.[183]
Ossetians such as Vasilii Tsoraev and Daniel Chonkadze used
Uslar's alphabet to publish collections of Ossetian folk tales and
proverbs.[184] Russia's Orientalists equipped mountain peoples with
written versions of their spoken tongues.

DRAWING BORDERS

Ethnographers, geographers, linguists, and other scholars who attributed a culture and a potential cultural and intellectual life to the
mountaineers presented a picture that was still fairly controversial at
the mid-nineteenth century. As Uslar hinted in his defence of his
work, not all Russians in the Caucasus were comfortable with the implications of comparative linguistics. Officials in St Petersburg and
the Caucasus, convinced of the virtues of empire-wide administrative
consistency and of the universality of Russian customs and forms of
rule, routinely objected to the special concessions of military-native
administration (*voenno-narodnoe upravlenie*) and the special mountain
courts. The views of ethnographers and other scholars discussed here
were especially contested by administrators and military officials preoccupied with mountaineer affairs in unstable regions such as Terek
oblast. Captain Zolotarev advocated mass exile for the mountaineers
of Terek oblast in 1863 as a "final resolution" to the problem of administration, and he stressed the need for firm colonial control over
the North Caucasus in light of the "inevitable war with the European
powers."[185] Like Europeans, Russians grew increasingly intolerant of
ethnic and national differences as the century wore on, and the tradition of conquest and exile continued to pose an alternative attractive
to many Russian officials and members of educated society. Yet the
vision of empire suggested by ethnographers and other scholars left a
powerful legacy to the modern era.

By the late nineteenth century, all Russians in the Caucasus associated the mountaineers with particular cultural traditions, languages,
histories, and a bounded territory. A narod, Russians assumed, was

not, or should not be, dispersed throughout an empire or region as a result of exile, but should possess a historic homeland. Imperial administrative distinctions more or less corresponded to such a notion of a territorially defined and homogeneous ethnic identity. The mountaineers of Shamil's imamate were divided in the eastern Caucasus when Chechnia became part of Terek oblast and Dagestan oblast was formed from what had been the Transcaspian Region (minus Kubinskii district). The right and left flanks of the Caucasus Line became the boundaries for Kuban and Terek oblasts.[186] The military-native administration announced by Prince Bariatinskii in 1860 extended beyond Terek and Dagestan oblasts to Kuban oblast, to where the Adygei had been moved, Zakatal'skii okrug, and Sukhumi otdel, the central region of Abkhazia. The new Adygei settlements in Kuban oblast were composed of many different tribes. Fourteen settlements comprised as many as five to six tribes, and the villages of Khatazhukai and Urupskii contained nine different tribes. The surviving Shapsugs were dispersed among eight different villages of Ekaterinodar district, nine villages of Maikop district, and four villages of Batalpashin district.[187] Tribal affiliation among the Adygei became less important as a result of Russian rule. The general administrative structure of territorial division according to narod was in place, and it appeared as a result of Russian imperial rule.

The *okrugi* (districts) under military-native administration in Terek oblast included the Kabard, Ossetian, and Ingush districts of the Western Military Section and the Chechen, Argun, and Ichkerian districts of the Central Military Section. The Eastern Military Section, extending to the Caspian Sea, included a district for the Kumyks.[188] In spite of the changing concerns of the imperial regime in the North Caucasus in the later nineteenth century, this process of administrative division according to narodnost' remained constant. In 1883 Governor-General A.M. Dondukov-Korsakov formed a commission to provide recommendations to alleviate the deteriorating conditions among the Cossacks of the North Caucasus and to regulate the process of settlement so as to avoid conflicts between Cossacks, the new Russian emigrants from the southern provinces (the *inogorodnyi* population), and Greek and Armenian settlers. The members of this commission were far from sympathetic to the plight of the mountaineers. While Dmitrii Starosel'skii, of the Caucasus Mountain Administration, participated in the discussions, other individuals, such as V. Butyrkin, frequently warned their colleagues of the need to maintain the economic position and "military spirit" of the Cossacks, who had fought and won the war but still endured the thievery and attacks of armed mountaineers.[189] The commission declared entire villages responsible for crimes against Cossacks and Russian settlers and recommended "military expeditions" against the "guilty villages" until the problem was resolved.[190] Commission members were suspicious of the special mountain courts and the concessions of military-native administration.[191] Such measures, including the prospect of exile, were in the tradition of the Caucasus War. The immediate background to the militaristic response of this commission was the unexpected rebellion in Dagestan, Chechnia, and other mountaineer regions in the fall of 1877, which coincided with the announcement of another war between Turkey and Russia.

As a result of the recommendations of the commission, in 1888 Terek oblast was divided into three sections (the otdely of Piatigorsk, Kizliar, and Sunzhen) and four districts (the okrugi of Vladikavkaz, Khasav-Iurtov, Nal'chik, and Groznyi).[192] In 1905 another section (Mozdok) was added to the former group, and two more districts (Nazranovsk and Vedeno) to the latter.[193] The three western administrative units of Terek oblast again corresponded more or less to the Kabard, Ossetian, and Ingush populations, while the mountaineer districts to the east were inhabited by the Chechens. This was far from "Ingushetia for the Ingush," of course, as numerous other groups, such as Russians, Kabards, Ukrainians, and Kumyks also lived in Sunzhen section. Cossacks made up roughly 50 per cent of the entire population of the sections of Sunzhen, Kizliar, and Piatigorsk.[194] But 99 per cent of the Ingush population lived in the otdel of Sunzhen, just as 96 per cent of the Ossetians lived in Vladikavkaz district.[195] The 1888 administrative realignment changed Vladikavkaz district to include the Ossetian population previously in Sunzhen.[196] The administrative distinctions of the tsarist regime responded to the ethnographic vision of narodnost'.

In contrast to Uslar or Zisserman, Butyrkin and the commission were hostile rather than sympathetic, angry rather than curious. Even for Butyrkin, however, the Russian Empire was a conglomeration of peoples. His empire contained territorial distinctions that were borders and boundaries of exclusion, intended to mark segregated prisons rather than historic and legitimate homelands. He wanted mountaineers in distinct administrative groups in order to police them better. Such a vision of cultural conflict rather than cultural cooperation ironically called into question the very military expansion that had brought Russian rule to the region in the early nineteenth century. This was not a workable vision of empire but a retreat from the problem posed by the incorporation of non-Russian lands into the empire.

The boundaries of the west Caucasus did not need to be drawn so neatly, although only because the mountaineer population was so tragically decimated. Sukhumi otdel, eventually Sukhumi okrug (1883), became part of Kutaisi province, and the former Adygei lands of the north Black Sea shore were part of Chernomorsk okrug. Because of the absence of the mountaineers, the primary issues of administration in the west Caucasus were related to the difficulties of settlement and to the many conflicts between the immigrant groups mentioned above. Thus Dondukov-Korsakov's commission recommended attaching the northern portion of Chernomorsk okrug to Kuban oblast, and its southern portion to Sukhumi okrug of Kutaisi province (they were geographically divided by the Caucasus mountain range), because from the point of view of the regime, these regions presented similar administrative challenges.[197] In this case, geography prevailed, and Chernomorsk okrug was left intact and made a province. By the early twentieth century the population of Chernomorsk province included 85,968 Russians, 12,334 Greeks, 11,236 Armenians, and numerous other immigrant nationalities, but only 2,390 "Cherkes."[198] The mountaineers of the west Caucasus were gone.

Russia's preoccupation with national and cultural identity (*narodnost'*), originality, and the cultivation of indigenous tradition was extended by borderland communities to non-Russian regions such as the Caucasus. These interests were evident in the work of the local branch of the Geographic Society and other smaller scholarly societies in Tbilisi, which played a key role in prompting new questions about the purpose of expansion and the nature of imperial identity. "Originality" on the frontier, in the imperial conception, meant a vision of historically authentic and indigenous culture untouched by Islam. Georgian thinkers contributed to this debate by developing similar Romantic notions about historic Georgian identity and by depicting Islam as an impediment and threat to the flowering of the Georgian nation. They were especially alarmed by Islamic incursions into frontier regions that, in their view, had been inhabited by "Georgians" since antiquity.

The imperial perception of Islam as an ethno-historical dilemma stimulated the emergence of ethnography, which in turn contributed to an alternative vision of the Russian Empire. The new vision contrasted sharply with the historic traditions of Russian militarism and exile that had accompanied the expansion of the Russian state into the southern borderlands. Romantic literature and travel writing, while frequently criticized by ethnographers and other scholars for its failure to conform to the dictates of what they understood as "science," in fact served as an important source of inspiration for their work. Ethnographic description conformed more closely to the needs of the empire, as newly understood by ethnographers. While ethnographers offered a new means of conceptualizing cultural difference, they did not challenge its contemporary hierarchies. Their work, for example, was far from the radical perspectivism of twentieth-century modernism or the cultural relativism of much of contemporary anthropology. By the standards of our day, their ideas were chauvinistic and Russocentric. Mountain languages were to be transcribed and young mountaineers were to be educated in order for mountaineers to gain exposure to the cultural world of Russia and Europe. Uslar insisted on the use of Cyrillic rather than Georgian for the transcription of mountaineer languages, since the purpose of mountaineer literacy was, in his view, to facilitate their access to the literature of Russia.

In spite of their frequently profound criticism of the history of conquest, ethnographers still accorded to Russian culture and even to the Russian state a prominent educative and tutelary position.[199] In their vision of empire, Russia still remained a "great people," as Dostoevsky's Shatov put it, the benevolent caretaker of a diverse empire.[200] At the same time, however, the ethnographers' interests and assumptions about identity looked toward the twentieth century and illustrate the contradictions and tensions of Russian imperial society, simultaneously autocratic and reformist, in the last half of the nineteenth century. These interests and assumptions also illustrate the contradictions associated with the rethinking of the empire on its southern frontier. While the proliferation of "peoples" was still quite compatible with empire – indeed, the process of cultural discovery was fostered by the imperial experience – this compatibility could not be taken for granted in a nationalistic age when an ethnically defined "people" was understood as the foundation for political sovereignty. The incorporation of the frontier left the new empire with numerous "peoples" who might someday ask to be "nations."

5 Customary Law: Noble Peoples, Savage Mountaineers

> Why [did Kazbich kill Bela], what do you think? These
> Circassians have got thieving in their blood. They'll steal
> anything, given the chance. Even things they don't want – they'll
> take them just the same. They just can't help it. And besides he'd
> long had a fancy for her.
>
> Lermontov's Maksim Maksimych in *A Hero of Our Time*[1]

Historians of colonialism have convincingly added customary law to
the growing list of the many "invented traditions" of the modern age.[2]
Colonial administrators attempted to create a recognizable order in the
colonies, and in the process they transformed, as Kristin Mann and
Richard Roberts write, "fluid cultural and legal ideas and relationships
into reproducible rules."[3] From Africa to Southeast Asia, colonial administrators were interested in law for several related reasons: the administration of justice was a means of colonial control, law sometimes
served to introduce the new moral order of Foucault's "disciplined"
West, such order in turn promoted economic productivity, and the arrival of the rule of law served as evidence of Europe's civilizing and
beneficial work in the colonies.[4] The elaboration and consolidation of
tribal identities was one of the more significant results of this colonial
interest in the traditions of customary law.[5]

Russia's empire shared several important similarities with the general Western colonial experience. Like the French in Algeria, the
Russians fought a long war against insurgents based in the mountains,
and hence colonial control remained paramount in the minds of wary
officials in regions only recently "pacified," as the conquest was called
by officials of both victorious powers. Like many European colonial officials, Russian administrators were also notably proud of their introduction of new concepts of law in the borderlands. Alexander I
declared to the Georgians in 1801 that their annexation by the Russian
Empire was motivated, not by "greed" or for "the expansion of boundaries," but in order to "give everyone the protection of law" (*dat'*

kazhdomu zashchitu zakona).[6] This was long before the advent of the Great Reforms brought new attention to matters of legality and government among educated society and regime officials. Only the Russians, emphasized A. Lilov, a Tbilisi gymnasium director, ethnographer, and student of mountaineer customary law in the late nineteenth century, were set upon establishing the conditions for "peaceful, civil [*grazhdanskoi*] life" in the region, in contrast to the many imperial powers of the past. "That which the Greeks and Romans never did," he wrote, "has been left to the Russians to accomplish."[7]

On the other hand, regime officials in the Caucasus and other Russian frontier regions throughout the nineteenth century were far less absorbed with matters of the economy and the promotion of trade and industrial production than the Western colonial powers. Also in contrast to the Western experience, Russia's rapid expansion in the eastern and southern borderlands very quickly created a contiguous colonial empire and hence a multi-ethnic state.[8] The colonized peoples lived not in "colonies," as in the rest of the non-Western world, but in peculiarly Russian "borderlands." Russia itself had historically expanded in a similar fashion. As they considered matters of legality and customary law in the North Caucasus, Russian colonial officials were again sensitive to questions of ethnicity and its historical evolution, or more precisely the question of narodnost' and the relationship of the Russian Empire to its historical evolution. The ideas of Russian officials and members of educated society about customary law were again an outgrowth of uniquely Russian concerns with custom and tradition. From our perspective, customary law can best be viewed for the insight it allows into imperial identity and ideology.

LAW IN RUSSIA AND THE BORDERLANDS

By the time Russian officials began seriously to contemplate the administration of justice in the North Caucasus in the mid-nineteenth century, several different traditions of thinking about law vied for their attention. The first corresponded to the growth in power of the state itself. Legal codification in Russia, as in Europe, was first initiated directly by the rulers of the old-regime state. Law was understood by Russia's rulers as a means to increase the effectiveness of their rule. Peter the Great attempted to introduce the study of jurisprudence to military cadets, and Catherine eventually made law part of the curriculum at Moscow University.[9] The collection of laws initiated in the eighteenth century accelerated in the early nineteenth century, when Mikhail Speransky led the work that resulted in the publication in 1830 of the forty-volume *Polnoe sobranie zakonov Rossiskoi Imperii*. Work on the second edition was begun soon after, and the last volume of the third edition was issued in 1916, just a year before the collapse of the old regime.[10] Law and its history, Russian officials believed, not only increased the effectiveness of administration but also illuminated and glorified the history of the development of the state. Russia's administrators feared the implications of the French Revolution and understood legal codification as a means to strengthen the autocracy. Codification served the "needs of the state," as Nicholas I's 1833 manifesto declared – "justice and orderly rule."[11] As in other old-regime states, inequality was legally sanctioned by the judicial system. Different courts existed for each of the different estates.[12]

A challenge to this Russian version of the "well-ordered police state" was the *rechtsstaat*, or a state governed by the rule of law. Russian officials in the early and middle nineteenth century sought new methods to improve the administration of the empire, and in the process they contested the historical traditions of the police state.[13] Officials in the Ministry of Justice in particular, as Richard Wortman has shown, developed a "legal consciousness" that informed the implementation of the judicial reforms during the Great Reform period.[14] The concern of officials and members of educated society with the question of *zakonnost'* (legality) suggested a limitation upon the unlimited authority of the monarch.[15]

This latter tradition was complicated by the fact that the conceptions of the European-educated bureaucracy did not necessarily correspond to the judicial practices or conceptions of the Russian people. Students of the Russian peasantry were well aware that peasant judicial norms differed from the ideas and expectations of regime officials and legal specialists.[16] Throughout the nineteenth century, peasants often ignored the reformed township (*volost'*) courts and continued to resolve their disputes according to customary law, or the practices of *samosud* (self-adjudication).[17] For some Russians such practices were a source of curiosity and fascination and a matter of national identity, in the tradition of the fascination with the legends, songs, and folk tales of the unique Russian "people" that Hans Rogger dates from the later eighteenth century.[18] For Slavophiles like Khomiakov, customary law practices were another crucial reservoir of "originality," an expression of Russia's native soil far preferable to the rational abstractions and legal formulas that he associated with the Roman heritage. In contrast to the artificial character of law, wrote Khomiakov, custom "reflects within itself the most fundamental unity of society ... The deeper the sphere of custom, the stronger and healthier the society, and the more original and richer will be the development of law."[19]

Khomiakov hoped to see Russia draw from its own native soil, and by the mid nineteenth century he had access to a rapidly developing Russian ethnography that offered numerous catalogues of the customary legal practices of the Russian peasantry. The Imperial Russian Geographic Society, for example, initiated an ambitious project for the study of the judicial conceptions of the Russian peasantry in the eighteen different provinces of the empire. P.S. Efimenko completed one such study in 1869 in Arkhangel'sk. He prepared a "program" for the study of customary law, covering issues related to marriage, family relations, the authority of the father, and conceptions of crime, which he hoped to see employed by scholars throughout the empire.[20] The question of Russian identity was first among his interests. Were Russian peasant cultural practices part of a "general Russian" tradition, adopted from somewhere else (*chudskii*), or local to Arkhangel'sk?[21]

The ideas and administrative experimentation of the Great Reform period were easily compatible with the military expansion of the empire into the southern and eastern borderlands. While borderland officials and colonial communities were increasingly reluctant to justify their colonial rule according to the statist tradition of Russian imperial law, everyone could agree that notions of legality were to be found in the West rather than the East. The reformed Russian state might serve as the harbinger of zakonnost' to lands with long histories of *proizvol*, or "arbitrariness." The experience of the long Caucasus War, however, had taught military officials several important lessons. Earlier efforts to administer mountaineer regions according to Russian laws, such as in Dagestan in 1843, only intensified mountaineer opposition to the Russian presence.[22] Officials began experimenting with the use of customary law courts in Kabarda in 1822, in Ossetia in 1847, and in parts of Chechnia in 1852.[23] As the war against the mountaineers of the North Caucasus wound down in the early 1860s, some administrators hoped to introduce Russian courts in the region, but they were warned by officials such as General Boguslavskii in 1866 that such a measure would be "inconvenient and even dangerous."[24] The military committee formed to address administrative issues in what were now Terek and Kuban oblasts affirmed that purely Russian forms of administration would provoke "at first discontent and then straightforward rebellion."[25] The "mountaineer courts," announced by Viceroy Grand Duke Mikhail in 1869, were regulated by "temporary rules" to be used "until the total introduction of the judicial decree of 20 November 1864" was possible.[26] The North Caucasus was thus similar in this respect to other parts of the empire, such as Siberia and the Kazakh steppe, where the regime decreed, with some exceptions, that judicial conflicts could be resolved according to local traditions of customary law.[27]

Such tolerance was not simply born of fear or administrative realism, but was an important component of the set of concerns that shaped the making of the empire on the frontier. Judicial practices of the empire varied from region to region, officials of the regime conceded, but they did not understand this as a permanent situation. Different peoples possessed different levels of judicial consciousness. Less-developed peoples, Russian officials concluded, might progress in time and make the general application of the rule of law feasible for the entire empire. Governor-General A.M. Dondukov-Korsakov, the grand duke's successor, reminded officials in Tbilisi and St Petersburg that mountaineer societies were still "similar in social organization to the barbaric peoples of Europe at the beginning of the Middle Ages."[28] Russian practices and forms of rule, he emphasized for the benefit of officials who thought otherwise, were frequently inappropriate for borderland peoples such as the mountaineers or the Kyrgyz (Kazakh) of the Small and Middle Hordes. The language, the traditions, the nature of the charge, and the fact that the mountaineer "does not know or understand" the attorney of the crown left mountaineers, Dondukov-Korsakov argued, suspicious and uncomfortable in Russian courts. Bureaucratic uniformity, from St Petersburg to the isolated valleys of mountainous Dagestan, would in any case only be "illusory," he continued. "The mentality of a people [sklad narodnago kharaktera] cannot be changed simply through circulars, commands, or laws."[29]

Problematic "mentalities" could be changed, however, and the courts were understood by Russians as a means toward the achievement of such a goal. Ethnographers, of course, were self-proclaimed experts on the "character" of a people (what they termed narodnyi kharakter), and the regime frequently promoted their work in the Caucasus and throughout the empire, as we discussed in the last chapter. Dondukov-Korsakov turned to historical ethnography in his defence of administrative innovation in the North Caucasus before his many critics in the ministries of St Petersburg. Ethnographic study, he suggested, revealed the continuing presence of ancient tribal forms of administration and allegiance among the mountaineers. Each tribe in Dagestani villages, he explained, sent two or three representatives to a village meeting (the dzhamaat), which issued decisions called maslagat. The villages elected elders, who were helped by other respected figures. Justice, Dondukov-Korsakov emphasized to the minister of the interior, was adjucated according to customary law. Murder was increasingly resolved by the *diiat*, or a payment that purchased forgiveness from a victim who possessed the right of vengeance (*krovomshchenie*), a fine, or other methods. The remarkable aspect of Dondukov-Korsakov's presentation, a set of ideas also evident in numerous ethnographic discussions, was his respect for the traditions of mountaineer customary law. While the political purpose of his support for customary legal practices was clearly "to paralyze the influence of the main enemy of Russian power – Muslim law [the shari'a] and its representatives," as he put it, his position included a fair amount of respect for the manner in which conflict was resolved in mountaineer society. Customary law worked, and in most cases both parties abided by its terms. "[S]uch was the internal structure of the order of mountaineer society," Dondukov-Korsakov explained. "It has developed over centuries and has been preserved through the severe measures adopted by Shamil and his predecessors."[30] The governor-general's argument was a summary of ideas developed by ethnographers, whose work in turn was directly commissioned by the state.[31] High officials of the imperial state were not immune to questions of tradition, cultural authenticity, and native soil.

As in matters of faith, imperial service, and narodnost', the Georgian example again contributed to the climate and tenor of imperial culture and empire-building in the region. Georgia's Romantic exploration of its own traditions produced positive portrayals of peasant customary law practices, including those of the "mountain Georgians" such as the Tushin and Khevsur. "[O]ne of the more original customs" among the Khevsur, explained D. Pazliashvili in *Tsnomis Purtseli*, was their manner of resolving judicial disputes between families.[32] To illustrate this, he told an extended story of an unintended murder in a Khevsur village as a result of incorrect medical advice. The guilty individual and his family, however, were compelled yearly to sacrifice an animal in honour of the deceased and were prevented from receiving traditional forms of village communal labour help at key moments in the agricultural season. After a period of time the offended family declared that the penance had been properly performed, and the village council oversaw the matter and declared the case resolved. Pazliashvili portrayed customary law (*adati* in Georgian) as effective and an outgrowth of centuries of historic Georgian development.[33]

In the North Caucasus a notion of "custom" was at the centre of this colonial and administrative project on customary law. Like the reformed courts of rural Russia, the mountain courts were to be "based upon local customs [*obychai*]," as a judicial statute declared.[34]

Imperial educated society envisioned the courts as a site where mountaineer conflicts, complex and often incomprehensible to regime officials, might be resolved in the traditional terms of historic custom. They were for mountaineers only. Conflicts that included Russians or other nationalities, or those that included an accusation against a mountaineer from any "person not of native origin," or even conflicts that required the presence of a non-mountaineer as a witness, were sent on to district or oblast Russian courts.[35] Murder was also handled in the higher courts, as well as armed robbery for a significant sum of money and, of course, actions that officials took as a direct challenge to their authority.[36] Questions that the Russians identified as belonging to the realm of "custom," however, were to be resolved by mountaineers themselves. The *sud'i* (deputies) and *qadi* (Muslim judges) who sat on the courts were indirectly elected by the local populace, in that each tribe was allowed to choose two candidates to attend a conference to choose the deputies and judges for the district court. The process was carefully controlled by imperial officials, however, as the final list of choices was reviewed by the district commander or the Cossack section (*otdel*) *ataman* and then sent to the oblast commander, who possessed the final privilege of appointment. Any figure found inappropriate by the Russians could be arbitrarily removed from the list.[37] Muslim law was relegated to family matters of marriage and inheritance, for which the qadis were consulted.[38] As in other parts of the colonized world, customary law was codified by the regime in order to compel the mountaineers to follow their own "custom." "Custom became a resource of the instruments of government, rather than a resource of the people," writes Martin Chanock of central Africa.[39] Each case was recorded in a casebook (*nastol'nyi zhurnal*), as a written precedent that might in subsequent cases serve as a guide.[40]

These guides then sometimes took precedence over the wishes of villagers themselves, presumably the real makers of "custom." Elders, mullas, and other "respected figures" from a village in Kazikumukhsk district in Dagestan, for example, saw their ideas about transforming the resolution of horse thievery and other issues rejected by the military governor of Dagestan in 1907. The villagers apparently viewed adat as a flexible and fluid means of resolving conflict and village disputes. The military governor, however, was beholden to officials in Tbilisi, who were reluctant to change previously codified adat compilations or encourage too much administrative and legal variation in the already complex region.[41]

The regime was thus the protector of mountain customary law, which put it in the odd and ironic position of promoting the process of Romantic self-discovery by which people learn they are "peoples" (*narody*). Russian ideas about customary law were part of a widely held ethnographic vision about mountaineer identity and the significance of imperial rule. As in Russia, where customary law was portrayed as an attribute of a unique folk culture passed on through the generations, Russian ethnographers and other students of mountaineer customary law believed that they offered insight into the history of the mountaineer narody. That history was not, of course, one of written laws but a history of customs. Customary law, wrote Lilov in 1892, "in the eyes of the mountaineer has the sacred significance of a law."[42] Codifying customs, rather than collecting laws, was a means of writing the history of a people. As mountaineer customary law endured through the centuries, Russian ethnographers and administrators believed, so did mountaineer folk identities. The assumptions and interests of Russian educated society in the importance of peasant custom and its relationship to national identity was extended by ethnographers and regime officials to the borderlands.

"Peoples," according to this common view, had rulers, centralized adminstrations, and courts. Russians claimed, most forcefully when they had the aid of educated mountaineers, that the mountaineers possessed such a history. Shora Nogmov's *Istoriia Adygeiskago naroda* (The history of the Adygei people) of 1847 emphasized the court system and unified administration of the late-sixteenth-century ruler Prince Berslan Dzhankutov.[43] For N.F. Grabovskii, a Russian ethnographer of the late nineteenth century, such evidence was proof that contemporary Kabards ("eastern" Adygei) possessed the necessary historical prerequisites that made possible "the existence of a nation [*natsiia*]."[44] This was a problematical line of reasoning in a multi-ethnic empire, and Grabovskii must have been aware that in Europe the question of legal codification was closely related to the unification of the modern nation-state. Germany's National Liberals, for example, did not want to see the different states of the North German Confederation produce distinct legal codes, but advocated a single and unified German law code, which was to correspond to a united Germany.[45] But Kabard was a long way from Frankfurt, and Russians such as Grabovskii could justify their colonial rule if it served to encourage the mountaineers in the proper direction. Grabovskii was also uncommon in his use of this term – most Russians spoke of peoples (*narody*) rather than nations – and his historical memory was remarkably selective. Kabards, in his view, shared in the historical potential enabled by Berslan Dzhankutov, while the Adygei proper of the Black Sea coastal region, as he was surely aware, had been destroyed by the Russian army and exiled en masse to Ottoman Turkey in 1861–64.

For Grabovskii, the great impediment to the proper historical development of the mountaineers was not Russia's long colonial war, however, but Islam. Muslim traditions adopted by certain mountaineer princes, who, in the Russian view, were traitors to the genuine folk traditions of the mountaineers, introduced Muslim law and left judicial matters in the hands of the mulla.[46] Lilov also emphasized the cultural authenticity of the adat and its eleven-century history in the region, in contrast to the more recent intrusion of Islam and what he portrayed as Shamil's despotic efforts to replace the adat with the shari'a.[47] The region's genuine past, and hence proper future, was one free of the influence of Islam. This was another variant of the French "Kabyle myth" about the Berbers of the Maghrib. The ideas of administrators and imperial educated society about Islam, Orthodoxy, and customary law were shaped by a similar set of assumptions about history and cultural authenticity. European colonialism presumably meant the preservation or sometimes resurrection of tradition itself. French administrators hoped to revive and preserve a supposedly untainted Berber past, and they devoted significant efforts toward the codification of Berber customary law.[48]

Islamic judicial traditions challenged even the sporadic innovations of the regime that dated from the eighteenth century. In 1793 General Gudovich had established a "tribal court" for Kabard princes, subordinate to a court founded in Mozdok that functioned with the presence of Russian overseers.[49] In 1822 General Ermolov attempted to revive this institution. One of the statutes for his court proclaimed that all matters "shall be resolved according to ancient customs and rites," except in cases where they conflicted with Russian rule. The courts disappointed both Russians and Kabards, however. Ermolov complained that Kabards ignored the courts and instead resolved matters "in the homes of the clergy," and several Kabard princes informed the administration that the destructive raids so feared by the Russians in fact were provoked by the presence of the Russian courts.[50]

The primary contrast remained that between Islam and what the Russians called "custom." The latter began to emerge as a more important indicator of identity than "faith" in ethnographic texts in the eighteenth century.[51] "Custom" in the Russian view was pure, historically authentic, and pre-existant to the arrival of Islam in the North Caucasus, which, as the Russians emphasized, was brought by emissaries who were not native to the region. The adat belonged to the realm of "custom," and when properly chronicled (because peoples possessed histories of law), it would serve as evidence that mountaineers themselves belonged to "peoples." And "peoples," in the

Russian view, possessed unlimited potential for further development and growth, at least if they had the benefit of imperial rule. The codification of mountaineer customary law, Russians believed, illustrated this benevolence. It also allowed the regime to regulate and limit the perpetuation of the blood feud (*krovomshchenie*). One murder suspect was enough, unless "the victim received several wounds; then two [people could be accused], but not more."[52] The regime feared the initiation of several different and potentially interminable blood feuds.

Apparently not all customs were historically progressive and worthy of preservation. And clearly the blood feud, the "beginning and end of banditry," as General Mikheev of Terek oblast warned in the early twentieth century, was deeply woven into the very fabric of mountaineer society and remained impervious to the decree of 1859 by Viceroy Bariatinskii that declared it illegal.[53] Officials were well aware that the traditions of the blood feud carried on through the generations and usually predated Russian rule. The district court that investigated the murder of Ramazan Kirkhliar by Magomed-Ragim Gasan, for example, discovered that fifteen years previous to the 1868 event, when the Kiurin area (the Dargin area of Dagestan) was ruled by local khans, Ramazan and his brother had assaulted the brother of Magomed-Ragim in retaliation for what they supposed was an affair with the wife of Ramazan's brother.[54] The traditions of the blood feud represented a virtual shadow government, dispensing justice and resolving disputes according to terms and traditions mysterious to regime officials. Frequently the very relatives of the murder victim hid the circumstances of the case from the authorities because they expected and wanted to be recompensed according to the terms of the blood feud.[55] Was this not "custom" itself, the very basis of customary law?

There was an alternative view. "Within the character of the mountaineer and the conditions of his existence," wrote Lilov, "there are characteristics that sooner or later will lead, if not to the collapse of his society, at least to the weakening of its bonds."[56] The "character" of a people was more promising than the "character" of the individual mountaineer. "Peoples" remained pure; they were inhibited only by the character defects of the individual mountaineer. "These Circassians have got thieving in their blood," pronounced Lermontov's Maksim Maksimych of Bela.[57] Sometimes responsibility lay with their "military spirit" and "unrestrained passion," as E.P. Kovalevskii suggested, or their "inclination toward arguments, bravery, and shortness of temper," in the words of K. Borisevich.[58] In the Russian view, these character defects were magnified and encouraged by the unfortunate recent history of the North Caucasus, which included the intrusion of Islam, the absence of literacy, and a failure among mountaineers to respect the traditions of their own culture.

MOUNTAINEER CRIMINALITY

In describing these character defects of the individual mountaineer, the chief of which might be summed up as a general absence of restraint, Russian administrators and ethnographers developed a composite picture of mountaineer criminality. Russian interest in the question of mountaineer "savagery" (*dikost'*) was hardly new. As a sign of exoticism, it was a staple of Romantic literature. The Caucasus War also provided plenty of material for Russian newspapers and popular pamphlets, which featured detail on characters such as the naib Adalo, supposedly accustomed to killing defenceless women and children in his raids of Georgian villages, parading around villages with heads on stakes, cutting bodies in half, and so on.[59] *Prisoners of Shamil*, the widely read story by M. Verderevskii, discussed in the following chapter, featured the intrusion of such savagery into the domestic setting of the genteel Chavchavadze estate.[60]

Crimes in the North Caucasus were not a product of the Orientalist imagination. District reports from the region suggest that local officials spent the bulk of their time pursuing perpetrators of "robbery" and "banditry."[61] The isolated criminal event, however, was rendered by ethnographers, statisticians, and various regional scholar-officials into a story about mountain culture and the problems it posed for the administration of the empire. The Caucasus Mountain Administration played a key role in this transformation, in particular with its journal *Sbornik Svedenii o Kavkazskikh Gortsakh* (Collection of information about the Caucasus mountaineers), edited by the ethnographer and statistician Nikolai I. Voronov. This journal frequently published collections of vignettes on mountaineer crimes, under the heading of "mountaineer criminal statistics." These were short stories rather than statistical compilations in the modern sense and were published without editorial comment, as if to suggest that the moral of the story was self-evident – obvious to the educated reader. The archival remains of the Mountain Administration reveal that the journal published the court reports almost verbatim.[62] Officials wanted the proceedings to be known beyond the confines of the court, because they apparently believed that the judicial encounter revealed truths about mountain culture that justified imperial rule. The stories portrayed the mountaineers as excessively proud, quick to violence, and extremely jealous and overprotective in matters of family and sexuality. The quantity of literature inspired by the question of mountaineer criminality also suggests that colonial officials viewed law, to borrow from Antonio Gramsci, as a productive form of power, as an instrument useful to the state in its "educative" function of cultural transformation.[63]

The self-destructive cycle of violence that accompanied the blood feud was the chief expression of this lack of personal restraint that characterized the mountaineers. Adil-Girei, of the village of Kazanishchi in Temir-Khan-Shura okrug, shot and killed Abakar Bamat, who four years earlier had killed Almakhsuta Makhmud, the brother of Adil-Girei. He then approached the authorities with an explanation for his action, noting that "he had run into Abakar, one of his blood enemies," and killed him, as "according to tradition, he had the right to do this in vengeance for the blood of his brother."[64] Also in the village of Kazanishchi, Shuaib Khasai mistook a passerby on the street for a "blood enemy" and killed him because he failed to pay him proper respect according to the traditions of customary law. Before the administration of North Dagestan, Shuaib explained his "terrible mistake"; his intention to murder an "enemy," however, needed no explanation or apology.[65]

Clearly, these interpretations were examples of the vastly different ideas held by mountaineers about the proper means of resolving conflict – a different "custom."[66] Shuaib did not realize that his explanation was in fact what the Russians took to be a confession to a crime. But for imperial administrators and ethnographers the blood feud was a deviation from historic custom rather than custom itself. The diiat (a payment to the family of a murder victim by the guilty party), for example, was a customary law tradition that resolved a murder case. Escalating violence and the perpetuation of a blood feud, such as when Kuli Molla-oglu refused to recognize the diiat and murdered the son of the man who fifteen years earlier had killed his own father, resulted when mountaineers failed to recognize their own traditions.[67] What were officials and scholars to make of a people that did not know its own customs? Mired in an impoverished intellectual tradition that left them unable to comprehend the individual "criminal will" or to distinguish "between private and public interests," the benighted mountaineers savagely pursued the "eye for an eye, tooth for a tooth" mentality of the Muslim.[68] "Pride and touchiness," concluded Grabovskii, coupled with a lack of respect for human life fostered by centuries of conflict, "have given rise to their inclination to arguments and fights, which originate from mere trifles and insignificant reasons but which always conclude with a resort to the use of arms."[69]

Court proceedings illustrated numerous other examples of the daily life of the unrestrained mountaineer. The tradition among young men, for example, of gathering at the hut of newlyweds to listen in on their activities frequently ended in violence, as when Kalau Daurov fired his pistol through the wall of his dwelling to disperse the assembled group, injuring Taga Biataev in the leg.[70] Sometimes the problem at hand appeared to be a simple and immature lack of control. Abdukham Gichakaev, for example, while dancing at the wedding of a close friend, in celebration intended to fire his pistol in the air but instead wounded two girls.[71] Escalating violence was a more serious problem. In November 1868 in the Ingush village of Ekazhev the minor theft of grain resulted in seven wounded from dagger assaults; in Gaustkhi, another Ingush village, a battle over grazing lands prompted Esa Arzhivarov to stab to death Mustobi Kuzhgov, whose brother, Sustobi Kuzhgov, then shot the uncle of Arzhivarov. In despair his sister then plunged a dagger into her own stomach. Another woman present at this scene, the report informs us, removed the knife but seriously cut her hand in the process.[72] The presentation of these bloody events in succession is almost comic, but in the nineteenth century they must have confirmed for Russian readers their assumptions about the unrestrained savagery of the mountaineer. The results of these conflicts, of course, were extremely serious. A dispute between two families over grain in Tulizm, Kazi-Kumukh okrug (Dagestan), led to a stone-throwing fight that left nine wounded, including a young pregnant woman, Zaza Gasan, injured in the stomach and back. She died twenty-two days later.[73]

The absence of restraint and self-control that Russians associated with mountaineer culture apparently made North Caucasus peoples more susceptible to dramatic suicide. Suicide in response to unrequited love was only one of the better known varieties.[74] Alai Akhmed-oglu, of the village of Urari in Dargin okrug (Dagestan), wanted to marry his fiancée but was opposed in the match by his strong-willed mother, who repeatedly reminded her son of her opposition. Alai Akhmed resolved the issue by proclaiming to his mother, "If you will not leave me in peace, then I'll do it myself," and he shot himself in front of her.[75] The mountaineer home was presented as the site of irrationality. In October of 1869 a father and son argued in Kulidzh, Kaitak-Tabasaran okrug (Dagestan). The father refused the boy's request for forgiveness and forbade him from entering the family home. The young Murtuzali killed himself at the doorstep, and in despair his father stabbed himself to death.[76] The drunken Rabadan-Popala-Magomed-oglu, of Khodzhal-Makhi in Dargin okrug, repeatedly warned by his fellow villagers of the dangers of excessive drinking, finally declared, "If my stomach cannot make it without vodka, then I will have to punish him," and he too stabbed himself to death.[77] Magomed

Omar of Kaitak-Tabasaran okrug shot himself "after his mother scolded him for laziness."[78] Sixteen-year-old Gurdzhinat Omar-kizy of Dargin hanged herself after her older sister slapped her for failing to respond to her command to prepare dinner.[79]

Zaza Gasan died with child, pelted by stones and bricks around her mid-section. Women were frequently the victims of crimes or stood in one way or another at the centre of mountaineer conflicts. Gender and sexuality as problematic aspects of mountaineer culture were thus central to the way in which Russians justified their colonial rule in the Caucasus. On 19 October 1868, in the village of Gogaz in Dagestan, Selim Dervish stabbed Aga-Sultan Agaz to death after she refused his request that they elope together from the village. Selim explained his case to the Russian authorities: he had been having a relationship with Aga-Sultan Agaz, he said, and had given her 100 rubles and other presents in expectation that she would break with her husband, Ibragim. Upon meeting him, however, Aga-Sultan Agaz rejected Selim, "saying that many times she had deceived fools such as he." He stabbed her and fled, fearful of the wrath of her family. Selim Dervish expected to be exonerated by the court. In fact a different story surfaced, one that illustrated the powerlessness of women such as Aga-Sultan Agaz. She had been raped by Selim a year earlier and then divorced by her husband, Ibragim, because everyone in the village was aware of the event. Selim offered marriage, but Aga-Sultan and the family refused his proposal, and Selim killed her.[80]

The cycle of violence portrayed by the Russians as endemic to the mountaineer character often originated around women's sexuality. Gitino Magoma, of Gintlia in Gunib okrug (Dagestan), with the help of two relatives, murdered the man who had impregnated his daughter. Gitino-Gadzhi, the suspect youth, believed that he had done proper penance according to the traditions of customary law in this region. He had removed himself from the village, paid a sum to the family, and planned to marry Gitino Magoma's daughter. Her father, however, thought otherwise.[81] When Aktemir Choriev, of the Ingush village of Srednyi Achaluk, was rejected in his marriage proposal to Asharpi, the daughter of Beisultan Baichiev, he and several of his friends followed her late at night, attacked her, and dragged her to the dwelling of one of his relatives. Asharpi's family responded by surrounding the hut. In the pitched family battle eleven people were wounded.[82] Patima Iusup was murdered by her husband for using foul language and refusing to answer his queries about her recent whereabouts.[83] A twenty-two-year-old male in Dagestan responded to evidence produced by his close friend concerning his wife (she had supposedly received a mirror and some candy from her alleged lover) by stabbing her with his kinzhal fifteen times. Eight of the wounds were to the head.[84] In similar circumstances, Akhmed-khan Shikhali killed his wife, Kistaman Safi-kum, with a kinzhal.[85] Geidar Bek Gasan, of Kaitago-Tabasaranskii district (Dagestan), murdered his sister for marrying against the wishes of the men of the family.[86] Unfortunately, these gruesome stories could be endlessly compiled. In most cases, women suffered the most.

Both Russians and Georgians were quick to portray these events as a product of Muslim and mountain savagery, and they conceived of imperial expansion as a source of stability and support to domesticity and the family. Georgia's new nativists recognized the centrality of women to the making of a progressive and enlightened future, but only because they were "personally responsible for children and family."[87] Muslim families, however, faced significant impediments to progress, in the common imperial conception. Travellers, ethnographers, and administrators throughout the nineteenth century frequently noted the abuse endured by Muslim women, the "genuine slave[s]" and "working cattle" of the Muslim family, as several Russian commentators put it.[88] In "criminal statistics" documents women were all too often the primary victims of mountaineer cultural practices and traditions. The compilers of these reports implicated the mountaineer extended family in this repression of women, making it clear that women faced the prospect of kidnapping and rape if they declined a marriage proposal. In one case, relatives themselves participated in such a rape because they supported the family mariage alliance.[89] Women were not entirely helpless, however. Parida, from the village of Bakhlukh in Avar okrug, where she was raped by three men, managed to kill each of them with a dagger, one at a time, as she stalked them through the woods. Apparently in her defence, the published recounting of the event recorded her pain as a result of the rape, noting her "terrible dreams" and poor appetite during the month following the event.[90] Parida challenged her male persecutors, and in veiled terms, imperial educated society applauded her efforts.

Officials were doing the same thing in the courts. In numerous cases the regime was in effect prosecuting the male perpetrators and exonerating the women, even against the wishes of families and even entire villages. Rape victim Leila Magomed-Gusein saw her persecutor sent into administrative exile in spite of written support for the rapist from his influential family as well as from 160 people from the village of Maza in Samursk district (Dagestan).[91] The intervention of the higher-level oblast court in the workings of the district courts was often in response to these miscarriages of justice at the local level.

Officials had to intervene to ensure the prosecution of men guilty of these horrific crimes related to gender and sexuality.[92]

There were limits to this colonial support for the downtrodden, of course. Rape was a standard issue for students of customary law, but compilers of mountaineer traditions usually stipulated that female victims of rape needed to have their screams heard in order to lodge a complaint.[93] And further, "Women who are well known for their debauched behaviour are not allowed to charge someone with rape."[94] Not surprisingly, rape generally went unreported. Rape victim Patimat' Suleiman testified before the Kazi-Kumukh district court that she was reluctant to yell or scream because "if she had done this, then Gusein Ramazan would have run away but returned later to persecute her again, having threatened to kill both her and her husband if she told him."[95]

Patimat' only related the rape in court because she was expecting exoneration for what she claimed was sole responsibility for the murder of Gusein. Officials aware of the traditions of the blood feud, however, felt that they were on the scent of a more complex murder, in spite of the fact that alleged witnesses were reluctant to get involved in a matter they understood to be between two families. Where was the blood on Patimat's dress? Was she strong enough to deliver the six kinzhal wounds to Gusein's chest? The court explained to Patimat' that her status as a victim of abduction and rape did not give her the right to murder the criminal, and it convicted her, along with two male family members, of the crime.[96] For Patimat', historic "custom" justified retaliatory homicide; officials knew this and looked to unravel the circumstances of the event and the family conflict they knew it would provoke.

These many horrible events were not fictions of the colonial imagination. Educated officials administering the courts and following these events were understandably disturbed by problems and relationships they were at a loss to understand. The composite picture of mountaineer criminality that emerges from the work of the courts and a journal such as *Sbornik Svedenii o Kavkazskikh Gortsakh*, however, served to justify colonial rule and explain in a particular way the sources and causes of crime. Impulsive, quick to anger, self-destructive, excessively macho, and exhibiting a pronounced lack of personal self-control, mountaineers predictably appeared incapable of self-government. The family, the home, and women's sexuality often provided the background and setting for this drama of mountaineer criminality. Ethnographers and administrators, however, did not attribute these characteristics to the realm of "custom." The publication of "mountaineer criminal statistics" was not a contribution to the collection of mountaineer folklore but a compilation of criminal incidents that posed difficulties for the regime's administration of justice in the region. The gender question raised the problem of Islam as well, because imperial readers tended to associate such views and treatment of women not with indigenous and "natural" custom but with the heritage of Islam. True "custom" remained sacrosanct. Criminal events were frequent, but they could be explained by other factors, chief of which was the absence of Russia's imperial presence in the region in the past.

These assumptions continued to govern Russian thinking about mountaineer criminality until the end of the imperial era, with a minor but interesting exception. By the turn of the century, with Russian culture and rule no longer novel to the North Caucasus, it was increasingly difficult for Russians to portray Islam as the wrecker of culture and Russia, by contrast, as its preserver. Some Russians and non-Russians identified other processes and developments as sources of the decline and erosion of custom as well. General Mikheev of Terek oblast criticized new mountaineer habits such as smoking, drinking, and the wearing of new clothes and jewellery, and noted with chagrin that such practices were inspired by the exposure of the mountaineers to Russian culture.[97] The city, source of cultural decline and corruption, was intruding into the village, and the irony was obvious that Russian rule had served to facilitate this intrusion. Ethnographers and travellers such as A. Krasnov visited Svan villages and were disappointed to find store-bought rather than handmade clothes.[98] Ossetian contributors to Russian ethnographic publications such as Dzhantemir Shanaev suggested that Ossetian judicial traditions such as the historic sanctity of the oath (*ard*; in Russian, *prisiaga*) had actually declined with the onset of Russian rule. The continuing demise of tribal solidarity, Shanaev maintained in 1873, was eroding a historic tradition that resolved disputes as well as any European manner of administering justice.[99] The colonizing state that was preoccupied with the preservation of the past was of course simultaneously responsible for the diverse changes we generally call "modernization."

LEGAL RUSSIFICATION

More important to the fate of customary law in the North Caucasus was the statist tradition described earlier. Such views had not disappeared. In 1883 Ivan Tukheev, of the Ministry of State Domains, emphasized the tragedy of the many Russian losses in the course of the long Caucasus War and advocated the abolition of the special courts and the special form of military-native rule (*voenno-narodnoe upravlenie*) that had been established by Bariatinskii in the mountain regions. The North Caucasus must be "ruled like the entire general State Property of the Empire," Tukheev wrote.[100] By the turn of the century there was greater pressure from St Petersburg to abolish the special courts and make uniform the judicial practices of the empire. After the disturbances of 1905–07 such pressure came from the new viceroy himself, Count I.I. Vorontsov-Dashkov, who was sent to the Caucasus to apply political pressure on the many increasingly radical groups of the region. Vorontsov-Dashkov told the Ministry of Justice in 1907 that Russian courts could now be used in the North Caucasus to help the mountaineers work toward "the beginning of a general-Russian conception of law [*pravosoznaniia*]."[101] He continued to press the issue six years later, by then disappointed that little progress had been made.[102] It was possible, Vorontsov-Dashkov wrote to I.G. Shcheglovitov in 1913, for Russians and mountaineers to participate together in the "general legal culture" of the empire.[103]

Such was the goal of the commission chaired by N.M. Reinke of the Ministry of Justice in St Petersburg in 1912–14. Besides the Ministry of Justice, the ministries of War, Internal Affairs, and State Domains and the office of the viceroy in Tbilisi participated in the study he headed.[104] His commission criticized the functioning of the special mountain courts. Reinke claimed that the special courts were slow to act, possessed no authority among the population, usually sent the guilty away free, and functioned poorly because of a dearth of qualified deputies. All of this, he wrote, had created a situation of "legal anarchy."[105] In spite of his criticism of the courts, the commission was oddly, perhaps cynically, optimistic about the state of mountaineer judicial consciousness. Reinke asserted that years of exposure to Russian rule and culture had actually prepared the mountaineers for full participation in the legal culture of the empire.[106] The special concessions, he claimed, actually served to impede the further progress of the mountaineers, since they preserved archaic forms of culture associated with the mountaineer past.[107] "In a conflict between groups at two opposing moral and social levels, the higher world view cannot subordinate itself to the lower," Reinke maintained.[108] The end of Russian tolerance and administrative concession was in the interest of the mountaineers themselves.[109] Russian administrative practices were to faciliate the "uniting [*splocheniiu*] of this borderland with the centre of the state."[110] The ethnographic and geographic diversity of the region, presented in the introduction to his report, was offered, not in the spirit of respect for the cultural differences that complicated the administration of the region, but as an excuse for the inability of the state to establish adminstrative uniformity in legal affairs.

This push for bureaucratic uniformity and centralized rule on the part of officials in St Petersburg represented a return to the earlier and statist tradition of thought about the purpose of legal codification. In contrast to the Romantic tolerance and interest in the discovery of the unique cultural practices of a "people," the statist tradition was primarily concerned with the maintenance of order and the strengthening of the authority of the state itself. This process has perhaps been misnamed "Russification." It was not an effort to impose "Russian" traditions upon other parts of the empire (Russian peasants too had customary law courts) but an effort to extend the imperial legal norms of the European-educated bureaucracy to everyone. This tradition shared similarities with the French colonial notion of "assimilation" to the universal practices of the European Enlightenment. "A good law is good for all men," argued Condorcet, and hence Algerians and other North Africans were to be deprived of the right to practise their local and customary ways.[111] In the spirit of the Great Reforms, Vorontsov-Dashkov still referred to "legal consciousness" (*pravosoznaniia*), but he and other officials were no longer willing to wait out the discrepancies of comparative historical development. They considered the level of mountaineer autonomy over the judicial process to be too high. Vorontsov-Dashkov probably would have responded in a similar fashion to judicial questions among Russian peasants, but it would be senseless to speak of the "Russification" of Russian peasants. The relationship between educated society (*obshchestvo*) and people (*narod*) bore important similarities to the colonial encounter in the borderlands.

By the early twentieth century, Russian officials had lost patience with their continuing inability to monitor the administration of justice in the North Caucasus. Village elders frequently concealed their knowledge of local crimes from Russian officials;[112] mullas and qadi maintained the predominant influence over the workings of the courts and pointedly conducted affairs in Arabic, a language inaccessible to the majority of Russian officials;[113] and insufficient resources left many cases for the mountaineers to resolve themselves.[114] In response, the regime attempted to require each village to maintain within its village administration a clerk (*pisar'*) literate in Russian.[115] Colonial officials were hoping for direct communication with reasonably loyal mountaineer figures who possessed no ties to Muslim religious leaders. For this reason the regime took seriously its appointment of village elders. Frequently, however, the Russians were manipulated by such figures, while in other cases mountaineers trustworthy to the Russians turned out to be "the most mediocre natives" without influence and prestige in the village, as General Mikheev complained.[116] In times of rebellion, elders who cooperated too closely with the regime found themselves in great physical danger.[117]

The remarkable hostility expressed by many late-imperial officials toward the different judicial practices and traditions of the mountaineer perhaps exemplified their concern, even fear, that the centre might no longer hold. The "judicial norms" of Russia were the judicial norms of the empire, claimed the chair of the Council of Ministers in 1913, and a useful and "strong cement for the uniting of the separate parts of the state into a single unit."[118] Commissions continued to study the possibility of abolishing the courts and military-native administration through 1914 and 1915, but by this time officials in St Petersburg were distracted by more pressing matters, such as the prosecution of the First World War and the influx of refugees from Turkey and Persia into the Russian Caucasus.[119]

Opponents of this statist imperial mentality countered with the logic and patience of the customary law tradition, mixed with a greater knowledge of the local situation, which led them to question the wisdom of dictating local affairs in the terms of St Petersburg. While the oblast governors in Kars and Batumi found Reinke's ideas promising, both the military governor of Dagestan and the commander of Zakatal'skii okrug countered his view of the courts and, more importantly, questioned the implications of these ideas. In their eyes, Reinke's ambitious ideas about cultural transformation appeared viable only if undertaken through violent measures. These officials convinced Vorontsov-Dashkov that such a policy would not increase respect for Russian rule among the mountaineers.[120] More theoretically, A.V. Moskalev reminded his colleagues in the Ministry of Justice in 1913 that "these people possess a legal consciousness of the 14th or 15th century."[121] The mountaineers were relics of the past, he said, with a world view "completely contradictory" to the Russian judicial system.[122]

The imperial regime did not have four or five centuries to spare, and the debate was quickly overtaken by the events of 1914–17. After the continuation of the concessionary policies through the 1920s, the Soviet authorities decisively resolved the matter with the astonishing announcement in 1927 that both the shari'a and the adat were unacceptable guides to the administration of justice in the North Caucasus.[123] Their French colonial counterparts in the Maghrib and other parts of the colonial world would never have dreamed of such high-handedness. The new ideology of progress propagated by the Soviet regime, univeralist in pretension, bore many similarities to the imperial mentality of Reinke and his colleagues at the Ministry of Justice from 1911 to 1914. Soviet administrators called "backwardness" what nineteenth-century ethnographers had identified as "custom," and they anticipated a future unburdened by the legacy of the past. P. Tabolov associated "all customary law and tradition" with "stagnation," a "weapon of deception" in the hands of the kulaks.[124] The power of the Soviet state in the North Caucasus quickly exceeded the ambitions of even imperial proponents of the statist legal tradition.

6 The Russian Shamil, 1859–1871

European civilization, with railroads, steam cars, gas lighting, the comforts of life, and so on, opened a new world to these savages, who have previously never seen anything but the pitiful poverty and rags of Dagestan.

S. Ryzhov, 1859[1]

The encounter of Russia's nobility and cultural elite with European culture coincided with the eastern and southern expansion of the empire. Russians brought the cultural confidence of the West to their southeastern borderlands, where "half-savage peoples, … [u]nused to the laws and habits of civilized life," as Pushkin wrote of the Bashkirs, challenged the work of Russian officials and the civilizing potential of Russian culture.[2] Like Tbilisi and the region as a whole, which were to be transformed by their exposure to civilization and the culture of Russia, Shamil himself was to undergo a personal transformation as a result of his stay in Kaluga from 1859 to 1871. The conquered Shamil of the Russian press and popular literature was an imaginary figure, supposedly transformed by his exposure to the wonders of culture and civilization. Throughout his exile in Kaluga, however, Shamil was persistent in his efforts to arrange a hajj for himself and his family to Mecca, and after his death his family remained in the Ottoman Empire. The Russian Shamil, however, was a different figure, supposedly eager to shed his past and participate in the traditions of imperial obshchestvo.

SHAMIL IN RUSSIAN LETTERS

The Caucasus War was a literary event, in part because some of the most talented Russian writers of the early nineteenth century chose it as a setting for their works. Russian readers were therefore highly interested in the events that led up to the conclusion of the war, such as the flight of Shamil, the exchanges between Bariatinskii and the imam, and the behaviour of Shamil in captivity. The most intriguing question for Russian readers was his response to the world of Russia itself. In this encounter between backwardness and civilization, as the Russians imagined it, the intrigue for them lay in Shamil's moment of recognition of the veracity of this contrast. He was to see the future and, as a result, re-evaluate his own past and self. The encounter was limited and self-congratulatory for the Russians, in that it merely served to confirm the assumptions of Russian readers about the differences between West and East.

In the former Soviet Union, scholars have devoted little time to this aspect of the encounter. Soviet scholarship initially treated Shamil as the leader of a "national liberation" war and then, in a dramatic reversal, as one of the many "henchmen" of "Anglo-Turkish agents," as S.K. Bushuev wrote during the Cold War.[3] Later Soviet scholars tended to ignore not only Sufism but also the character of Shamil himself, and instead attempted to determine the structural changes in mountaineer society that had precipitated the colonial war. They concluded that the development of the mountaineer "raiding system," related to the transition of mountaineer society from a feudal to a bourgeois economy, had prompted mountaineer attacks upon the expanding Russian presence in the Caucasus. Socio-economic change, rather than a holy war, in this view inspired mountaineer hostility to the Russians.[4] Only very recently have post-Soviet scholars in Dagestan and the North Caucasus begun to rediscover Shamil.[5] In the West there has been far more interest in the Russian creation of Shamil.[6]

For Russian readers, 1859 marked a dividing line in the imam's personal history. His past belonged to the Romanticized world of exotic savagery. Shamil's relationship to his mother, for example, was described in a 1859 pamphlet published in Moscow called *Shamil: A Description of His Life, His Capture and Imprisonment and How He Endured 95 Blows to the Back from a Whip at the Will of the Prophet.*[7] This story described an 1843 effort by the Chechens to abandon the war and submit to the Russians. They sent four deputies to Shamil to request further aid or be allowed to end their resistance. Fearful of his response, they convinced his mother to intercede on their behalf and offered her a present worth 2,000 rubles in silver for her effort. Like all mountaineers, A. Kuzanov claimed, she was devoted to Shamil but suffered from "greed for money."[8] Shamil somehow deciphered this state of affairs, however, and retreated to a mosque for three days to seek guidance from Allah. He finally emerged, his face pale, his eyes red with tears, to announce the treachery of the Chechens and his own mother to the people of Dargo. "Weak, like all woman," Shamil said of his mother, "she submitted to their request and wanted me to be well-disposed to these unfaithful Chechens."[9] The worse was yet to come: Allah had commanded Shamil to punish, with a hundred lashes, the person who had informed him of the "shameless suggestions" of the Chechens. "And this was, unfortunately, my own mother," the burdened Shamil told the crowd. He began to beat his own mother, who was senseless after five blows. Dropping to his knees, after long and dramatic prayer, Shamil rose to announce that Allah had permitted him to stand in for his mother and receive the remaining ninety-five blows to the back. His Dargo audience was then surprised to see him grant the four Chechen deputies their lives and their freedom. "Return home," he announced before the crowd, as in a parable from the life of Christ, "and instead of an answer to the thoughtless request of your people, explain to them everything that you have seen and heard here with your own eyes and ears."[10]

A more famous source of information about Shamil was M. Verderevskii's dramatic rendition of the capture and imprisonment of the Chavchavadze and Orbeliani princesses in 1855.[11] The commander of the Lezgin Line insisted that the details of the event be communicated to the tsar himself.[12] But more significant was the public fascination with the story. Verderevskii's version was even translated into English and published in London, and probably was the most well known Russian contribution to this sort of popular Orientalist genre.[13] To tantalize the Russian reader in the Caucasus, Verderevskii excerpted the first three chapters in the main Tbilisi newspaper, *Kavkaz*, in 1855. Advertisements in large type in that newspaper announced the arrival of the complete edition.[14] In his introduction to the drama Verderevskii informed those of "enlightened contemporary society" that the following events would strike them as "almost fairy-tale-like legends from a long-lost time of barbarism," similar to the "bloody horrors" that had accompanied the efforts of European settlers to colonize the plains of North America.[15] These events, however, took place nearby, "in the borderlands of immense Russia."[16]

The Chavchavadze and Orbeliani families were among the most important in Georgia. The two princesses were the granddaughters of the last spouse of the Georgian tsar, Giorgi xii. The Chavchavadze family was especially well connected to the world of Russian letters. Lermontov's aunt, Praskovaia Akhverdova, was close to the family, and he and many other Russian officers frequently visited the estate while serving in the Caucasus. Nino, the daughter of Major Prince

Aleksandr Chavchavadze, married Aleksandr Griboedov, author of *Woe from Wit*.[17] Their gravesite on the side of the mountain overlooking Tbilisi (Mtatsminda) stood, as the Georgian press often reminded its readers, as a monument to these links of nobility and culture.[18] Aleksandr was the son of Gersevan Chavchavadze, the diplomatic representative to Russia at the time of the 1783 treaty marking the incorporation of Georgia into the empire, another reminder of the historic links between Russia and Georgia in the formation of the empire on the southern frontier. The preface to this literary encounter with mountaineer savagery thus pointed to the cultural world of the reader, which was the high culture of multi-ethnic educated society. The setting for the story was the wealthy Chavchavadze family estate at Tsinandali in Kakheti, Georgia. In this idyllic setting the Chavchavadze children learned to play the piano and to speak foreign languages.

Vulnerable women left unprotected by their husbands was one of the central themes of Vederevskii's story. When the mountaineers descended upon the Chavchavadze estate, they found only a large number of women and children. The frightened group awaited their capture in the belvedere and heard only "the smashing of glass, and the thumping of the robbers' fists on the keys of the pianoforte whenever it attracted the attention of a fresh party."[19] When Prince Chavchavadze returned to his burning and looted mansion, no one remained save an elderly wet nurse, who cried, "David, David, ... Why are you not here to help your family?"[20] Madame Dranse, the governess from France who had only been in the Caucasus eighteen days but who was to gain fame by telling this story to a Parisian audience, found herself "in the arms of a man with a bare shaven head, a red face, and an indescribable odour."[21] The mountaineers were particularly savage in their destruction of icons, bibles, and religious works. The pursuit of Captain Khitrov of the Caucasus Army was too late and caused Princess Chavchavadze tragically to drop Lydia, her four-month-old child, who died under the horses of the mountaineers. In transit, Nino, a young servant girl, was separated from the group and sinisterly disappeared, in spite of repeated assurances from a "benevolent" mulla.[22] Such were the central themes of this drama: mountaineer savagery and its threat to domesticity, female sexual vulnerability, the failure of men to protect this domestic and feminine world, and duplicitous Islam and its threat to Christianity. Such themes resonated with Vederevskii's Russian reading audience and with many government and church officials, who described the Chavchavadze episode in a similar way.[23]

Georgians reproduced this material in their press throughout the late nineteenth century with particular poignancy. Georgian domesticity and Georgian Christianity, emphasized Barbare Jorjatsisa in *Iveria* in 1893, found themselves in a precarious position on a Georgian frontier threatened by Islam and aggressive mountaineers. Aleksandr Chavchavadze's military miscalculation proved fatal for the family, and from too far away to help, he learned from a subordinate: "Sir! The enemy is on its way! Shamil is at the head of an army headed our way, and mountaineers are pillaging the countryside beyond the river!"[24] According to this account, Davit (David) Chavchavadze at least made a valiant effort, organizing Georgian peasants from the surrounding countryside for their holy struggle against the barbaric intruder.[25]

In Verderevskii's (Russian) account, Shamil was somewhat peripheral to the main events of the drama. Once he presided over an animal sacrifice in preparation for the feast of Bairam, and on another occasion he dramatically left for battle on his white horse, with his tunic, coloured boots with braids, and white turban.[26] In this costume "Shamil looked magnificent, and even imposing," Verderevskii said. He depicted the imam as generally humane to his prisoners but out of touch with the activities of his enormous household.[27] This household, rather than Shamil, became the primary setting for the remainder of the story. Zaidat, his Tatar wife and frequent persecutor of the captives, contrasted with the friendly and honest Shuanet, whose fate was of great interest to Russian readers. She, along with her wealthy Armenian merchant family from Mozdok by the name of Ulukhanov, had been captured by the mountaineers in an invasion of that town. Shamil refused to accept a ransom for the return of the family, but the then-sixteen-year-old Shuanet nobly pledged to become Shamil's wife in return for the safety of her family. In time she studied the Qur'an and adopted Islam as her faith.[28] Was she happy, the Princess Chavchavadze wondered? "I persisted in not abjuring my own religion, but at last I got to know Shamil, and for love of him consented to everything. At present I am happy, but I sometimes cannot help regretting –," she was reported to confide.[29] In any event, after Shamil's death in 1871, Shuanet did not return to Mozdok but joined the rest of Shamil's family in Turkey.[30]

Eight months and many negotiations later, the twenty-two captives were returned to the Russians. As Princess Chavchavadze left, she saw a young Georgian girl, held by the mountaineers since she was young and apparently intended as a future wife of Shamil. "If you should grow up here, never forget that you are a Georgian, and whenever you have an opportunity, help the Christians," the princess told the girl. Dzhemaledin (Jamal al-Din), Shamil's son, previously surrendered to the Russians and now an officer in the regiment of the Grand Duke Mikhail, was returned to Shamil along with

40,000 rubles in silver from the Chavchavadze family. He lamented the end of his exposure to a European education and the twists of fate that were now to leave him in "the midst of ignorance," where he would forget what he had learned and "go backwards like a crab."[31] Kazi-Magomet, Verderevskii claimed, was greatly influenced by Dzhemaledin's respect for a European education and was secretly imitating his brother. "May it be attended with success!" Verderevskii exclaimed.[32] The early infective influence of Europe was to be planted within Shamil's very household, though Vederevskii's enthusiasm was not warranted. Dzhemaledin soon died in 1858 of tuberculosis ("galloping consumption"), in spite of Shamil's attempt to enlist a Russian doctor to administer to him, and years later Kazi-Magomet left for Turkey and eventually returned to oppose the Russians in the war of 1877–78.[33] The significance attached to the household's exposure to "civilization" was obviously overrated by Verderevskii and his Russian readers, yet the images contributed significantly to Russian ideas about the famous imam and his family.

THE JOURNEY OF 1859

Russian writing about Shamil in 1859 celebrated his introduction to the world of progress, technological advance, consumer prosperity, the high culture of the Western world, and different notions of gender and the family. Russian culture and standards of behaviour, as writers emphasized in the newspaper accounts of the 1859 journey, were more humane and elevated than the savage and fanatical traditions of the mountaineers.[34] This difference impressed Shamil immediately after the capture, Russians reported, as observers claimed he was visibly transformed upon hearing Viceroy Aleksandr Bariatinskii announce the tsar's benevolent sparing of his life.[35] In the tradition of mountain culture, he expected to be executed on the spot. Not long after the capture, Colonel Karl Kh. Trampovskii, part of the entourage that accompanied Shamil to St Petersburg, intervened to settle the "explosion of Asian passion" that surrounded the conflict over the fate of Kerimat, the wife of Kazi-Magomet (now Shamil's eldest living son, who was also headed to Kaluga), but also the daughter of Daniel-Bek, who was present at Shamil's capture in the role of an interpreter for the Russians.[36] Daniel-Bek threatened to cut off the hands of his own daughter. The paternal presence of a Russian served to resolve the irrational and violent domestic dispute of mountaineers who were now to live in the Russian Empire.

Newspaper and pamphlet writers emphasized that Shamil's encounter with the material and technological aspects of Russian culture began immediately after his removal from his mountain hideout of Gunib. After descending from the mountains, Shamil for the "first time became acquainted with the comforts of European life" in Temir-Khan-Shura, in the home of Baron Wrangel.[37] "Europe" was present in Dagestan in the form of Wrangel's hospitality, the tablets for a stomach ache he received from a local Russian doctor in Temir-Khan-Shura, and the photograph collection of Count Nostigr in Gir-Iurt.[38] The fascinated Shamil requested that copies of photographs of himself be sent to his wives, who remained in Temir-Khan-Shura. Crowds of the curious gathered here and in Mozdok, where the imam spent 5 September with the family of his Armenian wife, Shuanet, as they did in Georgievsk and Ekaterinograd.[39]

Stavropol, however, was to be "the first European city" that Shamil had ever seen, as a Russian newspaper commentator put it, and crowds of the curious assembled to witness his arrival. "As happens with all powerful natures, Shamil carries himself extraordinarily well and does not reveal his feelings," the newspapers reported.[40] Shamil calmly looked at "the buildings, and at our wonderful boulevard."[41] Kazi-Magomet, however, was astonished. "And can it be that Petersburg is still better than Stavropol?" he was reported to ask naively.[42] The next day in Stavropol, Shamil was visited by a school director, who was accompanied by a mountaineer student from the Stavropol gymnasium. They spoke in Kumyk without a translator, but not for long, the observant Russians noted. Was Shamil put off by the educated youth, who did not kiss his hand and recognize him as his imam? The Russians of Stavropol exhibited for Shamil what they assumed was most impressive: the Vorontsov Gardens, the theatre, evening balls, a vaudeville.[43] The *Stavropol Provincial News* reported his smile and curiosity when exposed to the vaudeville and his satisfaction with the choirs that had been arranged for an 8 p.m. performance in the Vorontsov Gardens. He spent less time at the ball, however, apparently "surprised at the social freedoms of Russian society" or, as it was reported in St Petersburg, "scandalized by the customs of the *giaour* [unbelievers]."[44]

In Khar'kov, Shamil was introduced to a similar world, visiting the university, the circus, a ball given by the Khar'kov provincial governor, and the home of a local notable on Ekarinoslav Street. Such a display was beginning to have its intended effect. Shamil supposedly confessed his disappointment that he had waged war against Russia for so many years. "I am sad," he was reported to say, "that I did not know Russia and did not earlier seek out its friendship."[45] Again amazed by Russian women and the social conventions of Russian balls, this time Shamil was intrigued rather than deterred. At a ball

held by the governor of Khar'kov province, the stunned Shamil retreated several paces upon seeing the dresses of the Russian women.
"You will not go to heaven," he told his hosts after he performed a
quick prayer, as "you have here on earth that paradise which
Muhammad has promised us in the sky."[46]

By mid-September Shamil was in Kursk, where his exposure to the
world of Russia continued. He told the provincial governor, Nikolai
Petrovich Bibikov, that his previous estimation of Stavropol as the
most beautiful and remarkable city he had ever seen now had to be
reserved for Khar'kov and Kursk.[47] There he listened with great interest to stories about the railroad and the telegraph and other "suc-
cesses of our civilization," as I. Besiadovskii of Kursk said.[48] Shamil
thanked Bibikov for his fine treatment and then, "according to European custom," performed a "chake-hands [sic]" with his host.[49]
Shamil's trip to the Kursk Theatre was of particular interest to Besiadovskii: "Is this not a dream? Is this not amazing? Shamil is in Kursk!
... at the theatre! ... at the Italian opera!" "Una voce poco fa!" rather
than the sounds of Russian artillery met the ears of Shamil.[50] He
enoyed Italian opera scenes from *Il trovatore*, *Il barbiere di Seviglia*, and
Columello. During intermission the crowd whispered to one another
in the lobby and boxes:

"Voyez ce grand Chamil!"
"Qu'il est beau! Qu'il est magnifique!"
"Voilà le type d'un héros!"
"D'un brigand!"
"D'un martyr!"
"How he is so sadly silent!"
"How he grandly muses!"
"Quel sublime silence!"

Upon leaving the theatre, Shamil informed the crowd that he preferred the tragic scenes to the comic ones, since in them the "strength
of feeling and energy of passion" were most evident.[51] He moved on,
leaving Kursk to more mundane matters and the Italian opera to
emptier houses in the typically slow summer season.[52]

The culmination of this exposure to Western culture and the world
of Russia took place in St Petersburg. The inhabitants of the city were
by this time well prepared for Shamil's arrival. A poem called "The
Subjugation of the Caucasus," accompanied by a portrait of the
imam, appeared on the St Petersburg streets, and books such as *The
History of the Transcaucasus*, Verderevskii's *Prisoner of Shamil*, and
Shamil in Paris and *Shamil Close Up* were prominently displayed in the

St Petersburg bookstores. Newspaper writers joked that they expected to see Shamil caps, Shamil bracelets, and Shamil cloaks soon on the streets.[53] Shamil finally arrived at the Nikolaev Station on the morning of 26 September and promptly informed the crowd that had gathered to see him: "If I had earlier known Russia and all that I have now seen and see, I would have submitted [pokorilsia] a long time ago."[54] He visited the general of the Main Staff, the St Petersburg military governor-general, and the Military Topographical Department, where he was shown a number of maps of the Caucasus.[55] On the 28th he was taken to the Academy of Sciences Museum and the Italian Opera, and the following day to the Bolshoi Theatre.[56] At the Public Library on Nevskii Prospect, Shamil admired works of Russian scholarship, viewed portraits of previous Russian tsars and maps of the Caucasus, and in particular examined a portrait of General Paskevich.[57] At St Isaac's Cathedral he carefully examined the massive dome and requested details on its construction.[58]

Rumours of Shamil's location quickly spread among the residents of the city, often causing crowds to gather in vain. Large crowds nightly appeared at all the St Petersburg theatres, unsure of which one he was to attend.[59] Shamil had finally been exposed to the most European of Russian cities, and his every reaction to the details of European life was of interest to the Russian public. In his room at the Znamenskii Hotel the Russians observed "with what curiosity he looked over the gas burner," apparently convinced that a source of oil must be hidden somewhere. He was similarly intrigued by the street lights, and at the Italian opera he was surprised and curious when the lights dimmed.[60] S. Ryzhov, in a passage that we have quoted at the start of this chapter, summarized the cumulative effect of such exposure upon the great mountaineer: "European civilization, with railroads, steam cars, gas lighting, the comforts of life, and so on, opened a new world to these savages, who have previously never seen anything but the pitiful poverty and rags of Dagestan." Shamil, Ryzhov was comforted to discover, was "surprised at everything he sees."[61] Russia, of course, to Ryzhov's thinking, belonged to "European civilization."

On 10 October Shamil and his party finally reached Kaluga. Huge Russian crowds, the local newspaper reported, were delighted by his smiling face, fur coat, and beautiful white turban at the Kulon Hotel window, and they were pleased to know that "Shamil really liked our city" and claimed that it reminded him of Chechnia.[62] The residents of Kaluga had played host to other prominent and non-Russian exiles in the past. The last Crimean khan, Shahin-Girei, had resided first in Voronezh and then in Kaluga in 1786; the sultan of the Small Kirgiz Horde, Arungiz Abulgaziev, had arrived in Kaluga in 1823 and stayed for ten years; and the widow of the Georgian king Irakli was in Kaluga with her children in 1834–35.[63] In the three-storey home of a landlord by the name of Sukhotin, which was to be his residence, Shamil inspected in detail all its conveniences and luxuries, including its adjoining barn and well, and he was in particular enamoured of two bronze busts of Greek church fathers.[64] His visits around Kaluga included exposure to magnets, air pumps, and other various new technological devices.[65] On 12 October he witnessed the annual celebration of the Procession of the Cross (*krestnyi khod*) across from the main cathedral in Kaluga, in memory of the city's liberation from the French. For Russian readers, Shamil's Kaluga possessed important symbols of Russification: the heritage of Byzantium, Orthodoxy, modern technology, and Russian military power. Shamil spent time reading Colonel Boguslavskii's translation of Verderevskii's *Prisoners of Shamil*, which had immediately disappeared from the libraries and bookstores of Kaluga. Aside from a few mistakes in his historical biography, "Shamil verified everything that was said in this book."[66] Happy, contented, and settled in Kaluga, this imaginary Shamil affirmed that the image was indeed accurate.

A few commentators dissented from this 1859 version of the imam. How could "educated society" feel this way about him, A. Gariainov wondered, when he "himself stood outside their laws," and was responsible for the loss of many Russian lives in the course of the long war? Gariainov reminded Russians of the incarceration of Prince Orbeliani, and he suggested that Shamil was a cunning manipulator of the mountaineers and their claims of freedom, nationality, and religion. The imam, he concluded, should be shot, just as he had executed many Russians. "He can't expect any better."[67] Petr Egorov doubted the many stories of Shamil's asceticism and courage and his claims about his lack of knowledge and understanding of the genuine character of Russia. Egorov believed that Shamil was feigning interest in Russian society and culture: "Palaces, the wonders of science and culture, the balls, theatres, and all the brilliance of European life is for him only a temporary pastime, while all of Russia [remains for him] an enormous prison."[68] Egorov doubted the stories of Shamil's honesty and naïveté, and he emphasized instead the savage events of the Caucasus War, complete with grisly detail: the naib Adalo, who invaded the Georgian village of Kvareli and killed defenceless women and children, paraded around the head of a boy on a stake, and cut a girl in half in order to resolve an argument about who would acquire her as booty. On another occasion, mountaineers descended upon "some village" in Georgia, attacked an imperial official, and cut off and took away his hand as a trophy; upon returning home and discovering that they had mistakenly cut off his left hand rather than his right, they returned to cut off his other hand.[69]

This dissenting voice of 1859 was in the minority, however, and was roundly and quickly criticized by numerous other commentators. Gariainov was chastised for his lack of humanity and for embarrassing Russian society by reproducing the gutter talk of uneducated soldiers in a Russian newspaper.[70] The promise of Shamil in 1859 lay in his potential for cultural transformation. Like the conduct of the tsar and Bariatinskii, whose polite treatment after the capture Shamil found surprising, Russian society intended to inspire the imam's respect and admiration. The spitefulness and anger of Gariainov and Egorov were incongruous with the purpose of Shamil's trip to Russia.

SHAMIL IN KALUGA, 1859–1871

Once he was finally settled in Kaluga, Russians expected to witness a new direction in Shamil's family history. A. Runovskii's replacement of Boguslavskii as the *pristav* (police officer) responsible for Shamil and his household afforded him a special opportunity to encourage generational cultural change. Runovskii was especially interested in the fate of the younger generation of men within Shamil's household, such as Kazi-Magomet's younger brother, Magomet-Shefi, Khadzhio, a close but young murid of Shamil, and Abdurrakhman and Abduragim, the sons-in-law of Shamil. Khadzhio, he believed, epitomized the younger generation of muridism, whose ideas about their faith, women and gender, the Caucasus War, and the situation of the mountaineers of the North Caucasus were in flux and distinguishable from the ideas of Shamil and the older generation.[71] Khadzhio in particular, Runovskii claimed, was fascinated and intrigued by the greater pleasures of Russian society, and in Kaluga he took up smoking, frequented Russian social events, and courted a number of Russian women, activities that served to motivate his efforts to acquire Russian.[72] "Regarding the shari'a," Runovskii's Khadzhio confided, "I'll repeat what I've said before: it forbids all that is good and permits the bad."[73] Pavel G. Przhetsslavskii, a subsequent family pristav, also noted a similar openness on the part of Abduragim, who "worried little about a trip to Mecca and Medina."[74] Abduragim once exclaimed in exasperation, according to Przhetsslavskii, "I am unable and do not want to be a 'murid' – not of Kaluga or Dargo!"[75] Like Khadzhio, Abduragim attended the theatre in Kaluga in the company of Russian women.[76]

Reform of the views of Shamil's party about gender and the family were central to Runovskii's notion of cultural progress. The younger generation, he was proud to report, as a result of their exposure to Russia, began to understand that women need not play the role of a "pack animal" (v'iuchnyi skot) in the household, veil their faces, or be ignored by and excluded from male society.[77] Numerous Russian travellers, ethnographers, and administrators in the Caucasus at this time also drew attention to the situation of Muslim women within the household. The promise, to their own minds at least, of alleviating the domestic injustices of Muslim culture served as a partial justification of the Russian colonial presence, as we discussed in the previous chapter. On one occasion Runovskii took up the matter with Shamil, who affirmed that female inferiority in all respects was ordained by Allah. Runovskii countered with his version of domestic gender relations: the man was to protect and defend the woman, from danger as well as from hard labour, and the woman was charged with the "raising of children, looking after the domestic household, [and] loving her husband."[78] Like most other Russians, he upheld a version of female propriety and domesticity as a mark of progress and civilization. To Russian thinking, this image of the oppressed Muslim woman was complemented by the aggressive sexual threat posed by the male mountaineer. Both characteristics were absent from the family life of civilized cultures.

Imperial educated society was highly optimistic in its 1859 vision of Shamil in the process of cultural change. In reality, he tried to maintain contact with Sufi leaders in the North Caucasus throughout his stay in Kaluga and consistently pressed various Russian officials and the tsar himself regarding his request to visit Mecca before his death.[79] Shamil concluded that pristav Pavel Przhetsslavskii was obstructing his efforts to arrange a trip to Mecca. In the fall of 1863 he informed the Kaluga governor of his "extreme dissatisfaction" with the work of Przhetsslavskii and claimed that the Polish pristav was informing him of events in Poland in 1863.[80] Kazi-Magomet approached the Russians with a request from Shamil that Przhetsslavskii be replaced with an officer of "pure Russian background," and General Kartsov was concerned enough to suggest that Przhetsslavskii be replaced with a "Russian officer of Orthodox faith."[81] That Shamil would make such a claim, and that Russian officials would respond so quickly, is an indication of the fears and sensitivities of Russian officials about their rule in the borderlands. Przhetsslavskii was eventually exonerated of the charge, but not before several anxious moments when he was forced to emphasize that he and all of his family had left the Polish provinces twenty-five years earlier and that he held "nothing in common with my compatriots [sootechestvenniki]."[82]

"I can endure him no longer," wrote Shamil of Przhetsslavskii to Governor Spasski of Kaluga province in August 1865.[83] The imam was mistaken, however, in his belief that lower-level officials were obstructing his efforts to petition the tsar.[84] Caucasus viceroy Grand Duke Mikhail and other high officials were opposed because they feared that word of such an event would further inspire North Caucasus mountaineers to rebellion.[85] There were other reasons for Shamil to be dissatisfied with the work and interests of Przhetsslavskii. Like many other Russians who wrote about Shamil, Przhetsslavskii took a particular interest in the younger generation and encouraged Abduragim, the imam's son-in-law, to leave the family for a place in Russian service. Shamil and Kazi-Magomet opposed such a plan and stalled matters by insisting upon the consent of Abduragim's father, who lived in Turkey and could not be reached.[86] Przhetsslavskii spent far more time with Abduragim and others of the younger generation than with Kazi-Magomet and Shamil. In spite of the renewed confidence of Ministry of War officials in his trustworthiness, they relieved him of his position in 1866. Surveillance was only half the task of a pristav, and Przhetsslavskii had failed at maintaining a close, helpful relationship with Shamil.[87]

More serious was the declining health of the imam's family. "My family is also thankful to the Great Emperor," wrote Shamil to Dmitrii Miliutin in April of 1867, "but it has gradually diminished."[88] Kazi-Magomet's wife, Kerimat, died in 1862 from tuberculosis at age twenty-five. Next to die was Nafisat, the wife of Abdurrakhman and supposedly Shamil's favourite daughter. In all, seventeen members of the party were to die in Kaluga, most of them from tuberculosis.[89] In desperation, Shamil's letters to the tsar became increasingly obsequious.[90] The regime finally granted him his wish, and the family journeyed from Kaluga to Kiev and then to the Ottoman Empire, where most of the family stayed even after the death of Shamil in 1871.

THE DESCENDANTS OF SHAMIL

En route to Russia and in captivity in Kaluga, Shamil and his family had found themselves at the centre of several colonial mythologies, all of them characterized by a confidence in the transformative power of Russian culture upon Shamil and the mountaineers. "Russian" culture in this context signified progress, European enlightenment generally, and the high culture and traditions of imperial educated society. Georgian watchers of Shamil in Tbilisi imagined the encounter in a way similar to the Russian press in St Petersburg and Moscow.[91] The purpose of the extended voyage to Russia was to expose the imam to cultural monuments such as St Isaac's Cathedral and cultural artifacts such as works of literature and theatre productions. As a result, Shamil and, in particular, the younger generation were to become "civilized," which in addition meant they were to absorb new ideas about technology, consumerism, education, and gender and the family. The fate of the younger generation was of particular interest to Russian readers, as they had spent less time in the North Caucasus and could look foward to a longer future within the Russian Empire. Their personal histories were to take a new direction, as the North Caucasus in general was offered a different future as a result of its incorporation into the Russian Empire.

Like the southern borderlands, the lives of those members of the younger generation who stayed in the Russian Empire did change. For Russian readers, one career worth following was that of Magomet-Shefi, the son of Shamil, who as a boy in Kaluga appeared to Russians to exhibit great promise.[92] From Kaluga, Magomet-Shefi found a place in Russian service, and in 1865 he was sent to the Caucasus for the purpose of assembling an escort squadron of mountaineers from Dagestan and Chechnia. At the wedding of the tsar's daughter in 1866, the emperor himself was said to be particularly impressed by this son of Shamil. Magomet-Shefi grew up to achieve more than Khadzhio, who eventually served in the Russian bureaucracy in Dagestan, or Abdurrakhman, who achieved the rank of lieutenant-colonel and retired to live in Kazi-Kumukh.[93] He eventually rose to the rank of general-maior, briefly lived in Paris, and served as the governor-general of Kazan province (although he was not sent to the Caucasus in 1877).

At the turn of the century, Magomet-Shefi, like a member of obshchestvo, was vacationing at the mineral waters of Kislovodsk. There he met for conversation and reminiscence with two aging Russians whose past experience was also closely tied to the Caucasus War and the Russian colonization of the region. I.N. Zakhar'in was an officer in the Russian army who had had the opportunity of visiting Shamil and his family in Kaluga on two occasions in 1860–61. Magomet-Shefi at that time was just fifteen. General V.A. Potto was a prolific military historian who published one of the more prominent histories of the war and various essays on characters such as Shamil and Hadji Murat.[94] As Shamil's son approached the seated Potto and Zakhar'in in the Kislovodsk park, Potto characterized the significance and purpose of the occasion: "My, how many tales we could share about the former heroes of the Caucasus War!"[95] Magomet-Shefi was thus privy to what had become a common and particularly Russian pastime of the later nineteenth century for those with a history related to the Caucasus. Memoir writers made heroes of themselves and the Russians who had fought the mountaineers, and ignored the conflict of faiths and cultures in favour of a glorification of combat and battle against the savage mountaineers.[96] Other writers reminded Russians that they were the first citizens of a colonial power by sharing stories of the inadequacies of hotel service and the difficulties of transport, of amusing stories and local colour provided by "native" guides, of conversations with aging mountaineers who claimed to have fought for Shamil, and of begging Ossetians along the Georgian Military Road.[97]

Magomet-Shefi was quick to compliment Zakhar'in's work and favourably compared it to the "fabrications" published by Pavel Przhetsslavskii.[98] The former pristav drew the ire of several Russian writers as well.[99] True to his diary reports prepared for the Ministry of War, Przhetsslavskii had published a series of essays in *Russkaia Starina* in 1877–78 that emphasized the importance of Islam to the character of Shamil.[100] He challenged the version of the civilized Shamil presented to Russian readers in 1859 and raised a series of difficulties, not only for the Russian reading public but also for Russian administrators in the Caucasus. While in Kaluga, Przhetsslavskii publicly pointed out, Shamil was consistent in his desire to leave and flooded his pristav, various military commanders, and the tsar himself with a barrage of requests to be allowed a trip to Mecca. Talk of "holy places" was never far from Shamil's mind, Przhetsslavskii wrote, and if denied a trip to the lands of the sultan, the imam hoped as a second choice to be relocated from Kaluga to either Crimea or Kazan.[101] In Przhetsslavskii's story the far reaches of the empire were present as places of significant cultural and religious difference, in contrast to the 1859 image of Shamil well known to Russians.

The presence of Magomet-Shefi in Russia instead reminded Russians that exposure to Russia might make educated "natives" out of misled and uninformed mountaineers. Culture in the service of conquest created colonial elites throughout the colonized world in the nineteenth century. The regime founded schools for Muslim and mountaineer children in the larger cities of the region, which eventually produced students willing and able to participate in the educated colonial community in the Caucasus, sometimes as teachers, translators, and administrators for the regime. While Russian success stories such as Magomet-Shefi received prominence in the Russian press, less attention was devoted to the fact that the primary source of education in places such as Dagestan remained the Muslim primary and secondary schools.[102]

A vision of empire accompanied and inspired the Russian conquest of the North Caucasus. Shamil's long history of "savagery," Sufism, and military opposition presented no particular obstacle to his eventual imagined participation in the world of imperial educated society. The former guerilla war leader from the frontier was to be remade. Russian and Georgian writers and readers believed that exposure to the world of Western consumerism, technology, and high culture and to Western conceptions of gender and the family would initiate an immediate process of profound cultural self-awakening on the part of Shamil and members of his family. He was to acquire a new "poddanstvo" and allegiance to the world of Russia, but inspired by a genuine appreciation and recognition of the virtues of that world. He was to live as a "Russian" noble (*rossiiskaia* rather than *russkaia*) in Kaluga and sympathize with the cultural interests and aspirations of this multi-ethnic corporate body. His Kaluga home included direct references to patristic Orthodoxy. The Russian Shamil was a still noble military leader from the frontier who had left behind his lifelong association with Sufi Islam.

Even his departure from Russia in favour of the holy lands of Islam did not deter the hopeful from among Russians, some of whom, such as M.N. Chichagova, continued even later in the century to reproduce the 1859 version of Shamil in the process of cultural change and the many stories that were discredited by subsequent events in both the North Caucasus and Kaluga.[103] "Shamil very much loved children," wrote Chichagova, the wife of yet another official associated with the imam's surveillance, "and such a man cannot be evil."[104] Shamil was noble at heart, she stressed, generous with his family, admiring of the tsar, and even impressed by the beauty and pathos of the Christian faith.[105] Kazi-Magomet, Chichagova claimed, was deeply devoted to the Russian tsar, but perhaps faltered as a result of the grief caused by the death of his father. "I simply cannot get used to the idea that Kazi-Magom[et] was with the Turkish troops in the last war!" she mused.[106] Islam remained perpetually foreign and even inconceivable for the creators of the Russian Shamil.

7 Russification and the Return of Conquest

> The colonization of the Caucasus by the native Russian element will create in this rich borderland a firm bulwark in support of the state, and will link [the region] more closely to the other parts of the empire.
>
> Holy Synod report, 1900[1]

"Russification" in the Caucasus was not so much a particular policy as a broad series of trends, explored here in regard to intellectual history, memoir writing, international competition, and colonization policy, which challenged the ideologies of a multi-ethnic empire developed by educated society from the 1840s on. They emerged in a belligerent way at the turn of the twentieth century in response to basic Russian dilemmas about its simultaneous identity as both nation and empire, but they were of course never far from the surface.[2] For some military officials, it was simply a return to the long Caucasus War, which in their view had never ended; for others, it was a comforting resurrection of the traditional symbols of empire. When Tsar Alexander III and his family travelled to Vladikavkaz in 1888, in the tradition of a monarchy aware of the "ceremonial possibilities of travel," as Richard Wortman writes, his purpose was to illustrate imperial power and benelovence to provincial and borderland regions far from St Petersburg.[3] The tsar approached a young Ossetian pupil supported by the Society for the Restoration of Orthodoxy. "Do you understand Russian?" "I understand, Your Imperial Highness," the boy replied, and the tsar was visibly pleased. In Vladikavkaz the imperial family was greeted with a rendition of "God Save the Tsar" from the choir of the Ossetian Girls' School.[4] Tsar, Orthodox Christianity, and Russian culture and language still served in his mind as the basis of empire. The "national myth," emphasizes Wortman, stood as the foundation of empire for Russia's last two tsars and their advisers.[5]

The fears and concerns that prompted Russification in the border-lands were numerous, although the impulse was not just an attempt to return to tradition. For some officials, it was a product of their continuing effort to extend the authority and practices of their version of the enlightened "well-ordered police state" to the edges of the empire. "The All-Russian State is unitary and indivisible," proclaimed the first article to the Fundamental Laws (Osnovnyie Zakony) issued on 23 April 1906. As. B.E. Nol'de pointed out before the revolution, in fact, that claim illustrated the centralizing efforts of the modern Petrine state to end previous forms of autonomy and privilege. The tsar historically allowed "privileges and rights" to endure on the frontier, in a way similar to the relationship of the early modern French monarchy to its provinces.[6]

This history of negotiation and concession that accompanied the formation of the empire left the "all-Russian" political order "vastly heterogeneous," as Kappeler wrote, a patchwork quilt created by many hands.[7] Nobilities throughout the empire continued to exercise their traditional forms of authority, universities such as the one in Dorpat used German as the language of instruction until 1893, Bashkirs and others served in special military squadrons, the Finns basically maintained their own army, native Siberians and other inorodtsy were exempt from military service, colonies of Indian and German traders had special privileges in Astrakhan, and peoples from the Kazakhs in Central Asia to the Chechens practised customary legal traditions.[8] But by the early twentieth century, officials in and from St Petersburg had become impatient with the many administrative concessions and special scholarly projects sponsored by the Caucasus administration in Tbilisi. Reinke and other officials who attacked the customary law courts in the North Caucasus perceived the region as undergoverned, chaotic, and far too distant from the reach of St Petersburg. In search of administrative "fusion" (sliianie), the Council of Ministers in St Petersburg abolished the Caucasus Committee and the namestnichestvo (viceroyalty) itself, established for Vorontsov in 1845.[9] The model of unity and cultural and administrative conformity adopted by nation-states both new and old, from Italy to Germany to France, influenced the Russian outlook as well.[10] State-building in "Russia," as in France, meant administrative and central uniformity and the effort to silence regional "savagery" from the frontier.[11]

The drive for administrative fusion was bound to provoke problems in a distant region that remained basically unintegrated into the imperial system in the first place. Mountain village elders maintained a high degree of independence from Russian officials in the North Caucasus, numerous crimes were still adjudicated according to mountain customary law, and of course, mountaineers often took matters into their own hands and resolved them beyond the court system anyway. Mountain peoples were generally exempt from military service, and families were slow to respond to the educational initiatives of the regime. The absence of an ecclesiastical administration in the North Caucasus left regime officials unable to monitor the activities of Sufi murids and their followers, and Sufi-inspired rebellions continued throughout the imperial era. Even the captive Shamil and his family proved recalcitrant, immune from what Russians took to be the cultural wonders of St Petersburg and Kaluga. He preferred Mecca, and his son Kazi-Magomet maintained Sufi contacts in the Ottoman Empire and North Caucasus and returned to fight the Russians in 1877. Vedeno, famous during the Caucasus War as the residence of Shamil, whence he fled during his final retreat and capture in the summer of 1859, remained relatively untouched by Russian rule.[12] Conservative frustration with such cultural and administrative challenges at the *fin de siècle* was common throughout the colonial world. French colons in Algeria, for example, such as Eugène Étienne of Oran, the deputy to the French Chamber, presented themselves as champions of French culture in a hostile, Muslim land. They attacked the Muslim courts and educational system, and portrayed Algerian Jews and even other European settlers as unreliable and untrustworthy.[13]

Russification collided with new forms of regionalism and even nationalism from the frontier, which were themselves partially the outgrowth of imperial policy. Native language instruction for missionaries in the 1850s meant access to the Gospel, but the climate had changed several decades later. Even the Georgians, long-time contributors to the discourse on empire, were frustrated by the apparent limits on their access to culture. The theatre established by Vorontsov, explained a commentator in 1882, was a sign of the "strengthening of our national conscience and the awakening of our motherland." "I want a theatre," he continued, "– only a Georgian theatre." "I want schools – [but] Georgian schools."[14] Georgian scholars such as G. Kipshidze took their cue from Petr Uslar and his respect for antiquity and native tradition as they outlined plans to recover ancient manuscripts and cultivate a national memory.[15] It was now conceivable that non-Russians might employ their newly written languages, the lessons of the Russian educational system, or the notion of civilization to criticize the regime. For later officials, increased literacy was not necessarily progress, and by the turn of the century the regime was in the business of restricting writing rather than promoting it. Russian officials such as Governor-General A.M. Dondukov-Korsakov, newly arrived from the western provinces and no doubt keenly aware of Polish dissent, exercised a more careful censorship over non-Russian newspapers and closed several Georgian newspapers (such as *Droeba* in 1885 and the smaller and populist *Imedi* and *Shroma* in Kutaisi in 1883).[16] Even traditionally "colonial" publications suffered. In 1898 the regime began to issue *Kavkaz* directly from the office of the governor-general.[17] Chavchavadze, however, careful to distance himself from the emerging Georgian radicalism, was able to publish *Iveria* on a daily basis from 1886, and several other cultural and literary journals endured as well.[18]

The extraordinary events surrounding the 1905 revolution for borderland communities posed the prospect of imperial fragmentation. Labour activism, peasant rebellion, the growing disillusionment of educated society with the state, and other familiar developments made for a dramatically different climate throughout the empire in the years preceding the First World War. The question of empire was now the "nationalities question," and recently established newspapers openly debated the dilemmas and viabilities of new forms of regional arrangements such as separatism, autonomy, and national independence.[19] Georgian intellectuals now recalled an oppressive history of empire and colonial domination instead of the shared cultural and social experience that had characterized the earlier period. At a Duma meeting in January 1909, for example, G.D. Chkheidze looked back to the inattention to the Georgian language in imperial schooling as a history of "pedagogical terror." Ignoring or offering a different interpretation of the history of non-Russian participation in the imperial service, he criticized the history of Georgian noble collaboration in the conquest of the Caucasus.[20]

Incidents in precarious frontier regions such as the North Caucasus complemented events in the Russian capital cities that contributed to the fear felt by many regime administrators and members of educated society at the prospect of the disintegration of the empire. For the imperial educated community in the Caucasus, the mountaineer rebellion of 1877 was an important moment in the waning of their confidence in their capacity to influence the future of the region. The rebellion and subsequent pacification exacerbated an already fragile relationship, perhaps similar to the "enduring bitterness and suspicion" left in the wake of the Berber revolt in 1871 in Algeria.[21] And the Russian *narod* itself appeared as the potential victim of this enduring mountaineer savagery in the Caucasus, especially to those who remembered how rebellious mountaineers in 1877 had threatened Russian populations in larger Dagestani cities such as Temir-Khan-Shura and appeared particularly intent on destroying all traces of Russian culture and the presence of the regime in the North Caucasus.[22]

BIG PEOPLES AND SMALL PEOPLES

Conservative writers in the capital cities of Russia were particularly concerned about cultural competition on the frontier, and their ideas found an audience among frontier officials in daily contact with different "cultural-historical types." "Native soil conservatives" and proponents of Pan-Slavism drew on the heritage of Romantic and Slavophile thought, but reworked the Slavophile focus on Russian tradition into an ideology of ethnic essentialism, religious exclusivity, and imperial expansion and conquest.[23] Inspired by Nikolai Danilevskii, thinkers such as Dostoevsky and Nikolai Strakhov apoc alyptically worried about European geopolitics.[24] Russia was still a young and energetic people destined to "work out its own culture and fulfill its historical tasks," argued general and Pan-Slavist M.G. Cherniaev, but its principal task was the realignment of the map of Europe and the destruction of the Ottoman Turks.[25] The Slavic Benevolent Society throughout the late imperial era offered inflammatory denunciations of the historic role of Ottoman Turks in both the Byzantine Empire and the Russian borderlands.[26]

This new climate of competitive nationalism and imperialism held out a belligerent discourse that many frontier officials found especially compelling. Both Slavophiles and Westerners drew upon the heritage of the German Romantics and liked to measure civilizations and their respective contributions to "universal history," although they were never particularly belligerent about the implications of such differences.[27] This was not the case with later Slavophiles such as Ivan Aksakov, for example, who regularly voiced his fears of Bismarck and the Germans in *Rus'* throughout the 1880s.[28] Aksakov had been exposed at an early age to Khomiakov, Kireevskii, and Slavophile circles and then far outlived them to witness further conflicts with the Ottoman Turks and the emergence of the various Pan-Slavic committees. He was obsessed with international competition and the need for Russia to counter its rivals in the Balkans and on its various frontiers. He was instrumental in the formation of the Slavic Benevolent Society in Moscow, served briefly as its secretary in 1862 and treasurer until 1868, and was close to General Cherniaev.[29] Slavic visitors to the 1867 Slavonic Ethnographic Exhibit, Aksakov wrote in *Moskva*, strengthened "their spiritual and moral ties to Russia" as preparation for subsequent struggle with Magyars, Germans, and Turks.[30]

These were the competing big civilizations in borderland regions that threatened to divert small peoples from the correct path. While the preoccupation of conservative writers with Russia's relationship to the West is well known, scholars have paid less attention to the implications of these ideas within the context of empire. The influence of Nikolai Danilevskii was particularly important. As was the case with Khomiakov and Kireevskii, Russia in the portrayal of Danilevskii was unique and special, and the key to its unusual strength lay in its continuing reservoir of indigenous culture and "originality" (*samobytnost'*), untainted even by the reforms of Peter the Great.[31] A "world-historical type" in its tribal phase underwent a "long preparatory period" for its "future conscious activities." During the "ethnographic period" its "tribal particularities," such as the development of its language, the expression of myth and legend, and its way of life, percolated in the background of the world stage, awaiting their entrance.[32] Russia might have been a latecomer to the world stage, but its time had arrived.

But not all civilizations could boast of such a future. Thinkers who drew on the Romantic heritage in the late nineteenth century were far more explicit about just who qualified and who did not to benefit from these ideas about historically young peoples and their future cultural expression. The Westerners had been accustomed to making similar distinctions, although according to a different set of criteria. Belinskii, for example, made note of those peoples with "fewer sources of spiritual life," by which he meant a less-fertile soil of proverbs, sayings, parables, songs, tales, and legends from which literature might emerge – in short, a less-developed sphere of custom. These peoples would never "rise to the significance of a universal-historical people."[33] Belinskii notably excluded even Ukrainians from this picture.[34]

Danilevskii, as well, emphasized that not all peoples were capable of "originality" or of attaining significant levels of culture and civilization; they "are born, achieve their various levels of development, age, deteriorate, and die." Predictably, the Slavs, headed by the Russians, were one of those "cultural-historical types" destined, in Danilevskii's view, to play a decisive role in the history of the world. Small peoples on the Russian frontier such as those of the Middle Volga, on the other hand, were to play the role of "ethnographic material," "that is, something like inorganic matter that makes up the composition of historical organisms."[35] Danilevskii did not consider this process of assimilation a cultural insult or certainly not a political conquest, and instead felt that peoples at the mere stage of "ethnographic material" were in fact fortunate to contribute to the strength and richness of a genuine "cultural-historical type." Mountaineers in the Caucasus did not even make it this far, and instead, with their "fanatical religion, their way of life and habits, and even the land they inhabit," they were little more than "natural [*prirodnye*] predators and robbers."[36] For Danilevskii, they were apparently like animals, lacking even the rudiments of culture and not worthy of much consideration.

Conservative thought in the age of Russification reserved cultural "originality" and authenticity for the Russians and offered little to the small peoples of the empire, such as those of the North Caucasus. Danilevskii denied the heritage of conquest that had created the empire in places such as the Middle Volga, the Caucasus, and Turkestan, argued that the state could only (and should only) represent the resident "cultural-historical type" (the Russians), advocated the assimilation or "fusion" (*sliianie*) of various small peoples with the Russians, denied that Russia possessed colonies, defended the activities of settlers, and attributed the (supposed) weaknesses of the French national character to the historic mixing of Germanic and Roman cultural influences.[37] Similarly, Strakhov defended the formation of the Russian Empire as a sharp contrast to European colonial empires, British Ireland, and American slavery.[38] He also associated the expansion of the state into numerous borderland regions and its growing power in relation to Europe with the emergence of Russian "originality," and he emphasized that the state drew its sustenance from "russkie" rather than "rossiiskie."[39] Ivan Aksakov suggested that any "genuine nationalities policy for Russia" must be based on a recognition that the empire's Slavic (by which he meant Russian) heritage was its true source of vitality.[40] He was suspicious of the emerging discussions about federalism in what was soon to be the Austro-Hungarian Empire after 1867, which would not help the Czechs, for example, who would remain "deprived of their tribal originality [*samobytnost'*]" in the Germanic world.[41]

Strakhov adopted many of Danilevskii's views about the nature of different "cultural-historical types." Thus he was alarmed by John Stuart Mill's focus on culture and character formation in his work on gender differences; instead for Strakhov, like Danilevskii, cultural (and social) differences were the natural outgrowths of the organic process of history itself. Different peoples represented different "cultural-historical types," and they were far from equal in their "spiritual strengths."[42] Within the context of the multi-ethnic empire, conservative thinkers felt the need to emphasize the limits of the "reverse Orientalism" implicit in the rethinking of the Russian past and its relationship to Europe initiated by the Slavophiles. Russia's historic "backwardness" was suddenly a virtue; Chechen or Abkhaz "savagery," however, remained just that.

The question of "world-historical types" and "historical peoples," which in the 1830s and 1840s was self-evidently a debate about the big civilizations of the Hebrews, Latins, Germanic peoples, and so on, needed further clarification in an empire unique for its growth of nationalism more advanced among the periphery peoples (Balts, Ukrainians, Georgians, Armenians) than among the "imperial" people. Uslar's 1881 work on ancient myths about the Caucasus possessed the vocabularly and assumptions of Danilevskii.[43] He explored antiquity in order to come to conclusions about the hierarchy of peoples in the present. Peoples and civilizations were not all the same: "The doctrine of the brotherhood of all peoples is not a doctine about their equality."[44] "Negroes," for example, regardless of their individual accomplishments or level of education, could never "become Europeans"; Huns, Turks, and Mongols had been and would always be "hostile to any human progress," as they were not among the select "historical peoples" chosen to play a leading role on the stage of "universal history."[45] In Uslar's view, the mountain peoples were obviously not "historic peoples," but they did possess a historic antiquity that demanded preservation against the weathering impact of time. But was it obvious to a linguistic specialist on the region that Russia was indeed the "historical" people when Georgia and Armenia possessed literary languages from the fourth and fifth centuries? Eastern languages such as Turkish or Arabic were obviously out of the question as potential alphabets for the transciption of mountain languages, but Uslar and his colleagues were well aware of the fact that the guttural sounds of Georgian made the Georgian script a reasonable candidate. Cyrillic, however, might eventually give small peoples access to the civilization of a "world-historical people."

THE EASTERN QUESTION AT HOME

Militant Pan-Slavism and a belligerent approach to the "Eastern question" was an important expression of conservative thought in international politics, with major implications for the blurring of the boundaries between domestic and foreign policy. If imperial identity was essentially Slavic identity, and if smaller Slavic peoples risked losing their "tribal particularities" if abandoned to the pernicious influence of other civilizations, then the Russian state had much work to do in eastern Europe, the Balkans, and maybe even Constantinople. Ottoman and Muslim influence in the Balkans, for example, according to Aksakov, severed the ability of small peoples such as the Chernogortsy, who according to him faced extinction "to the last person" as a result of "pressure from Asian hordes," to maintain and preserve their links to the past.[46] The Chernogortsy, in his view, were at the forefront of the battle against Islam and the Turks, in a way similar to Cossacks within the empire, "pioneers of Slavic freedom!"[47]

Yet the Chernogortsy, in spite of Russia's negligence and the absence of support from abroad, "remained true to their faith and Slavic narodnost', not once confusing themselves with change."[48] The essence of the "Eastern question" lay in the heroic capability of small Balkan peoples to preserve and maintain their faith and customs over time in the face of the illegitimate cultural threat brought by Ottoman Islam. The role and purpose of imperial rule, simultaneously a civilizing and a Christianizing mission, was to preserve and maintain indigenous mountain tradition in the face of these Ottoman and Muslim threats. Educated society in the Caucasus, as we have discussed, came to similar conclusions about the relationship between tradition and Islam regarding the North Caucasus mountain peoples.

Imperial competition and the limited nature of borderlands integration sustained interest in frontier security. A conservative writer and veteran of the Caucasus such as Rostislav A. Fadeev, described by Edward Thaden as "probably the most important popularizer of social and political realism during the 1860s and 1870s," found his audience by playing on these fears and concerns.[49] Fadeev's experience was similar to that of many other members of imperial obshchestvo in the Caucasus. His father occupied a post in the administration of Viceroy Vorontsov and was later a friend of Bariatinskii. Fadeev secured an appointment as an ensign in the Caucasus Army, served in southern Dagestan in the 1850s, participated in the final campaigns against Shamil, and advanced quickly to the rank of major general by 1864.[50]

In his essays he thought primarily in terms of geopolitics, imperial competition, and conquest. Georgia, he claimed, might have been conquered some three centuries earlier if the will of the tsars had been stronger.[51] The conquest of the North Caucasus meant that there were no natural barriers to the expanse of Russia, which depended "only on the will of Russia itself."[52] Fadeev was keenly aware of European colonialism throughout the globe and of foreign threats to Russian interests in the borderlands. The mountaineer resistance was "our Algeria," he wrote, and Russian enemies in the Caucasus included the Turks, English, and other foreigners, who intended to dominate the region and interfere in Russia's "domestic matters."[53] In Fadeev's view, the destruction of the Adygei was justified because of their strategic location along the Black Sea.[54] He looked to "Cossack settlers," whom he depicted variously as "genuine Russians," "one of the formative forces of our history," and a "means of conquest," to transform the Black Sea shore region into "Russian land."[55] The economic potential of the region might then serve Russia, with the small offshoots of the Black Sea serving the hinterland "like the Nile for Egypt." Fadeev thought primarily of military security and the power of the state.

In spite of his conservatism and glorification of the Russian tradition of conquest in the borderlands, Fadeev used modern means to promote his vision of the empire. He was a publicist, like Zisserman, Berzhe, and numerous other figures who rethought the empire and were determined to educate the emerging Russian public about the significance of colonial expansion. His goal, however, was a different one. He opposed state censorship, notes Thaden, because he wanted to witness the emergence of a public sphere aggressive about questions of expansion and international politics.[56] Fadeev took to the pen to remind Russians about the significance of colonial expansion, the potential of the Russian military, and the importance of a strong state in Russia and the borderlands. Only the Russians and the French in Algeria, he wrote, managed to penetrate to the depths of Asia, "to the depths of barbarian countries."[57] These belligerent writers were primarily interested in glorious traditions of Russian conquest, rather than visions of a multi-ethnic imperial community united by a common set of assumptions about Europe and enlightenment.

MEMOIR AND TRAVEL WRITING

Other genres of Russian writing about the North Caucasus and the Transcaucasus and their history contributed to the conservative turn of the late nineteenth century. The proliferation of memoir literature in glorification of the conquest, though not a regime policy of course, might also be considered as another aspect of this general atmosphere of "Russification."[58] While educated society in the 1850s worked to establish a foundation for imperial rule unrelated to military conquest, numerous Russian writers by 1900 were committed to maintaining the myth of the righteous conquest. The sixty-year-long Caucasus War, wrote the editor of a 1904 collection of essays about the event, "reminds every Russian about the glorious activities of his ancestors."[59] The volume offered not only an introduction to the ethnography, geography, and history of the region, but "most importantly, to those heroic Russian people" who conquered the Caucasus.[60] These numerous "old Caucasian veterans" and their encounter with "strange wild tribes" and "constant danger" might finally get a chance to share their story. In 1830 Lermontov had written that "one can only regret that so little of this is ever put down on paper."[61] By the late nineteenth century, however, his Maxim Maximych had come of age.

There were some very important dissenters from this glorification of conquest, such as Leo Tolstoy. In *Hadji Murat* Tolstoy returned to the topic that had shaped his own youthful experience and criticized the emerging mythology of conquest and colonial benevolence.[62] Although he had participated in the Caucasus War as a young man in the 1850s, he portrayed Hadji Murat as the tenacious and "terribly strong" thistle, stepped upon by Russian rule.[63] Tolstoy became an avid reader of *Sbornik Svedenii o Kavkazskikh Gortsakh* as well as a subscriber to other ethnographic publications from his estate at Yasnaya Polyana.[64] He consulted with Arnol'd Zisserman, who by this time had retired to an estate just twelve kilometres from Yasnaya Polyana.

Tolstoy, on this issue as on many others, offered a minority view, however. Most Russians felt the need to emphasize that the primary identity of the region was as "one of the best decorations of our dear Orthodox mother Rus'."[65] By the turn of the century, chauvinistic works were more popular for many readers throughout the empire, who were accustomed to a long tradition of writing about heroism, conquest, and the savagery of the borderlands. Often left by former participants of the war by then well advanced in years but nostalgic for the adventure of their own youth, memoirs recalled a past that was increasingly irrelevant to the concerns of the present. They contributed to the climate of intolerance in the borderlands in the late nineteenth century.

Arnol'd Zisserman had pursued adventure and travel in the Caucasus in order to contribute to ethnography, to a more effective colonial administration, and to a better-informed public about borderland affairs. By the late nineteenth century, Russian readers were extraordinarily interested in the drama of the exploits of colonial discovery but without the lessons of Zisserman's experience. *Fin-de-siècle* travel writing drew on the tradition of the Romantic fascination with the exotic East but possessed a painfully imperial style, in particular because of the new colonial relationship and situation of the later nineteenth century. For Romantic writers, the savage was also noble, unburdened by the artifice of civilization. Young Zisserman sometimes learned from and admired the Khevsur. Later Russian travel writers such as A. Krasnov complained about inadequate hotel service and transportation, luggage delays, and too much time spent in Sochi among "Turks" and Georgians.[66] There was no longer genuine adventure and danger in the region, only writers who turned out a stale reproduction of the danger associated with the Caucasus War. Mostly they complained about the "natives," as did A.V. Pastukhov, who climbed Mount Ararat in the company of nine Cossacks in 1893.[67] In Romantic fashion, N.Ia. Dinnik pondered his own "powerlessness and insignificance" in the face of glaciers in Terek oblast in 1884 and then enjoyed several stories and anecdotes provided by his "native" guide.[68] Lermontov was a historical icon and guide to later writers, but mountaineers were neither noble nor savage.[69] During Filipov's trip along the Georgian Military Road, his guide explained the significance of the occasional crosses visible from the highway. These were places of death as a result of either crime, accident, or a natural catastrophe. The region again spoke of its dangerous past to the Russian reader. And suddenly, "as if from underground," a group of Ossetian youths appeared alongside the road. Now, however, their presence was more pitiful than threatening: " 'What do they need? – I turn to our coachman. 'They're asking for money.' " Filipov tossed some copper coins out behind him onto the road.[70] The waning of the Romantic vision of historic recovery and restoration in the region had left behind languid and even pitiful "natives" to haunt the colonial imagination of the *fin de siècle*.

COLONIZATION

Imperial policy in the age of Russification coincided with the hostile attitudes common to conservative writers and the producers of travel literature. If mountaineers were "savages" or "ethnographic material" or languid natives who obstructed imperial progress, they might best be replaced by energetic and productive Russian settlers. Imperial policy on the question of colonization evolved in this direction from roughly 1850 to 1900.

For the proponents of conquest during the long Caucasus War, settler colonialism was the logical complement to the exile of the indigenous population. As Grand Duke Mikhail Nikolaevich made plans for the final "cleansing" of the North Caucasus in 1863, he assumed that his work was preparation for the eventual arrival of Russian settlers.[71] But in fact the regime had been surprisingly open-minded in its notions of colonization on the North Caucasus frontier. From the 1830s to the 1850s it encouraged "Little Russian" (Ukrainian) Cossacks, Germans, Greeks, Armenians, and Old Believers and other sectarians from Russia to emigrate to the North Caucasus.[72] For most officials, the ethnic origin of the new immigrants was inconsequential. As late as 1857, important officials such as Bariatinskii still conceived of the North Caucasus as a distant frontier that might even serve the internal provinces of the empire by relieving them of sectarians and as a place welcome to any economically productive person.[73] Other officials, however, were beginning to wonder about the political consequences of potentially unreliable settlers on the frontiers of the empire. The commander of Chernomorsk district raised the "Russian question" to his colleagues in 1868. "Might we not admit the possibility of primarily allowing the Russian element [to immigrate]?"[74] At his initiative the administration tried to advertise the advantages of settlement to the interior provinces of the empire. "With the final conquest of the Caucasus a beautiful and rich country fell into the hands of the government," announced the administration in 1867 to those "wishing to resettle to Chernomorsk district."[75]

The problem was that Russian settlers were not up to the task. After the expulsion of the Adygei, most Russian administrators in the Caucasus were reluctant to allow even Russian peasants to attempt to colonize the northwest Caucasus since they often were unable to navigate the unfamiliar conditions of mountain geography and either died from fever or ended up in need of government care in Tbilisi. Even decades after the conquest, officials were still warning the interior that Russians needed to be of "strong spirit and body" to handle the experience.[76] Instead, administrators in Tbilisi found Armenians, Greeks, Czechs, Moldavians, and Chukhovs more likely to adapt to the cattle-raising, wine-growing, and beekeeping traditions of the northwest Caucasus.[77] They enticed Greeks and Chernogortsy from the Ottoman Empire, who were at least "religiously sympathetic to us," and offered them freedom from military service and an eight-year exemption from taxation.[78] Especially valuable, reported General Murav'ev, were "mountain tribes that professed Christianity," by which he meant people from mountain Imeretia and Guria (Georgia).[79] Officials granted the Georgian migrants from Kutais province 20 rubles per family to purchase provisions for the trip, provided food for the travellers and their livestock along the way, and guided them through Sukhumi, the Gagra fortress, and then on to river valleys in Abkhazia, where they supplied them with food for the first year.[80] The politics of the imperial state inadvertently had a strong hand in encouraging Georgian colonization of Black Sea regions such as Abkhazia.

The tide was turning in favour of strictly Russian colonization, however, especially after the rebellion of 1877 made "loyalty to the government" a critical criterion in the minds of officials.[81] Ivan Zolotarev, an official close to the issue of colonization, complained that Germans maintained their schools and churches and passed on their "Germanness" to subsequent generations.[82] Ministry of Agriculture officials lamented that Armenians and Greeks "preserved their tribal peculiarities" and proved "hostile to all things Russian." They "lived separately" from the Russian population, "not assimilating with it but only exploiting it for their own use."[83]

The imperial state openly declared its preference for the Russians. By the turn of the century only Russian settlers were welcome. On

31 March 1897 for Chernomorsk province and 15 April for the rest of the Caucasus, the government decreed that only "Orthodox settlers of native Russian background" be allowed to immigrate.[84] New settlers generally to the Kuban grew from 30,000 in 1870 to 800,000 by 1900.[85] Borderland settlement was facilitated by a decree of 13 July 1889 that reduced the restrictions of the commune upon peasant mobility and then by the 6 June 1904 decree that permitted the free movement of the subjects of the tsar throughout the empire.[86] In places such as the North Caucasus and Kazakhstan, however, the subjects of choice were by 1897 ethnically Russian.

Officials associated with the problems of settlement stressed that the state needed to discriminate according to ethnic background in the borderlands and offer greater financial support to ethnic Russians over the many other non-Russian immigrants. This policy was "necessary for the strengthening of the Russian element amid the different and not always reliable peoples [narodnosti] in order to raise the prestige of the name of Russia [and] its faith, language, and civilization in the region."[87] The settlement legislation issued in 1901 for the Caucasus was a means for the regime at least to attempt to ensure that reliable and capable Russian families populated available lands. Thus after the departure of the Doukhobors from Kars oblast to North America, a regulated process of settlement allowed administrators of the regime the satisfaction of knowing that in the shuffle the oblast "lost not one Russian person."[88] The borderlands might even serve as a tool of assimilation within the settler community, where "Little Russians" (Ukrainians) would become "Great Russians."[89]

The transformation of imperial policy and sentiment meant an unprecedented preoccupation with ethnicity and Russian identity. For conservative officials in particular, like the conservative thinkers discussed above, Russia was losing ground in an empire of competing peoples. The state was duty bound, in their view, to protect, preserve, and favour Russian tradition and culture. V.G. Butyrkin, a member of an official commission to survey the situation of the Cossacks, was shocked that more recent Russian settlers to the North Caucasus were encroaching upon Cossack lands. How could Russians conflict with their own kind in the borderlands? "Russians are not Jews, living according to the Talmud," he explained, "but brothers by blood and faith."[90] We must prevent "foreigners" (inostrantsy) from engaging in agriculture in Chernomorsk province, warned Aleksei Bereznikov, the provincial governor, in 1909.[91] Who was a "foreigner" along the Black Sea coast in 1909? The empire's southern borders with Ottoman Turkey and Iran had been drawn almost one hundred years earlier in 1828, as a result of Russian military conquest. Butyrkin and Bereznikov drew new kinds of borders, but within the empire. Such distinctions were fraught with peril in the Caucasus, historically recognized by everyone including Russians as a place of inconceivable diversity. The state's open advocacy of Russians in the business of settlement was one of the many fateful and mistaken aspects of Russification.

THE DILEMMA OF RUSSIAN ETHNIC SETTLEMENT

Russification as ethnic Russian settlement disappointed even the Russian officials who formulated and implemented the policy. They were dismayed to discover that Russian settlers in the North Caucasus themselves needed frequent reminders about the values and characteristics of Russian culture and the tasks and duties of colonization. As the Ministry of Agriculture pointed out in 1895, the tasks of the "pacification" and "cleansing" of the former Adygei lands of savage mountaineers had been successfully accomplished by Russian soldiers in the 1860s, but the secondary tasks of settlement and the "reviving" (ozhivlenie) of the Black Sea shore were yet to be realized.[92] Russians fought with Russians, Russians impeded the development of the Cossack settlements, and Russians competed with other immigrant communities often better able to adapt to the new conditions. New settlers to Kuban oblast in particular suffered from landlessness.[93] The different origins of the peasants sometimes led to confusion in the villages. Russians clashed with Ukrainians, peasants from wooded regions with peasants from the steppe. Cattle brought from Russia quickly died in the Caucasus from the climate or from predators, and many of the agricultural implements useful in Russia proved useless in the new situation. Daunted by the mountains, many peasants clung to the foothills and settled on the shores of the Black Sea or on the rivers that fed it, exposing themselves to fever.[94] Frequently one-third to even one-half of the population of many of the new emigrant villages either died or left for other prospects within a few years of their founding.[95] Lands granted at reduced prices to Russian officials and military officers serving in the region, the fate of some of the best Adygei lands, sat unused and unproductive – a real estate investment for Russians uninterested in living so far from Tbilisi.

Russian rule, as Ministry of Agriculture officials painfully admitted, had been a disaster for the agricultural productivity of the Black Sea littoral. When the Adygei ruled themselves, numerous mountain villages were surrounded by rich gardens and fruit orchards, and mountain communities carried on an active trade on the Black Sea. Russian officials hoped that imperial rule might even increase fruit and vegetable produce for export to the capital cities of Russia, decreasing the need to import such things from Constantinople, Algeria, or Egypt.[96] In their haste, ignorance, and lack of respect for their new surroundings, however, early immigrants actually chopped down the trees in order to gather the fruit more easily. Early in the new century some 17,000 Russians and other immigrants were reckoned to be starving or suffering from fever in "that very same region where the mountaineers lived well and developed advanced agriculture [*zanimalis' vysokoiu kul'turoiu*] ... How are we to explain this strange and sad phenomenon?" asked agricultural officials.[97] Given the history of war, the tragic exile of the Adygei, and now the languishing lands of the Black Sea littoral, whose "culture" was more advanced? The commander of Kuban oblast answered the question in 1896 when he suggested that many of the new Russian settlers "in fact belong neither here nor there and have acquired that cut-off character of nomads."[98] Nomadism, of course, traditionally referred to the frontier and its borderland peoples on the margins of true faith and culture.

The influence of Russian culture might even be negative. The early-twentieth-century commander of Terek oblast, General Mikheev, heir to the position of Loris-Melikov, suggested to the tsar in 1909 that the influence of Russian culture itself was one of the many problems which complicated the administration of the oblast, an unusual complaint from a Russian general, oblast commander, and Cossack ataman.[99] Mikheev explained that "half-savage races" were unable to distinguish between the positive and negative sides of more civilized cultures and frequently adopted the less-admirable characteristics during the initial stages of cultural contact. This phenomenon explained why more natives were smoking and frequenting restaurants, and why native women seemed overly interested in fancy boots, beaded jewellery, and other luxuries; "in a word, the requirements of the household have been transformed."[100] Exposure to the world of Russia and greater contact with the institutions and practices of the empire meant that the mountaineers, he said, were "gradually losing all their best old traditions."[101] Russian rule, Mikheev complained, was slowly eroding traditional sources of authority in mountain villages, leaving the mountaineers without the benefit of their traditional sources of cohesion. Village elders were seen by the mountaineers as compromised because of their association with Russian rule and hence lacked authority and the respect of the populace.[102] Traditional culture was a source of stability in a time of difficult social and cultural change.

Russian settlers in the early twentieth century were suspect not only as models of high culture and economic productivity. Old Belief presented an additional dilemma, reminding us that the imperial preoccupation with the maintenance of cultural tradition and authenticity was applied to both Russians and non-Russians. The influence of sectarianism among settler communities suggested to regime officials that institutional reminders of the nature of Orthodoxy were sorely needed. Cossacks, the Terek oblast commander warned in 1890, in particular were in need of greater access to the rituals and literature of Orthodoxy. The presence of Old Belief threatened to erode the primary source of stability for the regime in the precarious mountain regions of the North Caucasus. In 1890, 6,621 new members of different sectarian groups moved into Terek oblast alone. Kizliar otdel contained 20,407 Old Believers in that year. The Terek oblast commander suggested that sectarian proselytizing be made illegal in Cossack settlements, that funds for Orthodox religious education be increased for the Cossacks, and that special lists of sectarians be compiled in order to identify and counter their activities. "Religious-moral education," he warned, was crucial to containing the spread of such deviance.[103] Russian peasant settlers in the borderlands also faced the risk of religious and cultural "apostasy."

Missionaries, in particular, but officials generally also blamed Old Believers for providing an inadequate religious example to non-Russians populations and hence contributing to the expansion of Islam. In the Middle Volga, Nikolai Il'minskii partially attributed the return of many "baptized Tatars" to Islam to this failing on the part of Orthodox settlers.[104] In the Caucasus the difficulties and trials of settlement, the many threats posed by the mountaineers, and the unfamiliar climate and geography of the region, Governor-General Golitsyn informed the Ministry of the Interior in 1901, left new Russian settlers particularly in need of reminders of their Russian past. Small and temporary prayer houses were not enough, he argued; they were unable to provide the "moral strength" offered by a vast and well-built cathedral.[105] Immigrants needed symbolic reminders of the importance of Orthodoxy as well as religious support in the face of the temptation presented by the many sectarians who were populating the North Caucasus. Golitsyn wanted greater attention from the government and the Holy Synod to the construction and maintenance of Orthodox churches in newly settled villages. Of fifty-four new immigrant villages in the Caucasus in 1902, only six had churches, while five possessed temporary prayer houses. Thirty-year waits for the construction of churches, he wrote to Pobedonostsev, left Russian peasants in the "obscurity of religious ignorance and moral wildness [*odichanie*] and exposed to the harmful influence of those of other faiths and sectarians."[106] Russian peasants, in the eyes of officialdom apparently close to being "savages" themselves, were especially in need of guidance on the distant frontier.

Golitsyn's successor, Viceroy Vorontsov-Dashkov, continued to bring attention to this issue and even feared that new immigrants might adopt the "religious views and mistakes" of their non-Russian and non-Orthodox neighbours.[107] Potential conversion to Islam stood at the end of this path of cultural betrayal. Settlement villages grew rapidly in the early twentieth century, from the 54 in 1902 (as noted above) to 288 by 1910, containing a population of more than 62,000.[108] Funding for church construction from the Ministry of Finance, the Holy Synod, or other ministries of the government could not keep up with this remarkable growth. Pobedonostsev allocated 10,000 rubles per year for church construction in the new settlements, and this fig-ure was increased to 20,000 per year in 1906.[109] Such an amount could support only a handful of churches, prayer houses, and combination school–prayer houses, however, and Viceroy Vorontsov-Dashkov pushed the Holy Synod to increase the yearly allocation to 60,000.[110] His request was rejected in 1913.[111] A State Duma law of 3 December that year allocated a mammoth increase in such support, from 20,000 rubles yearly to 341,500 rubles, and authorities even planned to in-crease this sum to 550,000 in 1914, 725,000 in 1915, and 900,000 in 1916.[112] Such measures were not forthcoming because of the demands of the First World War, and in retrospect they appear as a somewhat desperate means of attempting to influence the future of the Caucasus.

This version of Orthodox missionary work, tied to the question of increased ethnic settlement, evoked medieval Rus' in conflict with hostile Muslims on its many frontiers. The Russian community in Vedeno and its concerned supporters resorted to military imagery in their requests for the construction of an Orthodox church.[113] After many appeals to different Russian institutions and officials, the Russian inhabitants of Vedeno wrote directly to Grand Princess Elisaveta Fedorovna in 1915. They supported their request with refer-ences to the price that Russia had already paid for securing Vedeno – the "Russian blood" that had flowed in its capture; the many battles which "brought to their graves thousands of Russian warriors" – and by emphasizing the paucity and isolation of Russians in Vedeno dis-trict and hence the significance of a strong or increased cultural pres-ence of the Russian state and Russian culture.[114] "Living among the Chechen Muslims, in villages with beautifully painted mosques, we Russians, Orthodox people, cut off by a large distance from the Russian population, are embarassed in front of the Chechens by our squalid [*ubogii*] Christian church."[115] They could no longer bear, the Russians of Vedeno pleaded, the mockery and ridicule of their Chechen neighbours.[116] Military officials supported the aspirations of the Russian villagers of Vedeno as a stern reminder to the Chechens that Russian rule was "unshakable" in Chechnia, and other officials agreed that the matter was of great symbolic significance.[117] Increased funding was a necessity, argued a church official in Vladikavkaz, since Vedeno was located in the "very centre of Chechnia and was surrounded on all sides by those of other tribes and faiths [*inorodnye* and *inovercheskie*]."[118] This was the historical language of conquest in the borderlands. Officials visualized mountain peoples as aliens, only capable of understanding a show of force and strength from the Russians.

The policies and attitudes of Russification partially drew on the continuing administrative drive to extend the virtues of the "well-ordered police state" to the borderlands. By the turn of the century this effort brought the state into conflict with the sundry practices of the borderlands and an increasingly vocal nationalism from especially the Georgians which was also partially a product of the impact of the Russian state. Russification drew on the heritage of conquest in the region, in keeping with the new climate of fear and phobia that inspired ethnic nationalism throughout Europe. This aspect of Russification was a conservative return to the traditional symbols and themes of tsar, church, army, and imperial competition discussed in chapter 2, complemented by a preference for ethnic Russian settlement. Conservative thought contributed to this climate of hostility and fear, and justified the increasing tendency of officials to identify the imperial state explicitly with Russia and the Russians. Russification as ethnic Russian settlement and a belligerent glorification of conquest was obviously a far cry from the efforts of imperial educated society to visualize a multi-ethnic imperial community committed to a common civilizing endeavour on the frontier.

Conclusion: Empire
and Nativism in
the Russian Caucasus

And indeed, were not [the interests of Russia and Georgia] one
and the same? Those were the years of the terrible battle with
Shamil, and all Georgians, with just a few exceptions, considered
it their duty to bring about a Russian victory.

Akaki Tsereteli, 1894–1909[1]

"God forbid," wrote Nikolai Raevskii to Minister of War Chernyshev
in 1841, "that the conquest of the Caucasus might leave a similar
bloody legacy to Russian history, such as that left by [Pizarro and
Cortés] to the history of Spain."[2] In such criticism of Russia's violent
and coercive relationship toward the North Caucasus, Raevskii and
other officials took their cue from literary figures such as Aleksandr
Pushkin. The lives of the two individuals indeed intersected.
Pushkin's trip with the Raevskii family through the Caucasus and
Crimea in the spring and summer of 1820 served as the inspiration
for *Prisoner of the Caucasus*. Pushkin became close to Nikolai and once
served in St Petersburg with his brother, Aleksandr Raevskii. The two
Raevskii daughters, Ekaterina Nikolaevna and Mariia Nikolaevna,
married the Decembrists M.O. Orlov and S.G. Volkonskii.[3] On the
southern frontier the rethinking of the tradition of Russian autocracy
went hand in hand with the posing of new questions about the heritage and purpose of empire.

Yet both Pushkin and Raevskii belonged to their time. Even as they
explored the possibilities of primitive nobility, Romantic writers
viewed conquest and the civilizing process as an inevitable part of
the inevitable expansion of the Russian Empire. Even Joseph Conrad,
as Said points out, was unable to imagine an alternative to European
rule over the Congo. Raevskii remained a strong advocate of Russian
expansion and was eventually enamoured of the Pan-Slavs and
General Cherniaev. Conquest, however, was not simply war and coercive exile; it was to have a well-defined purpose and mission. This

study has explored a series of related stories about the identity of the mountain peoples and the purpose and mission of Russian imperial rule. These discussions emerged as a reaction to Russia's long history of destructive conquest on the early modern steppe, as well as the very recent reminder of this heritage in the massive exile of many mountaineers that accompanied the conclusion to the Caucasus War. Frontier lands were historically inhabited by "evil" and "godless" infidels, or they were places without people, "empty lands" where "till now no fields have been ploughed, no homesteads have stood, and no tax has arrived to the tsar's treasury," as Ivan the Terrible's 1558 charter suggested to Grigorii Stroganov.[4] The population transfers from the North Caucasus again left "empty land," as an 1860 imperial decree put it, now to be used to reward the military service of loyal Georgian princes in the course of the Caucasus War.[5] The modern and enlightened empire was to be based on something other than the historic "gathering of the lands" of the Muscovite tsar, army, and church.[6] Borderland communities such as educated society in the Caucasus were the important voices that shaped the new consciousness of empire which emerged in Russia from the middle nineteenth century.

The makers of this empire were not only Russians, and even the Russians were not so much "Russian" as they were members of imperial educated society, with names like Berzhe, Uslar, Zisserman, and Radde. These "Europeans" served in numerous frontier locations of the Russian Empire, the heirs of the transformative project of Westernization and Enlightened rule initiated by the eighteenth-century state. "I would not have guessed in 1700," wrote Voltaire to Catherine II, "that Reason, one day would come to Moscow, at the voice of a princess born in Germany, and that she would assemble in a great hall idolaters, Moslems, Greeks, Latins, Lutherans, who would all become her children."[7] Imperial expansion was no longer to be associated with the establishment of fortresses with imposing names such as Groznyi ("menacing" or "terrifying"), but with the establishment of outposts of European culture on the borders of Asia. The borderland communities understood Russia to be the cultural conduit from Europe to the Russian frontier, in which the presence of a transformative Russia might help to chart the path from savagery to civil society. "Orientalism," or the extended scholarly preoccupation with the empire and its diverse peoples, emerged as a product of this nexus of Europeanization, reform, and expansion.

Native peoples from the Caucasus contributed to the formation of the empire. The multi-ethnic service elite of privilege and status was well prepared to contribute to the discourse of empire as well. A

Russian-language newspaper such as *Kavkaz* and its obschestvo of readers sometimes directly appealed to a Georgian-language newspaper such as *Droeba* and its community of sazogadoeba. "It is good and useful when our genuinely intelligent and interesting (societies) join forces," affirmed the editorial staff of *Droeba* in 1870.[8] The possibilities of cooperation especially concerned matters of education, learning, and institutions of high culture such as theatres and libraries. Georgian educated society identified civilizing projects of uplift that were similar to the concerns of educated society throughout the empire.[9] The shared concerns among Russians and Georgians about civilization and culture found especially fertile soil in the North Caucasus highland regions, long famous for their remoteness and distance from civilized society. Georgians not only served in the imperial administration but proved to be important contributors to imperial discussions about Christian antiquity, customary law, Shamil, Islam, and other topics that especially pertained to the North Caucasus.

The idea of "Europe" was a powerful notion affecting not just Russians on the frontier but also Georgians and many other smaller peoples in the Caucasus. Even the children of Shamil were to be incorporated into not just this world of privilege but also a world united by their common assumptions about Enlightenment and the prospect of progress in Russia and the transformation of its backward frontier in particular.[10] Mikhail Shervashidze, the Abkhaz ruler-administrator, was deeply sensitive to the hierarchy of civilization that separated Europeans from Russians, Russians from Georgians, Georgians from Abkhaz, and even Abkhaz from Adygei. "[I]n his words, he had been driven out of Abkhazia like some sort of Ubykh," he complained.[11] Russians were proud of the assimilation of "Enlightenment" on the part of the Georgian nobility, evident, for example, in their attendance at the new Tiflis Theatre, and Georgians in turn felt this distinguished them from their frontier peoples. "Try to imagine what sort of life is here," complained a Georgian teacher in Abkhazia in 1872. "Where is polite society? Where is the theatre?"[12] The Tiflis Theatre established by Vorontsov symbolized Russia's benevolent extension of the fruits of the Enlightenment to its southern frontier and offered a location where the cohesive and integrative role of Enlightenment (i.e., "imperial") culture might contribute to the work of empire-building. In 1869 Loris-Melikov, the Armenian commander of Terek oblast, established a theatre in Vladikavkaz.[13] "[A]lready hundreds of us, thanks to the government, have joined the ranks of obshchestvo," claimed Adygei Khan-Girei already in 1846.[14] Like Europe, obshchestvo too was an idea, with integrative and cohesive possibilities in the multi-ethnic borderlands.

Georgia's relationship to Islam and the East was an outgrowth of its relationship to the idea of a Europe that included Russia. Its historic location on one of the fault lines of Christianity and Islam (but a frontier vastly under-researched compared to the Balkans or Spain) obviously produced a ready reservoir of hostility toward the Islamic empires and their faith, most often remembered in frightening references to the sack of Tbilisi in 1795 by the Persians. Mountain peoples were similarly menacing, threatening faith, family, high culture, and everything Georgian, as the extraordinary literary reproduction of the Chavchavadze episode illustrated.[15] Russians, Georgians, and imperial educated society generally were quick to portray the influence of Islam in the North Caucasus as something that obstructed social development from primitive to civil life, tragically distorted gender relations within the family, destroyed authentic legal tradition, inhibited the reorientation of Shamil and his family toward Russia, and offered only "savagery" and "fanaticism" in place of enlightened civilization. This familiar form of "Orientalism" flourished in the Russian Empire.

The unique Russian imperial context, however, produced a specific form of Orientalism that shaped the evolution of the empire and even contributed to the formation of the eventual Soviet state. The Romantic preoccupation with narodnost', "originality," and authentic historic custom that influenced the climate of imperial educated society especially shaped imperial discourse on the eastern borderlands. Islam posed the question of "apostasy," in this case a "falling away" not just from the correct faith but from correct custom and the past itself. Georgians, Russians, and many others portrayed Islam as an impediment to the preservation and cultivation of tradition. Cataloguing customs, the ethnographic impulse that flourished throughout the empire, was an act of "correct faith," a means to counter the "heresy" of foreign borrowing and imitation. Disciplines such as ethnography and geography in Russia emerged from the unique context of imperial competition among Christian and Islamic states. Georgians were especially interested in the "rescue" of a "literature of the people" under threat not just from the corrosive influence of time but also from external threats – indeed, "ferocious enemies."[16] Georgians valorized their own mountain peoples such as the Khevsur, whose history they portrayed as a story of beleaguered but preserved Georgian custom and culture under threat from the vicious Kistebi (Chechens).[17] The Georgian experience on the frontier of Islam shaped the imperial purpose and mission in the North Caucasus.

The visualization of empire thus emerged as a product of multiple influences and contexts. The frontier itself was most important. Local borderland perceptions of the historic clash between Christianity and Islam were the most important context that produced the discourse on empire. Russia's Orientalism was never simply a product of official discourse and historiography in St Petersburg. On the other hand, the general cultural dilemmas familiar to historians of Russia proper were also significant in the borderlands. The interests of conservative thinkers in uniquely Russian traditions resonated among officials on the frontier accustomed to thinking about Russia's role in the world and its relationship to other civilizations. Russia's famous dilemmas regarding the West were also especially acute on the frontier, and even shared by non-Russian peoples such as the Georgians. The rethinking of empire in the wake of the destructive conquest drew on Russia's Romantic exploration of its own special spirit, language, history, and potential contribution to world civilization. The purpose of empire was to extend this vision of progress to backward borderland peoples and to foster and encourage true and authentic culture liberated from the influence of Islam and the general "savagery" of the past.

Such was the self-professed project of numerous ethnographers, travellers, geographers, and statisticians of diverse ethnic backgrounds on the imperial frontier. Linguists such as Petr Uslar emphasized that mountain languages were in no way inferior to the languages of Europe and were capable of expressing ideas of complexity and beauty. He and other linguists, supported by the Geographic Society and other branches of the administration in the Caucasus, worked to transcribe mountaineer languages into a script based on Cyrillic. The regime introduced readers in these mountain languages into primary schools that it founded for the mountaineers and encouraged educated mountaineers to work as teachers, serve in the Russian bureaucracy, and even contribute essays to journals and ethnographic publications. In such essays, educated mountaineers usually attested to the importance of education and literacy and to Russia's role in allowing the mountaineers access to the world of "culture." Uslar visualized a "renaissance" for the mountain peoples, in the tradition of medieval Europe's cultural awakening and rediscovery of antiquity in the early modern era.[18] Ethnographers ventured into mountaineer villages to record the cultural traditions of the mountain peoples (narody), and the regime even established territorial units for the mountaineers based on what they took to be these cultural identities.

Historic "custom," in this imperial view, was the key to mountain identities in the present. The regime would preserve custom and thus foster, in the tradition of Herderean Romanticism, the cultural

development of the mountain peoples. The special courts established by the colonial regime in the moutain regions were primarily
based on the adat, or customary law, instead of the shari'a, or
Muslim law. To a certain extent this practice was politically self-
serving, of course, since the regime intended to counter the influence
of Islam and the mullas, the Muslim religious leaders. But it was far
more than politically manipulative and was an important component of this set of ideas about Russia's relationship to the historic
customs and traditions of the non-Russians. As in Russia, where customary law was portrayed as an attribute of a unique folk culture
passed on through the generations, Russian ethnographers and
other students of mountain customary law believed that they offered
insight into the history of the mountain narody. The regime could
codify the customs of the non-Russians and hence contribute to the
recovery of "indigenous" history. Like customary law, identity endured through the centuries, and the contribution of Russian ethnographers was to clarify its authentic character. Fyodor
Dostoevsky's discovery of his "Russian" heart, which accompanied
the "regeneration of [his] convictions" after his return from prison
exile in the 1850s, coincided with the general interest from the different elements of educated opinion in the moral and spiritual values
and way of life of the Russian peasant.[19] The expansion of the
Russian state meant the extension to the borderlands of the interests
and assumptions of Russian educated society about the importance
of peasant custom and its relationship to identity.

Russification in the borderlands was a product of more assertive
yet frightened imperial administrators in the last decades of the tsarist era. With renewed efforts, officials worked to achieve administrative uniformity and end the diverse and heterogeneous practices of
the frontier. Non-Russians were not necessarily to "become Russian"
(obrusenie), but borderland institutions, schools, regulations, and directives ideally were to correspond to practices at the centre. The
push for administrative conformity was accompanied by the increasingly hostile climate of competitive nationalism and imperialism that
also shaped European culture of the fin de siècle. Major thinkers in the
big cities of Russia were explicit about the relationship of small peoples ("ethnographic material") to the Russians (the "great people"),
as Danilevsky and Dostoevsky wrote. Some borderland officials in-
stinctively welcomed these warnings about the dangers of other
"alien spirits" and instead preferred Russia's historic identity of tsar,
church, and army. Alexander III liked to travel to borderland out-
posts such as Vladikavkaz to query Ossetians about their knowledge
of the Russian language and to hear the Ossetian Girls' School sing

"God Save the Tsar."[20] Russian readers lost interest in criticism of the militaristic imperial conquest and instead wanted to learn about "the glorious activities of [their] ancestors."[21]

In a frustrating search for stability, officials explicitly identified the interests of the state with Russian colonists in the borderlands. In ways similar to German efforts in the Polish lands of the eastern marches, the Russian regime adopted settlement laws in 1896 and 1897 which declared that only "Orthodox settlers of native Russian background" would be allowed to immigrate.[22] General Sheremetev applauded the results of ethnic colonization and enthusiastically claimed that certain regions of the North Caucasus were now little different from many "native parts of the empire."[23] Loris-Melikov, the consummate imperial administrator from the region and veteran of tough Terek oblast who had repeatedly doused fires as part of numerous "special commissions," was now suspect in the eyes of the right, who considered him unlikely to understand that the imperial state in fact belonged to Orthodox Russians.[24] This was not a promising development in a society where Russians composed only 44.3 percent of the population according to the 1897 census, and only 2.3 per cent of an oblast such as Dagestan.[25] Russification recalled the disturbing history of conquest that had historically served as the foil for the Orientalists and visionaries of imperial community. Richard Wortman portrays the new "national myth," which he dates from 1881, as a frustrated response from the ruling house and its court to the failures of the previous "European myth" to contain the emerging world of modern political contestation.[26] Georgians too were victims of this new trend, and could no longer so easily contribute as they once had to the shared discourse on empire.

Multi-ethnic educated society in the borderlands visualized an "imagined community" of the empire rather than the nation, although "Orientalism" in the Caucasus, as we have seen, suggested a process of nativistic culture-building that might be viewed as proto-nationalism.[27] Georgians in particular were adept at placing archaeological exploration, the study of history, and new cultural institutions at the service of a project of national recovery. Because of the perceived threat of Islam, nativism was easily compatible with empire. With the support of the regime, Georgians encouraged Georgian theatre, Georgian history writing, and the "homeland's tongue," and their example was important for the rest of the region.[28] In his work on Dagestan, Abdulla Omarov wrote for those inspired by "patriotic and national feelings."[29] Uslar considered the primary virtue of empire to be the granting of the gift of literacy to the mountaineers, as the Russians had once received it from Cyril and Methodius in the tenth century, or the Armenians from

St Mesrob Mashtots in the fifth century. Greek (Byzantine) missionaries in the early centuries after Christ had failed to encourage literacy in the native languages of the Caucasus, and hence had failed to respect, Uslar emphasized, the important issue of "national independence."[30] In a secular fashion he envisioned local expressions of culture as a mark of progress and a sign of the benevolent and modern character of imperial Russian rule. Missionaries, by contrast, like Il'minskii in the Middle Volga and Central Asia, viewed the use of local languages as a more effective means to provide access to the Christian message. Whatever the motivation, the imperial regime was quite serious about its promotion of native language literacy among the "small peoples" of the frontier, an interesting contrast to its restrictive policies in the western borderlands. And Georgian officials participated in the promotion of literacy and education for frontier peoples such as the Abkhaz and Ossetians who in the past decade have sought greater autonomy from Georgia. The "national question," however, remained on the distant horizon. Educated society in the borderlands throughout the nineteenth century was thinking through the problem of empire, and the question of cultural "originality" was compatible with – indeed, fostered by – imperial rule. Most Russians and non-Russians, especially before 1905, were primarily interested in a nativistic cultivation of custom and tradition, rather than political statehood and independence.

Reformist visionaries of empire were proud of Russia's leading and guiding role within the empire. And obviously, the many small peoples of the empire were not "nationalities." They did not possess the extended histories of statehood, military conquest, and written national literary and administrative languages that excluded even many European peoples from consideration for this status.[31] Imperial educated society on the Caucasus frontier in its own way drew on Russia's encounter with the West and its location between West and East to imagine a multi-ethnic imperial community. This imagined community was invariably a product of the concerns of the educated, of course, as was common in such encounters throughout the globe. "What is denied is the existence of a human substance truly other," suggests Tzvetan Todorov of the attitudes of Columbus toward the Natives of the Americas, "something capable of being not merely an imperfect state of oneself."[32] If Russians once emerged from the closed and limited life of the family to develop "civic connections" in public, as the historian Nikolai Karamzin wrote, so too might the Abkhaz.[33] The captive Shamil and his large extended family might cultivate new attitudes and interests in their new home of Kaluga. The Chechens might have been without a nobility, but nonetheless officials would locate "people who by virtue of their position should naturally exercise the rights of this estate."[34] Russian villages and administrative traditions in Saratov province might transform "savages" from Dagestan into peaceful and productive subjects of the empire. Theatre might flourish in Tbilisi, accompanied by the emergence of a "Georgian Molière." Mountain peoples might learn to cultivate their "native soil" and, with imperial guidance, develop their true and indigenous sources of identity, such as Orthodoxy, narodnost', and customary legal traditions. Georgians and other non-Russians were regular contributors to these notions of imperial identity. This vision of Russia in the borderlands as the preserver and restorer of true culture and tradition was a "Russian" (rossiiskii) contribution to the history of European Orientalism. While the varied aspects of the vision signified at the time the virtues of empire rather than the emergence of the nation, it is obvious that the workings of the imperial era contributed to the transformation of identity in the twentieth century and to the formation of the Soviet ethno-territorial state.

When North Caucasus scholars began to cultivate local ethnic identities after the revolution, they drew on the work of imperial linguists and ethnographers. The Abkhaz language, for example, was modified by Abkhaz philologists but remained based on the Bzyb dialect chosen by Uslar in the nineteenth century.[35] Ethnographers and museum collectors generally obtained their cultural artifacts themselves from pre-revolutionary collections. The founders of the Regional Museum of the North Caucasus Peoples in Rostov-na-Donu in 1926 journeyed to St Petersburg to acquire artifacts that would allow them to realize their goal of enabling every mountaineer to enter the museum and find his own "corner, depicting the life of his people along with the peoples [narodnosti] of other oblasts."[36] The purpose of the 1909 exhibit sponsored by the Museum of Ethnography and Anthropology, constructed with the support of the Caucasus Museum in Tbilisi, was identical. New institutes formed in the wake of revolutionary change were dedicated to the study of the "languages, way of life, and antiquities" of the Caucasus peoples. The multi-ethnic group of scholars (nine Georgians, four Armenians, four Russians, and one Ossetian) active at the Caucasus Historical Archaeological Institute drew on the work of imperial institutions and their scholarly predecessors from the earlier era.[37] The Terek Oblast Museum, which had been founded in 1893 in Vladikavkaz and which had survived the civil war, was maintained by the new Soviet North Caucasus Institute of Regional Studies.[38] Revolutionary change meant a return with renewed vigour to the questions of multi-ethnic community and identity. Nativistic culture-building again proved to be an important aspect of the vision of progressive officials and members of Soviet educated society, whose new community was no longer an "empire" but a "union."

Afterword: Visualizing the Multi-ethnic Community in the Soviet Union

We must write our own literature and show our faces
[to the world].

Paranuk Karim (Adygei), 1928

The era of transformation and modernity promised by the Russian Revolution in imperial context meant a repudiation of "Russification" coupled with an appreciation of "progressive" imperial officials and their policies, which in the Soviet view at least offered a form of benevolent colonialism in the borderlands. The process began in the summer of 1917, when officials of the Provisional Government began to look into the possibility of establishing congruence between the region's "ethnic composition" and its administrative borders.[1] Soviet officials granted administrative and territorial legitimacy to the mountain peoples and used ethnic criteria to establish the "autonomous regions," or what were often referred to as the eight separate "national regions" (*natsional'nye oblasti*) of the North Caucasus.[2] New officials such as Anastas Mikoian, Armenian and close to the centre of authority like Loris-Melikov, explicitly contrasted their work to that of oppressive "Russian tsarist bureaucrats" of the past.[3]

In conception and practice, the continuities with the imperial era were greater than the contrasts, however. In "nationalities" studies, as in other areas of cultural history, the revolution can no longer be viewed as "some sort of big bang."[4] As in the nineteenth century, the new regime battled illiteracy, the lack of roads that prevented a greater cultural penetration of mountain communities, the abundance of festivals that reduced economic productivity, or simply the "remnants of savagery."[5] The new Soviet officials understood not only the shari'a but also the adat as obstacles to progress, and they declared both traditions illegal in 1927.[6] They first Latinized and then

Cyrillicized alphabets, built schools to replace the Muslim medresses and mektebs, and attempted to foster the growth of a new "native" intelligentsia.[7] "It's as if the mountaineer peoples were beginning their history anew," wrote the editors of a new journal, founded in 1928, *Revolution and the Mountaineer*.[8]

The ultimate sign of progress and contrast to the imperial past, in the Soviet view, was the genuine flowering of the native traditions of the region. Theatrical productions, newspapers, and literature in the native languages of the Caucasus were important instruments for the realization of the Soviet conception of progress in the region, as Stalin himself affirmed on many occasions.[9] "We must write our own litera-ture," explained a teacher of the Adygei language, Paranuk Karim, to ethnographer A.M. Ladyzhenskii, "and show our faces [to the world]."[10] The first Chechen newspaper was established in 1925.[11] The new regime sponsored cultural festivals and informational meet-ings about mountain cultures, and chastised the educated public for failing to appreciate sufficiently the unique cultures of the North Caucasus.[12] Drawing upon the experience of Uslar, close to 40 per cent of the schools in the North Caucasus by the late 1920s possessed teachers who knew and taught in the local language.[13]

Again as in the nineteenth century, Islam to administrators posed the spectre of illegitimacy, an alien tradition divorced from the genu-ine folk traditions of the region. In spite of the reduction in Muslim schools and mosques, the brotherhoods of Sufi Islam possessed a re-markable ability to retreat "underground" and continue their activi-ties, which for many of them even included armed opposition to the regime.[14] Rumours about the return of Kunta Haji's, the Kumyk who had introduced the Sufi Qadiriya order to the North Caucasus in the 1850s and who was prominent in the rebellion of 1877, persisted into the 1930s in spite of the fact that he had died in the late nineteenth century.[15] Like its imperial predecessor, the Soviet regime worried about the continuing popularity of the holy places and preachers of Sufi Islam.[16] Drawing upon the experience of the tsars, the Soviet rul-ers maintained Muslim Ecclesiastical Administrations to administer the profession of the faith. No longer interested in the "restoration" of a presumed Christian past to the North Caucasus, and even more fearful of any independent form of religious, social, or political ex-pression, the new regime extended the reach of the ecclesiastical administration to the North Caucasus. The four Muslim Ecclesiastical Administrations (Musul'manskie Dukhovnye Upravleniia) were or-ganized in 1942, based in Tashkent, Ufa, Makhachkala, and Baku.[17] Throughout the Soviet era, state and party officials worried about the activities of "unregistered cult members" in places such as Dagestan, carefully appointed the most important figures in the Muslim religious hierarchy, and limited and regulated the hajj, or pilgrimage to Mecca, among Muslim believers from the borderlands.[18]

While discouraging and restricting Islamic expression, officials of the mature Soviet state simultaneously and constantly emphasized their support for the nativistic practices of cultural nation-building. The Western example of Wilsonian self-determination in the wake of the Treaty of Versailles was an important source of inspiration, but more significant were the terms of debate and ideas about cultural authenticity and identity familiar to Soviet officials from the pre-revolutionary discourse on empire. The "rooting" of peoples accompanied the closing of mosques. Soviet scholars explained that the hierarchy of cultural development progressed from "tribe" to "narodnost'" to "nation" (natsional'nost'). Though some narodnosti were closer to becoming a nation than others, all of them possessed the potential for such development, in particular as a result of the progressive policies of Soviet rule.[19] Economic development was judged to be crucial to this process, as well as "self-awareness of ethnic background," which grew as a result of Soviet rule.[20] Always but usually incorrectly distinguishing themselves from their imperial predecessors, Soviet officials were proud to exhibit "the extent to which the former borderlands of tsarist Russia had ... in the course of one generation finished with backwardness, poverty, disease, and ignorance," as they declared at an international exhibit held in Moscow in 1967.[21] The Soviet exhibit showcased a "Pavilion of the Soviet Republics."

By the 1960s and 1970s Soviet scholars were proud to note what they called the "consolidation of peoples" stimulated by the revolution and Soviet rule. In place of pre-revolutionary "ethnic fragmentation," and in contrast to the course of national development in the West, they believed that Soviet rule had resulted in the formation of "socialist peoples" (narodnosti), a prelude to the formation of "socialist nations" and then the eventual "fusing of nations" (sliianie natsii), which meant the disappearance of nations within the international community of "Soviet people" (Sovetskii narod).[22] Khadzhi-Murat Salmanov, for example, heralded the "new self-conception of 'Dagestani,'" which united the more than thirty ethnically different and isolated groups of pre-revolutionary Dagestan.[23] N.G. Volkova, a Soviet historian of the North Caucasus peoples, emphasized that an oppressive Ottoman Turkish nationalities policy in the nineteenth century had resulted in a loss of the "national distinctiveness" (samobytnost') of many of the North Caucasus peoples who emigrated from the Russian Empire.[24] In the Soviet Union, by contrast, she implied, samobytnost' endured and flourished. Nativistic culture-building preceded and allowed for an eventual contribution to "universal" Soviet culture.

The ambiguities and contradictions of imperial policy continued through the Soviet era, as repression and exile were combined with the promotion of non-Russian cultures and literatures. In the tradition of Berzhe, Uslar, Bakradze, and many others who had rethought the character and purpose of the Russian Empire, Soviet officials promoted "nativization" (korenizatsiia) and took measures to facilitate the increased cultural expression of the peoples of the North Caucasus. Opportunity, advancement, and cultural growth, however, uneasily coexisted with the tradition of conquest and the tragedy of exile.[25] Stalin was simultaneously capable of drawing on several traditions from the history of the empire on the southern frontier. The tradition of conquest and exile in the southeastern borderlands also cast its shadow over the Soviet era. In 1943–44, 397,966 Chechens and Ingush, 32,248 Balkars, and 60,656 Karachais were deported, the Chechen-Ingush ASSR was abolished, the Karachai autonomous province was also abolished (resulting in an enormous gain of territory for the republic of Georgia), and the Kabardino-Balkar ASSR was relieved of the Balkars and became the Kabard ASSR.[26] The Meskhetians of southern Georgia, strongly influenced by Islam and Turkish culture, were also sent to Central Asia.[27] Over 2,000 Georgians were settled in what was previously Karachai territory, now called the Klukhori district of the Georgian Republic.[28]

The 1944 exile reports testify not to the vision of imperial community but to the heritage of conquest and exile, the very tradition that Raevskii feared would leave a "bloody legacy" to Russian history. The reports from the NKVD (secret police responsible for internal security) might have been produced by angry officers in the Caucasus Army at the time of the Caucasus War. Officials implicated entire peoples in their version of a betrayal of "poddanstvo," with the dreaded foreign influence now posed by Germans and Turks. "Terrorist groups," "bandits," and "hostile elements" haunted the Soviet imagination on the frontier.[29] Georgian and Kabard officials sometimes offered their special "knowledge of the customs and habits" of the North Caucasus peoples to the NKVD.[30] Soviet practice and the ferocious twentieth century were obviously the immediate context to the 1944 exile. Lavrenti Beria (from Mingrelia), for example, made explicit references in a July 1944 letter to Molotov to the regime's previous experience with the deportation of the kulaks.[31] But the impact of the imperial background was just as significant. In actions similar to the events of 1864, roughly 600,000 mountaineers were driven to an early death or, at best, a precarious existence in a foreign land.

Approximately 25 per cent of them died within just four years.[32] Orthodox Georgia benefited from the incident, and the exiled mountaineers were all Muslims, sent to their fate by a Russified Georgian who had attended the Tiflis Orthodox Seminary as a young man. The maverick Bolshevik rulers from Moscow contributed to the traditional ambiguities of empire on Russia's southern frontier.

Notes

PREFACE

1 Aleksandr Kondrashov, "S kem voiuiut nashi soldaty?" *Argumenty i Fakty* 5, no. 1006 (February 2000): 5.
2 Nino Chekhoshvili, "Zdes' khoteli zhit'," *Kavkazskii Aktsent*, no. 10 (1–15 May 2000): 4.
3 Islam Saidaev, "Vinovaty li Chechentsy v tom, chto vynuzhdeny zashchish-chat' svoiu zhizn'," *Chechenskaia Pravda* 3, no. 3 (February 2000): 11. See also Alf Grannes, " 'Persons of Caucasian Nationality' – Russian Negative Stereo-types," in Høiris and Yürükel, *Contrasts and Solutions in the Caucasus*, 18–33.
4 Yekaterina Grigoryeva, "No Talks with Aslan Maskhadov," *Moscow News*, no. 16 (26 April–2 May 2000): 2.
5 Cited in Lars Funch, "Cultural Boundaries and Identity Building in the North Caucasus," in Høiris and Yürükel, *Contrasts and Solutions in the Caucasus*, 108–9.

CHAPTER ONE

1 GVIARF, f. VUA, op. 1, 1841–42, d. 6440, Delo "Po raportu Raevskago," Report from Raevskii to Chernyshev, 15 March 1841, l. 2.
2 SSSA, f. 433, op. 1, 1872–73, d. 19, Delo "Sochinenie uchitelei shkoly Obshchestva za 1872 god," Report, 1872, l. 4.
3 Ibid., l. 5.
4 Ibid., l. 6.
5 On the literary construction of the region, see Layton, *Russian Literature and Empire*; Halbach, "Die Bergvölker (*gorcy*) als Gegner und Opfer"; Ram, "Prisoners of the Caucasus." For a discussion of imaginative litera-ture and history writing, see Wiener, "Treating 'Historical' Sources as Literary Texts."
6 See Altstadt, *The Azerbaijani Turks*; Swietochowski, *Russian Azerbaijan*; Suny, *The Making of the Georgian Nation*; Suny, *Looking toward Ararat*.
7 Narochnitskii, *Istoriia narodov severnogo Kavkaza*, 55; *Peoples and Languages of the Caucasus*; Betrozov, *Etnicheskaia istoriia Adygov*, 45–6.
8 Volkova, *Etnicheskii sostav naseleniia severnogo Kavkaza v* XVIII-*nachale* XX *veka*, 15–44. On the history of the term "Cherkes," probably of Turkic ori-gin, see Betrozov, *Etnicheskaia istoriia Adygov*, 225–6.
9 G.V. Sollogub, "Predislovie," ZKOIRGO 1 (1852): 11.
10 Said, *Orientalism*. Note Roland Barthes's attention to the place in the Western imagination of exotic Easterners, who served not as "the object, the term of genuine consideration, but simply a cipher, a convenient sign of communication" (from *A Barthes Reader*, 155), and of course Michel Foucault's sustained interest in epistemological order and the importance of exclusion to the formation of identity.

11 Stoler and Cooper, "Between Metropole and Colony: Rethinking a Research Agenda," in Cooper and Stoler, *Tensions of Empire*, 1–56; Mitchell, *Colonising Egypt*; Pratt, *Imperial Eyes*; Fabian, *Language and Colonial Power*; Mudimbe, *The Invention of Africa*; Cohn, *Colonialism and Its Forms of Knowledge*; Metcalf, *Ideologies of the Raj*; Conklin, *A Mission to Civilize*. A similar method inspires scholars of the earlier Spanish conquest of the New World, such as Greenblatt, *Marvelous Possessions*; Todorov, *The Conquest of America*.

12 Wolff, *Inventing Eastern Europe*.

13 Godlewska and Smith, *Geography and Empire*; Livingstone and Withers, *Geography and Enlightenment*; Clifford and Marcus, *Writing Culture*; Stocking, *Victorian Anthropology*.

14 Stoler and Cooper, "Between Metropole and Colony," in Cooper and Stoler, *Tensions of Empire*, 11.

15 Said, *Orientalism*, 92. Also see MacKenzie, *Orientalism*, 58–67.

16 Metcalf, *Ideologies of the Raj*, 12–15.

17 See Algeron, *Les algeriens Musulmans et la France (1871–1919)*, vol. 1; Lorcin, *Imperial Identities*.

18 Bassin, "Russia between Europe and Asia." See also various discussions in Brower and Lazzerini, *Russia's Orient*; and Burbank and Ransel, *Imperial Russia*.

19 Unfortunately, Said's appropriation of Foucault and various currents within French post-structuralism and some of his extreme epistemological positions have sometimes generated more interest than his attention to the history of colonialism, thus diverting historians from the subject at hand and simultaneously turning them into mediocre literary critics. For a discussion of the dilemmas, see Clifford, "Review Essay"; Clifford, *The Predicament of Culture*, 255–76; Pagden, *European Encounters with the New World*, 183–8; and Slezkine, *Arctic Mirrors*, 390–5. Recently from the Russian field, see Knight, "Grigor'ev in Orenburg, 1851–1862," and the subsequent exchange: Khalid, "Russian History and the Debate over Orientalism"; Knight, "On Russian Orientalism"; and Todorova, "Does Russian Orientalism Have a Russian Soul?" For earlier and pioneering works on European ideas about non-Western peoples, without any radical claims about intertextuality, see Baudet, *Paradise on Earth*; Kiernan, *The Lords of Human Kind*; Diamond, *In Search of the Primitive*; and more recently, Bitterli, *Cultures in Conflict*.

20 LeDonne, *The Russian Empire and the World, 1700–1917*; Kappeler, *La Russie*; Rhinelander, *Prince Mikhail Vorontsov*.
    See also von Hagen, "Writing the History of Russia as Empire"; Barkey and von Hagen, *After Empire*; Nolde, *La formation de l'Empire russe*; Raeff, "The Style of Russia's Imperial Policy and Prince G.A. Potemkin"; Raeff, "Patterns of Russian Imperial Policy toward the Nationalities"; Rieber,

"Persistent Factors in Russian Foreign Policy"; Rieber, "Struggle over the Borderlands"; Rieber, *The Politics of Autocracy*; Sarkisyanz, "Russian Imperialism Reconsidered"; Starr, "Tsarist Government"; Jersild, "'Russia,' from the Vistula to the Terek to the Amur." On popular literature and new conceptions of the empire, see Brooks, *When Russia Learned to Read*, 214–45.

Recent work on the Volga-Urals includes Dowler, *Classroom and Empire*; Werth, "The Limits of Religious Ascription"; Geraci, "Ethnic Minorities, Anthropology, and Russian National Identity on Trial"; Kefeli-Clay, "L'Islam populaire chez les Tatars chrétiens orthodoxes au xixe siècle"; and Steinwedel, "The 1905 Revolution in Ufa."

On the conquest and incorporation of the Caucasus, see Atkin, "Russian Expansion in the Caucasus to 1813"; Atkin, *Russia and Iran, 1780–1820*; Gammer, *Muslim Resistance to the Tsar*; Henze, "Fire and Sword in the Caucasus"; Henze, "Circassia in the Nineteenth Century."

On colonial administration in the Caucasus, see Rhinelander, "Russia's Imperial Policy"; Rhinelander, "The Creation of the Caucasian Vicegerency"; Esadze, *Istoricheskaia zapiska ob upravlenii Kavkazom*; less valuable is Esadze's military history commemorating the fiftieth anniversary of the end of the Caucasus War: *Pokorenie zapadnogo Kavkaza i okonchanie Kavkazskoi voiny.*

21 Zhigarev, *Russkaia politika v vostochnom voprose.*
22 Consider, for example, the socio-economic determinism that shaped the efforts of scholars in the former Soviet Union to explain the origins and course of the Caucasus War. The terms of debate included wars of "national liberation" (Shamil's), economies characterized by a "feudal social-economic" level of development (the mountaineers) or a "feudal-serf system [undergoing] a deep crisis" (Russia), and historical moments of "progress" (alignment with Russia) and "backwardness" (the influence of Turkey and Persia). See Ibragimbeili, "Narodno-osvoboditel'naia bor'ba gortsev severnogo kavkaza"; Ortabaev and Totoev, "Eshche raz o kavkazskoi voine"; Bliev, "K probleme obshchestvennogo stroia gorskikh (vol'nykh) obshchestv"; Bliev, "Kavkazskaia voina." For examples of post-Soviet scholarship, see *Kavkazskaia voina*; and Georgiev et al., *Sbornik russkogo istoricheskogo obshchestva*. Less scholarly but intriguing is Dziuba, *'Kavkaz' Tarasa Shevchenko.*
23 Baddeley, *The Russian Conquest of the Caucasus*; Gammer, *Muslim Resistance to the Tsar*. Nineteenth-century studies of the war include Romanovskii, *Kavkaz i Kavkazskaia voina*; Dubrovin, *Istoriia voiny i vladychestva russkikh na Kavkaze*; and Potto, *Kavkazskaia voina v otdel'nykh ocherkakh, epizodakh, legendakh i biografiiakh.*
24 "bibliografia," *droeba*, no. 19 (19 May 1872):1; "iveriis redaktsiisagan," *iveria*, no. 1 (January 1882):3.

25 "sakartvelo," *droeba*, no. 31 (24 March 1876):1–2.

26 "stsavlis sakme chvenshi," *kvali*, no. 2 (10 January 1893):7–10.

27 ilia chavchavadze, "chveni ubeduri mtsibnobroba am saukuneshi," *droeba*, no. 2 (15 January 1870):1.

28 Ibid.

29 This interesting tension shapes the discussion of Jewish, Central Asian, and Ukrainian history writing by Benjamin Nathans, "On Russian-Jewish Historiography"; Adeeb Khalid, "The Emergence of a Modern Central Asian Historical Consciousness"; and Zenon E. Kohut, "The Development of a Ukrainian National Historiography in Imperial Russia," in Sanders, *Historiography of Imperial Russia*, 397–477. On various reformers in Islamic regions and their relation to Russia, see Lazzerini, "Ismail Bey Gasprinskii (Gaspirali)"; Lazzerini, "Defining the Orient"; Jersild, "Rethinking Russia from Zardob"; and Khalid, *The Politics of Muslim Cultural Reform*.

30 Cited in Rayfield, *The Literature of Georgia*, 198.

31 g. tsereteli, "mtiulni," *kvali*, no. 3 (1893):10.

32 ingalo janashvili, "istoriuli da geograpiuli agtsera heretisa," *mogzauri*, nos. 1–4 (1903):65–75.

33 Hosking, *Russia: People and Empire, 1552–1917*, 9.

34 The phrase belongs to LeDonne, *The Russian Empire and the World, 1700–1917*.

35 Bassin, *Imperial Visions*, 263.

36 "Novyi shag k vostoku," *Chernomorskii vestnik*, no. 1 (1 January 1900):3.

37 Schwab, *The Oriental Renaissance*, 186.

38 For earlier works of Bassin and other explorations of imperial ideology, see Bassin, "Inventing Siberia"; Bassin, "Turner, Solov'ev, and the 'Frontier Hypothesis'"; Becker, "The Muslim East in 19th-Century Russian Popular Historiography"; Becker, "Russia between East and West"; Kristof, "The Russian Image of Russia," in Fisher, *Essays in Political Geography*; Riasanovsky, "Asia through Russian Eyes"; Whittaker, "The Impact of the Oriental Renaissance in Russia"; Slocum, "Who, and When, Were the *Inorodtsy*?"; and the collection of essays in the *Russian Review* 53, no. 3 (July 1994): Rieber, "Russian Imperialism"; Hokanson, "Literary Imperialism, *Narodnost'* and Pushkin's Invention of the Caucasus"; Barrett, "The Remaking of the Lion of Dagestan"; Brower, "Imperial Russia and Its Orient."

39 Booker, *Colonial Power, Colonial Texts*, 19. For an exploration of this concept in the Russian imperial context, see Werth, "From Resistance to Subversion." For a social history of shared material culture on the frontier, see Sunderland, "Russians into Iakuts?"; and Barrett, *At the Edge of Empire*.

40 The reference is to Werth, "From Resistance to Subversion."

CHAPTER TWO

1 GVIARF, f. 400, op. 1, 1864, d. 4736, Delo "Otchet po glavnomu shtabu o voennykh deistviiakh voisk Kavkazskoi armii," Emigration of natives of Kuban oblast to Turkey, l. 61.

2 "Vziatie v plen Shamilia," *Zhurnal dlia chteniia vospitannikam voenno-uchebnykh zavedenii* 142, no. 566 (15 January 1860):179.

3 Griboedov, *Sochineniia*, 497–519, citation from 519.

4 Lantzeff, *Siberia in the Seventeenth Century*, 30–87.

5 Cited in Anisimov, *The Reforms of Peter the Great*, 259.

6 Nolde, *La formation de l'Empire russe*, 2:347.

7 P.A. Tomarov, "Obzor Stavropol'skoi gubernii za 1894 g.," ZKOIRGO 19 (1897):97–9; Nolde, *La formation de l'Empire russe*, 2:349.

8 B.V. Vinogradov, "Nekotorye aspekty Kavkazskoi politiki Pavla I," in *Kavkazskaia voina*, 183.

9 For the history of the Russian conquest of the southern borderlands, see Nolde, *La formation de l'Empire russe*, vol. 2; Kappeler, *La Russie*, 150–63; LeDonne, *The Russian Empire and the World, 1700–1917*, 89–129; Atkin, "Russian Expansion in the Caucasus to 1813"; Atkin, *Russia and Iran, 1780–1820*; Kazemzadeh, "Russian Penetration of the Caucasus"; Gammer, *Muslim Resistance to the Tsar*; Zelkina, *In Quest for God and Freedom*, 52–74, 121–88; Kohut, *Russian Centralism and Ukrainian Autonomy*; Fisher, *The Crimean Tatars*; Fisher, *The Russian Annexation of the Crimea, 1772–1783*; Georgiev et al., *Sbornik russkogo istoricheskogo obshchestva*.

10 Gammer, "Russian Strategies in the Conquest of Chechnia and Daghestan, 1825–1859," 46. For a different perspective on Ermolov, see L.V. Shatokhina, "Politika Rossii na severo-zapadnom Kavkaze v 20–e gody XIX veka," and Iu.Iu. Klychnikov, "Deiatel'nost' A.P. Ermolova na severnom Kavkaze (1816–1827)," in Georgiev et al., *Sbornik russkogo istoricheskogo obshchestva*, 58–83.

11 Barratt, "A Note on the Russian Conquest of Armenia (1827)," 409. The border with Ottoman Turkey was further amended after the war of 1877–78.

12 *Tiflisskiia Vedomosti*, no. 13 (26 September 1828):1.

13 On Georgian opposition to imperial rule, such as the noble conspiracy of 1832, see Suny, *The Making of the Georgian Nation*, 71–2; Jones, "Russian Imperial Administration and the Georgian Nobility"; Kipiani, "Zapiski Dmitriia Ivanovich Kipiani," *Russkaia Starina* 50 (1886):270–2.

14 Dzidzariia, *Makhadzhirstvo*, 102–3; Megrelidze, *Zakavkaz'e v Russko-Turetskoi voine 1877–1878 gg.*, 50–2.

15 Degoev, *Kavkazskii vopros v mezhdunarodnykh otnosheniiakh*, 8–22.

16 SPbFIV RAN, f. 6, op. 1, d. 33a, Delo "V.S. Ruban: Adol'f Petrovich Berzhe, stranitsy iz zhizni, kn. 1," l. 317.

17 Bell, *Journal of a Residence in Circassia during the Years 1837, 1838 and 1839.*
18 SPBFIRI RAN, f. 36, op. 2, 1839, d. 32, Delo "Zhurnal voennykh deistvii otriada Raevskago," Report by Raevskii, 23 July 1839, ll. 23–6, citation from l. 25.
19 Ibid., Report by Raevskii, l. 50; Report by Serebriakov, l. 57.
20 E.D. Felitsyn, "O kontrabande i eia prekrashchenii," *Kubanskiia Oblastnyia Vedomosti*, no. 10 (10 March 1890):1.
21 GVIARF, f. 14719, op. 1, 1828, d. 97, Delo "Vozzvanie-proklamatsiia ... generala Emanuelia k Zakubanskim narodam po sluchaiu obiavleniia voiny Turtsii," Proclamation, 25 April 1828, l. 1.
22 Ibid., ll. 1–2.
23 GVIARF, f. VUA, op. 1, 1843, d. 6485, Delo "O deputatsii ot Kavkazskikh gortsev plemen v Konstantonopil' v 1843 g.," Report to commander of Black Sea Line, 6 November 1843, l. 29.
24 Kappeler, *La Russie*, 35; Ivanov et al., *Etnicheskaia istoriia i Kul'tura Chuvashei Povolzh'ia i Priural'ia*, 22–3.
25 Kappeler, "Czarist Policy toward the Muslims of the Russian Empire," 143–6. Also see Zenkovsky, *Pan-Turkism and Islam in Russia*, 16–18.
26 Gritsenko, *Goroda severo-vostochnogo Kavkaza*, 75–8.
27 G.A. Vertepov, "Obzor Terskoi oblasti za 1894 god," ZKOIRGO 19 (1897):164, 168.
28 Baddeley, *The Russian Conquest of the Caucasus*, 222–3.
29 See Nolde, *La formation de l'Empire russe*, 2:358–84; "Napadenie na Gruziiu," *Tiflisskiia Vedomosti*, no. 1 (4 June 1828):3.
30 On Tsitsianov, see Rhinelander, "Tsitsianov, Pavel Dmitrievich," in Joseph L. Wieczynski, ed., *The Modern Encyclopedia of Russian and Soviet History* (Gulf Breeze, Fl: Academic International Press), 40:51–5.
31 "Predsmertnoe Pis'mo," *Kavkaz*, no. 17 (16 February 1846):28.
32 "8 Fevralia 1806 g.–8 Fevralia 1846 g.," *Kavkaz*, no. 6 (8 February 1846):22–3.
33 GVIARF, f. 14719, op. 2, 1841–43, d. 878, Delo "Postavlenie Raevskogo," Letter from Colonel Murav'ev to General Kotsebu, 26 March 1841, l. 1. For a 1832 listing of yearly payments in silver to Kabardan, Chechen, and Adygei princes, see GVIARF, f. 14719, op. 1, 1832, d. 153, Delo "Spisok Aziatsam naznachennykh k nagrade," ll. 1–2.
34 Dzidzariia, *Makhadzhirstvo*, 108.
35 GVIARF, f. VUA, op. 1, 1856–58, d. 6662, Delo "O chastom poiavlenii na vostochnom beregu Chernago moria Angliiskikh i Turetsskikh sudakh," Letter to minister of war, 14 November 1856, ll. 3–4.
36 GVIARF, f. 14719, op. 3, 1826, d. 8, Delo "Prisiaga Karachaevskogo naroda russkomu pravitel'stvu," Letter of mulla, trans. from Arabic, 25 July 1826, l. 2.
37 Raeff, *The Well-Ordered Police State*, 221; Jones, *The Emancipation of the Russian Nobility, 1762–1785.*

38 Kappeler, *La Russie*, 213; also see 41, 105–28, 155–6; and Kappeler, "Czarist Policy toward the Muslims of the Russian Empire," 142–3.

39 Nolde, *La formation de l'Empire russe*, 1:185–7, 2:301–31; Lantzeff, *Siberia in the Seventeenth Century*, 91–3; Chantal Lemercier-Quelquejay, "Co-optation of the Elites of Kabarda and Daghestan in the Sixteenth Century," in Broxup, *The North Caucasus Barrier*, 18–44; Kohut, *Russian Centralism and Ukrainian Autonomy*; Menning, "The Emergence of a Military-Administrative Elite in the Don Cossack Land, 1708–1836."

40 Lang, *A Modern History of Soviet Georgia*, 37. For a discussion of the "social assimilation" of the "ruling elites" in the Caucasus by the "feudal-patriarchal" empire, see A.M. Avramenko, O.V. Matveev, P.P. Matiush-chenko, V.N. Ratushniak, "Ob otsenke Kavkazskoi voiny s nauchnykh positsii istorizma," in *Kavkazskaia voina*, 24–43.

41 Esadze, *Istoricheskaia zapiska*, 1:59–60; Rhinelander, "Russia's Imperial Policy," 224–5; Nolde, *La formation de l'Empire russe*, 2:384; Kappeler, *La Russie*, 156.

42 PFA AN, f. 32, op. 1, 1828–30, d. 66, Delo "Materialy po deiatel'nosti russkikh voisk na Kavkaze pod nachal'stvom gen. Emmanuelia," l. 5.

43 Letter from Paul I to General Kotliarevskii, 27 June 1799, in Korolenko, *Dvukhsotletie Kubanskago Kazach'iago voiska, 1696–1896*, 76; also see RGIA, f. 565, op. 6, 1905, d. 24843, l. 6.

44 GVIARF, f. 14719, op. 2, 1845–46, d. 920, Delo "Perepiska po khodataistvu maiora Danielia Beka," Letter from Grigorii Shvarts to Vladimir Osipovich, l. 1.

45 GVIARF, f. VUA, 1841, d. 6411, Delo "Raport ... Raevskago," Reports from Raevskii to Chernyshev, 27 August 1840, l. 1; Ol'shevskii to Raevskii, 10 March 1840, ll. 2–4; Ol'shevskii to General Kotsebu, 10 March 1840, l. 6.

46 GVIARF, f. 14719, op. 2, 1845–46, d. 920, Letter from General Gurko to commander of Dzharo-Belokanskii Military District, 19 September 1845, l. 2–7.

47 SSSA, f. 4, op. 3, 1846–55, d. 181, Delo "O Zakavkazskiia urozhentsakh ... v raznye stolichnye uchebnye zavedeniia," Report from Orbeliani to Vorontsov, 20 January 1847, l. 22; Letters to S.V. Safonov, April, March 1847, ll. 34–41.

48 SSSA, f. 1437, op. 1, 1912, d. 35, Delo "Khodotaistvo glavnokomandiuush-chego," Letter to Vorontsov-Dashkov, October 1912, l. 5; also SSSA, f. 1437, op. 1, 1883, d. 4, and 1884, d. 5, Dela "Pis'ma Baratova."

49 SSSA, f. 7, op. 8, 1861–74, d. 2, Delo "O ssylke v g. Voronezh," Letter to General Kartsov, l. 8.

50 SSSA, f. 229, op. 1, 1884–85, d. 127, Delo "O dostovlenii ... spisok na ofitse-rov iz tuzemtsev za 1883 god," ll. 24–37; f. 229, op. 1, 1886, d. 183, Delo "Spisok ofitseram Karsskoi militsii," List, ll. 1–2.

51 SSSA, f. 5, op. 1, 1874, d. 3480, Delo "Po otnosheniiu kavkazskago gorsk-ago upravleniia," List, l. 1.

52 sssa, f. 229, op. 1, 1888–89, d. 256, Delo "O peremenakh, proizshidshikh mezhdu ofitserami iz tuzemtsev," ll. 20–30.

53 Henze, "Fire and Sword in the Caucasus," 16; i. khatiashvili, "dagestnis imamebi," *mogzauri*, nos. 1–4 (1903):29–44; nos. 7–8 (1903):192–208; V.A. Georgiev and N.G. Georgieva, "Kavkazskaia voina (1829–1864 gg.)," in Georgiev et al., *Sbornik russkogo istoricheskogo obshchestva*, 158–71; Bennigsen and Wimbush, *Mystics and Commissars*, 18–20; on North Caucasus Sufism and a discussion of the diversity of views that made up the North Caucasus notion of ghazavat, see Zelkina, *In Quest for God and Freedom*; Halbach, " 'Heiliger Krieg' gegen den Zarismus"; Kemper, "Einige Notizen zur Arabischsprachigen Literatur."

54 Voll, *Islam*, 59–61. Also see Martin, *Muslim Brotherhoods in Nineteenth - Century Africa*; and O'Brien and Coulon, *Charisma and Brotherhood in African Islam*.

55 Green, "Political Attitudes and Activities of the Ulama in the Liberal Age," 217. This generalization, of course, does not always hold, and certain Sufi orders closely cooperated with the French in West Africa and the Maghrib.

56 Ruedy, *Modern Algeria*, 57–65; Danziger, *Abd al-Qadir and the Algerians*; Dekmejian and Wyszomirski, "Charismatic Leadership in Islam"; Voll, "Mahdis, Walis, and New Men in the Sudan"; Voll, "The British, the 'Ulama,' and Popular Islam in the Early Anglo-Egyptian Sudan."

57 See Rhinelander, *Prince Michael Vorontsov*, 145 and 250n49.

58 Danziger, *Abd al-Qadir and the Algerians*, 79.

59 Esadze, *Pokorenie zapadnogo Kavkaza i okonchanie Kavkazskoi voiny*, 68; Boratav, "La Russie dans les Archives ottomanes in Dossier ottoman sur l'imam Chamil"; Henze, "Circassia in the Nineteenth Century," 256; Prozritelev, *Posol'stvo ot Shamilia k Abadzekham*.

60 Ruedy, *Modern Algeria*, 65; Danziger, *Abd al-Qadir and the Algerians*, 238–47.

61 The letter written by Abd al-Qadir was translated from Arabic into French by Russian officials in Constantinople and can be found in gviarf, f. 400, op. 1, 1866, d. 14, Delo "Zapiska vitse kantslera na imia voennogo ministra o poezdke Shamilia v Mekku," l. 3.

62 gviarf, f. 38, op. 7, 1865, d. 507, Delo "O dozvolenii voenno-plennomu Shamiliu vyekhat' v Turtsiiu," Ignat'ev, 12 September 1865, l. 4.

63 M. Ia. Ol'shevskii, "Kavkaz i pokorenie vostochnoi ego chasti," *Russkaia Starina* 27 (1880):290–5.

64 A. Zisserman, "Lager u ozera Iani-am," *Kavkaz*, no. 59 (30 July 1859):316.

65 A. Zisserman, "O poslednikh sobytiiakh v Dagestane," *Kavkaz*, no. 72 (13 September 1859):398–9.

66 Gadzhi-Ali, "Skazanie ochevidtsa o Shamile," *ssokg* 7 (1873), part 1:63.

67 "Vziatie v plen Shamilia," *Zhurnal dlia chteniia vospitannikam voenno-uchebnykh zavedenii* 142, no. 566 (15 January 1860):179.

68 Ryzhov, "Puteshestvie Shamilia ot Guniba do Sanktpeterburga," *Sanktpe-terburgskiia Vedomosti*, no. 212 (1 October 1859):923.

69 *Pokorenie Kavkaza i vziatie Shamilia*, 7.

70 Potichnyj, "The Struggle of the Crimean Tatars," 302.

71 PFA AN, f. 100, op. 1, 1777, d. 100, Delo "Ukazy Ekateriny II o zaselenii iuzhnykh gubernii i obespechenii bezopasnikh granits," Letter from Potemkin to Catherine, 24 April 1777, l. 8.

72 Adol'f P. Berzhe, "Vyselenie gortsev s Kavkaza," *Russkaia Starina* 33 (January 1882):341–2; Totoev, "K voprosu o pereselenii Osetin v Turtsiiu (1859–1865)," 26.

73 Berzhe, "Vyselenie gortsev s Kavkaza," 338.

74 GVIARF, f. 400, op. 1, 1864, d. 4736, Emigration of natives of Kuban oblast to Turkey, l. 68; and Changes in the administration of Kuban oblast, 1863–64, ll. 58–9. Also RGIA, f. 1268, op. 15, 1870, d. 56, Delo "Vsepoddaneishii otchet glavnokomanduiushchago kavkazskago armieiu po voenno-narodnomu upravleniiu za 1863–1869 gg.," l. 23.

75 Dzidzariia, *Makhadzhirstvo*, 188; B.M. Dzhimov, "Politika vedushchikh derzhav i ee otrazhenie v khode Kavkazskoi voiny (konets XVIII–pervaia polovina XIXv.)," in *Kavkazskaia voina*, 17.

76 Dzidzariia, *Makhadzhirstvo*, 58.

77 Ibid., 161.

78 Volkova, *Etnicheskii sostav*, 220–2; A.Kh. Kasumov, "Okonchanie Kavkazskoi voiny i vyselenie Adygov v Turtsiiu," in *Kavkazskaia voina*, 63–79.

79 GVIARF, f. 400, op. 1, 1866–68, d. 49, Delo "O polozhenii dela po vodvoreniiu v Turtsiiu Chechenskikh pereselentsev," General Mikhail to Miliutin, 28 December 1865, ll. 4–12; and Captain Zelenyi to Dmitrii Starosel'skii, 8 October 1866, ll. 25–6. A rosier view of the Ottomans is offered by Magomeddadaev, "Die Dagestanische Diaspora in der Türkei und in Syrien." See also Karpat, "The Status of the Muslims under European Rule."

80 Volkova, *Etnicheskii sostav*, 222.

81 GVIARF, f. 400, op. 1, 1864, d. 4736, Emigration of natives of Kuban oblast to Turkey, ll. 68–74.

82 N. Drozdov, "Poslednaia bor'ba s gortsami na zapadnom Kavkaze," *Kavkazskii Sbornik* 2 (1877):456.

83 Ibid., 452.

84 Ibid., 453.

85 A.N. D'iachkov-Tarasov, "Abadzekhi," ZKOIRGO 22 (1903), part 4:50.

86 "More than 50%," according to Kumykov, *Vyselenie Adygov v Turtsiiu – posledstvie Kavkazskoi voiny*, 18.

87 Dzidzariia, *Makhadzhirstvo*, 209–10.

88 On Evdokimov, see Berzhe, "Vyselenie," 341; Megrelidze, *Zakavkaz'e*, 55; and Kasumov, "Okonchanie Kavkazskoi voiny," in *Kavkazskaia voina*, 66.

On other regime officials, see GVIARF, f. 14719, op. 4, 1864, d. 87, Delo "O podgotovke desanta k Ubikhskim beregam na sluchai voiny s Turtsiei," Letter from commander of Main Staff of Caucasus Army to commander of Artillery, 17 December 1863, ll. 1–2.

89 Dzidzariia, *Makhadzhirstvo*, 191, 283.

90 "Izvestie o poslednikh voennykh deistviiakh na zapadnom kavkaze," *Kavkaz*, no. 44 (11 June 1864):265.

91 GVIARF, f. 400, op. 1, 1864, d. 4736, Delo "Otchet po glavnomu shtabu o voennykh deistviiakh voisk Kavkazskoi armii," General situation in the Caucasus, 1863, ll. 9–10.

92 Ibid., Military activities, 1863, ll. 26–30; Information about our [Russian] losses, 1864, l. 34.

93 Ibid., Emigration of natives of Kuban oblast to Turkey, l. 61.

94 K. Geins, "Pshekhskii otriad," *Voennyi Sbornik*, no. 1 (January 1866):8.

95 A. Lilov, "Poslednye gody bor'by Russkikh s gortsami na zapadnom Kavkaze," *Kavkaz*, no. 19 (15 March 1867):110.

96 Dzidzariia, *Makhadzhirstvo*, 210.

97 Volkova, *Etnicheskii sostav*, 221, and confirmed by a document from SSSA reproduced in Kumykov, *Vyselenie Adygov v Turtsiiu – posledstvie Kavkazskoi voiny.*

98 Berzhe, "Vyselenie gortsev s Kavkaza," 162; Megrelidze, *Zakavkaz'e v Russko-Turetskoi voine 1877–1878 gg.*, 56; Dzidzariia, *Makhadzhirstvo*, 210.

99 Sherbin, *Istoriia Kubanskogo kazach'ego polka*, 2:14 (470,000); Esadze, *Istoricheskaia zapiska*, 1:51–2 (418,000).

100 N.I. Voronov, "'Kavkaz,' gazeta politicheskaia i literaturnaia za 1863, 1864 i 1865 gody," ZKOIRGO 7, no. 1 (1866), part 2:6.

101 GVIARF, f. 400, op. 1, 1864, d. 4736, Information about the number of exiled mountaineers of Kuban oblast, l. 77–9.

102 High figures are provided by Totoev, "K voprosu o pereselenii Osetin v Turtsiiu (1859–1865)" (700,000 to 750,000 from 1859 to 1865); Laipanov, "K istorii pereseleniia," 113–14 (307,000 for the Cherkes emigration from 1859 to 1865, 800,000 for all of the Caucasus in the 1860s, and 1,800,000 for all of the Caucasus throughout the nineteenth century); Berhok, *Tarihte Kafcasya*, 528 (1 million); Karpat, "The Status of the Muslims under European Rule," 11 (1.2–2 million from 1862 to 1870); and A.Kh. Kasumov, "Okonchanie Kavkazskoi voiny i vyselenie Adygov v Turtsiiu," in *Kavkazskaia voina*, 76 (398,955 western Adygei from 1858 to 1864 and perhaps 1 million from 1800 to 1864). For figures from Western scholarship, see Lang, *A Modern History of Soviet Georgia*, 98 (600,000); Kazemzadeh, "Russian Penetration of the Caucasus," 262 (250,000); Henze, "Fire and Sword in the Caucasus," 32–5 (400,000 "Circassians" and 600,000 people from the North Caucasus generally); Henze, "Circassia in the Nineteenth Century," 269 (1 million "Circassians");

Bennigsen and Broxup, *The Islamic Threat to the Soviet State*, 20 ("over a million Cherkess" in the 1860s); Brock, "The Fall of Circassia," 425 (400,000); Fisher, "Emigration of Muslims from the Russian Empire in the Years after the Crimean War," 364 (700,000–900,000 Muslim Crimeans and North Caucasus peoples from 1856 to 1864).

103 Volkova, *Etnicheskii sostav*, 221.

104 Berzhe, "Vyselenie," 164.

105 RGIA, f. 1268, op. 15, 1870, d. 56, ll. 23, 59; Berzhe, "Vyselenie," 347.

106 I.Ia. Kutsenko, "Kavkazskaia voina i problemy preemstvennosti politiki na severnom Kavkaze," in *Kavkazskaia voina*, 55.

107 Drozdov, "Poslednaia bor'ba," 416; Megrelidze, *Zakavkaz'e*, 54.

108 Berzhe, "Vyselenie," 176, 345–6.

109 Megrelidze, *Zakavkaz'e*, 61; Dzidzariia, *Makhadzhirstvo*, 93–118; Totoev, "K voprosu o pereselenii," 34–9; Laipanov, "K istorii pereseleniia," 114–15.

110 SSSA, f. 5, op. 1, 1873, d. 3011, Delo "Po prosheniiu Cherkesskoi deputatsii iz Maloi Azii," ll. 1–3.

111 SSSA, f. 7, op. 1, 1876, d. 1756, Delo "… o vozrashchenii na rodinu iz Turtsii," Report, November 1876, ll. 9–12.

112 Bennigsen and Wimbush, *Mystics and Commissars*, 9, 20–1.

113 SSSA, f. 7, op. 8, 1861–74, d. 2, Report of Ministry of War, 22 December 1861, ll. 13–15; Mal'sagova, *Vosstanie gortsev v Chechne v 1877 godu*, 4; Magomedov, *Vosstanie gortsev Dagestana v 1877 g.*, 26; Kosven, *Ocherki istorii Dagestana*, 1:246; RGIA, f. 932, op. 1, 1882, d. 303, Delo "Doklad nachal'nika Terskoi obl. kn. A.M. Dondukovu-Korsakovu," l. 4; Bennigsen and Wimbush, *Mystics and Commissars*, 21.

114 A.P. Ippolitov, "Uchenie 'zikr' i ego posledovateli v Chechne i Argunskom okruge," SSOKG 2 (1869):3.

115 Megrelidze, *Zakavkaz'e*, 66.

116 "Po povodu vozstaniia v Zakatal'skom okruge v 1863-m godu," *Kavkazskii Sbornik* 10 (1886):585–607.

117 RGIA, f. 1268, op. 15, 1870, d. 56, l. 56.

118 Dzidzariia, *Vosstanie 1866 v Abkhazii*, 184.

119 RGIA, f. 1268, op. 15, 1870, d. 56, ll. 48, 60–2.

120 P.G. Przhetsslavskii, "Shamil' v Kaluge," *Russkaia Starina* 20 (1877):497, 506.

121 Ramazanov and Ramazanov, *Shamil'*, 77.

122 RGIA, f. 565, op. 1, 1859–66, d. 2441, Delo "O priniatii na schet kazny izderzhek na soderzhanie … Shamilia," ll. 10–50, 79, 86, 89, 98, 109, 119, 122, 125; also GVIARF, f. 400, op. 1, 1865–66, d. 8, Delo "Po predstavlenii podpolkovnika Przhetsslavskago," Reports of 26 May and 29 July 1865, ll. 4, 21. Przhetsslavskii claimed that the government spent 200,000 rubles in silver on Shamil from 1860 to 1868; see Przhetsslavskii, "Shamil' i ego sem'ia v Kaluge," *Russkaia Starina* 21 (1878):266.

123 Ibid., l. 42; RGIA, f. 1268, op. 10, 1859–61, d. 197, Delo "O naznachenii vziatomu v plen Shamiliu pensii po 10/5 rub ser. v god i ob opredelenii dlia prismotra ego osobago pristava s pomoshchnikom," l. 6.

124 For example, GVIARF, f. 400, op. 1, 1869, d. 39, Delo "Po pros'be Shamilia ob uvolnenii ego v Mekku dlia pokloneniia grobu Magometa," Letter of Shamil to tsar, 19 December 1868.

125 GVIARF, f. 400, op. 1, 1869, d. 39, Viceroy Mikhail to Dmitrii Miliutin, 25 January 1869, ll. 1–2.

126 VIARF, f. 400, op. 1, 1867–70, d. 23, Delo "Po predmetu pereseleniia Shamilia s semeistvom v iuzhnuiu Rossiiu," Shamil to Miliutin, 15 April 1867, l. 20; RGIA, f. 1286, op. 20, d. 1507, ll. 55–7.

127 Zakhar'in, Shamil v Kaluge, 40; S. Shul'gin, "Razskaz ochevidtsa o Shamile i ego sovremennikakh," Sbornik Materialov dlia opisaniia mestnostei i plemen Kavkaza, no. 32 (1903), part 1:24.

128 GVIARF, f. 400, op. 1, 1871–72, d. 266, Delo "O vydache sostoiashchemu za perevodnika pri semeistve Shamilia ... Onuflievu," Report from Kiev commander, 23 January 1871, l.1.

129 Ramazanov and Ramazanov, Shamil, 78–82. Shuanet was Anna Uvanovna Ulusova, born to an Armenian merchant in Mozdok and captured in the 1840 invasion of Mozdok. Przhetsslavskii described her as "Tatarized" (otataralas'); see Przhetsslavskii, "Shamil' i ego sem'ia v Kaluge," Russkaia Starina 21 (1878):262.

130 Zakhar'in, Shamil v Kaluge, 42; Chichagova, Shamil' na Kavkaze i v Rossii, 206.

131 RGIA, f. 1286, op. 20, d. 1507, l. 62.

132 GVIARF, f. 400, op. 1, 1870–72, d. 243, Delo "Perepiska s ministerstvami," Letter from Ignat'ev to Aleksandr Mikhailovich, 28 January 1871, l. 16.

133 Ibid., Letter from Ignat'ev to director of Asian Department, 2 March 1871, l. 32.

134 GVIARF, f. 400, op. 1, 1875, d. 403, Delo "O povedenii v Turtsii syna Shamilia," Commander of Caucasus Mountain Administration to Ignat'ev, 24 December 1874, ll. 2–3.

135 Bennigsen and Wimbush, Mystics and Commissars, 22.

136 "Voenno polozhenie v Terskoi oblasti," Kavkaz, no. 97 (24 May 1877):1.

137 I.D.V., "Bezporiadki v Dido," Kavkaz, no. 109 (7 June 1877):3; I.D.V., "Eshche o bezporiadkakh v Dido," Kavkaz, no. 128 (29 June 1877):3.

138 Mal'sagova, Vosstanie gortsev, 23.

139 "Iz Dagestana," Kavkaz, no. 212 (21 October 1877):3.

140 Kosven, Ocherki istorii Dagestana, 1:248; RGIA, f. 932, op. 1, 1882, d. 297, Delo "Vedomosti i spravki o kolichestve mestnykh zhitelei, vyslannykh v administrativnom poriadke s Kavkaza za uchastie v vostaniiakh 1877 g. i ugolovnye prestupleniia v 1874–1882," l. 4.

141 "S severnago Kavkaza," Kavkaz, no. 225 (6 November 1877):1.

142 See the series of documents collected in *Agrarnyi vopros i krest'ianskoe dvizhenie 50–70-kh godov XIX v.*, 343–52.

143 Mal'sagova, *Vosstanie gortsev*, 19.

144 P.P. Korolenko, "Na beregakh Abkhazii," *Voennyi Sbornik*, no. 7 (July 1891):333.

145 Mal'sagova, *Vosstanie gortsev*, 12–13, 17–18; Magomedov, *Vosstanie gortsev Dagestana v 1877 g.*, 7; Kosven, *Ocherki istorii Dagestana*, 1:242.

146 N. Semenov, "Iz nedavniago proshlago na Kavkaze: Razskazy – vospominaniia o Chechenskom vozstanii v 1877 g.," *Kavkazskii Vestnik*, no. 4 (April 1900):26.

147 SSSA, f. 229, op. 1, 1888, d. 20, Delo "So vsepoddanneishim otchetem ...," Report of military governor, 1888, ll. 13–14.

148 Kosven, *Ocherki istorii Dagestana*, 1:248–9.

149 Megrelidze, *Zakavkaz'e*, 256.

150 Ibid., 257.

151 "Nekotoryia statisticheskiia i etnograficheskiia dannyia o Karsskoi oblasti," ZKOIRGO 18 (1896):323, 354–5.

152 SSSA, f. 416, op. 3, 1878, d. 190, Delo "Zapiska ob ... naseleniia Abkhazii," Report from the Office of the Viceroy, 1878, l. 1.

153 Mal'sagova, *Vosstanie gortsev*, 31.

154 Saltykov-Shchedrin Public Library, Manuscripts Department, f. 73, d. 844, Delo Butkevich, "Musul'manskii vopros na Kavkaze," 23 November 1877, ll. 34–40.

155 RGIA, f. 565, op. 5, d. 19814, Letter from Minister of the Interior Timashev to MF, 18 October 1877, l. 1.

156 RGIA, f. 1286, op. 39, d. 362, ll. 12–15.

157 RGIA, f. 1282, op. 1, 1880–81, d. 970, Delo "O gortsakh vyslannykh s Kavkaza v Saratovskuiu guberniiu," Letter of Timiriazev, 15 September 1880, l. 12.

158 Ibid., MVD report of Baron von Geiking, 11 November 1880, l. 204; Timiriazev to commander of Saratov Provincial MVD, 22 October 1880, l. 20. For more on this, see Jersild, "Imperial Russification."

159 Andreevskii, *O namestnikakh, voevodakh i gubernatorakh*, 107–9; Got'e, *Istoriia oblastnogo upravleniia*, 2:260. On Russia within the empire, see Szporluk, "The Imperial Legacy and the Soviet Nationalities Problem," 1–4; Szporluk, "The Fall of the Tsarist Empire and the USSR."

160 Subtelny, *Ukraine*, 201–4; Ivanov et al., *Etnicheskaia istoriia i Kul'tura Chuvashei Povolzh'ia i Priural'ia*, 58; Kappeler, *La Russie*, 240, 242.

161 GVIARF, f. 38, op. 7, 1858, d. 358, Delo "O smerti Alagar-Beka," Letter from high commander to minister of war, 15 August 1858, ll. 1–3; SSSA, f. 416, op. 3, 1863, d. 201, Delo"Otnoshenie ... ob udalenii iz Avarii ... polkovnika Ibragim Khana," Viceroy to Miliutin, 29 March 1863, ll. 1–3;

SSSA, f. 416, op. 3, n.d., d. 205, Delo "Zapiska o Dagestane," Memorandum, n.d., ll. 8–9.

162 RGIA, f. 1268, op. 15, 1870, d. 56, ll. 40–6.

163 RGIA, f. 932, op. 1, 1855–80, d. 288, Delo "Kratkii ocherk rezultatov pravitel'svennoi deiatel'nosti," l. 3.

164 RGIA, f. 1268, op. 10, 1859, d. 176, ll. 9–11; GVIARF, f. 38, op. 7, 1858, d. 358, ll. 1–3.

165 Doyle, Empires, 133, 162–7, 198–201, 226.

166 SSSA, f. 416, op. 3, 1864–65, d. 182, Delo "Perepiska ob udalenii iz Abkhazii vladetelia Abkhazii," Letter from Sviatopolk-Mirskii to viceroy, 20 December 1864, l. 5.

167 Ibid.

168 SSSA, f. 416, op. 3, 1863–65, d. 178, Delo "Perepiska o vvedenii v Abkhazii russkago upravleniia," Letter from Mikhail Shervashidze to Sviatopolk-Mirskii, 21 June 1864, l. 60.

169 SSSA, f. 416, op. 3, 1847–67, d. 177, Delo "Perepiska ob udalenii vladetelia Abkhazii," Letter from Georgi Shervashidze to viceroy, 10 February 1865, l. 117.

170 SSSA, f. 416, op. 3, 1864–65, d. 182, l. 6.

171 Ibid., Letter from Sviatopolk-Mirskii to viceroy, 30 September 1864, ll. 13–17.

172 SSSA, f. 229, op. 1, 1883–84, d. 33, Delo "Po pros'be raznykh lits Dagestanskoi oblasti," Letter to commander of troops, 10 December 1883, ll. 5–7.

173 GVIARF, f. 400, op. 1, 1866–70, d. 68, Memorandum by Dmitrii Miliutin, 17 May 1866, l. 3. Also see V.N. Mal'tsev, "Vlianie Kavkazskoi voiny na administrativno-sudebnye reformy na severnom Kavkaze vtoroi poloviny XIX v.," in Kavkazskaia voina, 269.

174 See Perkins, Qaids, Captains and Colons.

175 "sakartvelo: kalakis sazogado gamgeobize," droeba, no. 23 (12 June 1870):1; droeba, no. 23 (5 August 1866):1; RGIA, f. 565, op. 6, 1905, d. 24843, l. 3; f. 1604, op. 1, 1890, d. 271, l. 19; Suny, The Making of the Georgian Nation, 96–112.

176 See the documents in Georgiev et al., Sbornik russkogo istoricheskogo obshchestva, 172–208.

177 Conklin, A Mission to Civilize, 96–116.

178 RGIA, f. 1158, op. 1, 1913, d. 268, Delo "O prekrashchenii zavisimykh otnoshenii poselan' Dagestanskoi oblasti," Report, 9 February 1913, l. 9; f. 1604, op. 1, 1890, d. 271, Memorandum by Dondukov-Korsakov, l. 13.

179 RGIA, f. 1158, op. 1, 1913, d. 268, Report of A. Nikol'skii to viceroy, 9 February 1913, l. 15. Also see f. 565, op. 6, 1905, d. 24843, Letter from Baron Nol'de to Ivan Pavlovich, 24 December 1905, ll. 2–3, and subsequent lists; f. 1278, op. 2, 1910–12, d. 5270, Delo "O zaprose ministru

vnutrennykh del po povodu zavisimykh otnoshenii" Report from I.A. Kurakin to MVD, 1911, l. 7; f. 408, op. 1, 1913, d. 426, Delo "Po delam sluzhaiushchisia v sovete ministrov," Journal of Soviet of Ministers, 24 January 1913, ll. 54–61; P.V. Gidulianov, "Soslovno-pozemel'nii vopros i raiiatskaia zavisimost v Dagestane," part 3, *EO*, no. 3 (1901):108.

180 RGIA, f. 1158, op. 1, 1913, d. 268, Rules about the ending of dependency, l. 4.

181 Ibid., Report, 9 February 1913, l. 7.

182 Petin, *Sobstvennyi Ego Imperatorskago Velichestva Konvoi, 1811–1911*, 2–3, 49–51, 91. Their dress code was formalized in 1835.

183 See Baumann, "Subject Nationalities in the Military Service of Imperial Russia."

184 RGIA, f. 866, op. 1, 1860, d. 40, Bariatinskii, Proclamation to the Chechen people, 1860, l. 13.

185 RGIA, f. 1246, op. 16, 1880–81, d. 11, Delo "Ob otmene osobago polozheniia o prieme v voennuiu sluzhbu kavkazskikh tuzemtsev," 1880–81, l. 1; RGIA, f. 1341, op. 13, 1864, d. 308, Delo "O pravakh Kavkazskikh tuzemtsev, postupaiushchikh po dobrovol'nomu zhelaniiu na sluzhbu v reguliarnyia voiska," 29 April 1864, ll. 1–5; RGIA, f. 1149, op. 11, 1891–93, d. 1, Delo "O summe naloga, podlezhashchago vzimaniiu v 1892 i 1893 g.g. s abkhhaztsev-khristian, vzimen otbyvaniia imi voinskoi povinnosti," 1891–92, ll. 2–3.

186 Vorontsov-Dashkov, *Vsepoddanneishii otchet za vosem let upravleniia Kavkazom*, 12; RGIA, f. 396, op. 7, 1914, d. 168, Delo "O privlechenii k otbyvaniiu voinskoi povinnosti," Letter from Ministry of War to Resettlement Administration, 11 December 1913, ll. 1–3. On the Terek Mountain Irregular Horse Regiment, established in 1876, for example, see Mutaliev, *V Odnom stroiu*, 34–5.

187 Pypin, *Istoriia Russkoi literatury*, 4: 25; Black, *Citizens for the Fatherland*, 100.

188 G.G. Evangulov, *Mestnaia reforma na Kavkaze* (St Petersburg, 1914); cited in Gatagova, *Pravitel'stvennaia politika*, 16.

189 Gatagova, *Pravitel'stvennaia politika*, 22.

190 "Ocherk severnoi storony Kavkaza," *Kavkaz*, no. 2 (11 January 1847):7.

191 Gatagova, *Pravitel'stvennaia politika*, 43.

192 *Otchet po upravleniiu Kavkazskim kraem za 1846, 1847 i 1848 gody*, 192–6; RGIA, f. 1268, op. 10, 1859–62, d. 168, Delo "Ob utverzhdenii predpolozhenii Namestnika Kavkazskago otnositel'no ustroistva nachal'nykh shkol dlia detei Kavkazskikh mirnykh gortsev," ll. 6–10.

193 Gatagova, *Pravitel'stvennaia politika*, 27.

194 Gadzhiev, *Petr Karlovich Uslar*, 16–17.

195 There were some 5,000 students in the medresses of Dagestan in 1880; from RGIA, f. 932, op. 1, 1880–82, d. 292, Delo "Otchet nachal'nika

Dagestanskoi obl. namestniku na Kavkaze o politicheskom i ekonom-
icheskom sostoianii kraia," l. 1. On Muslim education and Arabic liter-
ary traditions, see Kemper, "Einige Notizen zur Arabischsprachigen
Literatur." On imperial education in the North Caucasus, see Dzidzariia,
Formirovanie dorevoliutsionnoi Abkhazskoi intelligentsii, 23–5; Kopachev,
"Razvitie prosveshcheniia v Kabarde v xix veke," 150; and Kazarina,
"Iz istorii razvitiia obrazovaniia v Kabarde v kontse xix i nachale xx
vv.," 164.

196 Esadze, *Istoricheskaia zapiska ob upravlenii Kavkazom*, 2:9–10, 72; "sakartvelo:
kalakis sazogado gamgeobize," *droeba*, no. 23 (12 June 1870):1.

197 See discussions in RGIA, f. 821, op. 8, d. 610 and d. 599.

198 Forsyth, *A History of the Peoples of Siberia*, 162; Baumann, "Universal
Service Reform and Russia's Imperial Dilemma," 40.

199 Dul'etta Mesxidze, "Die Rolle des Islams beim Kampf um die Staatliche
Eigenständigkeit Tschetscheniens und Inguschetiens 1917–1925," in von
Kügelgen, Kemper, and Frank, eds., *Muslim Culture in Russia and Central
Asia from the 18th to the Early 20th Centuries*, 2:457–481; also see
Bennigsen and Wimbush, *Mystics and Commissars*, 22–31.

200 GARF, f. 6991, op. 6, 1975, d. 743, Delo "Perepiska s upolnomochennym
Soveta po voprosam deiatel'nosti religioznykh organizatsii po
Dagestanskoi ASSR," Speech of mufti of Muslims of the North Caucasus,
l. 12; Letter from A. Nurullaev to M.S. Gadzhiev, 18 February 1975, l. 21.

201 Evans, *The Making of the Habsburg Monarchy, 1550–1700*, 158.

CHAPTER THREE

1 Dubrovin, *Istoriia voiny*, 1:1, 384.

2 Strakhovsky, *L'Empereur Nicolas Ier et l'esprit national russe*; Koyré, *La
philosophie et le problème national en Russie au début du xix siècle*, 164–202;
Arseniev, *La sainte Moscou*; Riasanovsky, *Russia and the West in the
Teaching of the Slavophiles*; Christoff, *An Introduction to Nineteenth-Century
Russian Slavophilism*, vol. 1; Chmielewski, *Tribune of the Slavophiles*;
Gleason, *European and Muscovite*; Walicki, *The Slavophile Controversy*.

3 Khomiakov, "Neskol'ko slov pravoslavnago khristianina o zapadnykh
veroispovedaniiakh," (1853), in Khomiakov, *Izbrannye Sochineniia*, 252–5.

4 Ibid., in Khomiakov, *PSS*, 2:39–40.

5 Khomiakov, "Aristotel' i vsemirnaia vystavka" (1851), in Khomiakov,
PSS, 1:181; Samarin, "Zamechaniia na zametki Russkago Vestnika"
(1856), in Samarin, *Sochineniia*, 1:151.

6 Khomiakov, "Zapiski o vsemirnoi istorii," part 2, in Khomiakov, *PSS*,
6:485–98.

7 Ibid., 499.

8 Ibid.

9 "K Serbam, poslanie iz Moskvy" (1860), in Khomiakov, *Izbrannye Sochineniia*, 176.

10 Khomiakov, "Zapiski o vsemirnoi istorii," part 2, in Khomiakov, *PSS*, 6:500.

11 Ibid., 503.

12 Khomiakov, "O starom i novom" (1839), in Khomiakov, *PSS*, 3:37.

13 Ibid., 44.

14 Ibid.

15 Christoff, *An Introduction to Nineteenth-Century Russian Slavophilism*, 33.

16 On early Russia and the Byzantine heritage, see Michael Cherniavsky, "Khan or Basileus: An Aspect of Russian Mediaeval Political Theory," in Cherniavsky, *The Structure of Russian History*, 65–79; and Dmitri Obolensky, "Russia's Byzantine Heritage," ibid., 3–28.

17 Cited in Davison, " 'Russian Skill and Turkish Imbecility,' " 37. Article VII of the 21 July 1774 Treaty of Kuchuk Kainardji is in Macfie, *The Eastern Question, 1774–1923*, 81.

18 Pypin, *Istoriia Russkoi literatury*, 4:64; Zhigarev, *Russkaia politika v vostochnom voprose*, 1:213.

19 Wortman, *Scenarios of Power*, 1:138–41; Jelavich, *Russia's Balkan Entanglements, 1806–1914*, 3–5; Zhigarev, *Russkaia politika v vostochnom voprose*, 1:208–14; Ragsdale, "Russian Projects of Conquest in the Eighteenth Century," 82.

20 Cited in Jelavich, *Russia's Balkan Entanglements, 1806–1914*, 172.

21 V.N. Vinogradov, "The Personal Responsibility of Emperor Nicholas I for the Coming of the Crimean War," in Ragsdale, *Imperial Russian Foreign Policy*, 159–70; David M. Goldfrank, "Policy traditions and the Menshikov mission of 1853," ibid., 119–58.

22 *Teatr v Tiflise s 1845–1856 god*, 86.

23 RGIA, f. 932, op. 1, 1846, d. 92, Delo "Proekt o vedenii khristianskoi very na Kavkaze mezhdu gorskimi narodami," Aleksandr Begichev, 30 September 1846, ll. 5–13, 31–4; also see report of Lieutenant Stamm of the Black Sea Shore Line in PFA AN, f. 100, op. 1, 1854, d. 195/2, Delo "Etnograficheskii ocherk Cherkesskogo naroda," l. 129.

24 Algeron, *Les algeriens Musulmans et la France (1871–1919)*, 1:267–76.

25 Dowler, "The Politics of Language in Non-Russian Elementary Schools," 517; Olcott, *The Kazakhs*, 19; Slezkine, "Savage Christians or Unorthodox Russians?"

26 Platonov, *Obzor deiatel'nosti*, 79.

27 Petr Khitsunov, "O Dukhovnoi Osetinskoi shkole v Mozdoke," *Kavkaz*, no. 17 (30 March 1846): 52. On the Ossetian commissions, see Tarran, "The Orthodox Mission in the North Caucasus."

28 Platonov, *Obzor deiatel'nosti*, 80–90.

29 SSSA, f. 492, op. 1, 1816, d. 43, Delo "O potrete knig Osetinskoi Dukhovnoi Komissii," Report, 29 January 1816, l. 4.

30 S.A. Razdol'skii, "Russkaia pravoslavnaia tserkov' v Kavkazskoi voine," in *Kavkazskaia voina*, 258.

31 Lilov, *Deiatel'nost' obshchestva vozstanovleniia*, 20.

32 RGIA, f. 796, op. 141, 1860, d. 2040, Delo "Raport pr. Evseviia, arkhepiskopa kartashnskhago, Ekzarkh Gruzii," Report from Evsevi to Holy Synod, 13 October 1860, l. 8.

33 *O deistviiakh*, 2.

34 *Po predlozheniiam namestnika Kavkazskago*, 31.

35 RGIA, f. 796, op. 205, 1860, d. 464, Delo "Pis'ma Bariatinskogo, N.I.; Namestnika na Kavkaze, Mitr. Isidoru o polozhenii pravoslaviia na Kavkaze," Letter from Bariatinskii to Isidor, 25 April 1860, l. 2. Isidor was the metropolitan of Novgorod, St Petersburg, Estonia, and Finland.

36 Platonov, *Obzor deiatel'nosti*, 92; on Miliutin's support, see SSSA, f. 493, op. 1, 1860–82, d. 1, Delo "O uchrezhdenii Obshchestva vosstanovleniia," Essay from journal of Caucasus Committee, 2 December 1857, l. 15.

37 Rieber, *The Politics of Autocracy*, 61.

38 RGIA, f. 796, op. 205, 1858–61, d. 464, Letter to Bariatinskii, 13 October 1858, l. 26; also letters of 3 November 1859, l. 31, and 5 September 1860, l. 32; also SSSA, f. 493, op. 1, 1860–82, d. 1, l. 9.

39 RGIA, f. 796, op. 205, 1858–61, d. 464, Letter to Bariatinskii, 13 October 1858, l. 30.

40 *O deistviiakh*, 2–4.

41 SPbFIRI RAN, f. 36, op. 2, 1839, d. 32, l. 3.

42 Dubrovin, *Istoriia voiny*, 1:1:92.

43 Ibid., 1:2:96. For a similar description of the Abkhaz, see 1:2:12.

44 Ibid., 1:2:93.

45 D.Z. Bakradze, "Svanetiia," *ZKOIRGO* 6 (1864), part 2:19.

46 R.D. Eristov, "O Tushino-Pshavo-Khevsurskom okruge," *ZKOIRGO* (1855):96.

47 Ibid., 95.

48 SSSA, f. 493, op. 1, 1860–82, d. 1, ll. 1–3.

49 P. Khitsunov, "O sostoianii nekogda byvshago khristianstva na Kavkaze," *Kavkaz*, no. 34 (24 August 1846): 135–6; no. 35 (31 August 1846): 139–40.

50 P. Khitsunov, "O Chakhkirinskom kreste," *Kavkaz*, no. 15 (13 April 1846): 59.

51 A fascinating example of continuity across the bridge of the revolution in this regard is the way in which Soviet writers in the 1920s defined the "narod" in the North Caucasus as the "productive forces," allowing them to exclude Muslim clerics, Sufi teachers, privileged elites, former *chinovniki*, the emerging intelligentsia, and anyone with any connection to the surrounding empires.

52 Dubrovin, *Istoriia voiny*, 1:1:112.

53 Ibid., 1:1:165.

54 L. Ia. Liul'e, "Verovaniia, religioznye obriady i predrazsudki u Cherkess," *ZKOIRGO* 5 (1862): 123.

55 Ibid., 124–8.

56 Dubrovin, *Istoriia voiny*, 1:2:13, 115.

57 G.N. Kazbek (Kazbegi), "Tri mesiatsa v Turetskoi Gruzii," *ZKOIRGO* 10, no. 1 (1876): 79, 33–5.

58 mose janashvili, "ninas jvari," *mtskemsi*, no. 7 (1884): 5–6.

59 "kidev oriode sitkva kutaisis momavali sasulieri seminariis daarsmgis gamo," *mtskemsi*, no. 7 (1 April 1884): 1–4; "kristianobis gavrtseleba sakartveloshi," *mtskemsi*, no. 10 (1884): 3–5.

60 "Religioznoe sostoianie Abkhazii," *Pastyr'*, no. 1 (1890): 11; nos. 15–16 (1889):9–10.

61 SSSA, f. 493, op. 1, 1861–67, d. 16, l. 13.

62 RGIA, f. 796, op. 141, 1860, d. 2040, Report from Evsevi to Holy Synod, 13 October 1860, l. 6. Also see RGIA, f. 796, op. 137, 1855–56, d. 1377, Delo "So otchetami osetinskoi dukhovnoi komissii za 1855," Report of Isidor to Holy Synod, 26 July 1856, l. 4.

63 RGIA, f. 796, op. 141, 1860, d. 2040, l. 6.

64 Khomiakov, "Zapiski o vsemirnoi istorii," part 2, in Khomiakov, *PSS*, 6:484–500.

65 Ivan Aksakov in *Rus'* (1882), in Aksakov, *Slavianskii Vopros, 1860–1886*, 560.

66 Il'minskii, *Pis'ma*, 122; Dowler, *Classroom and Empire*, 59.

67 Markov, *Ocherki Kavkaza*, 177. A similar discussion in the Georgian press is "tsot-tsota kvelaperzed," *mtskemsi*, no. 10 (31 March 1886): 11–12.

68 Dubrovin, *Istoriia voiny*, 1:1:405–6, 466.

69 V. Novitskii, "Anapa i zakubanskiia poseleniia," *ZKOIRGO*, 2 (1853): 15.

70 Dubrovin, *Istoriia voiny*, 1:1:95.

71 SSSA, f. 493, op. 1, 1861–68, d. 14, Delo "O vyzov iz vnutrennikh gubernii Rossii," Document, ll. 33–4.

72 SSSA, f. 433, op. 1, 1881, d. 157, Delo "Godovye otchety o shkolakh," Report, 11 April 1881, l. 19.

73 SSSA, f. 433, op. 1, 1870, d. 7, Delo "Ob uchiteliakh shkol Obshchestva i shkolakh," Letter to N.P. Zakharov, l. 71.

74 SSSA, f. 493, op. 1, 1887–88, d. 489, Report of Svan religious official, 1886, l. 39.

75 Ibid., Report to council, 30 January 1886, ll. 100–1.

76 SSSA, f. 493, op. 1, 1861–67, d. 16, Delo "O soderzhanii gorskago dukhovenstva," l. 7.

77 SSSA, f. 493, op. 1, 1899–1901, d. 951, Delo "Ob otkrytii dukhovnago uchilishcha v Abkhazii," Prince Golitsyn to Pobedonostsev, 27 February 1901, ll. 11–12.

78 SSSA, f. 493, op. 1, 1887–88, d. 489, Delo "Otchety o missionerskoi deiatel'nosti," Report, 12 June 1887, l. 10; ibid., 1893, d. 699, Delo "Po raportu Ingiloiskogo sviashchennika Okropiridze," Report, 6 September 1893, l. 2.

79 D.A. Tolstoi, "O merakh k obrazovaniiu naseliaiushchikh Rossiiu inorodt-sev," 1558; Dowler, *Classroom and Empire*, 63–80; Vorontsov-Dashkov, *Vsepoddanneishaia zapiska*, 108.

80 SSSA, f. 493, op. 1, 1899–1901, d. 951, Delo "Ob otkrytii dukhovnago uchilishcha v Abkhazii," Prince Golitsyn to Pobedonostsev, 27 February 1901, l. 11.

81 The 1870 regulations remained technically a directive from the Ministry of Education rather than part of the Code of Laws, and of course they were frequently challenged throughout the imperial era. See Dowler, *Classroom and Empire*, 83, 163–70.

82 SSSA, f. 493, op. 1, 1887–88, d. 489, Delo "Otchety o missionerskoi dei-atel'nosti," Report of Svan religious official, 1886, l. 38.

83 Ibid., Report, 12 June 1887, l. 2.

84 Michael Khodarkovsky, " 'Ignoble Savages and Unfaithful Subjects': Constructing Non-Christian Identities in Early Modern Russia," in Brower and Lazzerini, *Russia's Orient*, 18–20.

85 Slezkine, "Savage Christians or Unorthodox Russians?" 17.

86 SSSA, f. 493, op. 1, 1862–68, d. 33, Delo "O uspekhakh deistvii mission-erov," Report, 30 January 1862, l. 4.

87 Ibid., Report, ll. 9–10.

88 Ibid., Document from Gabriel to council of society, 13 December 1868, l. 38.

89 Ibid., 1887–88, d. 489, Delo "Otchety o missionerskoi deiatel'nosti," Report, 12 June 1887, l. 10.

90 Ibid., 1868, d. 186, Delo "O prikhodskikh shkolakh vedomstva Obshchestvo," Report of council of society, 16 January 1868, l. 3.

91 SSSA, f. 5, op. 1, 1865, d. 177, Delo "O deistviiakh … Soveta Obshchestva," Note from the printing house, June 8, 1865, l. 4; Letter from society to Financial Department, 4 June 1865, l. 44.

92 M. Iluridze, "Istoricheskii ocherk deiatel'nosti pravoslavnago missioner-stva na Kavkaze v xviii i xix st.," *Pastyr'*, no. 5 (1889):5.

93 SSSA, f. 433, op. 1, 1870, d. 7, Delo "Ob uchiteliakh shkol Obshchestva," Essay, l. 89.

94 Ibid., Document from teacher of Khumalagsk school, 3 December 1870, ll. 95–6.

95 SSSA, f. 433, op. 1, 1872–73, d. 19, Report, ll. 34–40.

96 SSSA, f. 493, op. 1, 1887–88, d. 489, Delo "Otchety o missionerskoi deia-tel'nosti," Report, 12 June 1887, l. 10.

97 Ibid., ll. 16–17.

98 See Eklof, *Russian Peasant Schools*.

99 American agents of the Department of the Interior were similarly frus-trated with the Native Americans. An agent to the Sac and Fox tribes com-plained in 1882 that the "Indians scare the children by telling them if they attend school they will be taken from their home and made soldiers" (from Adams, *Education for Extinction*, 29).

100 *Otchet ... za 1866 god*, 23; *Otchet ... za 1865 god*, 35; *Otchet ... za 1866 god*, 16.

101 SSSA, f. 433, op. 1, 1872–73, d. 19, Report of teacher of Chargar'sk school, 1872, l. 26.

102 Ibid., l. 23.

103 Ibid., 1872, d. 23, Delo "Rodovykh otchety uchitelei," Report, 1872, l. 7.

104 SSSA, f. 492, op. 1, 1840, d. 23, Delo "O predostavlenii sluzhby sviash-chennikom," Report, 31 October 1840, ll. 2–4.

105 RGIA, f. 797, op. 2, 1814, d. 5716, Delo "O otnosheniem arkhiepiskopa Telivskago i Gruzinsko-Kavkazskago [illegible] po Osetinskoi dukhovnoi kommissii," Letter of Parsadan Tsitsianov to Holy Synod, 5 April 1817, l. 1.

106 *Otchet ... za 1862 i 1863 gody*, 23.

107 SSSA, f. 4, op. 1, 1853, d. 1645, Delo "Po otnosheniu nachal'nikakh Gorskikh narodov," Report, l. 1.

108 SSSA, f. 493, op. 1, 1887–88, d. 489, Delo "Otchety o missionerskoi deiatel'nosti," Report, 12 June 1887, l. 10.

109 *Otchet ... za 1864 god*, 9.

110 SSSA, f. 493, op. 1, 1881–82, d. 384, Delo "O preobrazovanii shkol Obshchestva v Tionetskom uezde," Roster, 1 September 1880, ll. 10–13.

111 Ibid., 1886–87, d. 468, Delo "Ob otkrytii Osetinskago trekhklassnago uchilishcha," Explanation of rector, 17 May 1886, ll. 3–7; ibid., 1887–88, d. 489, Report of Svan religious official, 1886, l. 39.

112 SSSA, f. 5, op. 1, 1874, d. 3121, Delo "S vsepoddanneishim' otchetom nachal'nika Terskoi oblasti," Loris-Melikov, 1873, l. 6.

113 SSSA, f. 493, op. 1, 1871, d. 247, Delo "O revizii shkol Obshchestva," 1870, ll. 8–9.

114 Ibid., l. 13.

115 SSSA, f. 433, op. 1, 1872, d. 23, Delo "Rodovykh otchety uchitelei," Report, 1872, l. 5.

116 RGIA, f. 799, op. 13, 1885, d. 862, Delo "Ob ustroistve del i uluchshenii sredstv soderzhaniia obshchestva vozstonavleniia pravoslavnago khris-tianstva na Kavkaze," Journal of Committee of Ministers, 29 January, 5 February, and 12 February 1885, l. 2.

117 On the concerns of Pobedonostsev, see RGIA, f. 932, op. 1, 1882, d. 415, Delo "Perepiska kn. A.M. Dondukova-Korsakova s ober prokurom Sinoda Konst. Petr. Pobedonostsev," Letter from Pobedonostsev to Dondukov-Korsakov, 22 April 1882, ll. 5–8; RGIA, f. 799, op. 13, d. 862, Department of the Orthodox Faith by Pobedonostsev, 14 January 1885, ll. 7–8. On the financial difficulties of the society, see *Otchet ... za 1864 god*, 37–40; RGIA, f. 799, 1885, op. 13, d. 862, Department of the Orthodox Faith, Pobedonostsev, 14 January 1885, l. 28; Telegraph from Ekzarkh Pavel to Holy Synod, 10 May 1885, l. 112; Journal of Committee of Ministers, 29 January, 5 February, and 12 February, 1885, l. 4; and Information about the debts of the society, 18 February 1885, l. 65.

118 Ivan Aksakov, *Den'* (1862, 1865), in Aksakov, *Slavianskii vopros, 1860–1886*, 25, 52.
119 Khomiakov, "Zapiski o vsemirnoi istorii, part 1, in Khomiakov, *PSS*, 5:25.

CHAPTER FOUR

1 Belinskii, "Obshchee znachenie slova literatura" (1842–44), in Belinskii, *PSS*, 5:633.
2 Ibid., 622.
3 Khomiakov, "Mnenie inostrantsev o Rossii" (1845), in Khomiakov, *Izbrannye Sochineniia*, 85–6; Samarin, "Dva slova o narodnosti v nauke" (1856), in Samarin, *Sochineniia*, 1:111.
4 Pypin, *Kharakteristiki literaturnykh mnenii ot dvadtsatykh do piatidesiatykh godov*, 231.
5 Kireevskii, "Nechto o kharaktere poezii Pushkina" (1828), in Kireevskii, *PSS*, 2:3–12; Kireevskii, "Bibliograficheskiia stat'i" (1845), ibid., 122.
6 Belinskii, "Literaturnye mechtaniia" (1834), in Belinskii, *PSS*, 1:35; Kireevskii, "Nechto o kharaktere poezii Pushkina" (1828), in Kireevskii, *PSS*, 2:12.
7 Tsereteli, *Perezhitoe*, 139; Surguladze, *I.G. Chavchavadze*, 119–20.
8 Reisner, "Die georgische Alphabetisierungsgesellschaft," 69.
9 ilia chavchavadze, "chveni ubeduri," *droeba*, no. 2 (15 January 1870):1.
10 ilia chavchavadze, "chveni ubeduri mtsibnobroba am saukuneshi," *droeba*, no. 3 (22 January 1870): 1.
11 ilia ponteli, "tavad rapiel eristavis 50 tslis literaturul mogvatse obis dgesastsaulis bamo," *iveria*, no. 228 (22 October 1895):3. For similar sentiments about Baratashvili, see petre umikashvili, "t. lekan melikishvilis tserili poetze," *kvali*, no. 3 (1893): 7–8.
12 ponteli, "tavad rapiel eristavis," *iveria*, no. 228 (22 October 1895):2; also *tsnomis purtseli*, no. 180 (1 January 1904); *tsnomis purtseli*, no. 182 (8 January 1904).
13 See Reisner, "Die georgische Alphabetisierungsgesellschaft," 77n51; Lodzemskaia, *M.M. Ippolitov-Ivanov i gruzinskaia muzykal'naia kul'tura*; SSSA, f. 2094, op. 1, 1912–16, d. 11, delo "sazogadoebis krebis okmis amona," ll. 25–6; "khalkhuri," *kvali*, no. 2 (10 January 1893): 7.
14 Layton, *Russian Literature and Empire*; Layton, "Nineteenth-Century Russian Mythologies of Caucasian Savagery," in Brower and Lazzerini, *Russia's Orient*, 89–91; Ram, "Prisoners of the Caucasus."
15 Gershenzon, *Istoriia Molodoi Rossii*, 21.
16 The reference is to Layton, "The Creation of an Imaginative Caucasian Geography." Also see Halbach, "Die Bergvölker (*gorcy*) als Gegner und Opfer."
17 "Letopis otdela," *ZKOIRGO*, 1 (1852):215.

18 Kapieva, "Kavkaz v russkoi poezii pervoi poloviny XIX veka";
   Bez'iazychnyi, "Kavkaz v zhizni i tvorchestve A.I. Polezhaeva, (1829–
   1833)," 83.
19 Braginskii, "Zametki o zapadno-vostochnom sinteze v lirike
   Pushkina,"119.
20 SPbFIV RAN, f. 6, op. 1, d. 33a, l. 27.
21 "Letopis' otdela," ZKOIRGO (1853):208; "Smes': voskhozhdenie na goru
   Demavend," ZKOIRGO 2 (1853):269.
22 "Letopis' otdela," ZKOIRGO 5 (1862):54; "Deistviia otdela," ZKOIRGO 3
   (1855):242, 280; "Sostav i sposoby otdela," ZKOIRGO 2 (1853):220.
23 "Otchet o sostoianii i deistviakh otdela s 1859 po 1863 god," ZKOIRGO 6
   (1864):29.
24 Brooks, When Russia Learned to Read, 214–45; Brower, "Imperial Russia
   and Its Orient."
25 "Puteshestvie Spika i Granta k istochnikam Nila," VP, no. 22 (1867):2;
   "Raznyia izvestiia: Novaia Kaledonia," VP, no. 28 (1867):112; "Raznyia
   izvestiia: belye i indeitsy v Soedinenykh Shtatakh," VP, no. 39 (1867):29–
   32; "Puteshestviia i prikliucheniia Barona Vogana v Kalifornii," VP, no. 1
   (2 June 1867): 1–16; "Raznyia izvestiia: bystroe protsvetanie
   Avstraliiskikh kolonii Anglii," VP, no. 20 (1867): 29–32; "Raznyia
   izvestiia," VP, no. 3 (1867): 14–16.
26 "Tri goda v plenu u Patagontsev," VP, no. 1 (29 June 1867):10.
27 PFA AN, f. 100, op. 1, 1845, d. 430, delo "Perepiska Nikolaia I s Novoross-
   iskim gen.-gubernatorom M.S. Vorontsovym o naznachenii ego namestni-
   kom Kavkaza," Letter from Nicholas I to Vorontsov, 17 November 1845,
   l. 1.
28 Rhinelander, Prince Mikhail Vorontsov, 7–12, 57–120; Brooks, "Nicholas I as
   Reformer," 245–6.
29 From 25,000 in 1834 to 70,000 by 1863. In 1880 the population of Tbilisi
   was 86,455, which included 19,804 Russians, 22,285 Georgians, 38,513
   Armenians, 3,332 "Tatars," and 2,521 "other narodnosti"; from A.S.
   Nadezhin, "Dvizhenie naseleniia v Zakavkazskom krae," SSOK 9 (1885):1.
   On Vorontsov in Tbilisi, see also Kishmishev, Tiflis: Lichnyia vospominaniia;
   and Kishmishev, Tiflis 40-kh godov. On Vorontsov in Odessa, where he was
   governor-general from 1823 to 1845, see Herlihy, Odessa: A History, 1794–
   1914, 117–44. Herlihy, however, associates Vorontsov more with his family's private exploitation of the resources of the region than with the city's
   cultural and social development. Soviet scholarship takes a similar approach. Sh. Chkhetiia, for example, identifies 1865 as the significant
   departure for capitalist development, for which Vorontsov's efforts provided the groundwork. See Chkhetiia, Tbilisi v XIX stoletii: 1865 gody, 9–14,
   30; also Gasamov, Vzaimootnosheniia narodov Dagestana, 34. On Vorontsov
   as a supporter of Cossack trade with the mountaineers, see Degoev,

Kavkazskii vopros v mezhdunarodnykh otnosheniiakh, 63–4; Kumykov, *Vovlechenie severnogo Kavkaza vo vserossiiskii rynok v xix v.*, 74–81; G.G. Moshkovich, "General-Leitenant G.A. Rashpil' i ego rol' v reshenii problemy mezhdnatsional'nykh otnoshenii v period Kavkazskoi voiny (1817–1864)," in *Kavkazskaia voina*, 156–68.

30 Demkov, *Istoriia Russkoi pedagogii*, 2:16–17.

31 Tokarev, *Istoriia Russkoi etnografii*, 76; Vucinich, *Science in Russian Culture*, 59–60, 100–5, 152–4; Layton, *Russian Literature and Empire*, 75–85; Pypin, *Istoriia Russkoi literatury*, 4: 167–9; Tsibirov, *Osetiia v Russkoi nauke*, 15.

32 Vengerov, *Ocherki po istorii Russkoi literatury*, 4.

33 *Rossiiskaia Azbuka dlia obucheniiu iunoshestva chteniiu*, 35; also see Pypin, *Istoriia Russkoi literatury*, 4:80

34 Raeff, "Les Slaves, les Allemands et les 'Lumières'"; Raeff, *The Well-Ordered Police State*, 37, 23.

35 Raeff, *Siberia and the Reforms of 1822*, 41, 109–10, 125; Slezkine, *Arctic Mirrors*, 82–8.

36 Jones, *The Emancipation of the Russian Nobility, 1762–1785*, 241.

37 Chechulin, *Russkoe provintsial'noe obshchestvo v vtoroi polovine xviii veka*, 27–8; Demkov, *Istoriia Russkoi pedagogii*, 2:678.

38 sssa, f. 4, op. 2, 1845–47, d. 19, Delo "O zhelanii … ustroit zavedenie dlia ochischeniia vody," Letter to Vorontsov, 30 May 1845, l. 1; ibid., Brochure, l. 9. Also see Rhinelander, "Viceroy Vorontsov's Administration of the Caucasus," 83–9; P. Sobol'shchikov, "Obshchestvennoe zdorov'e v Tiflise," in *Kavkazskii Kalendar' na 1846* (St Petersburg, 1846), 153–61.

39 "Neskol'ko slov," *Kavkaz*, no. 13 (13 February 1854):49–51; "Benefis Manokhina," *Kavkaz*, no. 6 (20 January 1854):11.

40 "Tiflisskiia vesti," *Kavkaz*, no. 39 (28 September 1846):153.

41 V., "Sneg v Tiflise," *Kavkaz*, no. 49 (6 December 1847):193–4.

42 spbfiv ran, f. 6, op. 1, d. 33a, l. 36.

43 sssa, f. 5, op. 1, 1863–67, d. 109, ll. 81, 170–3, 196; *Otchet po upravleniiu kavkazskim kraem za 1866 god*, 61.

44 g. tsereteli, "ormotsda sami tseli kartulis teatrisa," *kvali*, no. 2 (10 January 1893):10. Also see "kartuli teatri," *iveria*, no. 11 (1882):88–96.

45 Zisserman, *Dvadtsat' piat' let na Kavkaze (1842–1867)*, 1:5–18.

46 Ibid., 298.

47 Ibid., 188.

48 Ibid., 329.

49 Ibid., 270, 320–1.

50 Bassin, *Imperial Visions*, 94–101; Knight, "Science, Empire, and Nationality"; Lincoln, *In the Vanguard of Reform*, 91–101. Also see Vucinich, *Science in Russian Culture*, 350–3; Tokarev, *Istoriia Russkoi etnografii*, 214–84; Stepanov, "Russkoe geograficheskoe obshchestvo i etnografiia (1845–

1861)"; Berelowitch, "Aux origines de l'ethnographie russe"; Bassin, "The Russian Geographical Society"; Clay, "Ethos and Empire," 46–55; P.P. Semenov *Istoriia poluvekovoi deiatel'nosti Imperatorskago Russkago Geograficheskago Obshchestva, 1845–1895*.

51 "Letopis' otdela," *ZKOIRGO* 1 (1852):185.

52 *Kavkazskii Kalendar' na 1863*, 126–9; SPbFIVI RAN, f. 6, op. 1, d. 33a, l. 136.

53 Melikset-Bekov, *Vvedenie v istoriiu gosudarstvennykh obrazovanii Iugo-Kavkaza*, 18.

54 SSSA, f. 4, op. 3, 1846, d. 157, Delo "Po otnosheniiu russkago geograficheskago obshchestva," Letter from Lütke to P.A. Ladinskii, 20 July 1846, l. 3.

55 Ibid., Letter from Lütke to Vorontsov, 20 June 1846, ll. 1–2.

56 Ibid., Report, l. 4.

57 "Ot Imperatorskago Arkheologicheskago Obshchestva," *Kavkaz*, no. 52 (5 July 1850):208.

58 SSSA, f. 416, op. 1, 1864, d. 1, Delo "Ob uchrezhdenie Arkheograficheskoi komissii," Letter from Baron Nikolai to viceroy, 19 February 1864, l. 7.

59 "Deistviia otdela," *ZKOIRGO* 3 (1855):250–4; "Otchet o sostoianii i deistviiakh otdela s 1859 po 1863 god," *ZKOIRGO* 6 (1864):9; "Letopis otdela," *ZKOIRGO* 5 (1862), part 2:70.

60 SPbFIV RAN, f. 6, op. 1, d. 22, l. 1; d. 23, l. 1.

61 Ibid., d. 331, ll. 246–55. His report was Berzhe, "Etnograficheskoe obozrenie Kavkaza," in Grigor'ev, *Trudy tret'iago mezhdunarodnago s'ezda Orientalistov*, and published separately as Berzhe, *Etnograficheskoe obozrenie Kavkaza*.

62 N.I. Voronov, "Predislovie," *SSOK* 1 (1869):11.

63 SSSA, f. 5, op. 1, 1869–74, d. 1096, Delo "O drevnostiakh, naidennykh v Kubanskoi Oblasti," Letter from Gustav Radde to viceroy, 5 February 1870, l. 6; Letter from Radde, 6 January 1873, l. 46; SSMA, f. 3, 1870, Delo "Kavkazskago muzeia po raznym predmetam," Letters to director, ll. 12–13, 64.

64 SSSA, f. 5, op. 1, 1869–74, d. 1096, Plan, 2 February 1859, l. 58.

65 Bakradze, *Arkheologicheskoe puteshestvie po Gurii i Adchare*, v; see also Bakradze, *Istoriia Gruzii na osnovanii novykh izyskanii*.

66 Uslar, "Drevneishiia skazaniia o Kavkaze," 239.

67 Bakradze, *Arkheologicheskoe puteshestvie po Gurii i Adchare*, v.

68 Uslar, "Drevneishiia skazaniia o Kavkaze," 326–407. See also F. Baiern, "O drevnikh sooruzheniiakh na Kavkaze," *SSOK* 1 (1871):298–325.

69 Berzhe, *Chechnia i Chechentsy*, 76–8.

70 Ibid., 16, 38, 48.

71 Ibid., 69–75.

72 Ibid., 88.

73 SSSA, f. 419, op. 1, 1881, d. 1, Delo "Zhurnaly," ll. 5–11; ibid., d. 3, Delo "Perepiska," ll. 47–9.

74 "soplis mgudlis tserili tavis motsmetadmi," *mtskemsi*, no. 30 (30 October 1886): 2; "K pamiati pokoinago arkheologa D.Z. Bakradze," *Pastyr'*, nos. 9–10 (1890): 7–8.

75 SSSA, f. 493, op. 1, 1905, d. 1108, I. Aleksei, l. 38.

76 Bakradze, *Arkheologicheskoe puteshestvie po Gurii i Adchare*.

77 ingalo janashvili, "istoriuli da geograpiuli agtsera heretisa," *mogzauri*, nos. 1–4 (1903):67.

78 z. mtatsmindeli, "khalkhis hazri karsze da batumze," *droeba*, no. 218 (16 December 1877):2.

79 "khevsurebis chveneba imat mitsa-tsulis shesakheb kavkasiis keds ikit," *krebuli*, no. 7 (1872):133–41.

80 Rogger, *National Consciousness in Eighteenth-Century Russia*, 126–85.

81 Belinskii, "Literaturnye mechtaniia," in Belinskii, *PSS*, 92; Frank, *Dostoevsky: The Years of Ordeal, 1850–1859*, 228–33; Frank, *Dostoevsky: The Stir of Liberation, 1860–1865*, 104–5; Pypin, *Istoriia Russkoi literatury*, 4: 626; Vengerov, *Ocherki po istorii Russkoi literatury*, 413–16; Gleason, *Young Russia*, 1–4; 32–76; Slezkine, *Arctic Mirrors*, 75. For discussions of ethnography and its relationship to colonialism in other parts of the world, see Hymes, *Reinventing Anthropology*; Asad, *Anthropology & the Colonial Encounter*; Kuper, *Anthropologists and Anthropology*, 123–49. On French ethnography and French colonial policy in Morocco in the early twentieth century, see Burke III, "Fez, the Setting Sun of Islam." For discussions of ethnography as a form of self-reflexive fiction, see Clifford and Marcus, *Writing Culture*; Clifford, *The Predicament of Culture*; Marcus and Fischer, *Anthropology as Cultural Critique*. For the traditional Soviet approach to ethnography, see Tokarev, *Istoriia Russkoi etnografii*. On ethnography sponsored by the Naval Ministry, see Clay, "Russian Ethnographers in the Service of Empire, 1856–1862." On ethnography and the Geographic Society, see Knight, "Science, Empire, and Nationality."

82 Note the "Program" used by Efimenko, *Sbornik Narodnykh Iuridicheskikh obychaev Arkhangel'skoi Gubernii*, 305–29.

83 a.k., "mtserloba," *droeba*, no. 32 (28 March 1876):1.

84 A. Zisserman, "Poezdka v Shatil," *Kavkaz*, no. 18 (3 May 1847):69; A. Zisserman, "Poezdka v s. Tioanety," *Kavkaz*, no. 20 (17 May 1847):77; Arnol'd Ziserman [*sic*], "Iz moikh zapisok," *Kavkaz*, no. 22 (1 June 1846): 88. For Marlinsky's descriptions of combat, see "Pis'ma iz Dagestana," 17–19, and "Pokhod v Dagestan General-Ad'iutanta Pankrat'eva v 1831 godu," 25–6, 31, 52, in Bestuzhev-Marlinskii, *Sochineniia v dvukh tomakh*, vol. 2. On Marlinsky and ethnographic description, see Layton,

"Marlinsky's 'Ammalat-Bek' and the Orientalisation of the Caucasus in Russian Literature," 39–40; and Kosven, "A.A. Bestuzhev-Marlinskii."

85 Zisserman, *Dvadtsat' piat' let na Kavkaze (1842–1867)*, 1:1.
86 A. Zisserman, "Poezdka v Shatil'," *Kavkaz*, no. 18 (3 May 1847):69.
87 Arnol'd Ziserman [*sic*], "Iz moikh zapisok," *Kavkaz*, no. 22 (1 June 1846): 88.
88 Note Irina Paperno's description of "romantic consciousness" as a "tangible (though at times vehemently denied) presence, a substratum of the consciousness of the realist" in Paperno, *Chernyshevsky and the Age of Realism*, 7. The characterization might also be applied to the relationship of ethnographers in the Caucasus to the Romantic tradition. On the relationship between ethnography and travel literature, see Mary Louise Pratt, "Fieldwork in Common Places," in Clifford and Marcus, *Writing Culture*, 34–8.
89 G.V. Sollogub, "Predislovie," *ZKOIRGO* 1 (1852):ii–v.
90 Ibid., xiv.
91 "Ot redaktsii," *Kavkaz*, no. 1 (5 January 1846):1.
92 "Obiavlenie," *Kavkaz*, no. 2 (12 January 1846):8.
93 A. Zisserman, "Ocherki Khevsuri," *Kavkaz*, no. 22 (20 March 1851):88; *Kavkaz*, no. 23 (23 March 1851): 92–3; *Kavkaz*, no. 24 (27 March 1851): 96–7.
94 Zisserman, *Dvadtsat' piat' let na Kavkaze (1842–1867)*, 1:42.
95 "Materialy dlia izucheniia Kavkaza," *Kavkaz*, no. 96 (7 December 1858): 505.
96 SPbFIRI RAN, f. 36, op. 2, 1839, d. 32, Report by Serebriakov, l. 63; Journal by Kashutin, 1839, ll. 12–27a, 56–65; PFA AN, f. 100, op. 1, 1854, d. 195/2, Stamm, l. 48.
97 SPbFIRI RAN, f. 36, op. 2, 1839, d. 32, Report by Raevskii, 1839, l. 9.
98 GVIARF, f. VUA, op. 1, 1841–42, d. 6440, Delo "Po raportu Raevskago," Report from Raevskii to Chernyshev, 15 March 1841, l. 2; also cited in Bliev, *Osetiia v pervoi treti XIX veka*, 6. On Raevskii's later Pan-Slavic activities with General Cherniaev, see MacKenzie, *The Lion of Tashkent*, 97.
99 PFA AN, f. 32, op. 1, 1828, d. 66, l. 3.
100 PFA AN, f. 100, op. 1, 1854, d. 195/2, ll. 9–11.
101 Ibid., l. 44.
102 Ibid., l. 47; Trennert, *Alternative to Extinction*, 13.
103 PFA AN, f. 100, op. 1, 1844, d. 57, Delo "Obshchii vzgliad na prichiny i posledstviia besporiadkov vozniknuvshikh v Dagestane ot rasprostraneniia fanatizma v sekty miuridov mezhdu gortsami, 1823–1843," by Neverovskii, ll. 5–17, citation from l. 17.
104 SSSA, f. 433, op. 1, 1872–73, d. 19, Report, 12 January 1873, l. 53.
105 Ibid., Report from Levan Abelov, 6 February 1873, l. 17.

106 Ibid., Report, l. 7.

107 Ibid., Report, ll. 34–40.

108 SSSA, f. 433, op. 1, 1881, d. 157, Delo "Godovye otchety o shkolakh," Document, l. 89.

109 Harley, "Maps, Knowledge, and Power," 282.

110 GVIARF, f. VUA, op. 1, 1770, d. 19844, Delo "General'naia karta vsei Rossiiskoi Imperii, 1770."

111 RGIA, f. 187, op. 2, 1744, d. 1399, Delo "Kartina Kabardy."

112 RGIA, f. 932, op. 1, d. 495, Delo "Karta Kavkaza, sostavlennaia dlia obiavleniia deistvii gen. A.P. Ermolova v 1816–1825 gg."

113 GVIARF, f. VUA, op. 1, 1830, d. 20592, Delo "Karta Gorskikh za Kubanskikh narodov sostavlennaia po rasprosam ... vo vremia ekspeditsii protivu sikh narodov v oktiabr mesiats 1830 goda."

114 GVIARF, f. VUA, op. 16, 1806, d. 6715, Delo "Karta Kavkazskoi Gubernii"; ibid., Delo "Karta zemle Chechenskoi."

115 GVIARF, f. VUA, op. 16, n.d., d. 25485, Delo "Karta."

116 Volkova, *Etnicheskii sostav,* 16.

117 RGIA, f. 932, op. 1, 1842, d. 42, Delo "Karta Kavkazskogo kraia so svedeniiami o kolichestve naseleniia po natsional'nostiam i veroispovedaniiam."

118 PFA AN, f. 100, op. 1, 1870, d. 195/13, Delo "Karta Kavkazskago kraia."

119 GVIARF, f. VUA, op. 16, 1790, d. 20482, Delo "Gen. Karta kavkaza, 1790."

120 GVIARF, f. 38, op. 7, 1852, d. 203, Delo "Po otnosheniiu Glavnokomanduiushchago ... o vykhode iz gor urozhentsa Nagornago Dagestana Khalat Efendi," l. 5.

121 On the "quite recent" history of the term "ethnie" in Europe, see Hobsbawm, *Nations and Nationalism since 1780,* 160.

122 "Predislovie," SSOKG 1 (1868):1; "Obzor deiatel'nosti statisticheskikh komitetov Kavkazskago namestnichestva s 1862 po 1867 god," SSSOK 1 (1869), part 3:75.

123 "Etnograficheskiia zametki," EO, no. 3 (1889):11.

124 P.S. Nazarov, "K etnografii bashkir," EO, no. 1 (1890): 169–70.

125 Gustav Radde, "Khevsuriia i Khevsury," trans. and ed. E.G. Veidenbaum, ZKOIRGO 11, no. 2 (1880):57–63.

126 Arnol'd Ziserman [sic], "Iz moikh zapisok," Kavkaz, no. 22 (1 June 1846):88.

127 A. Zisserman, "Ocherki Khevsuri," Kavkaz, no. 22 (20 March 1851):89.

128 Radde, "Khevsuriia i Khevsury," ZKOIRGO 11, no. 2 (1880):72.

129 K. Borisevich, "Cherty nravov pravoslavnikh osetin i ingush severnago Kavkaza," EO, no. 1–2 (1899): 262–3; "Iz gorskoi kriminalistiki," SSOKG 4, part 4 (1870):53–86.

130 Raeff, *Siberia and the Reforms of 1822,* 108–10.

131 "Deistviia otdela," ZKOIRGO 3 (1855), 289; "Sostav i sposoby otdela," ZKOIRGO 3:298–9.

132 "Sostav i sposoby otdela," ZKOIRGO 3 (1855):300; "Otchet o sostoianii i deistviiakh otdela," ZKOIRGO 6 (1864):24–8; SSSA, f. 5, op. 1, 1864, d. 149, Delo "Ob uchrezhdenii v Tiflise Kavkazskago Muzeuma," Report of A. Berzhe, Radde, and N. Baronovskii, ll. 1–25; Zhordaniia, *Istoriia vozniknoveniia Kavkazskago Muzeia*, 125.

133 "Letopis' otdela," ZKOIRGO 5 (1862), part 2:68.

134 "Deistviia otdela," ZKOIRGO 4 (1857), part 2:240.

135 Zhordaniia, *Istoriia vozniknoveniia Kavkazskago Muzeia*, 115–25.

136 Radde, *Kratkii putevoditel' po Kavkazskomu Muzeiu*, 28–40.

137 SPbFIV RAN, f. 6, op. 1, d. 33a, Delo "V.S. Ruban: Adol'f Petrovich Berzhe, stranitsy iz zhizni," kn. 1, ll. 246–55.

138 SSSA, f. 5, op. 1, 1880, d. 6085, Delo "O kollektsii tipov Kavkazskikh plemen'," Letter from Academy of Sciences president, ll. 1–2.

139 SSMA, f. 3, 1909–19, d. 35/36, Delo "O pozhertvovanii raznymi litsami natsional'nykh kostiumov," Letter of Vorontsov-Dashkov, 14 December 1909, l. 1.

140 Ibid., Letters from district commanders, ll. 6–10.

141 Ibid., Vorontsov-Dashkov, l. 2.

142 For example, ethnographer E. Lineva obtained a phonograph in 1897 for the purpose of recording traditional folk songs in Russian villages. The peasants disappointed her, however, and protested: "We don't play those any more; those songs are dull; we have all the fashionable ones now." From E. Lineva, "Pribavlenie k otchetu," EO, no. 3 (1897):222. On Russian collection in the face of industrialization and social change, see discussions in *Etnografichesko Obozrenie*, such as "Voprosy i otvety," EO, no. 3 (1898):206–7; A. Grigor'ev, "Kritika i bibliografiia," EO, no. 3 (1899):182; N. Kharuzin, "K voprosu o bor'be Moskovskago Pravitel'stva s narodnymi iazycheskimi obriadami i sueveriiami v polovine XVII v.," EO, no. 1 (1897):151; "Izvestiia i zametki," EO, no. 2 (1890):259; "Ot redaktsii," EO, no. 1 (1890), VII.

143 A.I. Stoianov, "Puteshestvie po Svaneti," ZKOIRGO 10, no. 2 (1876):286.

144 Berzhe, *Chechnia i Chechentsy*, 67, 107; Nichols, "Who Are the Chechen?"

145 "Smes: material dlia etnografi vostochnogo Kavkaza," ZKOIRGO 7, no. 1 (1866), part 3:26–34; Berzhe, *Chechnia i Chechentsy*, 107.

146 Troinitskii, ed. *Pervaia vseobshchaia perepis' naseleniia Rossiiskoi Imperii, 1897 g.*, part 2:xxviii; Bauer, Kappeler, and Roth, *Die Nationalitaten des Russischen Reiches in der Volkszahlung von 1897*, 1:137–44; Kappeler, *La Russie*, 243.

147 A.P. Berzhe, "Etnograficheskoe obozrenie Kavkaza," in Grigor'ev, *Trudy tret'iago mezhdunarodnago s'ezda Orientalistov*, 298.

148 Berzhe, *Chechnia i Chechentsy*, 67.

149 Berlin, "Herder and the Enlightenment," 99; Hayes, "Contributions of Herder to the Doctrine of Nationalism"; Kohn, *The Idea of Nationalism*, 427–45; Kohn, *Pan-Slavism*, x, 132.

150 Cited in Kohn, *The Idea of Nationalism*, 432.

151 Rogger, *National Consciousness in Eighteenth-Century Russia*, 85–125.

152 L.P. Zagurskii, "Petr Karlovich Uslar i ego deiatel'nost' na Kavkaze," *ZKOIRGO* 12 (1881):ix–xi.

153 P.K. Uslar, "O rasprostranenii gramotnosti mezhdu gortsami," *SSOKG* 3 (1870):28.

154 "Essay on the Origin of Language," in Herder, *J.G. Herder on Social and Political Culture*, 152.

155 "kartuli teatri," *droeba*, no. 11 (13 May 1866):1.

156 "kalebis sakhelosno shkola tpilisshi," *droeba*, no. 3 (22 January 1870):4.

157 SSSA, f. 493, op. 1, 1865, d. 97, Delo "O sostavlenii programy azbuki i knigi dlia chteniia na gruzinskom iazyke," Document from main inspector of educational institutions, l. 2.

158 b. petriashvili, "am droebis kartvelebi," *droeba*, no. 24 (12 August 1866): 1–2.

159 "tsneli dro dagvidga da ra zomebi unda vismarot khalkhshi zneobis asamagleblad," *mtskemsi*, no. 9 (20 March 1886):1–3.

160 "sakartvelo," *droeba*, no. 20 (27 May 1872):1.

161 Reisner, "Die georgische Alphabetisierungsgesellschaft"; Reisner, "The Tergdaleulebi."

162 PFA AN, f. 94, op. 2, d. 2, Delo "Spisok russkikh slov s perevodom na andiiskii i ingushskii iazyki (russkaia transkriptsiia)," ll. 1–12; ibid., d. 114, Delo "Spisok russkikh slov s perevodom na cherkesskii iazyk," ll. 1–6; ibid., d. 61, Delo "Slova Cherkes Kabardinskikh (russkaia transkriptsiia)," ll. 1–5. Also see L. Zagurskii, "Neskol'ko slov po povodu novago lingvisticheskago truda akademika Shifnera," *SSOKG* 6 (1872), part 3:33–48.

163 "Deistviia otdela," *ZKOIRGO* 3 (1855):248; *Otchet o sostoianii i deistviiakh Kavkazskago Otdela*, 8.

164 Uslar, *Razbor sochineniia Barona P.K. Uslara*, 1.

165 "Deistviia otdela," *ZKOIRGO* 3 (1855):250–4; "Otchet o sostoianii i deistviiakh otdela s 1859 po 1863 god," *ZKOIRGO* 6 (1864):9; "Letopis otdela," *ZKOIRGO* 5 (1862): part 2:70.

166 Magometov, *P.K. Uslar*, 11; "Nechto ob azbukhakh kavkazskikh gortsev," *Kavkaz*, no. 20 (10 March 1863):124–6. On Uslar's life and work, see Zagurskii, "Petr Karlovich Uslar i ego deiatel'nost' na Kavkaze."

167 Zagurskii, "Petr Karlovich Uslar i ego deiatel'nost' na Kavkaze," xxxix–xlviii; Gadzhiev, *Petr Karlovich*, 7–10.

168 Khan-Girei, *Zapiski o Cherkesii*, 6, 17–18; D'iakov, "Zapiski o Cherkesii, sochinennye Khan-Gireem," 173.

169 Khan-Girei, *Zapiski o Cherkesii*, 105.

170 Abdulla Omar-oglu, "Vospominaniia Mutalima," *SSOKG* 1 (1868), part 7:13–64; reprinted in Omarov, *Dagestan: Vremia i sud'by*, 39–193.

171 Omarov, *Dagestan: Vremia i sud'by*, 40.

172 Ibid., 31–2.

173 Letter from Omarov to Suleiman, 10 April 1867, ibid., 285.

174 Muheddin Mahomed-Khanov, "Istinnye i lozhnye posledovateli tarikata," trans. A. Omarov, *SSOKG* 4 (1870):1.

175 Letter from Omarov to Suleiman, 25 October 1868, in Omarov, *Dagestan: Vremia i sud'by*, 292–3.

176 Mahomed-Khanov, "Istinnye i lozhnye posledovateli tarikata," 1–28. A similar work of clarification is "Uchenie o tarikate: Abdul-Marziia, soch. Sheikha Dzhemaleddina Kazikumukhskago," *SSOKG* 2 (1869):1–22.

177 Nogmov, *Istoriia Adygeiskogo naroda*.

178 Ibid., 18.

179 Bartolomeia, *Abkhazskii bukvar'*, 15–16, 40, 45–8, 71–2.

180 Ibid., 92.

181 Ibid., 15–16, 40, 45–8, 71–2.

182 Ibid., 92, 175–88.

183 *Chechenskii bukvar'*.

184 Tsibirov, *Osetiia v russkoi nauke*, 96–100; Abaev, *Tbilisi i Osetiia*, 16; Kokiev, "S.V. Kokiev," 134.

185 Dzagurov, *Pereselenie gortsev v Turtsiiu*, Captain Zolotarev, 14 June 1863, 11–12.

186 RGIA, f. 1268, op. 10, 1860, d. 40, Delo "Ob imenovanii kryl'ev kavkazskoi linii pravago-Kubanskoiu i levago-Terskoiu oblastniami," ll. 1–7. Terek oblast was technically called "Terskaia voiskovaia oblast'," after the Terek River and the Terek Cossacks (*Terskoe kazach'e voisko*).

187 Volkova, *Etnicheskii sostav*, 240–1.

188 RGIA, f. 1149, op. 7, 1869, d. 112, Delo "Ob ustroistve v Predkavkazskom krae dvukh oblastei Kubanskoi i Terskoi," Temporary establishment of military-native administration of Terek oblast, ll. 108–10.

189 RGIA, f. 560, op. 41, 1883, d. 143, Delo "Zhurnaly komissii po preobrazovaniiu upravleniia kavkazskimi kazach'imi voiskami," Letter of V. Butyrkin, 16 December 1883, ll. 4–5.

190 Ibid., Journal, 28 February 1884, l. 45.

191 Ibid., Journal, 6 March 1884, l. 51; Special opinion, 27 November 1884, l. 67.

192 RGIA, f. 37, op. 55, 1892–99, d. 69, Delo "O merakh k uporiadocheniiu razrabotok v kamenalomnakh," Report of commander of Terek oblast for 1890, l. 37. Previously Terek oblast had consisted of seven okrugi: Georgiev, Vladikavkaz, Groznyi, Argun, Vedeno, Kizliar, and Khasav-Iurtov. Virtually all the Terek oblast cities, such as Vladikavkaz, Groznyi, Kizliar, Piatigorsk, Georgiev, and Mozdok, were predominantly populated by Russian Orthodox Christians or other non-Russian Christians. See RGIA, f. 1290, op. 11, 1897, d. 2377, Delo "Materiialy Vserossiskoi perepis' po okrugam Terskoi oblasti," l. 6.

193 RGIA, Biblioteka, op. 1, 1884–1909, d. 99, Report for 1909, by General
     Mikheev, l. 42.
194 RGIA, f. 37, op. 55, 1892–99, d. 69, l. 44.
195 Volkova, *Etnicheskii sostav*, 245.
196 RGIA, f. 560, op. 41, 1883, d. 143, Journal, 23 February 1884, l. 44.
197 Ibid., 8 February 1884, l. 38. Also see RGIA, f. 1276, op. 21, 1895–97, d. 45,
     Delo "Materialy o Chernomorskom naberezh'i Kavkaza," Memoran-
     dum, ll. 1–10 (this RGIA file is mistakenly dated 1917).
198 RGIA, f. 1276, op. 17, 1911, d. 165, Delo "Otchety gubernatorov za 1909
     god," Report of Chernomorsk governor for 1909, ll. 95–6.
199 Thus many ethnographers are viewed favourably by Soviet scholars,
     who portray their critiques of Russian militarism as early examples of
     "democratic enlightenment" work that paved the way for the revolu-
     tionary radicalism of the early twentieth century and the events of 1917.
     For example, on Nikolai I. Voronov see Leiberov, *Tsebel'dinskaia nakhodka*,
     17, 25, 55–6, 84. Voronov offers a tempting target for this common Soviet
     teleology. He criticized Russian rule and studied mountaineers; his
     daughter, Liudmila Voronova, joined the Bolshevik Party in 1903. To the
     revolutionary teleology, Soviet scholars also added a respect for tsarist
     Russia as the "lesser evil" of the imperial powers in the region.
     "Progressive" officials at least introduced backward mountaineers to
     modern forms of schooling, administration, transportation, economy,
     and so on. See Shteppa, "The 'Lesser Evil' Formula." For the formula ap-
     plied to the North Caucasus, see Narochnitskii, *Istoriia narodov severnogo
     Kavkaza (konets xviiiv.-1917 g.)*, 5, 30, 60; and Tsulaia, "Iz istorii
     Kavkazovedeniia," 76.
200 Dostoyevsky, *The Possessed*, 255.

CHAPTER FIVE

1 Lermontov, *A Hero of Our Time*, 57.
2 The reference is to Hobsbawm and Ranger, *The Invention of Tradition*.
3 Roberts and Mann, "Law in Colonial Africa," in Mann and Roberts, *Law
   in Colonial Africa*, 4.
4 Ibid., 3.
5 See Chanock, *Law, Custom and Social Order*. The contrasting method,
   which was prevalent in both Soviet scholarship and traditional Western
   social science, was to treat colonial compilations of customary law as
   faithful expressions of an unchanging and historic culture. Soviet scholars in particular used the compilations as guides for their detection of
   "feudal relationships" and "patriarchal remnants." For example, see
   Edieva, "Formy zemlevladeniia i zemlepol'zovaniia po obychnomu
   pravu Karachaevtsy v pervoi polovine XIX veka"; Azamatov,

Sotsial'no-ekonomicheskoe polozhenie i obychnoe pravo Balkartsev v pervoi polovine XIX v; Luzbetak, *Marriage and the Family in Caucasia,* 168–82; and Grigolia, *Custom and Justice in the Caucasus,* 140–61. On frontiers as sites of judicial pluralism, see Bartlett, *The Making of Europe,* 197–220; and Dargo, *Jefferson's Louisiana.*

6 Manifesto of Alexander I, 12 September 1801, in Modzalevskii, *Khod uchebnago dela na Kavkaze s 1802 po 1880 god,* 4.

7 Lilov, "Ocherk byta Kavkazskikh gortsev," 2–3.

8 Kappeler, *La Russie,* 61, 276–7.

9 A.S. Lappo-Danilevskii, "Sobranie i svod zakonov Rossiiskoi Imperii," 8, 40.

10 Shebanov, "Polnoe sobranie zakonov Rossiiskoi Imperii," 4:299–300.

11 *Obozrenie Istoricheskikh svedenii o Svode Zakonov,* 191.

12 Chistiakov, *Rossiiskoe zakonodatel'stvo X–XX vekov,* vol. 8: *Sudebnaia reforma,* 31.

13 Lincoln, *In the Vanguard of Reform.*

14 Wortman, *The Development of a Russian Legal Consciousness.*

15 Lincoln, *The Great Reforms.*

16 Frierson, "Crime and Punishment in the Russian Village." For an interesting discussion of the"differences between the people and educated society,"see H.V.,"Iz domashnei khroniki,"*Delo* 17, no. 6 (1883):48–71.

17 Frank, "Popular Justice, Community and Culture among the Russian Peasantry, 1870–1900"; Lewin, "Customary Law and Russian Rural Society in the Post-Reform Era."

18 Rogger, *National Consciousness in Eighteenth-Century Russia,* 126–85.

19 Khomiakov, "Eshche o sel'skikh usloviakh" (1842), in his PSS, 3:75; cited in Riasanovsky, *Russia and the West in the Teaching of the Slavophiles,* 143. Also see Christoff, *An Introduction to Nineteenth-Century Russian Slavophilism,* 1:201.

20 Enfimenko, *Sbornik Narodnykh Iuridicheskikh obychaev Arkhangel'skoi Gubernii,* 305–29.

21 Ibid., 24.

22 Lilov, "Ocherk byta Kavkazskikh gortsev," 46.

23 Zh.A. Kalmykov, "Administrativno-sudebnye preobrazovaniia v Kabarde i gorskikh (Balkarskikh) obshchestvakh v gody Russko-Kavkazskoi voiny," in *Kavkazskaia voina,* 123.

24 GVIARF, f. 400, op. 1, 1866–70, d. 68, Delo "Ob administrativnom razdelenii Terskoi, Kubanskoi i Dagestanskoi oblastei," Memorandum of General Boguslavskii, 19 June 1866, l. 13.

25 Ibid., Explanatory memorandum about the situation in Terek and Kuban oblasts, l. 42.

26 GVIARF, f. 400, op. 1, 1870, d. 245, Delo "Vremennye pravila dlia gorskikh slovesnykh sudov," Temporary rules, Viceroy Mikhail, 18 December 1870, l. 1.

27 Raeff, *Siberia and the Reforms of 1822*, 108–11; Slezkine, *Arctic Mirrors*, 82–8.

28 RGIA, f. 1405, op. 532, 1912–14, d. 189, Materials on question of administration of justice for native population of the Caucasus, l. 8b.

29 Ibid., ll. 14–15.

30 Ibid., l. 13.

31 The findings of statistician A.V. Komarov in Dagestan, for example, became part of the adat collections sent to district commanders in Dagestan oblast; see A.V. Komarov, "Adaty i sudoproizvodstvo po nim," *SSOKG* 1 (1868):3. Or the process worked in the other direction. "Adaty Darginskikh Obshchestv," *SSOKG* 7 (1873), part 1:1–128, was prepared by the Dargin District Administration in Dagestan.

32 d. pazliashvili, "khevsurta zne-chveulebani," *tsnomis purtseli*, no. 266 (31 October 1904): 3–4. See also ibid., no. 222 (27 May 1904): 3–4; ibid., no. 223 (30 May 1904):3.

33 Ibid., no. 266 (31 October 1904):3–4. The publisher of the first Turkic newspaper in the Russian Empire, Hasan Melikov Zardabi from Azerbaijan, gradually developed a similar respect for village customary law traditions. See Jersild, "Rethinking Russia from Zardob."

34 GVIARF, f. 400, op. 1, 1870, d. 245, Temporary rules, Viceroy Mikhail, 18 December 1870, l. 5.

35 SSSA, f. 229, op. 2, n.d., d. 1, Delo "Proekt polozheniia," ll. 1–3.

36 GVIARF, f. 400, op. 1, 1870, d. 245, ll. 1–2; Kalmykov, "Administrativno-sudebnye preobrazovaniia v Kabarde," in *Kavkazskaia voina*, 123.

37 RGIA, f. 1276, op. 9, 1913, d. 849, l. 27; RGIA, f. 1405, op. 532, 1912–1914, d. 189, Short note, l. 8a.

38 GVIARF, f. 400, op. 1, 1870, d. 245, Temporary rules, l. 5.

39 Chanock, *Law, Custom and Social Order*, 47.

40 GVIARF, f. 400, op. 1, 1870, d. 245, Temporary rules, l. 5.

41 SSSA, f. 229, op. 2, 1907–08, d. 2846, Delo "S perepiskoi ob izmenenii adatov," Military governor, rural elders, mountain administration, ll. 1–12.

42 Lilov, "Ocherk byta Kavkazskikh gortsev," 6.

43 Nogmov, *Istoriia Adygeiskogo naroda*.

44 Grabovskii, "Ocherk suda i ugolovnykh prestuplenii v Kabardinskom okruge," 2.

45 John, *Politics and the Law in Late Nineteenth-Century Germany*, 36–50.

46 Grabovskii, "Ocherk suda i ugolovnykh prestuplenii v Kabardinskom okruge," 4–5.

47 Lilov, "Ocherk byta Kavkazskikh gortsev," 7. Also see Berzhe on the Chechen, in Berzhe, *Chechnia i Chechentsy*, 72–3.

48 Such as Hanoteau and Letourneux, *La Kabylie et les coutumes kabyles*.

49 Grabovskii, "Ocherk suda i ugolovnykh prestuplenii v Kabardinskom okruge," 6.

50 Ibid., 13–17.

51 Yuri Slezkine, "Naturalists versus Nations: Eighteenth-Century Russian Scholars Confront Ethnic Diversity," in Brower and Lazzerini, *Russia's Orient*, 27–57.

52 "Adaty Darginskikh Obshchestv," ssokg 7 (1873), part 1:12, 33–4.

53 rgia, Biblioteka, op. 1, 1909, d. 99, Delo "Otchety o sostoianii Terskoi oblasti za 1884–1886, 1909," Report of commander of Terek oblast by General Mikheev, l. 43.

54 "Iz gorskoi kriminalistiki," ssokg 3 (1870):11.

55 rgia, f. 1405, op. 532, 1912–14, d. 189, l. 15.

56 Lilov, "Ocherk byta Kavkazskikh gortsev," 28.

57 Lermontov, *A Hero of Our Time*, 57.

58 E.P. Kovalevskii, "Narody Zapadnogo Kavkaza," from *Vestnik Evropi* (1867), in Nadezhdin, *Priroda i liudi na Kavkaze*, 86; K. Borisevich, "Cherti nravov pravoslavnikh Osetin i Ingushei severnago Kavkaza," eo, no. 1–2 (1899):252.

59 Petr Egorov, "Neskol'ko slov o Kavkaze i Shamile," *Severnaia Pchela*, no. 248 (13 November 1859):993.

60 Verderevskii, *Plen u Shamilia*.

61 For example, sssa, f. 4, op. 1, 1847, dela 2222–62.

62 sssa, f. 229, op. 2, 1884–90, d. 41, Delo "O poselenii v Sibiri navsegda," Decisions of the Kurin District Court, 10 January 1884, ll. 1–10.

63 Gramsci, *Selections from the Prison Notebooks of Antonio Gramsci*, 246–7. On Foucault's contrast of "juridical" power versus law as a form of "positive knowledge," or a productive form of power, see Foucault, *Discipline and Punish*; and Foucault, *The History of Sexuality*, 1:85–91.

64 "Iz gorskoi kriminalistiki," ssokg 3 (1870):9.

65 Ibid., 12.

66 On contesting imperial and indigenous views of retaliatory horse theft on the Kazakh steppe, see Virginia Martin, "Barïmta: Nomadic Custom, Imperial Crime," in Brower and Lazzerini, *Russia's Orient*, 249–70.

67 "Iz gorskoi kriminalistiki," ssokg 4 (1870), part 4:78.

68 rgia, f. 1405, op. 532, 1912–14, d. 189, About the reorganization of justice in the Caucasus, 1913, by A.V. Moskalev, l. 30; ibid., Memorandum of N.M. Reinke, l. 97; Lilov, "Ocherk byta Kavkazskikh gortsev," 34.

69 Grabovskii, "Ocherk suda i ugolovnykh prestuplenii v Kabardinskom okruge," 20.

70 "Iz gorskoi kriminalistiki," ssokg 3 (1870):6.

71 Ibid., 6.

72 Ibid., 3–4.

73 Ibid., 2.

74 Ibid., 14.

75 Ibid., 8.

76 Ibid.

77 Ibid., 7.
78 Ibid.
79 "Iz gorskoi kriminalistiki," SSOKG 4 (1870), part 4:76.
80 "Iz gorskoi kriminalistiki," SSOKG 3 (1870):2.
81 Ibid., 8.
82 Ibid., 4.
83 SSSA, f. 229, op. 2, 1884–85, d. 64, Delo "O ssylke vo vnutreniia gubernii Imperii," Military governor of Dagestan to high commander, 7 January 1884, ll. 1–2.
84 Ibid., 1886, d. 367, Delo "O ssylke vo vnutreniia gubernii," Sentence, 14 May 1886, ll. 4–5.
85 Ibid., 1887, d. 514, Delo "O poselenii v Sibiri navsegda," Military governor of Dagestan, 22 December 1886, ll. 1–2.
86 Ibid., 1884–87, d. 32, Delo "O poselenie v Sibir' navsegda," Military governor to high Commander, 2 July 1884, l. 1.
87 "saliteraturo natsili: musha khalkhis kalis da ojakhis mdgomareoba evrokis tsinasaselmtsipo," droeba, no. 28 (14 July 1867):3–4.
88 E.P. Kovalevskii, "Narody Zapadnogo Kavkaza: Cherkesi, Abkhazi i Svaneti," in Nadezhdin, Priroda i liudi na Kavkaze i za Kavkazom, 87; L'vov, "O nravak i obychaiakh dagestanskikh gortsev," ibid., 134.
89 "Iz gorskoi kriminalistiki," SSOKG 4 (1870), part 4:77.
90 "Iz gorskoi kriminalistiki," SSOKG 3 (1870):13–14.
91 SSSA, f. 229, op. 2, 1888–93, d. 2025, Delo "O vysylke v odnu iz vnutrennikh gubernii imperii," Military governor of Dagestan, May 1888, ll. 1–16.
92 Ibid., 1886, d. 367, Military governor of Dagestan, 17 October 1886, l. 2.
93 "Adaty Darginskikh Obshchestv," SSOKG 7 (1873), part 1:20, 51.
94 Ibid., 21; also see 43.
95 SSSA, f. 229, op. 2, 1884, d. 43, Delo "O poselenii v Sibir' navsegda," Sentence of Dagestan People's Court, 22 December 1883, l. 8.
96 Ibid., ll. 10–16.
97 RGIA, Biblioteka, op. 1, 1909, d. 99, General Mikheev, l. 43.
98 A. Krasnov, "Svaneti," in Kruber et al., Aziatskaia Rossiia, 71.
99 Dzhantemir Shanaev, "Prisiaga po obychnomu pravu Osetin," SSOKG 7 (1873), part 1:5–8. On a similar change among the Karachai, see Boris Vs. Miller, "Iz oblasti obychnago prava Karachaevtsev," EO, no. 1 (1902): 18–19, 30. Shanaev served as a native collector of Ossetian folk tales in Dzhantemir Shanaev, "Iz Osetinskikh narodnykh skazanii," SSOKG 7 (1873), part 2:1–21.
100 RGIA, f. 560, op. 41, 1883, d. 143, Special opinion by official in Ministry of the Interior … about plan on military-native administration, l. 70.
101 RGIA, f. 1405, op. 532, 1912–14, d. 189, Notes from memorandum of Vorontsov-Dashkov, 10 February 1907, l. 23.

102 Ibid., Notes from report of Vorontsov-Dashkov, 11 July 1913, l. 25.

103 Ibid., Letter from Vorontsov-Dashkov to I.G. Shcheglovitov,
18 December 1913, l. 42.

104 Ibid., Memorandum ... of N.M. Reinke about creation of judiciary for
mountain population, ll. 78–105. His report is also in RGIA, f. 565, op. 9,
1914, d. 32428, Delo "Ob ustroistve sudebnoi chasti dlia tuzemnago naseleniia Kavkazskago kraia," ll. 40–67. A published version is Reinke,
Gorskie i narodnye sudy Kavkazskago kraia.

105 RGIA, f. 1405, op. 532, 1912–14, d. 189, Memorandum ... of N.M. Reinke,
ll. 87–91.

106 Ibid., l. 79.

107 Ibid., l. 91.

108 Ibid., l. 100.

109 Reinke, *Gorskie i narodnye sudy Kavkazskago kraia*, 3.

110 RGIA, f. 1405, op. 532, 1912–14, d. 189, l. 91.

111 Betts, *Assimilation and Association in French Colonial Theory, 1890–1914*,
15.

112 RGIA, f. 1149, op. 13, 1903, d. 126, Delo "O soderzhanii starshinam
tuzemnykh (aul'nykh) selenii Terskoi i Kubanskoi oblastei," Report from
General Korolev to Committee of Ministers, 23 May 1903, ll. 22–4.

113 RGIA, f. 1276, op. 9, 1913, d. 849, Delo "Ob uchrezhdenii osobogo
dukhovnogo upravleniia (muftiata) dlia musul'man severnogo
Kavkaza," State Duma legal supposition, 3 December 1913, l. 3; Zaikin,
Naselennyia mesta Dagestana, I–III.

114 RGIA, Biblioteka, op. 1, 1909, d. 99, Delo "Otchety o sostoianii Terskoi
oblasti za 1884–1886, 1909," Report of commander of Terek oblast for
1884 by General Iurkovskii, l. 16.

115 RGIA, f. 560, op. 41, 1883, d. 143, Delo "Zhurnaly komissii po preobrazovaniiu upravleniia Kavkazskimi kazach'imi voiskami," Journal, Report
by S.I. Pisarev and O.V. Margraf, 6 March 1884, l. 51.

116 RGIA, Biblioteka, op. 1, 1909 d. 99, Report on Terek oblast for 1909, by
General Mikheev, l. 43.

117 N. Semenov, "Iz nedavniago proshlago na Kavkaze: Razskazy –
vospominaniia o Chechenskom vozstanii v 1877 g.," *Kavkazskii Vestnik*,
no. 6 (June 1900):1–19.

118 RGIA, f. 1276, op. 9, 1913, d. 849, Delo "Ob uchrezhdenii osobogo
dukhovnogo upravleniia (muftiata) dlia musul'man severnogo
Kavkaza," State Duma legal statute on abolition of mountain courts,
3 December 1913, l. 28.

119 RGIA, f. 1405, op. 532, 1912–14, d. 189, Letter from Vorontsov-Dashkov,
18 December 1913, l. 135; Letter from official in office of the viceroy to
Aleksandr Verevkin, 13 January 1915, l. 148; Letter from Aleksandr
Khvostov to Tsar Nicholas II, 20 June 1916, l. 157.

120 RGIA, f. 1405, op. 532, 1912–14, d. 189, "Otzyvy po proektu," Letter from Vorontsov-Dashkov, 7 February 1913, ll. 123–4.
121 Ibid., About the reorganization of courts in the Caucasus, 1913, by A.V. Moskalev, l. 34.
122 Ibid., l. 30.
123 Bennigsen, "Islam and Political Power in the USSR," 71.
124 P. Tabolov, "Uzlovye voprosy sploshnoi kollektivizatsii sel'skogo khoziaistva gortsev," *Revoliutsiia i Gorets*, no. 1 (15) (January 1930):15.

CHAPTER SIX

1 Ryzhov, "Puteshestvie Shamilia ot Guniba do Sanktpeterburga," 923.
2 Pushkin, *The Captain's Daughter and Other Stories*, 47.
3 Bushuev, *Iz istorii vneshnepolitcheskikh otnoshenii v period prisoedineniia Kavkaza*, 18. Also see Tsagareishrili, *Shamil' – stavlennik sultanskoi Turtsii i Angliskikh kolonizatorov*. An earlier work by Bushuev, *Bor'ba gortsev za nezavisimost' pod rukovodstom Shamilia*, takes the opposite view. On Shamil in Soviet historiography, see Tillett, "Shamil and Muridism in Recent Soviet Historiography"; Tillett, *The Great Friendship*, 130–47, 194–221; Henze, "Unrewriting History – the Shamil Problem"; and "The Rehabilitation of Russia's Rebels." On Shamil as an inspiration against Soviet power for the Caucasus emigré community in Paris, see Gaidar Bammat, "1834–1934," *Kavkaz (Le Caucase)*, no. 7 (July 1934):1–3.
4 For this kind of discussion, see Ibragimbeili, "Narodno-osvoboditel'naia bor'ba"; Ortabaev and Totoev, "Eshche raz o kavkazskoi voine"; Bliev, "Kavkazskaia voina"; and Bliev, "K probleme obshchestvennogo stroia."
5 This process of rediscovery includes the reprinting of nineteenth-century Russian accounts of Shamil and the war. See Magomedov, *Shamil v otechestvennoi istorii*; Ramazanov and Ramazonov, *Shamil': Istoricheskii portret*; Zakhar'in, *Shamil' v Kaluge*; and Takhir, *Tri Imama*. Takhir was a personal secretary of Shamil. A bibliography of literature related to Shamil and the Caucasus War is Gammer, "Shamil and the Murid Movement, 1830–1859." Algerian nationalists and anti-colonialists incorporated Abd al-Qadir into their history of the development of Algerian nationalism, and his body was exhumed and brought to Algeria in 1968 (see Danziger, *Abd al-Qadir and the Algerians*, xii-xiv). The uses of Shamil in contemporary Dagestan remain to be seen. Magomedov (cited above), for example, in a time of ethnic tension and intolerance, emphasizes Shamil's acceptance of "national" differences, such as his Armenian wife, Shuanet, and his friend Akhverdi, an Armenian who converted to Islam (42). Magomedov's work has been influenced by the turns of Soviet historiography over fifty years. See Tillett, *The Great Friendship*,

146–7. For a recent discussion of captivity narratives, with reference to Shamil's Russian captivity after 1859, see N.V. Markelov, " 'Gde ryskaet v gorakh voinstvennyi razboi … ' (Kavkazskie plenniki)," in Georgiev, *Sbornik russkogo istoricheskogo obshchestva*, 98–108.

6 Barrett, "The Remaking of the Lion of Dagestan"; Gammer, "The Nicolay-Shamil Negotiations, 1855–1856"; Gammer, " 'The Conqueror of Napoleon' in the Caucasus"; Gammer, "Was General Kluge-von-Klugenau Shamil's Desmichels?"; and Layton, "Primitive Despot and Noble Savage."

7 *Shamil': Opisanie ego zhizni.*

8 Kuzanov, "Shamil' – politicheskii i dukhovnyi glava Dagestana," 890. This story is repeated in "Shamil'," *Vilenskii Vestnik* 94 (1 December 1859), 1081–4.

9 Kuzanov, "Shamil' – politicheskii i dukhovnyi glava Dagestana," 890.

10 Ibid.

11 Verderevskii, *Plen u Shamilia*; a Moscow edition was published in 1857, and the story was excerpted in *Otechestvennye Zapiski*, nos. 104–6 (1856).

12 sssa, f. 416, op. 2, 1854, d. 34, Delo "Raport nachal'nika Lezginskogo otriada," Report, 11 July 1854, l. 1.

13 Verderevsky, *Captivity of Two Russian Princesses in the Caucasus.*

14 "Obiavleniia," *Kavkaz*, no. 28 (5 April 1856):112.

15 E. Verderevskii, "Plen u Shamilia," *Kavkaz*, no. 50 (29 June 1855):203.

16 Ibid.; the story continued in *Kavkaz*, no. 51 (2 July 1855), 209–10, and no. 52 (6 July 1855):213–14.

17 Kelly, *Lermontov: Tragedy in the Caucasus*, 80–1, 86.

18 *tsnomis purtseli*, no. 188 (29 January 1904):1.

19 Verderevsky, *Captivity of Two Russian Princesses in the Caucasus*, 30.

20 Ibid., 22.

21 Ibid., 37.

22 Ibid., 47, 51–2, 99–100.

23 rgia, f. 796, op. 135, 1854–55, d. 1506, Delo "O vtorzhenii Shamilia soko-pishchami gortsev, lezginy i chechentsev v Kakhetiu i o razorenie ikh tserkvei i dukhovenstva," Report of Georgian ekzarkh, Isidor, 19 August 1854, ll. 1–4. On the sexual challenge to Russian men posed by the mountaineers, see Layton, *Russian Literature and Empire*, 146–55.

24 barbare jorjatsisa, "shamilis jaris chamosvlis dros kakhetshi 1854 ts. 4 ivliss," *iveria*, no. 68 (6 April 1893):1. Barbare Jorjatsisa was the sister of Rapiel Eristavi.

25 Ibid., *iveria*, no. 69 (7 April 1893):1–2; ibid., *iveria*, no. 77 (18 April 1893): 1–3.

26 Verderevsky, *Captivity of Two Russian Princesses in the Caucasus*, 183, 194.

27 Ibid., 194, 210, 244.

28 "Vesti s zapada," *Sanktpeterburgskiia Vedomosti*, no. 223 (15 October 1859): 979; "Shamil'," *Vilenskii Vestnik*, no. 93 (27 November 1859):1073.

29 Verderevsky, *Captivity of Two Russian Princesses in the Caucasus*, 220.
30 Prozritelev, *Shamil' v g.g. Stavropole*, 8.
31 Verderevsky, *Captivity of Two Russian Princesses in the Caucasus*, 303–4.
32 Ibid., 344.
33 Prozritelev, *Shamil' v g.g. Stavropole*, 8–9.
34 The complete journey was Kumtorkala–Chiriurt–Khasaviurt–
    Chervlennaia stanitsa–Mozdok–Georgievsk–Ekaterinodar–Stavropol–
    Khar'kov–Tula–Moscow–St Petersburg–Kaluga.
35 "Vziatie v plen Shamilia," *Zhurnal dlia chteniia vospitannikam voenno-ucheb-
    nykh zavedenii* 142, no. 566 (15 January 1860):184, 186.
36 Ryzhov, "Puteshestvie Shamilia ot Guniba do Sanktpeterburga," 923;
    "Shamil'," *Vilenskii Vestnik*, no. 93 (27 November 1859):1073.
37 Ryzhov, "Puteshestvie Shamilia ot Guniba do Sanktpeterburga," 924.
38 Ibid.
39 Ibid.
40 "Shamil' v Stavropole," *Sanktpeterburgskiia Vedomosti*, no. 210 (29 Septem-
    ber 1859):913.
41 Ibid.
42 Ibid.
43 A. Rudanovskii, "Kavkazskaia letopis': Stavropol," *Kavkaz*, no. 79
    (8 October 1859):457.
44 "O proezde Shamilia chrez Stavropol," *Stavropol'skiia Gubernskiia
    Vedomosti*, no. 37 (12 September 1859), chast neofitsial'naia, 215; "Shamil v
    Stavropole," *Sanktpeterburgskiia Vedomosti*, no. 210 (29 September 1859):
    913.
45 Z.Z., "Shamil' v Malorossii," *Sankpeterburgskiia Vedomosti*, no. 213
    (5 October 1859): 929.
46 Ryzhov, "Puteshestvie Shamilia ot Guniba do Sanktpeterburga," 924.
47 I. Besiadovskii, "Shamil' v Kurske," *Kurskiia Gubernskiia Vedomosti*, no. 43
    (24 October 1859), chast' neofitsial'naia, 248.
48 Ibid., 249.
49 Ibid.
50 Ibid.
51 Ibid.
52 Ibid., 250.
53 "Peterburgskaia letopis'," *Sanktpeterburgskiia Vedomosti*, no. 203 (20 Sep-
    tember 1859):885.
54 "Shamil' v Sanktpeterburge," *Severnaia Pchela*, no. 210 (29 September
    1859): 841.
55 "S. Peterburg," *Moskovskiia Vedomosti*, no. 231 (29 September 1859):1673;
    V. P-skii, "Shamil'," *Russkii Invalid*, no. 226 (21 October 1859):922.
56 "Shamil' v Sanktpeterburge," *Severnaia Pchela*, no. 210 (29 September
    1859):841.

57 Zhitel Petersburga, "Shamil' v publichnoi biblioteke," *Russkii Mir*, no. 54 (7 October 1859):945.
58 V. P-skii, "Shamil'," *Russkii Invalid*, no. 226 (21 October 1859):921.
59 "Peterburgskaia letopis'," *Sanktpeterburgskiia Vedomosti*, no. 214 (4 October 1859):933.
60 Ryzhov, "Puteshestvie Shamilia ot Guniba do Sanktpeterburga," 923; "O Shamile," *Severnaia Pchela*, no. 211 (30 September 1859):845.
61 Ryzhov, "Puteshestvie Shamilia ot Guniba do Sanktpeterburga," 923; and reprinted as "Puteshestvie Shamilia ot Guniba do Sanktpeterburga," *Russkii Mir*, no. 54 (7 October 1859):942.
62 "Mestnyia izvestiia," *Kaluzhskiia Gubernskiia Vedomosti*, no. 42 (17 October 1859), chast' neofitsial'naia, 528; reprinted as "Shamil' v Kaluge," *Severnaia Pchela*, no. 230 (25 October 1859):921
63 "Mestnyia izvestiia," *Kaluzhskiia Gubernskiia Vedomosti*, no. 40:507.
64 Ibid., no. 42 (17 October 1859):529.
65 Ibid., no. 43 (24 October 1859), chast' neofitsial'naia, 540–1.
66 Ibid., no. 42 (17 October 1859):529.
67 A. Gariainov, "O tom, chto vsekh zanimaet," *Severnaia Pchela*, no. 201 (18 September 1859):805.
68 Petr Egorov, "Neskol'ko slov o Kavkaze i Shamile," *Severnaia Pchela*, no. 248 (13 November 1859):994.
69 Ibid., 993.
70 "Peterburgskaia letopis'," *Sanktpeterburgskiia Vedomosti*, no. 209 (27 September 1859):909. Gariainov defended himself in A. Gariainov, "Otvet s Peterburgskim Vedomostiam," *Severnaia Pchela*, no. 239 (3 November 1859):957–8. The editors of *Severnaia Pchela* frequently offered a militaristic response to international events and matters of imperial security. It was one of the journals pronounced sufficiently loyal and patriotic by the commission of Prince Menshikov, which was assigned by Nicholas I to investigate and censor the press in response to the events of 1848 in Europe.
71 Runovskii, *Zapiski o Shamile*, part 2:7, 26.
72 Ibid., part 2:27–8, 52; part 4:8.
73 Ibid., part 4:8.
74 P.G. Przhetsslavskii, "Shamil' v Kaluge," *Russkaia Starina* 20 (1877): 257, 262; quote from 262.
75 Ibid., 275.
76 Ibid., 21 (1878):50.
77 Runovskii, *Zapiski o Shamile*, part 3:8.
78 Ibid., part 2:45. For an account of Shamil punishing unveiled women in Gimry, see Takhir, *Tri Imama*, 14.
79 For example, GVIARF, f. 400, op. 1, 1869, d. 39, Delo "Po pros'be Shamilia ob uvolnenii ego v Mekku dlia pokloneniia grobu Magometa," Letter of Shamil to tsar, 19 December 1868.

80 Ibid., 1863–66, d. 4, Delo "Ob otchislenii Kaluzhskago sekretaria Turminskago ot dolzhnosti pristava pri Shamile," Report from Kaluga governor to Dmitrii Miliutin, 1 September 1863, l. 21.

81 Ibid., Letter from E. Lerkh to N.I. Karlgof, 15 December 1863, l. 42.

82 Ibid., Letter from Pavel Przhetsslavskii to N.I. Karlgof, 28 January 1864, l. 52.

83 Ibid., 1865–67, d. 9, Delo "Po otnosheniiu Kaluzhskago Gubernatora o peremene drugim litsom nakhodiaschiisia pri voenno-plennom Shamil' pristava polkovnika Przhetsslavskago," Letter from Shamil to Governor Spasski, August 1865, l. 2.

84 Ibid., General Karlgof to Vladimir Nikiforovich, 29 October 1865, l. 5.

85 Ibid., 1869, d. 39, Viceroy Mikhail to Dmitrii Miliutin, 25 January 1869, ll. 1–2.

86 Ibid., 1863–67, d. 3, Delo "Perepiska ob opredelenii v voennuiu sluzhbu rodstvennikov voenno-plennogo Shamilia," Shamil to D.N. Skobelev, 3 September 1863, l. 8; Pavel Przhetsslavskii to N.I. Karlgof, 16 November 1863, l. 13.

87 Ibid., 1865–67, d. 9, Report, 5 January 1866, l. 72. The Ministry of War abolished the position itself after this affair.

88 Ibid., 1867–70, d. 23, Delo "Po predmetu pereseleniia Shamilia s semeistvom v iuzhnuiu Rossiiu," Shamil to Miliutin, 15 April 1867, l. 20.

89 Zakhar'in, Shamil' v Kaluge, 39–40.

90 For example, GVIARF, f. 400, op. 1, 1865–67, d. 9, Letter from Shamil to tsar, 8 April 1866, ll. 157–68. Also see Zakhar'in, Shamil v Kaluge, 15.

91 "shamilisa da misi ojasis ambivi," iveria, no. 253 (23 November 1895): 2–3.

92 Another son, Magomet, was born to Zaidat in Kaluga in 1861.

93 Zakhar'in, Shamil' v Kaluge, 15, 25. Khadzhio served in the Unkratl'skoe naibstvo of Betlinskii okrug in Dagestan oblast.

94 Potto, Kavkazskaia voina v otdel'nykh ocherkakh, epizodakh, legendakh i biografiakh; V. Potto, "Gadzhi-Murat," Voennyi Sbornik 76, no. 11 (November 1870):159–87.

95 Zakhar'in, Shamil' v Kaluge, 22.

96 For example, "Vospominaniia V.A. Poltoratskago," Istoricheskii Vestnik 52 (1893):355–72; Ogarkov, "Vorontsovy;" 86, "Sleptsov (Iz vospominanii kniazia Dondukova-Korsakova)," Starina i Novizna 5 (1902):155–7; "Moi vospominaniia, 1840–1844 gg. Kniazia Dondukova-Korsakova," Starina i Novizna 5 (1902):158–223.

97 A. Krasnov, "Sochi," in Kruber et al., Aziatskaia Rossiia, 74–8; N.Ia. Dinnik, "Gory i ushchel'ia Terskoi oblasti," ZKOIRGO 13, no. 1 (1884):1, 30, 10, 15–16; Vorontsov, "Devdoradskii lednik," in Kruber et al., Azoatskaia Rossiia, 26–32; Filippov, "Voenno-Gruzinskaia doroga," ibid., 19.

98 Zakhar'in, Shamil' v Kaluge, 23.

99 Chichagova, Shamil' na Kavkaze i v Rossii, 164–5, 176.

100 P.G. Przhetsslavskii, "Shamil' v Kaluge," *Russkaia Starina* 20 (1877): 253–76, 471–506. His memoirs continue as "Shamil' i ego sem'ia v Kaluge," *Russkaia Starina* 21 (1878):41–64, 265–80.

101 Ibid., 475–7.

102 RGIA, f. 932, op. 1, 1880–82, d. 292, l. 15.

103 Chichagova, *Shamil' na Kavkaze i v Rossii*, 15–16, 60–3, 113–26.

104 Ibid., 142. Her husband was Mikhail Nikiforovich Chichagov.

105 Ibid., 143, 181, 120.

106 Ibid., 223.

CHAPTER SEVEN

1 RGIA, f. 799, op. 25, 1900–15, d. 808, Report, 1900, l. 22.

2 Hosking, *Russia: People and Empire, 1552–1917*, 367–97.

3 Wortman, *Scenarios of Power*, 1:122.

4 Platonov, *Obzor deiatel'nosti*, 123.

5 Wortman, *Scenarios of Power*, vol. 2. Russification in the western provinces began earlier and was shaped by a different set of issues, chief among them the problem (for Russia) of the pretensions of the Poles to "Western" and "historic" status because of their Catholicism, Latin script, and general relationship to Europe. See Rodkiewicz, *Russian Nationality Policy in the Western Provinces of the Empire (1863–1905)*; Kappeler, *La Russie*, 214–25; Subtelny, *Ukraine*, 300–1; Thaden, *Russification in the Baltic Provinces and Finland, 1855–1914*; Weeks, "Defining Us and Them"; Weeks, *Nation and State in Late Imperial Russia*; Jersild, "'Russia,' from the Vistula to the Terek to the Amur."

6 Nol'de, *Ocherki Russkago Gosudarstvennago Prava*, 225–79. On Russification as an assault on previous forms of privilege, see Pearson, "Privileges, Rights, and Russification."

7 Kappeler, *La Russie*, 273.

8 Baumann, "Subject Nationalities in the Military Service of Imperial Russia"; Forsyth, *A History of the Peoples of Siberia*, 162; Golikova, *Ocherki po istorii gorodov Rossii kontsa xvii-nachala xviii v.*, 172–3.

9 SSSA, f. 416, op. 1, 1864, d. 1, Note, Council of Ministers, 3 February 1882, ll. 43–4; LeDonne, "La reforme de 1883 au Caucase."

10 Kappeler, *La Russie*, 213.

11 Weber, *Peasants into Frenchmen*, 292–302.

12 RGIA, f. 799, op. 26, 1915, d. 1701, Delo "O posobii na okonchanie tserkvi v sl. Vedeno, Terskoi oblasti," Letter from Construction Committee, village of Vedeno, to Elisaveta Fedorovna, 9 June 1915, l. 2.

13 Cooke, "Eugène Étienne and the Emergence of Colon Dominance in Algeria, 1884–1905"; Desvages, "La Chambre de 1898 et la crise algérienne"; Corre, "The Algiers Riot, January 1898."

14 "kartuli teatri," *iveria*, no. 11 (1882):90–1. For commentary on the propensity of the colonial powers to educate "natives" but then deny them access to positions of respect and authority within the colonial state, note Anderson, *Imagined Communities*, 140.

15 gr. kipshidze, "saistorio," *iveria*, no. 10 (October 1882):115–28.

16 z. chichinadze, "kartuli gazetebi," *sakartvelos kalendari* 1 (1897):466.

17 RGIA, f. 1263, op. 2, 1903, d. 5616, Memorandum, Golitsyn, ll. 207–8; Surguladze, *I.G. Chavchavadze*, 155.

18 See Rayfield, *The Literature of Georgia*, 162–3. On the Georgian press generally, see z. chichinadze, "kartuli gazetebi," *sakartvelos kalendari* 1 (1897):462–8.

19 "Spor ob avtonomii," *Vesennii potok*, no. 1 (19 April 1906):1; "Ot redaktsii," *Kavkazskaia zhizn'*, no. 1 (21 September 1906):1; M. N-dze, "Dva slova ob avtonomii," *Kavkazskaia zhizn'*, no. 3 (23 September 1906): 1; *Vozrozhdenie*, no. 1 (1 October 1905):1; *Spravedlivost'*, no. 2 (4 May 1906):1.

20 *Kavkazskii zapros' v gosudarstvennoi dume*, 67–71.

21 Confer, *France and Algeria*, 10. The impact of the 1857 revolt of the sepoys of the Bengal Army upon the British is another comparative example. See Metcalf, *Ideologies of the Raj*, 30–1.

22 RGIA, f. 573, op. 3, 1886, d. 4878, Report from Ministry of War to Council of Ministers, 19 November 1885, and subsequent lists, ll. 3–23.

23 Petrovich, *The Emergence of Russian Panslavism, 1856–1870*; Aksakov, *PSS*, 1:1–5, 14, 33–6, 50, 95, 132, 219.

24 Dowler, *Dostoevsky, Grigor'ev and Native Soil Conservatism*.

25 Cited in MacKenzie, *The Lion of Tashkent*, 198.

26 Bogdanovich, *Dvadtsatipiatiletie velikoi osvoboditel'noi voiny*.

27 Kireevskii, "Deviatnadtsatyi vek," in Kireevskii, *PSS*, 1:104; Khomiakov, "Zapiski o vsemirnoi istorii," part 2, in Khomiakov, *PSS*, 6.

28 For example, in *Rus'*, 12 January 1885, in Aksakov, *Slavianskii vopros, 1860–1886*, 606; also see Klier, *Imperial Russia's Jewish Question, 1855–1881*, 153–6.

29 Nikitin, *Slavianskie Komitety v Rossii v 1858–1876 godakh*, 33–9, 82–3, 291.

30 Aksakov, *Slavianskii vopros, 1860–1886*, 148.

31 Danilevskii, *Rossiia i Evropa*, 132.

32 Ibid., 111.

33 Belinskii, "Obshchee znachenie slova literatura" (1842–44), in Belinskii, *PSS*, 5:632–3.

34 Belinskii, "Istoriia Malorossii" (1842), in Belinskii, *PSS*, 7:44–65. See also Walicki, *A History of Russian Thought from the Enlightenment to Marxism*, 131–40. On Belinskii and Ukraine, see Rutherford, "Vissarion Belinskii and the Ukrainian National Question."

35 Danilevskii, *Rossiia i Evropa*, 93; also see 239.

36 Ibid., 37.

37 Ibid., 23–37, 237–8, 102–6, 237, 531–2, 259.

38 Strakhov, *Bor'ba s zapadom v nashei literature*, 2:ix.

39 Ibid., 27, 107.

40 Aksakov, *Moskva* (1867), in Aksakov, *Slavianskii vopros, 1860–1886*, 147.

41 Aksakov, *Den'* (1864), ibid., 46–9.

42 Strakhov, *Bor'ba s zapadom v nashei literature*, 1:173, 138–76.

43 Baron P.K. Uslar, "Dreveishiia skazaniia o Kavkaze," ssokg 10 (1881): 1–552.

44 Ibid., 43.

45 Ibid., 42–65.

46 Aksakov, *Den'* (1862), in Aksakov, *Slavianskii vopros, 1860–1886*, 25.

47 Aksakov, *Den'* (1865), ibid., 56.

48 Ibid., 56, 59.

49 Thaden, *Conservative Nationalism in Nineteenth-Century Russia*, 147.

50 Ibid., 148–56.

51 Fadeev, *Pis'ma s Kavkaza*, 7.

52 Ibid., 17, 204, 226.

53 Ibid., 33, 48, 115, 123, 199.

54 Ibid., 74–5.

55 Ibid., 75–6, 160.

56 Thaden, *Conservative Nationalism in Nineteenth-Century Russia*, 158.

57 Fadeev, *Pis'ma s Kavkaza*, 177–8.

58 For example, "Vospominaniia V.A. Poltoratskago," *Istoricheskii Vestnik* 51 (1893):54; ibid., 52 (1893):668–72; Ogarkov, "Vorontsovy: Ikh Zhizn i obshchestvennaia deiatel'nost," 86; "Sleptsov (Iz vospominanii kniazia Dondukova-Korsakova)," *Starina i Novizna* 5 (1902):155–7; "Moi vospominaniia. 1840–1844 gg. Kniazia Dondukova-Korsakova," *Starina i Novizna* 5 (1902):158–223."Far more balanced is "Kniaz Mikhail Semenovich Vorontsov (Vospominaniia Kniazia Dondukova-Korsakova)," *Starina i Novizna* 5 (1902):119–154. Vorontsov's memoirs were published as "Vypiski iz dnevnika svetleishnago kniazia M.S. Vorontsova," *Starina i Novizna* 5 (1902):74–118.

59 Kaspari, *Pokorennyi Kavkaz*, 2. A glorification of the many generals who served in the region is Begichev, *Iubileinyi Sbornik k stoletiiu prisoedineniia Gruzii k Rossii*.

60 Kaspari, *Pokorennyi Kavkaz*, 4.

61 Lermontov, "Bela," in Lermontov, *A Hero of Our Time*, 26.

62 Tolstoi, "Khadzhi-Murat," in Tolstoi, *Povesti i Rasskazy*, 2:412–524.

63 Ibid., 412–13.

64 Sergeenko, *'Khadzhi Murat' L'va Tolstogo*, 13; S. Shul'gin, "Iz vospominanii o gr. L.N. Tolstom," *Russkaia Mysl'*, 32, no. 2 (February 1911):72. The study by Sergeenko is an exhaustive account of the various works that Tolstoy was reading while composing his many drafts of *Hadji Murat*. On

Tolstoy, Russian imperialism, and the literary Caucasus, see Layton, *Russian Literature and Empire*, 258–87.

65 Kaspari, *Pokorennyi Kavkaz*, 5.

66 A. Krasnov, "Sochi," in Kruber, *Aziatskaia Rossiia*, 74–8.

67 A.V. Pastukhov, "Vokhozhdenie na Ararat, 2-go avgusta 1893 g.," *ZKOIRGO* 16 (1894):423–4. A more recent return to the mountain-climbing exploits of Pastukhov is Chumakov, *Priiut Pastukhova*.

68 N.Ia. Dinnik, "Gory i ushchel'ia Terskoi oblasti," *ZKOIRGO* 13, no. 1 (1884):1, 30, 10.

69 For example, see Markov, *Ocherki Kavkaza*; and Filipov, "Voenno-Gruzinskaia doroga," in Kruber et al., *Aziatskaia Rossiia*, 17. Vasilii Sidorov travelled with a copy of *A Hero of Our Time* in his pocket; see Sidorov, *Kavkaz: Putevyia zametki i vpechatleniia*, 11–12; 29–41.

70 Filipov, "Voenno-Gruzinskaia doroga," in Kruber et al., *Aziatskaia Rossiia*, 19.

71 SSSA, f. 416, op. 3, 1863, d. 216, Delo "Otnoshenie … o zaselenii," Mikhail Nikolaevich to Ministry of War, 10 December 1863, l. 1.

72 Ibid., 1865–77, d. 208, Delo "Vsepoddanneishii doklad," Memorandum, 26 July 1865, l. 1; "Svedeniia o nemetskikh poselentsakh v Zakavkazskom krae," *Kavkaz*, no. 40 (24 May 1850):159–60; SSSA, f. 4, op. 2, 1833, d. 2444, Delo "O poselenii raskol'nikov," governor-general of Novorossisk, 2 October 1833, l. 1; 1844, d. 831, Delo "O poselenii Russkikh pereselentsev," Report, 9 June 1848, l. 1.

73 Berzhe, *Akty Kavkazskoiu Arkheograficheskoiu Kommissieiu*, vol. 12, Bariatin-skii to Caucasus Committee, 15 August 1857, 12–13.

74 SSSA, f. 416, op. 3, 1867, d. 262, Delo "Doklad nachal'nika … i perepiska o zaselenii," Report of commander, 19 January 1868, l. 25.

75 Ibid., d. 222, Delo "O poselenii russkikh krest'ian," Announcement, 1867, l. 8.

76 RGIA, f. 932, op. 1, 1886, d. 316, Dondukov-Korsakov, 24 November 1886, l. 8.

77 Dukmasov, *O zaselenii Chernomorskago poberezh'ia Kavkaza kazach'im voiskom*, 8–9; RGIA, f. 1268, op. 15, 1870, d. 56, l. 28.

78 SSSA, f. 416, op. 3, 1864, d. 233, Delo "Dokladnaia zapiska … o pereselenii na Kavkaz khristianskikh vykhodtsev iz Turtsii," Memorandum of commander of troops of Kuban oblast, 27 August 1864, ll. 1–16.

79 Ibid., 1867, d. 262, Report, 29 March 1867, l. 2.

80 Ibid., l. 4. The file lists this 1867 colonization as between the rivers of Bzyb and Mzymt: 400 families; Mzymt and Sochi: 866 families; Sochi and Shakhe: 1,000 families; Shakhe and Ashe: 665 families; and Ashe and Tuapse: 445 families.

81 SSSA, f. 416, op. 3, 1878, d. 190, Delo "Zapiska ob … naseleniia Abkhazii," Office of Namestnik, 1878, l. 2.

82 SSSA, f. 5, op. 1, 1868, d. 770, Delo "Zapiska o zaselenii Kavkaza," l. 3.

83 RGIA, f. 1276, op. 21, 1895–97, d. 45, Memorandum of the Ministry of Agriculture, ll. 1–9.

84 RGIA, f. 1263, op. 2, 1903, d. 5616, ll. 157, 193.

85 Treadgold, *The Great Siberian Migration*, 74; Shatskii, "Russkaia kolonizatsiia," 40–1.

86 Olcott, *The Kazakhs*, 87–8; Treadgold, "Russian Expansion in the Light of Turner's Study of the American Frontier," 150.

87 RGIA, f. 1276, op. 21, 1895–97, d. 45, l. 10.

88 RGIA, f. 1263, op. 2, 1903, d. 5616, Memorandum, l. 197.

89 S.V. Farforovskii, "Statistichesko-geograficheskoe opisanie g. Maikopa i Maikopskago otdela," *Sbornik Materialov dlia opisanie mestnostei i plemen Kavkaza*, no. 41 (1910):37.

90 RGIA, f. 560, op. 41, 1883, d. 143, Letter of V. Butyrkin, l. 4.

91 RGIA, f. 1276, op. 17, 1911, d. 165, Report of Chernomorsk governor, l. 92.

92 RGIA, f. 1276, op. 21, 1895–97, d. 45, Notes of the Ministry of Agriculture, l. 1.

93 RGIA, f. 1263, op. 2, 1903, d. 5616, Memorandum, Golitsyn, l. 191.

94 RGIA, f. 1276, op. 21, 1895–97, d. 45, Notes of the Ministry of Agriculture, ll. 9–10. In 1901, settlement authorities were careful to incorporate the advice of a doctor familiar with malaria to guide the choice of location of new settlement villages; from RGIA, f. 1263, op. 2, 1903, d. 5616, ll. 193–5.

95 RGIA, f. 1276, op. 21, 1895–97, d. 45, Notes of the Ministry of Agriculture, l. 2.

96 Ibid., l. 3.

97 Ibid., l. 4.

98 *Otchet nachal'nika Kubanskoi oblasti … za 1895 god*, 15.

99 RGIA, Biblioteka, op. 1, 1909, d. 99, Report of commander of Terek oblast for 1909, General Mikheev, l. 41. By the early twentieth century the posts of commander of Terek oblast and ataman of the Terek oblast Cossacks were merged into a single position.

100 Ibid., l. 43.

101 Ibid., l. 44.

102 Ibid.

103 RGIA, f. 37, op. 55, 1892–99, d. 69, Delo "O merakh k uporiadocheniiu razrabotok v kamenalomnakh, "Report of commander of Terek oblast for 1890, ll. 46–7.

104 "Izvlechenie iz proekta 1849 g. o Tatarskoi missii," in Znamenskii, *Na Pamiat' o Nikolae Ivanoviche Il'minskom*, 331–5.

105 RGIA, f. 799, op. 25, 1900–15, d. 808, Delo "Ob assignovanii iz Gosudarstvennago kaznacheistva po finansovoi smety Sv. Sinoda summ na ustroistve pravoslavnykh tserkvei v pereselencheskikh seleniiakh Zakavkazskago kraia," Letter from Golitsyn to MVD, 4 October 1901, l. 9.

106 Ibid., Letter from Golitsyn to Pobedonostsev, 11 October 1902, l. 36.

107 RGIA, f. 799, op. 25, 1900–15, d. 808, Letter from viceroy to Sergei Mikhailovich Luk'ianov, 9 November 1910, l. 177.

108 Ibid.

109 Ibid., Decree signed by Pobedonostsev, 29 March 1902, l. 67; Letter from viceroy to ober-procurator, 3 October 1906, l. 111.

110 Ibid., Letter from Vorontsov-Dashkov to S.M. Luk'ianov, 9 November 1910, l. 179.

111 Ibid., From Department of Orthodox Faith to Office of the Viceroy, 2 October 1913, l. 231.

112 Ibid., From ober-procurator of Holy Synod to Holy State Synod, 4 July 1914, ll. 240–1.

113 RGIA, f. 799, op. 25, 1898–99, d. 450, Delo "Po khodataistvam ob otpuske summy na postroiku tserkvi v slobody Vedeno, Vladikavkazskoi eparkhii," Report from Episkop Vladimir of Vladikavkaz and Mozdok to Holy Synod, 5 October 1898, l. 2. ·

114 RGIA, f. 799, op. 26, 1915, d. 1701, Letter from Construction Committee, village of Vedeno, to Elisaveta Fedorovna, 9 June 1915, l. 2.

115 Ibid.

116 Ibid. For similar references to the demoralizing contrast between Russian prayer houses and beautiful Chechen mosques, see RGIA, f. 799, op. 25, 1898–99, d. 450, Letter from Aleksei Ofiptsov, 9 January 1898, l. 7.

117 RGIA, f. 799, op. 25, 1898–99, d. 450, Letter from commander of troops of Caucasus Military District to ober-procurator of Holy Synod, 28 November 1898, l. 4.

118 RGIA, f. 799, op. 26, 1915, d. 1701, Letter from official of Ved. Prav. Isp., Vladikavkaz, to Aleksandr A. Osetskii, l. 4.

CONCLUSION

1 Tsereteli, *Perezhitoe*, 182.

2 GVIARF, f. VUA, op. 1, 1841–42, d. 6440, l. 2.

3 Gershenzon, *Istoriia Molodoi Rossii*, 18–20, 40–7; Lobikova, "Kavkaz v tvorchestve Pushkina," 283.

4 Armstrong, *Yermak's Campaign in Siberia*, 52, 55, 68, 241, 281; Forsyth, *A History of the Peoples of Siberia*, 29; Nolde, *La formation de l'Empire russe*, 1:36.

5 *Polnoe sobranie zakonov Rossiiskoi Imperii*, vol. 35, part 1 (1860), no. 35519, 191.

6 See Kappeler, *La Russie*, 29, 37, 60.

7 Cited in Wolff, *Inventing Eastern Europe*, 211.

8 *droeba*, no. 5 (20 April 1870):1.

9 *iveria*, no. 1 (1 January 1886):1.

10 GVIARF, f. 38, op. 7, 1845, d. 115, Delo "Ob otpravlenii k Shamiliu pis'ma ot syna ego," Letter from Dzhemaledin to Shamil, 29 June 1845, l. 2.

11 SSSA, f. 416, op. 3, 1864–65, d. 182, l. 5.

12 SSSA, f. 433, op. 1, 1872–73, d. 19, ll. 34–40.

13 Jersild, "From Savagery to Citizenship," 108.

14 Girei, "Zamechaniia na stati'iu zakona i obychai Kabardintsev, *Kavkaz*, no. 11 (16 March 1846):37.

15 Verderevskii, *Plen u Shamilia*; jorjatsisa, "shamilis jaris chamosvlis," *iveria*, no. 68 (6 April 1893):1, no. 69 (7 April 1893), 1–2, and no. 77 (18 April 1893), 1–3.

16 "mtserloba," *droeba*, no. 32 (28 March 1876):1–3.

17 "khevsurebis chveneba imat mitsa-tsulis shesakheb kavkasiis keds ikit," *krebuli*, no. 7 (1882):134–41.

18 Uslar, "Prednolozhenie ob ustroistve gorskikh shkol," 33.

19 Frank, *Dostoevsky: The Years of Ordeal, 1850–1859*, 104–45; 223–35; Frank, *Dostoevsky: The Stir of Liberation, 1860–1865*, 104–5; Pypin, *Istoriia Russkoi literatury*, 4:626; Vengerov, *Ocherki po istorii Russkoi literatury*, 413–16; Gleason, *Young Russia*, 32–76; Slezkine, *Arctic Mirrors*, 75.

20 Platonov, *Obzor deiatel'nosti obshchestva*, 123.

21 Kaspari, *Pokorennyi Kavkaz*, 2.

22 RGIA, f. 1263, op. 2, 1903, d. 5616, ll. 157, 193.

23 GVIARF, f. 400, op. 1, 1897, d. 2093, Report by Golitsyn, 10 February 1897, l. 7.

24 Pobedonostsev, *K.P. Pobedonostsev i ego korrespondenty*, 53–8.

25 Kappeler, *La Russie*, 244, 252; Seton-Watson, *The Decline of Imperial Russia, 1855–1914*, 31; Ismail-zade, *Russkoe krest'ianstvo v Zakavkaz'e*, 18–19.

26 Wortman, *Scenarios of Power*, vol. 2.

27 On the "imagined community" of the nation in modern history, see Anderson, *Imagined Communities*.

28 g. tsereteli, "ormotsda sami tseli kartulis teatrisa," *kvali*, no. 2 (10 January 1893):10–14.

29 Mahomed-Khanov, "Istinnye i lozhnye posledovateli tarikata," 1.

30 P. Uslar, "Nachalo khristianstva v Zakavkaz'e i na Kavkaze," SSOKG 2 (1869):19–21.

31 Hobsbawm, *Nations and Nationalism since 1780*, 30–42; Fishman, *Language and Nationalism*, 26.

32 Todorov, *The Conquest of America*, 42.

33 Karamzin, *Istoriia gosudarstva Rossiiskago*, 1:48–52.

34 SSSA, f. 7, op. 8, 1861–74, d. 2, l. 8.

35 Kudriavtsev, *Sbornik materialov po istorii Akhazii*, 14; Guliia, *Materialy po Abkhazskoi grammatike*, 3–23; Ashkhatsav, *Puti razvitiia Abkhazskoi istorii*, 38–40. Ashkhatsav provided variations of Russian letters in order to express a wider variety of Abkhaz sounds.

36 L. Shirman, "Kraaevoi muzei sev.-kav. narodov i ego rabota," *Revoliutsiia i Gorets*, no. 2 (November 1928):84.

37 Zhordaniia, *Institut istorii, arkheologii i etnografii*, 6–19.

38 Semenov, *Gosudarstvennyi nauchnyi muzei gor. Vladikavkaza.*

AFTERWORD

1 RGIA, f. 1049, op. 1, 1917, d. 82, Delo "Protokol zasedanii komissii po voprosu o vozmozhnykh izmeniiakh granits gubernii i uezdov Kavkaza," Reports of 1, 2, 8 July 1917, l. 1.

2 A. Begeulov, "Sotsialisticheskaia stroika v gorskikh oblastiakh," *Revoliutsiia i Gorets*, no. 1 (October 1928):12.

3 Bugai and Gonov, *Kavkaz*, 89.

4 Clark, *Petersburg, Crucible of Cultural Revolution*, ix.

5 Ar. Tsekkher, "K zadacham 'Revoliutsii i gortsa'," *Revoliutsiia i Gorets*, no. 1 (October 1928):5; A. Lu-ch, "Dorozhnyi vopros v gorskikh oblastiakh," ibid., 23; A. Goozulov, "Problema ispol'zovaniia truda v krest'ianskom khoziaistve gortsev," ibid., no. 2 (November 1928):25–6; A. Begeulov, "Sotsialisticheskaia stroika v gorskikh oblastiakh," ibid., no. 1 (October 1928):10.

6 E.I. Khadartsev, "Adatnaia problema i zadachi kraevogo Gorskogo nauchno-issledovatel'skogo instituta," ibid., no. 1 (October 1928):50–2; Bennigsen, "Islam and Political Power in the USSR," 71.

7 "Na poroge dvenadtsatogo goda," *Revoliutsiia i Gorets*, no. 2 (November 1928):6.

8 Ibid., 7.

9 "The Policy of the Soviet Government on the National Question in Russia," in *Pravda*, no. 226 (10 October 1920): from Stalin, *Marxism and the National Question*, 81.

10 A.M. Ladyzhenskii, "K izucheniiu byta Cherkesov," *Revoliutsiia i Gorets*, no. 2 (November 1928):64.

11 G. Apresian, " 'Serlo' – Chechenskaia gazeta," ibid., 50.

12 "Debiuty Leila Khanum," ibid., 66; Amalatbek, "V dome pechati: 'Kazaki' – kino-film proizvodstvo Goskinprom Gruzii – glazami gortsa," ibid., 66–8.

13 The figure was higher in Ossetia (62.5%), lower in Adygei (25%), and 38.7% for the North Caucasus overall, according to "Khronika," ibid., 6. See also Islam Karachaily, "Rodnoi iazyk v natsiional'nykh oblastiakh severnogo Kavkaza," ibid., no. 1 (October 1928):39–43.

14 Bennigsen and Wimbush, *Mystics and Commissars*, 26–31.

15 Kolarz, *Russia and Her Colonies*, 186.

16 GARF, f. 6991, op. 6, 1975, d. 743, Delo "Perepiska s upolnomochennym Soveta po voprosam deiatel'nosti religioznykh organizatsii po

Dagestanskoi ASSR," Letter from M.S. Gadzhiev to A.A. Nurulaev, 8 April 1975, l. 25.

17 Bennigsen and Broxup, *The Islamic Threat to the Soviet State*, 71–2.

18 GARF, f. 6991, op. 6, 1975, d. 743, Letter from A. Nurullaev to M.S. Gadzhiev, 18 February 1975, l. 21.

19 See Wixman, *Language Aspects of Ethnic Patterns and Processes in the North Caucasus*, 21–30. Wixman suggests that the distinction in Soviet thinking between a "narodnost" and a "natsional'nost'" is a population of less (narodnost') or more than 300,000 people (natsional'nost'); see p. 23. Also see Rogachev and Sverdlin, "O poniatii 'natsiia'"; Dzhunusov, "Natsiia, kak sotsial'no-etnicheskaia obshchnost' liudei"; Kaltakhchian, "K voprosu o poniatii 'natsiia'"; Semenov, "Natsiia i natsional'naia gosudarstvennost' v SSSR"; Mnatsakanian, "Natsiia i natsional'naia gosudarstvennost'"; and the review of this discussion in Howard, "The Definition of a Nation."

20 Dzhunusov, "Natsiia, kak sotsial'no-etnicheskaia obshchnost' liudei," 23–9; Rogachev and Sverdlin, "O poniatii 'natsiia,'" 35–8, citation from 38. On the impact of Soviet rule upon the nationalities, see Slezkine, "The USSR as a Communal Apartment"; Suny, *The Revenge of the Past*; Kappeler, *La Russie*, 316–18; and Suny, "Transcaucasia," 234. On a similar process among the Tadzhiks of what Suny calls "cultural cohesion," see Rakowska-Harmstone, *Russia and Nationalism in Central Asia*, 76–9. Also see Breuilly, *Nationalism and the State*, 347–50; and Bennigsen and Lemercier-Quelquejay, *La presse et le mouvement national chez les Musulmans de Russie avant 1920*, 278. On the efforts of Soviet ethnographers to determine national identity based on census materials, see Hirsch, "The Soviet Union as a Work-in-Progress."

21 GARF, f. 9469, op. 1, 1960–67, d. 2, Delo "Perepiska s Sovetom Ministrov SSSR," Design meeting, 1967, l. 416.

22 Daniialov, "Ot narodnosti k natsii"; M. Ikhilov, "Ot razdroblennosti – k edinstvu," *Sovetskii Dagestan*, no. 1 (1970):4–8.

23 Salmanov, "O protsesse natsional'noi konsolidatsii narodov Dagestana," 289. For an example of the continuation of this debate into the post-Soviet era, with accusations of "genocide" countered by others who emphasize the relatively benevolent character of tsarist and Soviet policy, see Avramenko, Matveev, and Matiushchenko, "Ob otsenke Kavkazskoi voiny," and other essays in *Kavkazskaia voina*, 36–43.

24 Volkova, *Etnicheskii sostav naseleniia severnogo Kavkaza v XVIII–nachale XX veka*, 223.

25 On the paradox of "nation-building" and "nation-destroying" policy and thinking in Soviet history, see Martin, "The Origins of Soviet Ethnic Cleansing."

26 These figures are from GARF, f. 9401, op. 1, d. 435, l. 132, and f. 9479, op. 1, d. 436, ll. 119–20; cited in Bugai and Gonov, *Kavkaz*, 192–3. Also see Nekrich, *The Punished Peoples*, 185; Flemming, "The Deportation of the Chechen and Ingush Peoples"; and Kappeler, *La Russie*, 322.

27 Wimbush and Wixman, "The Meskhetian Turks."

28 Nekrich, *The Punished Peoples*, 42.

29 Bugai and Gonov, *Kavkaz*, 105–25, 153, 165; Bugai, *Iosif Stalin – Lavrentiiu Berii*, 9, 20, 67, 119, 343.

30 Bugai, *Iosif Stalin – Lavrentiiu Berii*, 111.

31 Bugai and Gonov, *Kavkaz*, 229. On the Soviet context to ethnic deportation, see Holquist, " 'Information Is the Alpha and Omega of Our Work' "; and Weiner, "Nature, Nurture, and Memory in a Socialist Utopia."

32 Bugai and Gonov, *Kavkaz*, 93.

Bibliography

ARCHIVAL SOURCES

SAKARTVELOS SAKHELMTSIPO SAISTORIO ARKIVI (SSSA;
GEORGIAN NATIONAL HISTORICAL ARCHIVE, TBILISI,
GEORGIA)

Fonds
4   Kantseliariia namestnika kavkazskogo
5   Kantseliariia nachal'nika glavnogo upravleniia glavnon-
    achal'stvuiushchego grazhdanskoi chast'iu na kavkaze
7   Departament glavnogo upravleniia namestnika kavkazskogo, 1859–82
12 Kantseliariia glavnonachal'stvuiushchego grazhdanskoi chast'iu na
    kavkaze
219 Vremennoe otdelenie po delam grazhdanskogo ustroistva kavka-
    zskogo i zakavkazskogo kraia, 1857–63
229 Kantseliariia namestnika na kavkaze po voenno-narodnomu upravle-
    niiu
416 Kavkazskaia arkheograficheskaia komissiia
419 Rasporiaditel'naia komissiia po organizatsii 5-go arkheologicheskogo
    s'ezda v g. Tiflise
433 Inspektsiia uchilishchu obshchestva vosstanovleniia pravoslavnogo
    khristianstva na kavkaze
481 kartvelta shoris tsera-kitkhvis gamovrtselebeli sazogadoeba
492 Osetinskaia dukhovnaia komissiia
493 Obshchestvo vostanovleniia pravoslavnogo khristianstva na kavkaze

1437   Lichnyi fond Baratova (N.N. Baratashvili)
2094   kartuli kulturis mokvarulta sazogadoeba

SAKARTVELOS SAKHELMTSIPO MUZEUMIS ARKIVI (SSMA;
ARCHIVE OF THE GEORGIAN STATE MUSEUM, TBILISI,
GEORGIA)

Fonds
    3   Kavkazskaia muzeia
  223   Spiski knig i literatury
  224   Tiflisskaia publichnaia biblioteka
  226   Tiflisskaia publichnaia biblioteka
  229   Tiflisskaia publichnaia biblioteka

GOSUDARSTVENNYI ARKHIV ROSSIISKOI FEDERATSII (GARF; STATE
ARCHIVE OF THE RUSSIAN FEDERATION, MOSCOW, FORMERLY TSGAOR)

Fonds
  649   Romanov, M.N.
  792   Lobanov-Rostovskii, M.B.
 5263   Komissiia po voprosam kul'tov
 6991   Sovet po delam religii pri sovete ministrov SSSR
 9469   General'nyi pravitel'stvennyi komissar vsemirnoi vystavki 1967 goda
        v Moskve

*GOSUDARSTVENNYI VOENNO-ISTORICHESKII ARKHIV ROSSIISKOI
FEDERATSII* (GVIARF; STATE MILITARY HISTORICAL ARCHIVE OF THE
RUSSIAN FEDERATION, MOSCOW, FORMERLY TSGVIA)

Fonds
   38   Departament general'nogo shtaba
  400   Glavnyi shtab, asiatskaia chast'
  644   Komanduiushchii voiskami Terskoi oblasti
14719   Glavnyi shtab kavkazskoi armii
 VUA   Voenno uchenyi arkhiv

SANKT-PETERBURGSKII FILIAL ARKHIVA ROSSIISKOI AKADEMII NAUK (PFA
AN; ST PETERSBURG BRANCH OF THE ARCHIVE OF THE RUSSIAN ACADEMY
OF SCIENCES, ST PETERSBURG, FORMERLY LO AAN)

Fonds
   32   Kupfer, A.Ia.
   94   Shegren, A.M.
  100   Dubrovin, N.F.

SANKT-PETERBURGSKII FILIAL INSTITUTA VOSTOKOVEDENIIA ROSSIISKOI
AKADEMII NAUK (SPBFIVRAN; ST PETERSBURG BRANCH OF THE
INSTITUTE OF ORIENTAL STUDIES OF THE RUSSIAN ACADEMY OF
SCIENCES, ST PETERSBURG, FORMERLY LO IVAN)

Fonds
6 Berzhe, A.P.

*SANKT-PETERBURGSKII FILIAL INSTITUTA ROSSIISKOI ISTORII ROSSIISKOI
AKADEMII NAUK* (SPBFIRI RAN; ST PETERSBURG BRANCH OF THE
INSTITUTE OF RUSSIAN HISTORY OF THE RUSSIAN ACADEMY OF SCIENCES,
ST PETERSBURG, FORMERLY LOII SSSR)

Fonds
36 Vorontsov

ROSSIISKII GOSUDARSTVENNYI ISTORICHESKII ARKHIV (RGIA; RUSSIAN
STATE HISTORICAL ARCHIVE, ST PETERSBURG, FORMERLY TSGIA)

Fonds
37 Gornyi departament MF
200 Shtab korpusa inzhenerov putei soobshcheniia MPS
381 Kantseliariia ministra zemledeliia
383 Pervyi departament MGI
385 Vremennyi otdel po pozemel'nomu ustroistvu gosudarstvennykh
krest'ian MGI
396 Departament gosudarstvennykh zemel'nykh imushchestv
408 Komitet po zemleustroitel'nym delam
560 Kantseliariia MF
565 Departament gosudarstvennogo kaznacheistva MF
573 Departament okladnykh sborov ministerstva finansov
727 Nol'de, E.Iu.
796 Kantseliariia sinoda
797 Kantseliariia ober-prokurora sinoda
799 Khoziaistvennoe upravleniia pri sinode
821 Departament dukhovnykh del inostrannykh ispovedanii MVD
832 Filaret (Drozdov Vasilii Imkheidovich) metropolit moskovskii
866 Loris-Melikov, M.T.
932 Dondukov-Korsakov, A.M.
1049 Sarkisov, G.S.
1149 Departament zakonov gossoveta
1152 Departament ekonomii gossoveta
1158 Finansovaia komissiia gosudarstvennogo soveta
1162 Gosudarstvennaia kantseliariia gosudarstvennogo soveta

1246 Osoboe prisutsvie o voinskom povinnosti pri gossovete
1263 Komitet ministrov
1268 Kavkazskii komitet
1276 Sovet ministrov (1905–17)
1278 Gosudarstvennaia Duma I, II, III, i IV sozyvov
1282 Kantseliariia ministra vnutrennikh del
1284 Kantseliariia MVD
1286 Departament politsii ispolnitel'noi MVD
1290 Statisticheskii komitet MVD
1291 Zemskii otdel tsentral'nogo statisticheskogo komiteta MVD
1341 Pervyi departament senata
1405 Ministerstvo iustitsii
1424 Karty, plani i chertezhi
1574 Pobedonostsev, K.P.
1604 Delianov, I.D.

RUKOPISNYI OTDEL, BIBLIOTEKA IMENI SALTYKOVA-SHCHEDRINA
(MANUSCRIPTS DEPARTMENT, SALTYKOV-SHCHEDRIN PUBLIC LIBRARY, ST
PETERSBURG)

Fonds
  73 Arkhiv V.A. Bil'basova i A.A. Kraevskago

NEWSPAPERS AND JOURNALS (RUSSIAN)

Bakinskii Rabochii
Biulleten' Severo-Kavkazskogo Biuro Kraevedeniia
Chechenskaia Pravda
Chernomorskii Vestnik
Delo
Etnograficheskoe Obozrenie (EO)
Istoricheskii Vestnik
Istoriia SSSR
Izvestiia Kavkazskago Otdela Imperatorskago Russkago Geograficheskago Obshchestva
Kaluzhskiia Gubernskiia Vedomosti
Kaspii
Kavkaz
Kavkazskaia zhizn'
Kavkazskii Aktsent
Kavkazskii Kalendar'
Kavkazskii Sbornik
Kavkazskii Vestnik

Kubanskiia Oblastnyia Vedomosti
Kurskiia Gubernskiia Vedomosti
Mir Islama
Moskovskiia Vedomosti
Novoe Obozrenie
Otchet obshchestva vozstanovleniia pravoslavnago khristianstva na Kavkaze
Pastyr'
Revoliutsiia i Gorets
Russkaia Mysl'
Russkaia Starina
Russkii Invalid
Russkii Mir
Sanktpeterburgskiia Vedomosti
Sbornik Materialov dlia opisaniia mestnostei i plemen Kavkaza
Sbornik Statisticheskikh Svedenii o Kavkaze (sssok)
Sbornik Svedenii o Kavkaze (ssok)
Sbornik Svedenii o Kavkazskikh Gortsakh (ssokg)
Severnaia Pchela
Sovetskii Dagestan
Spravedlivost'
Starina i Novizna
Stavropol'skiia Gubernskiia Vedomosti
Tiflisskiia Vedomosti
Tiflisskii Vestnik
Vesennii potok
Vilenskii Vestnik
Voennyi Sbornik
Voprosy Istorii
Vozrozhdenie
Vsemirnyi Puteshestvennik (vp)
Zapiski Kavkazskago Otdela Imperatorskago Russkago Geograficheskago
   Obshchestva (zkoirgo)
Zhivaia Starina
Zhurnal dlia chteniia vospitannikam voenno-uchebnykh zavedenii
Zhurnal Ministerstva Narodnogo Prosveshcheniia

NEWSPAPERS AND JOURNALS (GEORGIAN)

droeba
iveria (newspaper)
iveria (journal)
krebuli
kvali

mogzauri
mtskemsi
sakartvelos kalendari
tsnomis purtseli

BOOKS AND ARTICLES

Abaev, V.D. *Tbilisi i Osetiia*. Tbilisi, 1959.

Abdullaev, M. *Mysliteli narodov Dagestana xix i nachala xx v.v.* Daguchredgiz, 1963.

Abramishvili, A.Z. "Iz istorii Azerbaidzhanskoi periodicheskoi pechati." *Uchenye zapiski Azerbaidzhanskogo gosudarstvennogo universiteta im. S.M. Kirova*, no. 10 (1956): 69–80.

Adams, David Wallace. *Education for Extinction: American Indians and the Boarding School Experience, 1875–1928*. Lawrence: University Press of Kansas, 1995.

Agrarnyi vopros i krest'ianskoe dvizhenie 50–70-kh godov xix v. Moscow-Leningrad, 1936.

Aivazian, K.V. "'Puteshestvie v Arzrum' Pushkina (Pushkin v Armenii)." In K.V. Aivazian, ed., *Pushkin i literatura narodov sovetskogo soiuza*, 357–82. Erevan, 1975.

Aksakov, Ivan S. *Polnoe sobranie sochinenii*. Moscow, 1886.

– *Slavianskii vopros, 1860–1886*. Moscow, 1886.

Algeron, Charles-Robert. *Les algeriens Musulmans et la France (1871 1919)*. Vol. 1. Paris: Presses Universitaires de France, 1968.

Allen, W.E. D. *A History of the Georgian People*. London: K. Paul, Trench, Trubner & Co., 1932.

Altstadt, Audrey. *The Azerbaijani Turks: Power and Identity under Russian Rule*. Stanford: Hoover Institution Press, 1992.

Anderson, Benedict. *Imagined Communities: Reflections on the Origin and Spread of Nationalism*. London: Verso, 1991.

Andreevskii, Ivan. *O namestnikakh, voevodakh i gubernatorakh*. St Petersburg, 1864.

Anisimov, Evgenii V. *The Reforms of Peter the Great: Progress through Coercion in Russia*. Trans. John T. Alexander. Armonk, NY: M.E. Sharpe, 1993.

Anuchin, D.N. "O zadachakh russkoi etnografii." *EO*, no. 1 (1889):1–35.

Apsyrt, Aet-ipa. "On byl synom svoego vremeni." *Ekho Kavkaza*, no. 1 (1992):25–8.

Armstrong, Terence, ed. *Yermak's Campaign in Siberia: A Selection of Documents*. Trans. Tatiana Minorsky and David Wileman. London: Hakluyt Society, 1975.

Arseniev, Nicolas. *La sainte Moscou: Tableau de la vie religeuse et intellectuelle russe au xixe siècle*. Paris, 1948.

Asad, Talal, ed. *Anthropology & the Colonial Encounter*. London: Ithaca Press, 1973.

Ashkhatsav, S.M. *Puti razvitiia Abkhazskoi istorii*. Sukhum, 1925.

Atkin, Muriel. *Russia and Iran, 1780–1820*. Minneapolis: University of Minnesota Press, 1980.

– "Russian Expansion in the Caucasus to 1813." In Michael Rywkin, ed., *Russian Colonial Expansion to 1917*, 139–86. London, 1988.

Austin, Paul M. "The Exotic Prisoner in Russian Romanticism." *Russian Literature* 16, no. 3 (October 1984):217–74.

Azamatov, K.G. *Sotsial'no-ekonomicheskoe polozhenie i obychnoe pravo Balkartsev v pervoi polovine xix v.* Avtoreferat. Nal'chik, 1967.

Baddeley, John F. *The Russian Conquest of the Caucasus*. New York: Russell & Russell, 1908; repr., 1969.

Bakradze, Dm. *Arkheologicheskoe puteshestvie po Gurii i Adchare*. St Petersburg, 1878.

– *Istoriia Gruzii na osnovanii novykh izyskanii*. St Petersburg, 1873.

Barkey, Karen, and Mark von Hagen, eds. *After Empire: Multiethnic Societies and Nation- Building*. Boulder, Colo.: Westview Press, 1997.

Barratt, Glynn R. "A Note on the Russian Conquest of Armenia (1827)." *Slavonic and East European Review* 50, no. 120 (July 1972):386–409.

Barrett, Thomas M. *At the Edge of Empire: The Terek Cossacks and the North Caucasus Frontier, 1700–1860*. Boulder, Colo.: Westview Press, 1999.

– "Lines of Uncertainty: The Frontiers of the North Caucasus." *Slavic Review* 54, no. 3 (fall 1995):578–601.

– "The Remaking of the Lion of Dagestan: Shamil in Captivity." *Russian Review* 53, no. 3 (July 1994):353–66.

Barthes, Roland. *A Barthes Reader*. Ed. and introd. Susan Sontag. New York: The Noonday Press, 1982.

Bartlett, Robert. *The Making of Europe: Conquest, Colonization and Cultural Change, 950- 1350*. Princeton: Princeton University Press, 1993.

Bartolomeia, I., ed. *Abkhazskii bukvar'*. Tiflis, 1865.

Bassin, Mark. *Imperial Visions: Nationalist Imagination and Geographical Expansion in the Russian Far East, 1840–1865*. Cambridge: Cambridge University Press, 1999.

– "Inventing Siberia: Visions of the Russian East in the Early Nineteenth Century." *American Historical Review* 96, no. 3 (June 1991): 763–94.

– "Russia between Europe and Asia: The Ideological Construction of Geographical Space." *Slavic Review* 50, no. 1 (spring 1991):1–17.

– "The Russian Geographical Society, the 'Amur Epoch,' and the Great Siberian Expedition 1855–1863." *Annals of the Association of American Geographers* 73, no. 2 (1983): 240–56.

– "Turner, Solov'ev, and the 'Frontier Hypothesis': The Nationalist Signification of Open Spaces." *Journal of Modern History* 65, no. 3 (September 1993): 473–511.

Batsanadze, Asmat Sandroevna. *Gruzinskaia pressa i tsarskaia tsenzura v period vtoroi revoliutsionnoi situatsii i reaktsii (1879–1885 gg.)*. Avtoreferat. Tbilisi, 1990.

Baudet, E. H. P. *Paradise on Earth: Some Thoughts on European Images of Non-European Man*. Trans. Elizabeth Wentholt. New Haven, Yale University Press, 1965.

Bauer, Henning, Andreas Kappeler, and Brigitte Roth. *Die Nationalitaten des Russischen Reiches in der Volkszahlung von 1897*. Stuttgart: Franz Steiner Verlag, 1991.

Baumann, Robert F. "Subject Nationalities in the Military Service of Imperial Russia: The Case of the Bashkirs." *Slavic Review* 46, no. 3 (1987):489–502.

– "Universal Service Reform and Russia's Imperial Dilemma." *War and Society* 4, no. 2 (1986):31–49.

Baziiants, A.P. *Lazarevskii institut vostochnykh iazykov*. Moscow, 1959.

Becker, Seymour. "The Muslim East in 19th-Century Russian Popular Historiography." *Central Asian Survey*, 5, nos. 3–4 (1986):25–47.

– "Russia between East and West: The Intelligentsia, Russian National Identity and the Asian Borderlands."*Central Asian Survey* 10, no. 4 (1991):47–64.

Begichev, K.N., ed. *Iubileinyi Sbornik k stoletiiu prisoedineniia Gruzii k Rossii*. Tiflis, 1901.

Belinskii, V.G. *Polnoe sobranie sochinenii*. Moscow, 1953.

Belkin, D.I. "Tema zarubezhnogo vostoka v tvorchestve A.S. Pushkina." *Narody Azii i Afriki*, no. 4 (1965): 104–16.

Bell, James S. *Journal of a Residence in Circassia during the Years 1837, 1838 and 1839*. London: E. Moxon, 1840.

Bennigsen, Alexandre. "Islam and Political Power in the USSR." In Gustavo Benavides and M.W. Daly, eds., *Religion and Political Power*, 69–82. Albany, 1989.

– "The Qadiriyah (Kunta Haji) Tariqah in North-East Caucasus: 1850–1987." *Islamic Culture* 62, nos. 2–3 (April-July 1988): 63–78.

– "Un temoignage français sur Chamil et les Guerres du Caucase." *Cahiers du monde russe et soviétique* 7, no. 3 (1966):311–22.

– and Marie Broxup. *The Islamic Threat to the Soviet State*. New York: St. Martin's Press, 1983.

– and Chantal Lemercier-Quelquejay. "L' 'Islam parallele' en Union sovietique." *Cahiers du monde russe et soviétique* 21, no. 1 (janvier–mars 1980): 49–63.

– and Chantal Lemercier-Quelquejay. *La presse et le mouvement national chez les Musulmans de Russie avant 1920*. Paris: Mouton, 1964.

– and S. Enders Wimbush. *Mystics and Commissars: Sufism in the Soviet Union*. Berkeley: University of California Press, 1985.

Berelowitch, Wladimir. "Aux origines de l'ethnographie russe: La Société de geographie dans les années 1840–1850." *Cahiers du monde russe et soviétique* 31, nos. 2, 3 (avril–septembre 1990):265–74.

Berhok, I. *Tarihte Kafcasya.* Istanbul, 1958.

Berlin, Isaiah. "Herder and the Enlightenment." In Earl R. Wasserman, ed., *Aspects of the Eighteenth Century,* 47–104. Baltimore: Johns Hopkins University Press, 1965.

Berzhe, A.P., ed. *Akty Kavkazskoiu Arkheograficheskoiu Kommissieiu.* 12 vols. Tiflis, 1866–1912.

– *Chechnia i Chechentsy.* Tiflis, 1859; repr. Groznyi, 1991.

– *Etnograficheskoe obozrenie Kavkaza.* St Petersburg, 1879.

– "Vyselenie gortsev s Kavkaza."*Russkaia Starina* 33 (January 1882):161–76, 337–63.

Bestuzhev-Marlinskii, A.A. *Sochineniia v dvukh tomakh.* Vol. 2. Moscow, 1958.

Betrozov, Ruslan. *Etnicheskaia istoriia Adygov: s drevneishikh vremen do XVI veka.* Nal'chik, 1996.

Betts, Raymond F. *Assimilation and Association in French Colonial Theory, 1890–1914.* New York: Columbia University Press, 1961.

Bez'iazychnyi, V.I. "Kavkaz v zhizni i tvorchestve A.I. Polezhaeva (1829–1833)." *Izvestiia Groznenskogo Oblastnago instituta i muzeiia Kraevedeniia,* nos. 2–3 (1950):76–111.

Bgazhba, Kh. S. *Iz istorii pis'mennosti v Abkhazii.* Tbilisi, 1967.

Bitterli, Urs. *Cultures in Conflict: Encounters between European and Non-European Cultures, 1492–1800.* Trans. Ritchie Robertson. Oxford: Oxford University Press, 1989.

Black, J.L. *Citizens for the Fatherland: Education, Educators, and Pedagogical Ideals in Eighteenth Century Russia.* Boulder, Colo.: East European Quarterly, 1979.

Bliev, M.M. "Kavkazskaia voina: sotsial'nye istoki, sushchnost'." *Istoriia SSSR,* no. 2 (March–April 1983):54–75.

– *Osetiia v pervoi treti XIX veka.* Ordzhonikidze, 1964.

– "K probleme obshchestvennogo stroia gorskikh (vol'nykh) obshchestv severo-vostochnogo i severo-zapadnogo Kavkaza XVIII-pervoi poloviny XIX veka." *Istoriia SSSR,* no. 4 (July–August 1989):151–68.

Bogdanovich, Lev. *Dvadtsatipiatiletie velikoi osvoboditel'noi voiny.* Moscow, 1902.

Booker, Keith M. *Colonial Power, Colonial Texts: India in the Modern British Novel.* Ann Arbor: University of Michigan Press, 1997.

Boratav, Pertev. "La Russie dans les Archives ottomanes in Dossier ottoman sur l'imam Chamil." *Cahiers du monde russe et soviétique* 10, nos. 3–4 (juillet–décembre 1969):524–35.

Braginskii, I.S. "Zametki o zapadno-vostochnom sinteze v lirike Pushkina." *Narody Azii i Afriki,* no. 4 (1965):117–26.

Breuilly, John. *Nationalism and the State*. 2nd ed. Chicago: University of Chicago Press, 1993.

Brock, Peter. "The Fall of Circassia: A Study in Private Diplomacy." *English Historical Review* 71, no. 280 (July 1956): 401–27.

Brooks, E. Willis. "Nicholas I as Reformer: Russian Attempts to Conquer the Caucasus, 1825–1855." In Ivo Banac, John G. Ackerman, and Roman Szporluk, eds., *Nation and Ideology*, 227–63. New York, 1981.

Brooks, Jeffrey. *When Russia Learned to Read: Literacy and Popular Literature, 1861–1917*. Princeton: Princeton University Press, 1985.

Brower, Daniel.. "Imperial Russia and Its Orient: The Renown of Nikolai Przhevalsky." *Russian Review* 53, no. 3 (July 1994): 367–81.

– and Edward Lazzerini, eds. *Russia's Orient: Imperial Borderlands and Peoples, 1700–1917*. Bloomington: Indiana University Press, 1997.

Broxup, Marie Bennigsen, ed. *The North Caucasus Barrier*. New York: St. Martin's Press, 1992.

Bugai, N.F., ed. *Iosif Stalin – Lavrentiiu Berii: 'Ikh nado deportirovat'*. Moscow, 1992.

– and A.M. Gonov. *Kavkaz: Narody v eshelonakh (20–60-e gody)*. Moscow, 1998.

Burbank, Jane, and David L. Ransel, eds. *Imperial Russia: New Histories for the Empire*. Bloomington: Indiana University Press, 1998.

Burke, Edmund, III. "Fez, the Setting Sun of Islam: A Study of the Politics of Colonial Ethnography." *Maghreb Review* 2 (July–August 1977): 1–17.

Bushuev, S.K. *Iz istorii vneshnepoliticheskikh otnoshenii v period prisoedineniia Kavkaza k Rossii (20–70 gody XIX veka)* Moscow, 1955.

Chanock, Martin. *Law, Custom and Social Order: The Colonial Experience in Malawi and Zambia*. Cambridge: Cambridge University Press, 1985.

Chechenskii bukvar'. Tiflis, 1866.

Chechulin, N. *Russkoe provintsial'noe obshchestvo v vtoroi polovine XVIII veka*. St Petersburg, 1889.

Cherniavsky, Michael, ed. *The Structure of Russian History*. New York: Random House, 1970.

Chichagova, M.N. *Shamil' na Kavkaze i v Rossii: Biograficheskii ocherk*. St Petersburg, 1889.

Chistiakov, O.I., ed. *Rossiiskoe Zakonodatel'stvo X–XX vekov*. 9 vols. Moscow, 1988.

Chkhetiia, Sh. *Tbilisi v XIX stoletii: 1865 gody*. Tbilisi, 1939.

Chmielewski, Edward. *Tribune of the Slavophiles: Konstantin Aksakov*. Gainesville: University of Florida Monographs, 1962.

Christoff, Peter K. *An Introduction to Nineteenth-Century Russian Slavophilism: A Study in Ideas*. Vol. 1. The Hague: Mouton & Co., 1961.

Chumakov, S.V. *Priiut Pastukhova*. Moscow, 1977.

Clark, Katerina. *Petersburg, Crucible of Cultural Revolution*. Cambridge, Mass.: Harvard University Press, 1995.

Clay, Catherine Black. "Ethos and Empire: The Ethnographic Expedition of the Imperial Russian Naval Ministry, 1855–1862." PhD dissertation, University of Oregon, 1989.

– "Russian Ethnographers in the Service of Empire, 1856–1862." *Slavic Review* 54, no. 1 (spring 1995):45–61.

Clifford, James. *The Predicament of Culture*. Cambridge, Mass.: Harvard University Press, 1988.

– "Review Essay: Orientalism." *History and Theory* 19, no. 2 (1980):204–23.

– and George E. Marcus, eds. *Writing Culture: The Poetics and Politics of Ethnography*. Berkeley: University of California Press, 1986.

Cohn, Bernard S. *Colonialism and Its Forms of Knowledge: The British in India*. Princeton: Princeton University Press, 1996.

Confer, Vincent. *France and Algeria: The Problem of Civil and Political Reform, 1870–1920*. Syracuse: Syracuse University Press, 1966.

Conklin, Alice L. *A Mission to Civilize: The Republican Idea of Empire in France and West Africa, 1895–1930*. Stanford: Stanford University Press, 1997.

Cooke, James J. "Eugène Étienne and the Emergence of Colon Dominance in Algeria, 1884–1905." *Muslim World* 65, no. 1 (January 1975):39–53.

Cooper, Frederick, and Ann Laura Stoler, eds. *Tensions of Empire: Colonial Cultures in a Bourgeois World*. Berkeley: University of California Press, 1997.

Corre, Alan D. "The Algiers Riot, January 1898." *Maghreb Review* 5, nos. 2–4 (March–August 1980):74–8.

Cracraft, James. "Empire Versus Nation: Russian Political Theory under Peter I." *Harvard Ukrainian Studies* 10, nos. 3/4 (December 1986):524–41.

Cunynghame, Arthur T. *Travels in the Eastern Caucasus*. London, 1872.

Daniialov, G.D. "Ot narodnosti k natsii." In M.V. Vagabova, ed. *Oktiabr'skaia Revolutsiia i reshenie Natsional'nogo Voprosa v Dagestane*, 273–346. Makhachkala, 1967.

Danilevskii, N. *Kavkaz i ego gorskie zhiteli*. Moscow, 1846.

Danilevskii, Nikolai Ia. *Rossiia i Evropa*. St Petersburg, 1871.

Dantsig, B.M. *Blizhnii vostok v russkoi nauke i literature*. Moscow, 1973.

Danziger, Raphael. *Abd al-Qadir and the Algerians: Resistance to the French and Internal Consolidation*. New York: Homes & Meier Publishers, 1977.

Dargo, George. *Jefferson's Louisiana: Politics and the Clash of Legal Traditions*. Cambridge, Mass.: Harvard University Press, 1975.

Davison, Roderic H. *Reform in the Ottoman Empire, 1856–1876*. Princeton: Princeton University Press, 1963.

– "'Russian Skill and Turkish Imbecility': The Treaty of Kuchuk Kainardji Reconsidered." In Roderic H. Davison, *Essays in Ottoman and Turkish History, 1774–1923*, 29–50. Austin: University of Texas Press, 1990.

Degoev, V. V. *Kavkazskii vopros v mezhdunarodnykh otnosheniiakh 30–60-kh gg. XIX v.* Vladikavkaz, 1992.

Dekmejian, Richard H., and Margaret J. Wyszomirski. "Charismatic Leadership in Islam: The Mahdi of Sudan." *Comparative Studies in Society and History* 14 (1972):193–214.

Demkov, M.I. *Istoriia Russkoi pedagogii*. Vol. 2. St Petersburg, 1897.

Desvages, Hubert. "La Chambre de 1898 et la crise algérienne." *Revue d'histoire et de civilisation du Maghreb*, no. 5 (juillet 1968):90–120.

D'iakov, V.A. "Zapiski o Cherkesii, sochinennye Khan-Gireem." *Istoriia SSSR*, no. 5 (1958):173–8.

Diamond, Stanley. *In Search of the Primitive: A Critique of Civilization*. New Brunswick, N.J.: Transaction Books, 1974.

Diuma (Dumas), Aleksandr. *Kavkaz*. Trans. P.N. Roborovskii. Tbilisi, 1988.

Donogono-Korkmas, M. *Portrety Shamilia v Evrope*. Makhachkala, 1990.

Dostoyevsky, Fyodor. *The Possessed*. Trans. Constance Garnett. New York, 1936.

Dowler, Wayne. *Classroom and Empire: The Politics of Schooling Russia's Eastern Nationalities, 1860–1917*. Montreal: McGill-Queen's University Press, 2001.

– *Dostoevsky, Grigor'ev and Native Soil Conservatism*. Toronto: University of Toronto Press, 1982.

– "The Politics of Language in Non-Russian Elementary Schools in the Eastern Empire, 1865- 1914." *Russian Review* 54, no. 4 (October 1995):516–38.

Doyle, Michael W. *Empires*. Ithaca: Cornell University Press, 1986.

Drozdov, N. "Poslednaia bor'ba s gortsami na zapadnom Kavkaze." *Kavkazskii Sbornik*, 2 (1877):387–457.

Dubrovin, Nikolai F. *Istoriia voiny i vladychestva russkikh na Kavkaze*. 2 vols. St Petersburg, 1871.

Dukmasov, Iv. *O zaselenii Chernomorskago poberezh'ia Kavkaza kazach'im voiskom*. Moscow, 1887.

Dvadtsatipiatiletie Imperatorskago Russkago Geograficheskago Obshchestva. St Petersburg, 1872.

Dzagurov, G.A., ed. *Pereselenie gortsev v Turtsiiu: Materialy po istorii gorskikh narodov*. Rostov-Don, 1925.

Dzhibladze, Georgii. *Il'ia Chavchavadze: zhizn', poeziia*. Trans. N. Akkerman and S. Serebriakov. Tbilisi, 1984.

Dzhunusov, M.S. "Natsiia, kak sotsiial'no-etnicheskaia obshchnost' liudei." *Voprosy Istorii*, no. 4 (April 1966):16–30.

Dzidzariia, G.A. *Formirovanie dorevoliutsionnoi Abkhazskoi intelligentsii*. Sukhumi, 1979.

– *Makhadzhirstvo i problemy istorii Abkhazii XIX stoletiia*. Sukhumi, 1982.

– *Vosstanie 1866 v Abkhazii*. Sukhumi, 1955.

Dziuba, Ivan. *'Kavkaz' Tarasa Shevchenko: na fone neprekhodiashchego proshlogo*. Kyïv: Holovna spetsializovana redaktsiia literatury movamy natsional'nykh menshyn Ukraïny, 1996.

Edieva, F.D. "Formy zemlevladeniia i zemlepol'zovaniia po obychnomu pravu Karachaevtsy v pervoi polovine xix veka." In *Istoriia Gorskikh i Kochevykh Narodov Severnogo Kavkaza*, 1:49–66. Stavropol', 1975.

Eklof, Ben. *Russian Peasant Schools: Officialdom, Village Culture, and Popular Pedagogy, 1861–1914*. Berkeley: University of California Press, 1986.

Enfimenko, P.S. *Sbornik Narodnykh Iuridicheskikh obychaev Arkhangel'skoi Gubernii*. Arkhangel'sk, 1869.

Esadze, Semen. *Istoricheskaia zapiska ob upravlenii Kavkazom*. 2 vols. Tiflis, 1907.

– *Pokorenie zapadnogo Kavkaza i okonchanie Kavkazskoi voiny*. 1914; repr. Maikop, 1993.

Evans, R.J.W. *The Making of the Habsburg Monarchy, 1550–1700*. Oxford: Clarendon Press, 1979.

Fabian, Johannes. *Language and Colonial Power: The Appropriation of Swahili in the Former Belgian Congo*. Cambridge: Cambridge University Press, 1986.

Fadeev, R. *Pis'ma s Kavkaza*. St Petersburg, 1865.

Fisher, Alan W. *The Crimean Tatars*. Stanford: Hoover Institution Press, 1978.

– "Emigration of Muslims from the Russian Empire in the Years after the Crimean War." *Jahrbücher für Geschichte Osteuropas* 35, no. 3 (1987):356–71.

– *The Russian Annexation of the Crimea, 1772–1783*. Cambridge, Mass.: Harvard University Press, 1970.

Fishman, Joshua A. *Language and Nationalism: Two Integrative Essays*. Rowley, Mass.: Newbury House Publishers, 1972.

Flemming, William. "The Deportation of the Chechen and Ingush Peoples: A Critical Examination." In Ben Fowkes, ed., *Russia and Chechnia: The Permanent Crisis*, 65–86. London: MacMillan Press; New York: St. Martin's Press, 1998.

Fonvill, A. *Poslednii god voiny Cherkessii za nezavisimost', 1863–1864 g.* Krasnodar, 1927.

Forsyth, James. *A History of the Peoples of Siberia: Russia's North Asian Colony, 1581–1990*. Cambridge: Cambridge University Press, 1992.

Foucault, Michel. *Discipline and Punish: The Birth of the Prison*. Trans. Alan Sheridan. New York: Pantheon Books, 1979.

– *The History of Sexuality: An Introduction*. Vol. 1. Trans. Robert Hurley. New York: Vintage Books, 1990.

Frank, Joseph. *Dostoevsky: The Stir of Liberation, 1860–1865*. Princeton: Princeton University Press, 1986.

– *Dostoevsky: The Years of Ordeal, 1850–1859*. Princeton: Princeton University Press, 1983.

Frank, Stephen P. "Popular Justice, Community and Culture among the Russian Peasantry, 1870–1900." *Russian Review* 46 (1987):239–65.

Frierson, Cathy. "Crime and Punishment in the Russian Village: Rural Concepts of Criminality at the End of the Nineteenth Century." *Slavic Review* 46, no. 1 (spring 1987):55–69.

"From Ottoman Archives." *Central Asian Survey* 4, no. 4 (1985):7–12.

Frye, Richard N. "Oriental Studies in Russia." In Wayne S. Vucinich, ed., *Russia and Asia: Essays on the Influence of Russia on the Asian Peoples*, 30–51. Stanford: Hoover Institution Press, 1972.

Gabunia, Z. "General Uslar i Kavkazskie Iazyki." *Ekho Kavkaza*, no. 1 (1992):24–8.

Gadzhiev, A. *Petr Karlovich Uslar – Vydaiushchiisia Kavkazoved*. Makhachkala, 1966.

Gammer, Moshe. "'The Conqueror of Napoleon' in the Caucasus." *Central Asian Survey* 12, no. 3 (1993):253–65.

– *Muslim Resistance to the Tsar: Shamil and the Conquest of Chechnia and Daghestan*. London: Frank Cass, 1994.

– "The Nicolay-Shamil Negotiations, 1855–1856: A Forgotten Page of Caucasian History." *Central Asian Survey* 11, no. 2 (1992):43–70.

– "Russian Strategies in the Conquest of Chechnia and Daghestan, 1825–1859." In Marie Bennigsen Broxup, ed., *The North Caucasus Barrier*, 45–61. New York: St. Martin's Press, 1992.

– "Shamil and the Murid Movement, 1830–1859: An Attempt at a Comprehensive Bibliography." *Central Asian Survey* 10, nos. 1, 2 (1991):189–247.

– "Vorontsov's 1845 Expedition against Shamil: A British Report." *Central Asian Survey* 4, no. 4 (1985):13–33.

– "Was General Kluge-von-Klugenau Shamil's Desmichels?" *Cahiers du monde russe et soviétique* 33, nos. 2–3 (avril–septembre 1992):207–22.

Gasamov, Magomed Padzhabovich. *Vzaimootnosheniia narodov Dagestana i Gruzii v xix–nachale xx vv.* Avtoreferat dissertatsii na doktora istoricheskikh nauk. Tbilisi, 1986.

Gatagova, L.S. *Pravitel'stvennaia politika i narodnoe obrazovanie na Kavkaze v xix v.* Moscow, 1993.

Geins, K. "Pshekhskii otriad." *Voennyi Sbornik*, no. 1 (January 1866):3–5.

Georgiev, V.A., et al. *Sbornik russkogo istoricheskogo obshchestva*. No. 2 (150), *Rossiia i severnyi Kavkaz*. Moscow: Russkaia panorama, 2000.

Geraci, Robert. "Ethnic Minorities, Anthropology, and Russian National Identity on Trial: The Multan Case, 1892–96." *Russian Review* 59, no. 4 (October 2000):530–54.

Gershenzon, M. *Istoriia Molodoi Rossii*. Moscow, 1908.

Gerstein, Linda. *Nikolai Strakhov*. Cambridge, Mass.: Harvard University Press, 1971.

Gleason, Abbott. *European and Muscovite: Ivan Kireevsky and the Origins of Slavophilism*. Cambridge, Mass.: Harvard University Press, 1972.

– *Young Russia: The Genesis of Russian Radicalism in the 1860s*. New York: The Viking Press, 1980.

Godlewska, Anne, and Neil Smith, eds. *Geography and Empire*. Oxford: Blackwell Publishers, 1994.

Golikova, N.B. *Ocherki po istorii gorodov Rossii kontsa xvii–nachala xviii v.* Moscow, 1982.

Got'e, Iu. V. *Istoriia oblastnogo upravleniia v Rossii ot Petra I do Ekateriny II.* 2 vols. Moscow-Leningrad, 1941.

Grabovskii, N.F. "Ocherk suda i ugolovnykh prestuplenii v Kabardinskom okruge." *ssokg* 4 (1870):1–78.

Gramsci, Antonio. *Selections from the Prison Notebooks of Antonio Gramsci.* Ed. and trans. Quintin Hoare and Geoffrey N. Smith. New York: International Publishers, 1971.

Green, Arnold H. "Political Attitudes and Activities of the Ulama in the Liberal Age: Tunisia as an Exceptional Case." *International Journal of Middle East Studies* 7, no. 2 (April 1976):209–41.

Greenblatt, Stephen. *Marvelous Possessions: The Wonder of the New World.* Chicago: University of Chicago Press, 1991.

Griboedov, A.S. *Sochineniia.* Moscow, 1956.

Grigolia, Alexander. *Custom and Justice in the Caucasus: The Georgian Highlanders.* Philadelphia, 1939.

Grigor'ev, V.V., ed. *Trudy tret'iago mezhdunarodnago s'ezda Orientalistov.* St Petersburg, 1879–80.

Gritsenko, N.P. *Goroda severo-vostochnogo Kavkaza i proizvoditelnye sily kraia v seredina xix veka.* Rostov-na-Donu, 1984.

Grossman, Leonid. "Lermontov i kul'tury vostoka." *Literaturnoe Nasledstvo,* nos. 43–4 (1941): 673–744.

Guliia, D. *Materialy po Abkhazskoi grammatike.* Sukhum, 1927.

Halbach, Uwe. "Die Bergvölker (*gorcy*) als Gegner und Opfer: Der Kaukasus in der Wahrnehmung Ruslands." *Jahrbücher für Geschichte Osteuropas,* no. 5 (1991):52–65.

– "'Heiliger Kreig' gegen den Zarismus." In A.G. Kappeler et al., eds., *Die Muslime in der Sowjetunion und in Jugoslavien,* 213–34. Cologne: Markus Verlag, 1989.

Hanoteau, A., and A. Letourneux. *La Kabylie et les coutumes kabyles.* 3 vols. Paris: Imprimerie nationale, 1871.

Harley, J.B. "Maps, Knowledge, and Power." In Denis Cosgrove and Stephen Daniels, eds., *The Iconography of Landscape,* 277–312. Cambridge: Cambridge University Press, 1988.

Hayes, Carlton J.H. "Contributions of Herder to the Doctrine of Nationalism." *American Historical Review* 32, no. 4 (July 1927):719–36.

Henze, Mary L. "Thirty Cows for an Eye: The Traditional Economy of the Central Caucasus – An Analysis from 19th Century Travellers' Accounts." *Central Asian Survey* 4, no. 3 (1985):115–29.

Henze, Paul B. "Circassia in the Nineteenth Century." In Ch. Lemercier-Quelquejay et al., eds., *Turco-Tatar Past, Soviet Present,* 243–73. Paris: Éditions Peeters, 1986.

- "Circassian Resistance to Russia." In Marie Bennigsen Broxup, ed., *The North Caucasus Barrier*, 62–111. New York: St. Martin's Press, 1992.
- "Fire and Sword in the Caucasus: The 19th Century Resistance of the North Caucasian Mountaineers." *Central Asian Survey* 2, no. 1 (July 1983):5–44.
- "The Rehabilitation of Russia's Rebels." *Central Asian Survey* 4, no. 4 (1985):39–46.
- "Unrewriting History – The Shamil Problem." In Walter Laqueur, ed., *The Middle East in Transition*, 415–43. London, 1958.

Herder, J.G. *J.G. Herder on Social and Political Culture*. Trans. and introd. F.M. Barnard. Cambridge: Cambridge University Press, 1969.

Herlihy, Patricia. *Odessa: A History, 1794–1914*. Cambridge, Mass.: Harvard University Press, 1986.

Hirsch, Francine. "The Soviet Union as a Work-in-Progress: Ethnographers and the Category *Nationality* in the 1926, 1937, and 1939 Censuses." *Slavic Review* 56, no. 2 (summer 1997):251–78.

Hobsbawm, E.J. *Nations and Nationalism since 1780: Programme, Myth, Reality*. 2nd ed. Cambridge: Cambridge University Press, 1992.

- and Terence Ranger, eds. *The Invention of Tradition*. Cambridge: Cambridge University Press, 1983.

Høiris, Ole, and Sefa Martin Yürükel, eds. *Contrasts and Solutions in the Caucasus*. Aarhus, Denmark: Aarhus University Press, 1998.

Hokanson, Katya. "Literary Imperialism, *Narodnost'* and Pushkin's Invention of the Caucasus." *Russian Review* 53, no. 3 (July 1994):336–52.

Holquist, Peter. "'Information Is the Alpha and Omega of Our Work': Bolshevik Surveillance in Its Pan-European Context." *Journal of Modern History* 69, no. 3 (September 1997):415–50.

Hosking, Geoffrey. *Russia: People and Empire*. Cambridge: Mass.: Harvard University Press, 1997.

Hourani, Albert. *Islam in European Thought*. Cambridge: Cambridge University Press, 1991.

Howard, Peter. "The Definition of a Nation: A Discussion in 'Voprosy Istorii.'" *Central Asian Review* 15, no. 1 (1967):26–36.

Hunczak, Taras, ed. *Russian Imperialism from Ivan the Great to the Revolution*. New Brunswick: Rutgers University Press, 1974.

Hymes, Dell, ed. *Reinventing Anthropology*. New York: Panetheon Books, 1969.

Ibragimbeili, Khadzhi Murat. "Narodno-osvoboditel'naia bor'ba gortsev severnogo kavkaza pod rukovodstvom Shamilia protiv tsarisma i mestnykh feodalov." *Voprosy Istorii*, no. 6 (June 1990):151–60.

Il'minskii, Nikolai Ivanovich. *Pis'ma Nikolaia Ivanovicha Il'minskago*. Kazan, 1895.

Isaev, A.A. "O formirovanii i razvitii pis'mennosti narodov Dagestana." In *Sotsiologicheskii Sbornik* 1:173–232. Makhachkala: Dagestanskii filial AN SSSR Institut Istorii, Iazyka i Literatury im. G. Tsadasy, 1970.

Ismail-zade, Deliara Ibragim-Kyzy. *Russkoe krest'ianstvo v Zakavkaz'e.* Avtoreferat dissertatsii. Moscow, 1983.

Ivanov, V.P., et al. *Etnicheskaia istoriia i Kul'tura Chuvashei Povolzh'ia i Priural'ia.* Cheboksary, 1993.

Jelavich, Barbara. *Russia's Balkan Entanglements, 1806–1914.* Cambridge: Cambridge University Press, 1991.

Jersild, Austin. "From Savagery to Citizenship: Caucasian Mountaineers and Muslims in the Russian Empire." In Daniel Brower and Edward Lazzerini, eds., *Russia's Orient: Imperial Borderlands and Peoples, 1700–1917*, 101–14. Bloomington: Indiana University Press, 1997.

– "Imperial Russification: Dagestani Mountaineers in Russian Exile, 1877–1883." *Central Asian Survey* 19, no. 1 (March 2000):5–16.

– "Rethinking Russia from Zardob: Hasan Melikov Zardabi and the 'Native' Intelligentsia." *Nationalities Papers* 27, no. 3 (1999):503–17.

– "'Russia,' from the Vistula to the Terek to the Amur." *Kritika: Explorations in Russian and Eurasian Culture* 1, no. 3 (summer 2000):531–46.

– and Neli Melkadze. "The Dilemmas of Enlightenment in the Eastern Borderlands: The Theater and Library in Tbilisi." *Kritika: Explorations in Russian and Eurasian Culture* 3, no. 1 (2002, forthcoming).

John, Michael. *Politics and the Law in Late Nineteenth-Century Germany: The Origins of the Civil Code.* Oxford: Oxford University Press, 1989.

Jones, Robert E. *The Emancipation of the Russian Nobility, 1762–1785.* Princeton: Princeton University Press, 1973.

Jones, Stephen F. "Russian Imperial Administration and the Georgian Nobility: The Georgian Conspiracy of 1832." *Slavonic and East European Review* 65, no. 1 (January 1987):53–76.

Kaloev, B.A. *Zemledelie narodov severnogo Kavkaza.* Moscow, 1981.

Kaltakhchian, S.T. "K voprosu o poniatii 'natsiia.'" *Voprosy Istorii,* no. 6 (June 1966):24–43.

Kapieva, Natal'ia. "Kavkaz v Russkoi poezii pervoi poloviny XIX veka." *Literaturnyi Dagestan,* 1947:194–242.

Kappeler, Andreas. "Czarist Policy toward the Muslims of the Russian Empire." In Andreas Kappeler et al., eds. *Muslim Communities Reemerge,* 139–56. Durham: Duke University Press, 1994.

– *La Russie: empire multiethnique.* Trans. Guy Imart. Paris: Institut d'études slaves, 1994.

Karamzin, N.M. *Istoriia gosudarstva Rossiiskago.* Vol. 1. St Petersburg, 1892; Slavistic Printings and Reprintings, ed. C.H. Van Schooneveld, no. 189/1, The Hague: Mouton, 1969.

Karpat, Kemal H. "The Status of the Muslims under European Rule: The Eviction and Settlement of the Cerkes." *Journal, Institute of Muslim Minority Affairs* 2, no. 1 (1980):7–27.

Kaspari, A.A., ed. *Pokorennyi Kavkaz.* St Petersburg, 1904.

Kasumov, M.M. "G. Zardabi – vydaiushchiisia Azerbaidzhanskii prosvetitel' vtoroi poloviny xix veka." In *Trudy instituta istorii i filosofii*, 8:136–77. Baku: Akademiia nauk, 1955.

Kavkazskaia voina – uroki istorii i sovremennost'. Krasnodar: Kubanskii gos. universitet, 1995.

Kavkazskii zapros' v gosudarstvennoi dume. Tiflis: Elektropechatnia Kh.G. Khachaturov, 1909.

Kazarina, M.A. "Iz istorii razvitiia obrazovaniia v Kabarde v kontse xix i nachale xx vv." In *Uchenye zapiski Kabardino-Balkarskogo Gospedinstituta*, 13:161–80. Nal'chik, 1957.

Kazemzadeh, Firuz. "Russian Penetration of the Caucasus." In Taras Hunczak, ed., *Russian Imperialism from Ivan the Great to the Revolution*, 239–63. New Brunswick: Rutgers University Press, 1974.

– *The Struggle for Transcaucasia*. New York: Philosophical Library, 1951.

Kaznacheeva, T.P. "Esteticheskoe vliianie gorskoi material'noi kul'tury na kul'turu trudovogo Kazachestva severnogo Kavkaza." In A.V. Avksent'ev, ed. *Uchenye zapiski i nekotorye voprosy Kavkazovedeniia*, 1:188–206. Stavropol, 1971.

Kefeli-Clay, Agnès. "L'Islam populaire chez les Tatars chrétiens orthodoxes au xixe siècle." *Cahiers du monde russe* 37 (octobre-décembre, 1996):409–28.

Kelly, Laurence. *Lermontov: Tragedy in the Caucasus*. New York: G. Braziller, 1978.

Kemper, Michael. "Einige Notizen zur Arabischsprachigen Literatur der ;ab-Gihad-Bewegung in Dagestan und Tschetsche-Nien in der ersten Hälfte des 19. Jahrhunderts." In Anke von Kügelgen, Michael Kemper, and Allen J. Frank, eds., *Muslim Culture in Russia and Central Asia from the 18th to the Early 20th Centuries*, 2:63–99. Berlin: Klaus Schwarz, 1998.

Khalid, Adeeb. *The Politics of Muslim Cultural Reform: Jadidism in Central Asia*. Berkeley: University of California Press, 1998.

– "Russian History and the Debate over Orientalism." *Kritika: Explorations in Russian and Eurasian History* 1, no. 4 (fall 2000):691–9.

Khan-Girei. *Zapiski o Cherkesii*. Introd. V.K. Gardanov and G.Kh. Mambetov. Nal'chik, 1978.

Khomiakov, A.S. *Izbrannye Sochineniia*. Ed. N.S. Arsen'ev. New York: Izdatel'stvo imeni Chekhova, 1955.

– *Polnoe sobranie sochinenii*. 8 vols. 3rd ed. Moscow, 1900.

Kiernan, Victor G. *The Lords of Human Kind: Black Man, Yellow Man, and White Man in an Age of Empire*. Boston: Little, Brown, 1969.

Kireevskii, Ivan. *Polnoe sobranie sochinenii*. 2 vols. Ed. M. Gershenzon. Farnborough: Gregg, 1970.

Kishmishev, A. *Tiflis: Lichnyia vospominaniia*. Tiflis, 1909.

Kishmishev, S. *Tiflis 40-kh godov*. Tiflis, 1894.

Klier, John Doyle. *Imperial Russia's Jewish Question, 1855–1881*. Cambridge: Cambridge University Press, 1995.

Knight, Nathaniel. "Grigor'ev in Orenburg, 1851–1862: Russian Orientalism in the Service of Empire?" *Slavic Review* 59, no. 1 (spring 2000):74–100.

– "On Russian Orientalism: A Response to Adeeb Khalid." *Kritika: Explorations in Russian and Eurasian History* 1, no. 4 (fall 2000):701–15.

– "Science, Empire, and Nationality: Ethnography in the Russian Geographical Society, 1845–1855." In Jane Burbank and David L. Ransel, eds., *Imperial Russia: New Histories for the Empire*, 108–41. Bloomington: Indiana University Press, 1998.

Kohn, Hans. *The Idea of Nationalism*. New York: Macmillan Company, 1944.

– *Pan-Slavism: Its History and Ideology*. 2nd ed. New York: Vintage Books, 1960.

Kohut, Zenon E. *Russian Centralism and Ukrainian Autonomy*. Cambridge, Mass.: Harvard University Press, 1988.

Kokiev, G.A. "S.V. Kokiev – etnograf osetinskogo naroda." *Sovetskaia Etnografiia*, no. 3 (1946):133–7.

Kolarz, Walter. *Russia and Her Colonies*. New York: F.A. Praeger, 1952.

Kopachev, I.P. "Razvitie prosveshcheniia v Kabarde v xix veke." In *Uchenye zapiski Kabardino-Balkarskogo Gospedinstituta*, 13:147–60. Nal'chik, 1957.

Korolenko, P.P. *Dvukhsotletie Kubanskago Kazach'iago voiska, 1696–1896.* Ekaterinodar', 1896.

Kosven, M.O. "A.A. Bestuzhev-Marlinskii." In M.O. Kosven, *Etnografiia i istoriia Kavkaza*, 158–68. Moscow, 1961.

– ed. *Ocherki istorii Dagestana*. Vol. 1. Makhachkala, 1957.

Koyré, Alexandre. *La philosophie et le problème national en Russie au début du xix siècle*. Paris, 1929.

Kristof, Ladis K.D. "The Russian Image of Russia." In Charles A. Fisher, ed., *Essays in Political Geography*, 345–87. London: Methuen, 1968.

Kruber, A., S. Grigor'ev, A. Barkov, and S. Chefranov, eds. *Aziatskaia Rossiia*. Moscow, 1903.

Kudriavtsev, K. *Sbornik materialov po istorii Abkhazii*. Sukhum: Tipografiia asnkh Abkhazii imeni Lenina, 1926.

Kumykov, T. Kh. *Vovlechenie severnogo Kavkaza vo vserossiiskii rynok v xix v.* Nal'chik, 1962.

– *Vyselenie Adygov v Turtsiiu – posledstvie Kavkazskoi voiny*. Nal'chik, 1994.

Kuper, Adam. *Anthropologists and Anthropology: The British School, 1922–1972*. London: Allan Lane, 1973.

Kuzanov, A. "Shamil – politicheskii i dukhovnyi glava Dagestana." *Sanktpeterburgskiia Vedomosti*, no. 204 (22 September 1859):889–90.

Laipanov, Kh. O. "K istorii pereseleniia gortsev severnogo Kavkaza v Turtsiiu." *Trudy*, no. 5 (1966):111–31.

Lang, David. *A Modern History of Soviet Georgia*. New York: Grove Press, 1962.

Lantzeff, George V. *Siberia in the Seventeenth Century: A Study of the Colonial Administration*. Berkeley: University of California Press, 1943.

Lappo-Danilevskii, A.S. "Sobranie i svod zakonov Rossiiskoi Imperii, sostavlennye v tsarstvovanie Imperatritsy Ekateriny II." *Zhurnal Ministerstva Narodnago Prosveshcheniia*, January 1897, 1–59.

Layton, Susan. "The Creation of an Imaginative Caucasian Geography." *Slavic Review* 45, no. 3 (fall 1986):470–85.

– "Eros and Empire in Russian Literature about Georgia." *Slavic Review* 51, no. 2 (summer 1992):195–213.

– "Marlinsky's 'Ammalat-Bek' and the Orientalisation of the Caucasus in Russian Literature." In Derek Offord, ed., *The Golden Age of Russian Literature and Thought*, 34–57. New York: St. Martin's Press, 1992.

– "Primitive Despot and Noble Savage: The Two Faces of Shamil in Russian Literature."*Central Asian Survey* 10, no. 4 (1991):31–45.

– *Russian Literature and Empire: Conquest of the Caucasus from Pushkin to Tolstoy*. Cambridge: Cambridge University Press, 1994.

Lazzerini, Edward J. "Defining the Orient: A Nineteenth-Century Russo-Tatar Polemic over Identity and Cultural Representation." In Andreas Kappeler et al., *Muslim Communities Reemerge*, 33–45. Durham: Duke University Press, 1994.

– "Ismail Bey Gasprinskii (Gaspirali): The Discourse of Modernism and the Russians." In Edward A. Allworth, ed., *The Tatars of Crimea: Return to the Homeland*, 2nd ed., 48–70. Durham: Duke University Press, 1998.

LeDonne, John P. "La reforme de 1883 au Caucase." *Cahiers du monde russe et soviétique* 8 (1967):21–35.

– *The Russian Empire and the World, 1700–1917: The Geopolitics of Expansion and Containment*. New York: Oxford University Press, 1997.

Leiberov, I.P. *Tsebel'dinskaia nakhodka: iz istorii revoliutsionnykh sviazei mezhdu Peterburgom i Kavkazom*. Moscow, 1976.

Lemercier-Quelquejay, Chantal. "Cooptation of the Elites of Kabarda and Daghestan in the Sixteenth Century." In Marie Bennigsen Broxup, ed., *The North Caucasus Barrier*, 18–44. New York: St. Martin's Press, 1992.

– G. Veinstein, and S.E. Wimbush, eds. *Turco-Tatar Past, Soviet Present*. Paris: Éditions Peeters, 1986.

Leontovich, O.I. *Adaty kavkazskikh gortsev*. Vol. 2. Odessa, 1883.

Lermontov, Mikhail Yu. *A Hero of Our Time*. Trans. and introd. Paul Foote. New York: Penguin Books, 1966.

Lewin, Moshe. "Customary Law and Russian Rural Society in the Post-Reform Era." *Russian Review* 44 (1985):1–19.

Lilov, A. *Deiatel'nost obshchestva vozstanovleniia pravoslavnago khristianstva na Kavkaze za 1860–1870 god*. n.p., 1872.

– "Ocherk byta Kavkazskhikh gortsev." *Sbornik Materialov dlia opisaniia mestnostei i plemen Kavkaza* 14 (1892):1–57.

Lincoln, W. Bruce. *The Great Reforms: Autocracy, Bureaucracy, and the Politics of Change in Imperial Russia*. DeKalb: Northern Illinois University Press, 1990.

– *In the Vanguard of Reform: Russia's Enlightened Bureaucrats, 1825–1861.* DeKalb: Northern Illinois University Press, 1983.

Livingstone, David N., and Charles W.I. Withers, eds. *Geography and Enlightenment.* Chicago: University of Chicago Press, 1999.

Lobikova, N.M. "Kavkaz v tvorchestve Pushkina." In *Uchenye zapiski Kabardino-Balkarskogo Gospedinstituta,* 13:283–300. Nal'chik, 1957.

Lodzemskaia, L. *M.M. Ippolitov-Ivanov i Gruzinskaia muzykal'naia kul'tura.* Tbilisi: Izdatel'stvo soiuza pisatelei Gruzii 'Zaria vostoka', 1963.

Longworth, J.A. *A Year among the Circassians.* 2 vols. London: H. Colburn, 1840.

Lorcin, Patricia M.E. *Imperial Identities: Stereotyping, Prejudice and Race in Colonial Africa.* London: I.B. Tauris Publishers, 1995.

Luzbetak, Louis J. *Marriage and the Family in Caucasia: A Contribution to the Study of North Caucasian Ethnology and Customary Law.* Vienna: St. Gabriel's Mission Press, 1951.

Macfie, A.L. *The Eastern Question, 1774–1923.* Rev. ed. London: Longman, 1996.

MacKenzie, David. *The Lion of Tashkent: The Career of General M.G. Cherniaev.* Athens: University of Georgia Press, 1974.

MacKenzie, John M. *Orientalism: History, Theory and the Arts.* Manchester: Manchester University Press, 1995.

Magomeddadaev, Amirxan M. "Die Dagestanische Diaspora in der Türkei und in Syrien." In Anke von Kugelgen, Michael Kemper, and Allen J. Frank, eds., *Muslim Culture in Russia and Central Asia from the 18th to the Early 20th Centuries,* 2:281–98. Berlin: Klaus Schwarz, 1998.

Magomedov, R. *Vosstanie gortsev Dagestana v 1877 g.* Makhachkala, 1940.

Magomedov, R.M. *Shamil v otechestvennoi istorii.* Makhachkala, 1990.

Magometov, A.A. *P.K. Uslar – issledovatel' Dagestanskikh iazykov.* Makhachkala, 1979.

Mal'sagova, T.T. *Vosstanie gortsev v Chechne v 1877 godu.* Groznyi, 1968.

Mann, Kristin, and Richard Roberts, eds. *Law in Colonial Africa.* Portsmouth, N.H.: Heinemann Educational Books, 1991.

Marcus, George E., and Michael J. Fischer. *Anthropology as Cultural Critique: An Experimental Moment in the Human Sciences.* Chicago: University of Chicago Press, 1999.

Markov, Evgeniia. *Ocherki Kavkaza.* St Petersburg-Moscow, 1887.

Martin, B.G. *Muslim Brotherhoods in Nineteenth-Century Africa.* New York: Cambridge University Press, 1976.

Martin, Terry. "The Origins of Soviet Ethnic Cleansing." *Journal of Modern History* 70, no. 4 (December 1998):813–61.

Materialy po arkheologii Kavkaza: khristianskie pamiatniki. Vol. 3. Moscow, 1893.

Megrelidze, Sh.V. *Zakavkaz'e v Russko-Turetskoi voine 1877–1878 gg.* Tbilisi, 1972.

Melikset-Bekov, L.M. *Vvedenie v istoriiu gosudarstvennykh obrazovanii Iugo-Kavkaza*. Tiflis, 1924.

Menning, Bruce W. "The Emergence of a Military-Administrative Elite in the Don Cossack Land, 1708–1836." In Walter McKenzie Pintner and Don Karl Rowney, eds., *Russian Officialdom: The Bureaucratization of Russian Society from the Seventeenth to the Twentieth Century*, 19–45. Chapel Hill: University of North Carolina Press, 1980.

Metcalf, Thomas R. *Ideologies of the Raj*. The New Cambridge History of India, vol. 3, part 4. Cambridge: Cambridge University Press, 1997.

Mitchell, Timothy. *Colonising Egypt*. Cambridge: Cambridge University Press, 1988.

Mnatsakanian, M.O. "Natsiia i natsional'naia gosudarstvennost'." *Voprosy Istorii* 9 (September 1966):27–36.

Modzalevskii, L. *Khod uchebnago dela na Kavkaze s 1802 po 1880 god*. Tiflis, 1880.

Morison, David. "Shamil: New Documents and Correspondence," *Central Asian Survey* 4, no. 4 (1985):1–5.

Mudimbe, V.Y. *The Invention of Africa: Gnosis, Philosophy, and the Order of Knowledge*. Bloomington: Indiana University Press, 1988.

Murav'ev, N.N. *Voina za Kavkazom v 1855 godu*. St Petersburg, 1877.

Mutaliev, T. Kh.-V. *V Odnom stroiu (Chechentsy i Ingushi v Russko-Turetskoi Voine 1877–1878 godov)*. Groznyi, 1978.

Nadezhdin, P., ed. *Priroda i liudi na Kavkaze i za Kavkazom*. St Petersburg, 1869.

Narochnitskii, A.L., ed. *Istoriia narodov severnogo Kavkaza (konets xviiiv.–1917g.)*. Moscow, 1988.

Nechkina, M.V. *A.S. Griboedov i dekabristy*. Moscow, 1951.

Nekrich, Aleksandr M. *The Punished Peoples: The Deportation and Fate of Soviet Minorities at the End of the Second World War*. Trans. George Saunders. New York: Norton, 1978.

Nevskaia, V.P. "Karachaevo-Cherkesiia v sovetskoi istoricheskoi nauke." *Trudy*, no. 5 (1966):275–309.

Nichols, Johanna. "Who Are the Chechen?" *Newsletter, Center for Slavic Studies, Berkeley, California* 12 (spring 1995), no. 2:3–5.

Nikitin, S.A. *Slavianskie Komitety v Rossii v 1858–1876 godakh*. Moscow, 1960.

Nogmov, Sh.B. *Istoriia Adygeiskogo naroda*. 5th ed. Nal'chik, 1947.

Nol'de, B.E. *Ocherki Russkago Gosudarstvennago Prava*. St Petersburg, 1911.

– *Ocherk po istorii kodifikatsii mestnykh grazhdanskikh zakonov pri grafe Speranskom*. Vol. 1. St Petersburg, 1906.

Nolde, Boris. *La formation de l'Empire russe*. 2 vols. Paris: Institut d'études slaves, 1952–53.

Obozrenie Istoricheskikh svedenii o Svode Zakonov. St Petersburg, 1837.

O'Brien, Donal B., and Christian Coulon, eds. *Charisma and Brotherhood in African Islam*. Oxford: Oxford University Press, 1988.

O deistviiakh vysochaishe uchrezhdennago obshchestva vozstanovleniia pravoslavnago khristianstva na Kavkaze. St Petersburg, 1862.

Ogarkov, B.B. "Vorontsovy: Ikh Zhizn i obshchestvennaia deiatel'nost." In *Zhizn Zamechatel'nykh liudei,* 5–96. St Petersburg, 1892.

Olcott, Martha Brill. *The Kazakhs.* 2nd ed. Stanford: Hoover Institution Press, 1995.

Ol'shevskii, M. Ia. "Kavkaz i pokorenie vostochnoi ego chasti." *Russkaia Starina* 27 (1880):289–318.

Omarov, Abdulla. *Dagestan: vremia i sud'by.* Makhachkala, 1990.

Ortabaev, B Kh., and F.V. Totoev. "Eshche raz o kavkazskoi voine: o ee sotsial'nykh istokakh i sushchnosti." *Istoriia SSSR,* no. 4 (July–August 1988):78–96.

Otchet nachal'nika Kubanskoi oblasti i nakaznago Atamana Kubanskago Kazach'iago voiska o sostoianii oblasti i voiska za 1895 god. Ekaterinodar, 1896.

Otchet o deistviiakh Kavkazskago Otdela Imperatorskago Russkago Geograficheskago Obshchestva za 1852 god. Tiflis, 1853.

Otchet o sostoianii i deistviiakh Kavkazskago Otdela Imperatorskago Russkago Geograficheskago Obshchestva s 1859 po 1864 god. Tiflis, 1864.

Otchet po upravleniiu Kavkazskim kraem za 1846, 1847 i 1848 gody. Tiflis, 1849.

Otchet po upravleniiu Kavkazskim kraem za 1849, 1850, i 1851 gody. Tiflis, 1852.

Otchet po upravleniiu Kavkazskim kraem za 1865 god. Tiflis, 1865.

Otchet po upravleniiu Kavkazskim kraem za 1866 god. Tiflis, 1866.

Pagden, Anthony. *European Encounters with the New World: From Renaissance to Romanticism.* New Haven: Yale University Press, 1993.

Paperno, Irina. *Chernyshevsky and the Age of Realism: A Study in the Semiotics of Behavior.* Stanford: Stanford University Press, 1988.

Pearson, Raymond. "The Historical Background to Soviet Federalism." In Alastair McAuley, ed. *Soviet Federalism: Nationalism and Economic Decentralisation,* 13–32. Leicester, 1991.

– "Privileges, Rights, and Russification." In Olga Crisp and Linda Edmondson, eds., *Civil Rights in Imperial Russia,* 85–102. Oxford: Oxford University Press, 1989.

Peoples and Languages of the Caucasus. New York: Language and Communication Research Center, Columbia University, 1955.

Periodicheskaia pechat' na Kavkaze. Tiflis, 1901.

Perkins, Kenneth J. *Qaids, Captains and Colons: French Military Administration in the Colonial Maghrib, 1844–1934.* New York: Africana Publishing Company, 1981.

Petin, S. *Sobstvennyi Ego Imperatorskago Velichestva Konvoi, 1811–1911.* 2nd ed. St Petersburg, 1911.

Petrovich, Michael Boro. *The Emergence of Russian Panslavism, 1856–1870.* New York: Columbia University Press, 1956.

Platonov, A. *Obzor deiatel'nosti obshchestva vozstanovleniia pravoslavnago khristianstva na Kavkaze za 1860–1910 gg.* Tiflis, 1910.

Pobedonostsev, K.P. *K.P. Pobedonostsev i ego korrespondenty.* Vol. 1. Moscow, 1923.

Pokorenie Kavkaza i vziatie Shamilia. St Petersburg, 1859.

Polnoe sobranie zakonov Rossiiskoi Imperii. 2nd ed. St Petersburg, 1860.

Polozhenie o Kavkazskom Otdele Russkago Geograficheskago Obshchestva, Vysochaishe utverzhdennoe 27-go Iiulia 1850 goda. St Petersburg, 1851.

Po predlozheniiam namestnika Kavkazskago ob uchrezhdenii obshchestva vozstanovleniia pravoslaviia na Kavkaze. (n.p., n.d.).

Potichnyj, Peter J. "The Struggle of the Crimean Tatars." *Canadian Slavonic Papers* 17, nos. 2, 3 (1975):302–19.

Potto, V. A. *Kavkazskaia voina v otdel'nykh ocherkakh, epizodakh, legendakh i biografiiakh.* 5 vols. St Petersburg: Tipografiia R. Golike, 1885–91.

Pratt, Mary Louise. *Imperial Eyes: Travel Writing and Transculturation.* London and New York: Routledge, 1992.

Prozritelev, G. *Shamil' v g.g. Stavropole.* Stavropol, 1913.

Prozritelev, G.N. *Posol'stvo ot Shamilia k Abadzekham.* Makhach-kala, 1927.

Pushkin, Alexander. *The Captain's Daughter and Other Stories.* New York: Vintage Books, 1936.

Pypin, A.N. *Istoriia Russkoi literatury.* St Petersburg, 1903; Slavistic Printings and Reprintings, ed. C.H. Van Schooneveld, 92/4, The Hague: Mouton, 1968.

– *Kharakteristiki literaturnykh mnenii ot dvadtsatykh do piatidesiatykh godov.* St Petersburg, 1890.

Radde, G.I. *Kratkii putevoditel' po Kavkazskomu Muzeiu.* 5th ed. Tiflis, 1887.

Raeff, Marc. "Patterns of Russian Imperial Policy toward the Nationalities." In Edward Allworth, ed., *Soviet Nationality Problems*, 22–42. New York, 1971.

– *Siberia and the Reforms of 1822.* Seattle: University of Washington Press, 1956.

– "Les Slaves, les Allemands et les 'Lumières.'" *Canadian Slavic Studies* 1, no. 4 (winter 1967):521–51.

– "The Style of Russia's Imperial Policy and Prince G.A. Potemkin." In Gerald G. Grob, ed., *Statesmen and Statecraft of the Modern West: Essays in Honor of Dwight E. Lee and H. Donaldson Jordan*, 1–51. Barre, Mass.: Barre Publishers, 1967.

– *The Well-Ordered Police State: Social and Institutional Change through Law in the Germanies and Russia, 1600–1800.* New Haven: Yale University Press, 1983.

Ragsdale, Hugh. "Russian Projects of Conquest in the Eighteenth Century." In Hugh Ragsdale, ed., trans., and Valerii N. Ponaromarev, assistant ed., *Imperial Russian Foreign Policy*, 75–102. Cambridge: Cambridge University Press, 1993.

– ed., trans., and Valerii N. Ponaromarev, assistant ed. *Imperial Russian Foreign Policy.* Cambridge: Cambridge University Press, 1993.

Rakowska-Harmstone, Teresa. *Russia and Nationalism in Central Asia: The Case of Tadzhikistan.* Baltimore: John Hopkins Press, 1970

Ram, Harsha. "Prisoners of the Caucasus: Literary Myths and Media Representations of the Chechen Conflict." Working Paper, Berkeley Program in Soviet and Post-Soviet Studies, Summer 1999.

Ramazanov, Kh.Kh., and A. Kh. Ramazonov. *Shamil': Istoricheskii portret.* Makhachkala, 1990.

Rayfield, Donald. *The Literature of Georgia: A History.* Oxford: Clarendon Press, 1994.

Reinke, Nikolai. *Gorskie i narodnye sudy Kavkazskago kraia.* St Petersburg, 1912.

Reisner, Oliver. "Die georgische Alphabetisierungsgesellschaft: Schule nationaler Eliten und Vergemeinschaftung." *Jahrbücher für Geschichte Osteuropas* 48, no. 1 (2000):66–89.

– "The Tergdaleulebi: Founders of the Georgian National Identity." In Ladislaus Löb, István Petrovics, and György E. Szonyi, eds., *Forms of Identity: Definitions and Changes*, 125–37. Szeged, Hungary: Attila József University, 1994.

Rhinelander, L. Hamilton. "The Creation of the Caucasian Vicegerency." *Slavonic and East European Review* 59, no. 1 (January 1981):15–40.

– *Prince Michael Vorontsov: Viceroy to the Tsar.* Montreal: McGill-Queen's University Press, 1990.

– "Russia's Imperial Policy: The Administration of the Caucasus in the First Half of the Nineteenth Century." *Canadian Slavonic Papers* 17, nos. 2–3 (1975):218–35.

– "Viceroy Vorontsov's Administration of the Caucasus." In Ronald Grigor Suny, ed., *Transcaucasia: Nationalism and Social Change*, 87–104. Ann Arbor: University of Michigan Press, 1983.

Riasanovsky, Nicholas V. "Asia through Russian Eyes." In Wayne S. Vucinich, ed., *Russia and Asia*, 3–29. Stanford: Stanford University Press, 1972.

– *Nicholas I and Official Nationality in Russia, 1825–1855.* Berkeley: University of California Press, 1969.

– *Russia and the West in the Teaching of the Slavophiles.* Gloucester, Mass.: Peter Smith, 1952, 1965.

Rieber, Alfred J. "Persistent Factors in Russian Foreign Policy: An Interpretative Essay." In Hugh Ragsdale, ed., trans., and Valerii N. Ponomarev, assistant ed., *Imperial Russian Foreign Policy*, 315–59. Cambridge: Cambridge University Press, 1993.

– ed. *The Politics of Autocracy: Letters of Alexander II to Prince A.I. Bariatinskii, 1857–1864.* Paris: Mouton, 1966.

– "Russian Imperialism: Popular, Emblematic, Ambiguous." *Russian Review* 53, no. 3 (July 1994):331–5.

- "Struggle over the Borderlands." In S. Frederick Starr, ed., *The Legacy of History in Russia and the New States of Eurasia*, 61–89. Armonk, NY: M.E. Sharpe, 1994.

Rodkiewicz, Witold. *Russian Nationality Policy in the Western Provinces of the Empire (1863- 1905)*. Lublin, Poland: Scientific Study of Lublin, 1998.

Rogachev, P.M., and M.A. Sverdlin. "O poniatii 'natsiia.'" *Voprosy Istorii*, no. 1 (January 1966):33–48.

Rogger, Hans. *National Consciousness in Eighteenth-Century Russia*. Cambridge, Mass.: Harvard University Press, 1960.

Romanovskii, D.I. "General Fel'dmarshal kniaz' A.I. Bariatinskii i Kavkazskaia voina, 1815–1879." *Russkaia Starina* 30 (1881): 247–318.

- *Kavkaz i Kavkazskaia voina*. St Petersburg: Tipografiia Tovarishchestva 'Obshchestvennaia pol'za,' 1860.

Rossiiskaia Azbuka dlia obucheniiu iunoshestva chteniiu. St Petersburg, 1781.

Ruedy, John. *Modern Algeria: The Origins and Development of a Nation*. Bloomington: Indiana University Press, 1992.

Runovskii, A. *Zapiski o Shamile*. St Petersburg, 1860.

Rutherford, Andrea. "Vissarion Belinskii and the Ukrainian National Question." *Russian Review* 54, no. 4 (October 1995):500–15.

Ryzhov, S. "Puteshestvie Shamilia ot Guniba do Sanktpeterburga." *Sanktpeterburgskiia Vedomosti*, no. 212 (1 October 1859):923–4.

Said, Edward. *Orientalism*. New York: Vintage, 1978.

Salmanov, Khadzhi-Murat D. "O protsesse natsional'noi konsolidatsii narodov Dagestana." In *Sotsiologicheskii Sbornik* 1:279–95. Makhachkala: Dagestanskii filial AN SSSR Institut Istorii, Iazyka i Literatury im. G. Tsadasy, 1970.

Samarin, Iurii F. *Sochineniia*. Moscow, 1877.

Samurskii (Efendiev). *Dagestan*. Moscow, 1925.

Sanders, Thomas, ed. *Historiography of Imperial Russia: The Profession and Writing of History in a Multinational State*. Armonk, NY: M.E. Sharpe, 1999.

Sarkisyanz, Emanuel. "Russian Imperialism Reconsidered." In Taras Hunczak, ed., *Russian Imperialism from Ivan the Great to the Revolution*, 45–81. New Brunswick: Rutgers University Press, 1974.

Saunders, David B. "Historians and Concepts of Nationality in Early Nineteenth-Century Russia." *Slavonic and East European Review* 60, no. 1 (January 1982):44–62.

Schwab, Raymond. *The Oriental Renaissance: Europe's Rediscovery of India and the East, 1680–1880*. Trans. Gene Patterson-Black and Victor Reinking. New York: Columbia University Press, 1984.

Selimkhanov, A.K. "Iz istorii prosveshcheniia v Dagestane v xix veke." In *Uchenye Zapiski*, 1:137–56. Makhachkala: Dagestanskii gosudarstvennyi zhenskii pedagogicheskii institut imeni Gamzata Tsadasy, 1957.

Semenov, L.P. *Gosudarstvennyi nauchnyi muzei gor. Vladikavkaza*. Vladikavkaz, 1925.

– ed. *Kavkaz i Lev Tolstoi, 1828–1928.* Vladikavkaz, 1928.

Semenov, N. "Iz nedavniago proshlago na Kavkaze: Razskazy – vospomina-niia o Chechenskom vozstanii v 1877 g." *Kavkazskii Vestnik,* no. 4 (April 1900):21–37; no. 6 (June 1900):1–19.

Semenov, P.G. "Natsiia i natsional'naia gosudarstvennost' v SSSR." *Voprosy Istorii,* no. 7 (July 1966): 72–81.

Semenov, Petr Petrovich (Tian-Shanskii), ed. *Istoriia poluvekovoi deiatel'nosti Imperatorskago Russkago Geograficheskago Obshchestva 1845–1895.* 3 parts. St Petersburg, 1896.

Sergeenko, A.P. *'Khadzhi Murat' L'va Tolstogo.* Moscow, 1983.

Seton-Watson, Hugh. *The Decline of Imperial Russia, 1855–1914.* New York: F.A. Praeger, 1952.

– *The Russian Empire, 1801–1917.* London: Clarendon, 1967.

Shamil': Opisanie ego zhizni, o vziatii ego v plen, i o tom, kak on po vole proroka vyterpel 95 udarov plet'mi po spine. Moscow, 1859.

Shatskii, P.A. "Russkaia kolonizatsiia territorii Karachaevo-Cherkesii v XIX veke." In *Istoriia Gorskikh i kochevykh narodov Severnogo Kavkaza* 1:38–48. Stavropol', 1975.

Shebanov, A.F. "Polnoe sobranie zakonov Rossiiskoi Imperii." *Trudy* 4 (1970):277–304.

Sherbin, F.A. *Istoriia Kubanskogo kazach'ego polka.* Vol. 2. Ekaterinodar, 1913.

Shteppa, Konstantin F. "The 'Lesser Evil' Formula." In C.E. Black, ed., *Rewriting Russian History,* 107–20. New York, 1956.

Shul'gin, S. "Razskaz ochevidtsa o Shamile i ego sovremennikakh." *Sbornik Materialov dlia opisaniia mestnostei i plemen Kavkaza,* no. 32, part 1 (1903):1–76.

Sidorov, Vasilii. *Kavkaz: Putevyia zametki i vpechatleniia.* St Petersburg, 1897.

Slezkine, Yuri. *Arctic Mirrors: The Small Peoples of the North.* Ithaca: Cornell University Press, 1994.

– "Savage Christians or Unorthodox Russians? The Missionary Dilemma in Siberia." In Galya Diment and Yuri Slezkine, eds., *Between Heaven and Hell: The Myth of Siberia in Russian Culture,* 15–31. New York: St. Martin's Press, 1993.

– "The USSR as a Communal Apartment, or How a Socialist State Promoted Ethnic Particularism." *Slavic Review* 53, no. 2 (summer 1994):414–52.

Slocum, John W. "Who, and When, Were the Inorodtsy? The Evolution of the Category of 'Aliens' in Imperial Russia." *Russian Review* 57, no. 2 (April 1998):173–90.

Spencer, Edmund. *Travels in Circassia.* 2 vols. London: H. Colburn, 1839.

Stalin, Joseph. *Marxism and the National Question: Selected Writings and Speeches.* New York, 1942.

Starr, S. Frederick. "Tsarist Government: The Imperial Dimension." In Jeremy R. Azrael, ed., *Soviet Nationality Policies and Practices,* 3–38. New York: Praeger, 1978.

Steinwedel, Charles. "The 1905 Revolution in Ufa: Mass Politics, Elections, and Nationality." *Russian Review* 59, no. 4 (October 2000):555–76.

Stepanov, N.N. "Russkoe geograficheskoe obshchestvo i etnografiia (1845–1861)." *Sovetskaia Etnografiia*, no. 4 (1946):187–206.

Stocking, George W., Jr. *Victorian Anthropology.* New York: Free Press, 1987.

Stoler, Ann Laura, and Frederick Cooper. "Between Metropole and Colony: Rethinking a Research Agenda." In Frederick Cooper and Ann Laura Stoler, eds., *Tensions of Empire: Colonial Cultures in a Bourgeois World*, 1–56. Berkeley: University of California Press, 1997.

Strakhov, N. *Bor'ba s zapadom v nashei literature.* 3 vols. Kiev, 1897–98; Slavistic Printings and Reprintings, ed. C.H. Van Schooneveld, The Hague: Mouton, 1969.

– *Kriticheskiia stat'i ob I.S. Turgeneve i L.N. Tolstom (1862–1885).* 4th ed. Vol. 1. Kiev, 1901; Slavistic Printings and Reprintings, ed. C.H. Van Schooneveld, The Hague: Mouton, 1968.

Strakhovsky, L. *L'empereur Nicolas Ier et l'esprit national russe.* Louvain, 1928.

Subtelny, Orest. *Ukraine: A History.* Toronto: University of Toronto Press, 1988.

Sunderland, Willard. "Russians into Iakuts? 'Going Native' and Problems of Russian National Identity in the Siberian North, 1870s-1914." *Slavic Review* 55, no. 4 (winter 1996):806–25.

Suny, Ronald Grigor. *Looking toward Ararat: Armenia in Modern History.* Bloomington: Indiana University Press, 1993.

– *The Making of the Georgian Nation.* Bloomington: Indiana University Press, 1988.

– "'The Peasants Have Always Fed Us': The Georgian Nobility and the Peasant Emancipation, 1856–1871." *Russian Review* 38, no. 1 (January 1979):27–51.

– *The Revenge of the Past: Nationalism, Revolution, and the Collapse of the Soviet Union.* Stanford: Stanford University Press, 1993.

– "Transcaucasia: Cultural Cohesion and Ethnic Revival in a Multinational Society." In Lubomyr Hajda and Mark Beissinger, eds., *The Nationalities Factor in Soviet Politics and Society*, 228–52. Boulder, Colo.: Westview Press, 1990.

– ed. *Transcaucasia: Nationalism and Social Change.* Ann Arbor: University of Michigan Press, 1983.

Surguladze, Akakii. *I.G. Chavchavadze: Znamenosets natsional'no-osvobodi- tel'nogo dvizheniia Gruzinskogo naroda.* Tbilisi, 1987.

Swietochowski, Tadeusz. *Russian Azerbaijan, 1905–1920.* Cambridge: Cambridge University Press, 1985.

Szporluk, Roman. "The Fall of the Tsarist Empire and the USSR: The Russian Question and Imperial Overextension." In Karen Dawisha and Bruce Parrott, eds., *The End of Empire? The Transformation of the USSR in Comparative Perspective*, 65–93. Armonk, NY: M.E. Sharpe, 1997.

– "The Imperial Legacy and the Soviet Nationalities Problem." In Lubomyr Hajda and Mark Beissinger, eds., *The Nationalities Factor in Soviet Politics and Society*, 1–23. Boulder, Colo.: Westview Press, 1990.

Takhir, Mukhammed. *Tri Imama*. Makhachkala, 1990.

Tarran, Michel. "The Orthodox Mission in the North Caucasus – End of the 18th – Beginning of the 19th Century." *Central Asian Survey* 10, nos. 1, 2 (1991):103–17.

Teatr v Tiflise s 1845–1856 god. Tiflis, 1888.

Thaden, Edward C. "The Beginnings of Romantic Nationalism in Russia." *American Slavic and East European Review* 13 (1954):500–21.

– *Conservative Nationalism in Nineteenth-Century Russia*. Seattle: University of Washington Press, 1964.

– ed. *Russification in the Baltic Provinces and Finland, 1855–1914*. Princeton: Princeton University Press, 1981.

Tillett, Lowell R. *The Great Friendship*. Chapel Hill, 1969.

– "Shamil and Muridism in Recent Soviet Historiography." *American Slavic and East European Review* 20, no. 2 (April 1961):253–69.

Todorov, Tzvetan. *The Conquest of America: The Question of the Other*. Trans. Richard Howard. New York: Harper & Row, 1984.

Todorova, Maria. "Does Russian Orientalism Have a Russian Soul? A Contribution to the Debate between Nathaniel Knight and Adeeb Khalid." *Kritika: Explorations in Russian and Eurasian History* 1, no. 4 (fall 2000):717–27.

Tokarev, S.A. *Istoriia Russkoi etnografii*. Moscow, 1966.

Tolstoi, D.A. "O merakh k obrazovaniiu naseliaiushchikh Rossiiu inorodtsev." In *Sbornik Postanovlenii po Ministerstvu Narodnago Prosveshcheniia*, 4:1555–66. St Petersburg, 1871.

Tolstoi, L. *Povesti i Rasskazy*. Moscow, 1960.

Totoev, M.S. "K voprosu o pereselenii Osetin v Turtsiiu (1859–1865)." In *Izvestiia Severo-Osetinskogo nauchno-issledovatel'skogo instituta*, 13, no. 1:24–46. Dzaudzhikau, 1948.

Treadgold, Donald W. *The Great Siberian Migration: Government and Peasant in Resettlement from Emancipation to the First World War*. Princeton: Princeton University Press, 1957.

– "Russian Expansion in the Light of Turner's Study of the American Frontier." *Agricultural History* 26, no. 4 (1952):147–52.

Trennert, Robert A., Jr. *Alternative to Extinction: Federal Indian Policy and the Beginnings of the Reservation System, 1846–51*. Philadelphia: Temple University Press, 1975.

Troinitskii, N.A., ed. *Pervaia vseobshchaia perepis' naseleniia Rossiskoi Imperii, 1897 g*. St Petersburg, 1905.

Tsagareishirli, Sh. V., ed. *Shamil' – stavlennik sultanskoi Turtsii i Angliskhikh kolonizatorov*. Tbilisi, 1953.

Tsereteli, Akakii. *Perezhitoe*. Trans. Elena Gogoberidze. Moscow, 1940.

Tsibirov, G.I. *Osetiia v russkoi nauke*. Ordzhonikidze, 1981.

Tsulaia, G.V. "Iz istorii Kavkazovedeniia." In *Ocherki istorii Russkoi etnografii, fol'kloristiki i antropologii*, vol. 9. Moscow, 1982.

Uslar, Baron P.K. "Drevneishiia skazaniia o Kavkaze." *SSOKG* 10 (1881):1–552.

– "O rasprostranenii gramotnosti mezhdu gortsami." *SSOKG* 3 (1870):1–33.

– "Prednolozhenie ob ustroistve gorskikh shkol." In P.K. Uslar, *Etnografiia Kavkaza: Iazykoznania: Abkhazskii iazyk*, 30–44. Tiflis, 1887.

– *Razbor sochineniia Barona P.K. Uslara*. Ed. A. Shifner. St Petersburg, 1864.

Vateishvili, D.L. *Russkaia obshchestvennaia mysl' i pechat' na Kavkaze v pervoi treti xix veka*. Moscow, 1973.

Velichko, K.I., ed. *Voennaia Entsiklopediia*. Vol. 10. St Petersburg, 1912.

Vengerov, S.A. *Ocherki po istorii Russkoi literatury*. 2nd ed. St Petersburg, 1907; Slavistic Printings and Reprintings, ed. C.H. Van Schooneveld, no. 226, The Hague: Mouton, 1969.

Verderevskii, M. *Plen u Shamilia*. St Petersburg, 1856.

Verderevsky, M. *Captivity of Two Russian Princesses in the Caucasus*. Trans. H. Sutherland Edwards. London, 1857.

Villari, Luigi. *Fire and Sword in the Caucasus*. London, 1906.

Volkova, N.G. *Etnicheskii sostav naseleniia severnogo Kavkaza v xviii–nachale xx veka*. Moscow, 1974.

– and G.N. Dzhavakhishvili. *Bytovaia kul'tura Gruzii xix–xx vekov: Traditsii i innovatsii*. Moscow, 1982.

Voll, John O. "The British, the 'Ulama,' and Popular Islam in the Early Anglo-Egyptian Sudan." *International Journal of Middle East Studies* 2, no. 3 (July 1971):212–18.

– *Islam: Continuity and Change in the Modern World*. Boulder, Colo.: Westview Press, 1982.

– "Mahdis, Walis, and New Men in the Sudan." In Nikki R. Keddie, ed., *Scholars, Saints, and Sufis: Muslim Religious Institutions in the Middle East since 1500*, 367–84. Berkeley: University of California Press, 1972.

von Hagen, Mark. "Writing the History of Russia as Empire: The Perspective of Federalism." In Catherine Evtuhov, Boris Gasparov, Alexander Ospovat, Mark von Hagen, eds. *Kazan, Moscow, St. Petersburg: Multiple Faces of the Russian Empire (Kazan', Moskva, Peterburg: Rossiiskaia imperiia vzgliadom iz raznykh uglov)*, 393–410. Moscow: O.G.I., 1997.

von Kügelgen, Anke, Michael Kemper and Allen J. Frank, eds., *Muslim Culture in Russia and Central Asia from the 18th to the Early 20th Centuries*. Vol. 2. Berlin: Klaus Schwarz, 1998.

Voronov, N.I. "Kavkazskii otdel I.R. Geograficheskago Obshchestva s 1851 po 1876 g." In *Kavkazskii Otdel Imperatorskago Russkago Geograficheskago Obshchestva s 1851 po 1876*. Tiflis, 1876.

Vorontsov-Dashkov, Count. *Vsepoddaneishii otchet za vosem' let upravleniia Kavkazom*. St Petersburg, 1913.

– *Vsepoddanneishaia zapiska po upravleniiu Kavkazskim kraem*. Tiflis, 1907.

Vucinich, Alexander. *Science in Russian Culture*. Stanford: Stanford University Press, 1963.

Walicki, Andrzej. *A History of Russian Thought from the Enlightenment to Marxism*. Trans. Hilda Andrews-Rubiecka. Stanford: Stanford University Press, 1979.

– *The Slavophile Controversy*. Trans. Hilda Andrews-Rusiecka. Notre Dame: University of Notre Dame Press, 1975.

Weber, Eugen. *Peasants into Frenchmen: The Modernization of Rural France, 1870–1914*. Stanford: Stanford University Press, 1976.

Weeks, Theodore R. "Defining Us and Them: Poles and Russians in the 'Western Provinces,' 1863–1914." *Slavic Review* 53, no. 1 (spring 1994):26–40.

– *Nation and State in Late Imperial Russia: Nationalism and Russification in the Western Frontier, 1863–1914*. DeKalb: Northern Illinois University Press, 1996.

Weiner, Amir. "Nature, Nurture, and Memory in a Socialist Utopia: Delineating the Soviet Socio-Ethnic Body in the Age of Socialism." *American Historical Review* 104, no. 4 (October 1999):1114–55.

Werth, Paul W. "From Resistance to Subversion: Imperial Power, Indigenous Opposition, and Their Entanglement." *Kritika: Explorations in Russian and Eurasian History* 1, no. 1 (winter 2000):21–43.

– "The Limits of Religious Ascription: Baptized Tatars and the Revision of 'Apostasy,' 1840s–1905." *Russian Review* 59, no. 4 (October 2000):493–511.

Whittaker, Cynthia H. "The Impact of the Oriental Renaissance in Russia: The Case of Sergej Uvarov." *Jahrbücher für Geschichte Osteuropas* 26, no. 4 (1978):503–24.

Whittock, Michael. "Ermolov – Proconsul of the Caucasus." *Russian Review* 18, no. 1 (January 1959):53–60.

Wiener, Martin J. "Treating 'Historical' Sources as Literary Texts: Literary Historicism and Modern British History." *Journal of Modern History* 70, no. 3 (September 1998):619–38.

Wimbush, S. Enders, and Ronald Wixman. "The Meskhetian Turks: A New Voice in Soviet Central Asia." *Canadian Slavonic Papers* 17, nos. 2–3 (1975):320–39.

Wixman, Ronald. *Language Aspects of Ethnic Patterns and Processes in the North Caucasus*. Chicago: University of Chicago Press, 1980.

Wolff, Larry. *Inventing Eastern Europe: The Map of Civilization on the Mind of the Enlightenment*. Stanford: Stanford University Press, 1994.

Wortman, Richard S. *The Development of a Russian Legal Consciousness*. Chicago: University of Chicago Press, 1976.

– *Scenarios of Power: Myth and Ceremony in Russian Monarchy.* 2 vols. Princeton: Princeton University Press, 1995–2000.

Zagurskii, L.P. "Kratkii obzor 25-letnei deiatel'nosti Kavkazskago Otdela I.R. Geograficheskago Obshchestva po etnografii." In *Kavkazskii Otdel Imperatorskago Russkago Geograficheskago Obshchestva s 1851 po 1876.* Tiflis, 1876.

– "Petr Karlovich Uslar i ego deiatel'nost' na Kavkaze." zkoirgo 12 (1881):i-lxviii.

Zaikin, M. *Naselennyia mesta Dagestana.* Temir-Khan-Shura, 1917.

Zaionchkovsky, Petr A. *The Russian Autocracy in Crisis, 1878–1882.* Ed. and trans. Gary M. Hamburg. Gulf Breeze, Fl, 1978.

Zakhar'in, I.N. *Shamil' v Kaluge.* St Petersburg, 1902; repr. Groznyi, 1991.

Zapiski obshchestva liubitelei kavkazskoi arkheologii. Vol. 1. Tiflis, 1875.

Zavadskii, M.R. "Ob izdanii trudov P.K. Uslara." In P.K. Uslar, *Etnografiia Kavkaza. Iazykoznanie. Abkhazskii Iazyk,* v–xv. Tiflis, 1887.

Zelkina, Anna. *In Quest for God and Freedom: The Sufi Response to the Russian Advance in the North Caucasus.* New York: New York University Press, 2000.

Zenkovsky, Serge A. *Pan-Turkism and Islam in Russia.* Cambridge, Mass.: Harvard University Press, 1960.

Zhigarev, Sergei. *Russkaia politika v vostochnom voprose.* 2 vols. Moscow, 1896.

Zhordaniia, Givi. *Istoriia vozniknoveniia Kavkazskago Muzeia.* Tbilisi, 1951.

Zhordaniia, O.K. *Institut istorii, arkheologii i etnografii.* Tbilisi, 1988.

Zisserman, A.L. *Dvadtsat' piat' let na Kavkaze (1842–1867).* 2 vols. St Petersburg, 1879.

– *Fel'dmarshal Kniaz' Aleksandr Ivanovich Bariatinskii, 1815–1879.* Moscow, 1888.

– *Istoriia 80-go Pekhotnago Kabardinskago General-Fel'dmarshala Kniazia Bariatinskago polka (1726–1880).* 3 vols. St Petersburg, 1881.

Znamenskii, Petr Vasil'evich. *Na Pamiat' o Nikolae Ivanoviche Il'minskom.* Kazan,' 1892.

Index

Abadzeg, 4, 24
Abd al-Qadir, 20–1, 28. *See also* French Algeria
Abduragim, 120, 122. *See also* Shamil
Abdurrakhman, 120, 123. *See also* Shamil
Abkhaz, 8, 132, 147; borders of, 85; and Caucasus alphabet, 82–4; at Congress of Orientalists, 78; exile of, 23, 25–6; funeral, 3–4; Georgian settlers and, 138; maps of, 75–6; and native language instruction, 49–50, 52, 54–5, 152–3; princes and imperial service, 18, 33; rebellion of, 28, 31; religious identity of, 43, 45–6, 51
Academy of Sciences Museum of Ethnography and Anthropology, 78. *See also* ethnography
adat. See customary law
administration of North Caucasus, 32–3; and land reform, 35; and military service, 35. *See also* customary law; military-

native administration; *poddanstvo*; schooling; Society for the Restoration of Orthodoxy
Adrianople, 40; Treaty of, 15
Adygei, 4, 147; and archaeology, 68; borders of, 85; and Caucasus War, 15; and ethnography, 72–4; exile of, 23–5; and imperial service, 18–19; maps of, 76; and military service, 35; and native language, 156; religious identity of, 45–6, 48; and Russian settlement, 138, 140–1; in work of Khan-Girei, 82–3; in work of Nogmov, 96
Aga Mohammad, 16
Aksakov, Ivan: and Orthodoxy, 39, 47, 56; and Pan-Slavism, 130, 132–3
Alagar-Bek, 32
apostasy: and the Middle Volga, 48–50, 57, 142, 148. *See also* Il'minskii, Nikolai
archaeology, 8, 11, 75; and Christian history, 45;

and Georgia, 70, 151; and Imperial Archaeological Commission, 67–8, 70; and views on culture and the past, 67–71. *See also* Berzhe, Adol'f; Imperial Russian Geographic Society
Armenians, 4, 53, 155; as a Christian people, 16; imperial service of, 19; in Kars oblast, 31; and literacy, 151; and nationalism, 133; and settlement, 85, 137–8
Astrakhan, 18; and frontier security, 13; and *inorodtsy*, 36; khanate of, 15, 39; maps of, 75; and rebellion of 1877, 30; seminary of, 42
Avar, 4, 77, 82
Azerbaijanis, 4, 13; noble service of, 18

Baddeley, John, 7, 164
Bakradze, Dimitri, 158; and antiquity, 68, 70; on Svan, 45; *See also* archaeology
Baratashvili, Nikoloz, 60